岸本斉史

Lately, all over the world, there has been an upswing in terrorist acts—attacks by armed groups and the taking of hostages—by the worst kind of criminals. In an effort to resolve these situations with as little bloodshed and fanfare as possible, nations all over the globe are increasingly turning toward special operations forces, armed with the latest technologies and finely honed skills, giving them superlative intelligence-gathering capabilities. Such operatives are truly the modern analog to the type of warriors who, in the past, were known as ninja!

—*Masashi Kishimoto*, 2000

Author/artist Masashi Kishimoto was born in 1974 in rural Okayama Prefecture, Japan. After spending time in art college, he won the Hop Step Award for new manga artists with his manga **Karakuri** ("Mechanism"). Kishimoto decided to base his next story on traditional Japanese culture. His first version of **Naruto**, drawn in 1997, was a one-shot story about fox spirits; his final version, which debuted in **Weekly Shonen Jump** in 1999, quickly became the most popular ninja manga in Japan.

NARUTO VOL. 6
SHONEN JUMP Manga Edition

This graphic novel contains material that was originally published
in English in **SHONEN JUMP** #23–27. Artwork in the magazine
may have been slightly altered from that presented here.

STORY AND ART BY MASASHI KISHIMOTO

English Adaptation/Jo Duffy
Translation/Mari Morimoto
Touch-Up Art & Lettering/Heidi Szykowny
Design/Sean Lee
Series Editor/Joel Enos
Editors/Shaenon K. Garrity, Frances E. Wall

Printed in the U.S.A.

Published by VIZ Media, LLC
P.O. Box 77010
San Francisco, CA 94107

15
First printing, March 2005
Fifteenth printing, February 2016

www.viz.com

THE WORLD'S
MOST POPULAR MANGA
www.shonenjump.com

SHONEN JUMP MANGA EDITION

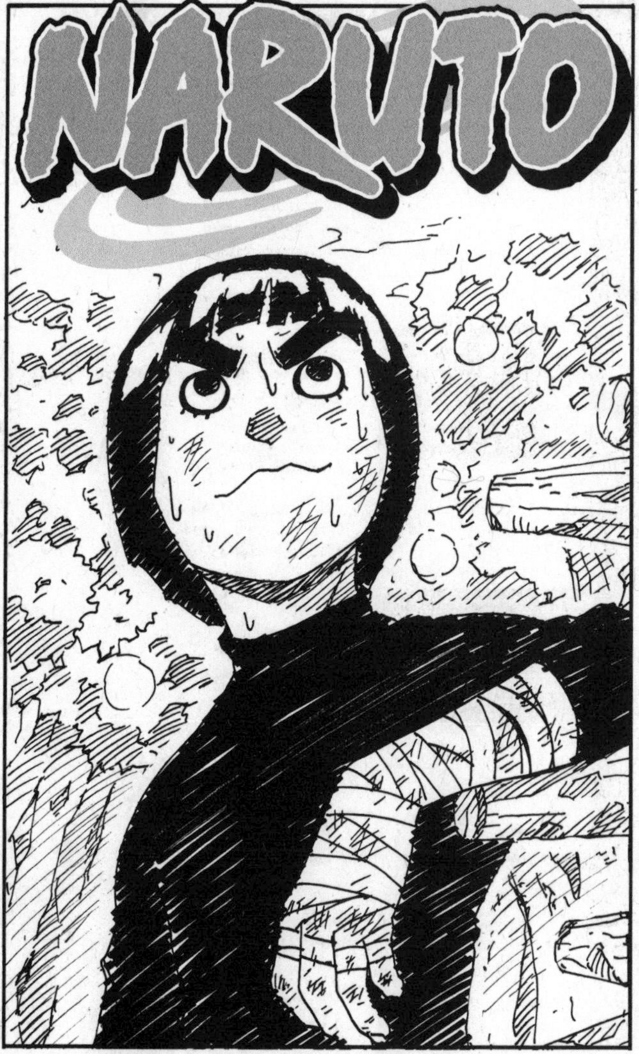
NARUTO

VOL. 6

PREDATOR

STORY AND ART BY

MASASHI KISHIMOTO

SAKURA サクラ

Smart and studious, Sakura is the brightest of Naruto's classmates, but she's constantly distracted by her crush on Sasuke. Her goal: to win Sasuke's heart!

NARUTO ナルト

When Naruto was born, a destructive fox spirit was imprisoned inside his body. Spurned by the older villagers, he's grown into an attention-seeking troublemaker. His goal: to become the village's next *Hokage*.

SASUKE サスケ

The top student in Naruto's class, Sasuke comes from the prestigious Uchiha clan. His goal: to get revenge on a mysterious person who wronged him in the past.

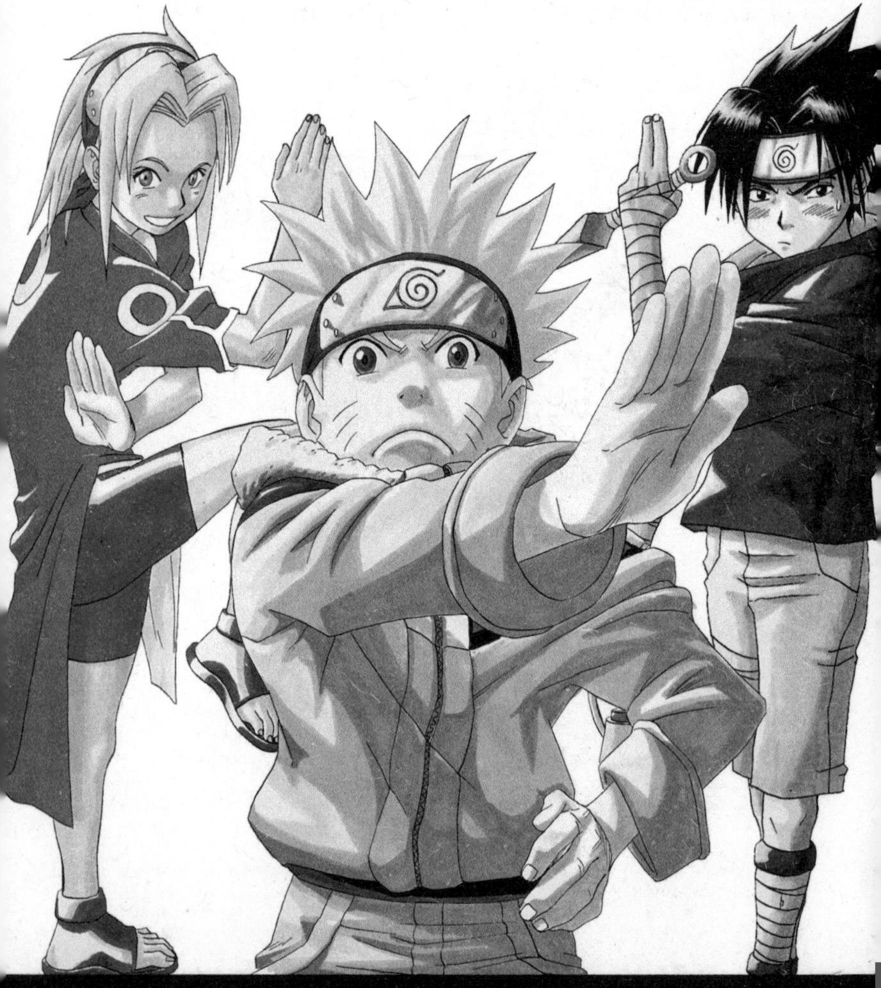

MITARASHI ANKO
みたらしアンコ

The Second Chief Examination Officer, responsible for the portion of the exam that takes place in the Forest of Death! She's determined to cut down the number of teams by half before the next segment of the test is complete, and she seems to relish the thought of watching the students go down in flames.

THE SOUND NINJA (OTONIN) 音忍

Are these mysterious ninja roaming the forest in search of their second scroll, or something else entirely?

ROCK LEE ロック・リー

Rock Lee, a devoted disciple of his teacher, Master Gai, is one of the most talented young shinobi around, and he's completely infatuated with Sakura.

THE ASUMA CELL
Choji チョウジ
Ino いの
Shikamaru シカマル

Sakura's rival Ino and her team hope to steal their second scroll from the weakest team in the bunch—Naruto's!

THE STORY SO FAR...

Twelve years ago, a destructive nine-tailed fox spirit attacked the ninja village of Konohagakure. The *Hokage*, or village champion, defeated the fox by sealing its soul into the body of a baby boy. Now that boy, Uzumaki Naruto, has grown up to become a ninja-in-training, learning the art of *ninjutsu* with his classmates Sakura and Sasuke.

Astonishingly, Naruto and his team passed the written section of the Chûnin (Journeyman Ninja) Selection Exam, but they face new dangers in the exam's second portion, which is conducted in the Forest of Death! The object of the exercise is to reach the tower in the center of the forest with two scrolls in hand, and all three team members alive, before five days elapse. Each of the 26 teams is given only one scroll, and must steal the second scroll from another team using any means necessary!

CONTENTS

Number 46: The Password Is...

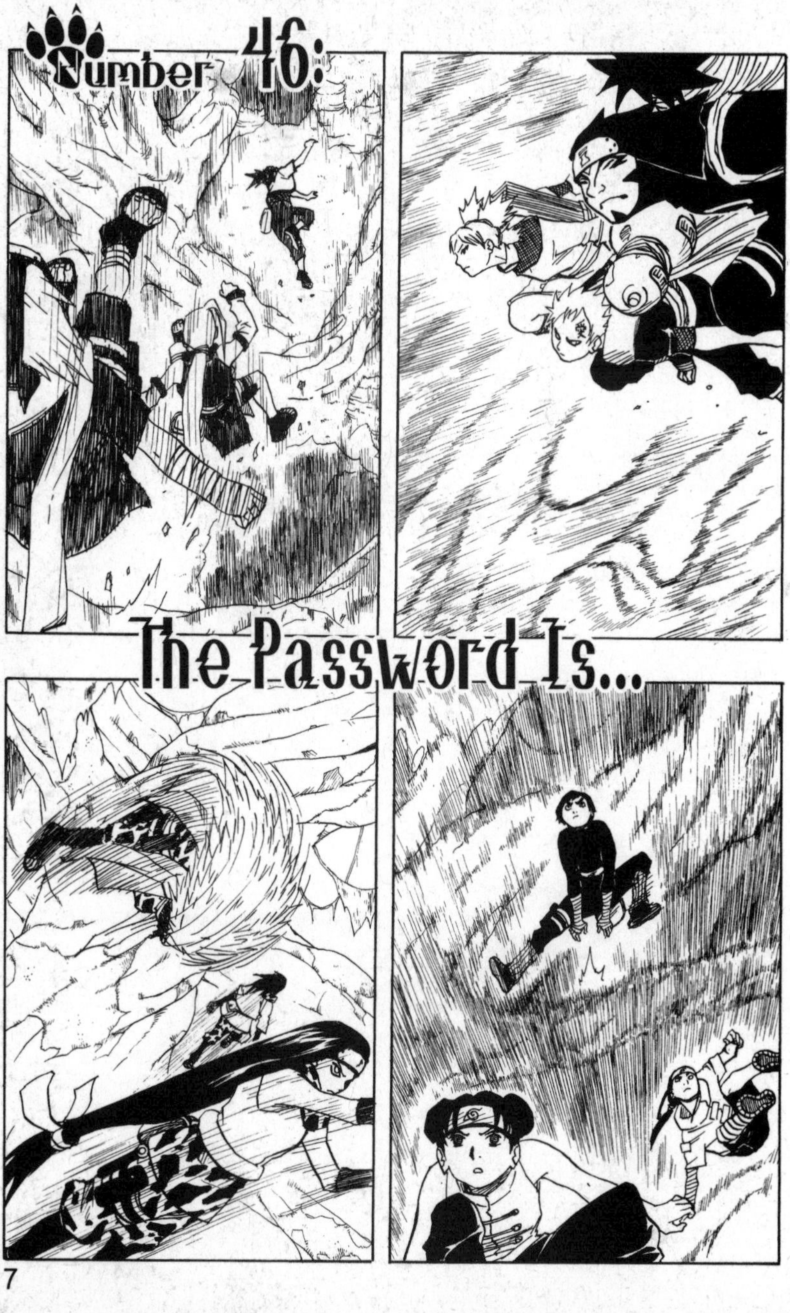

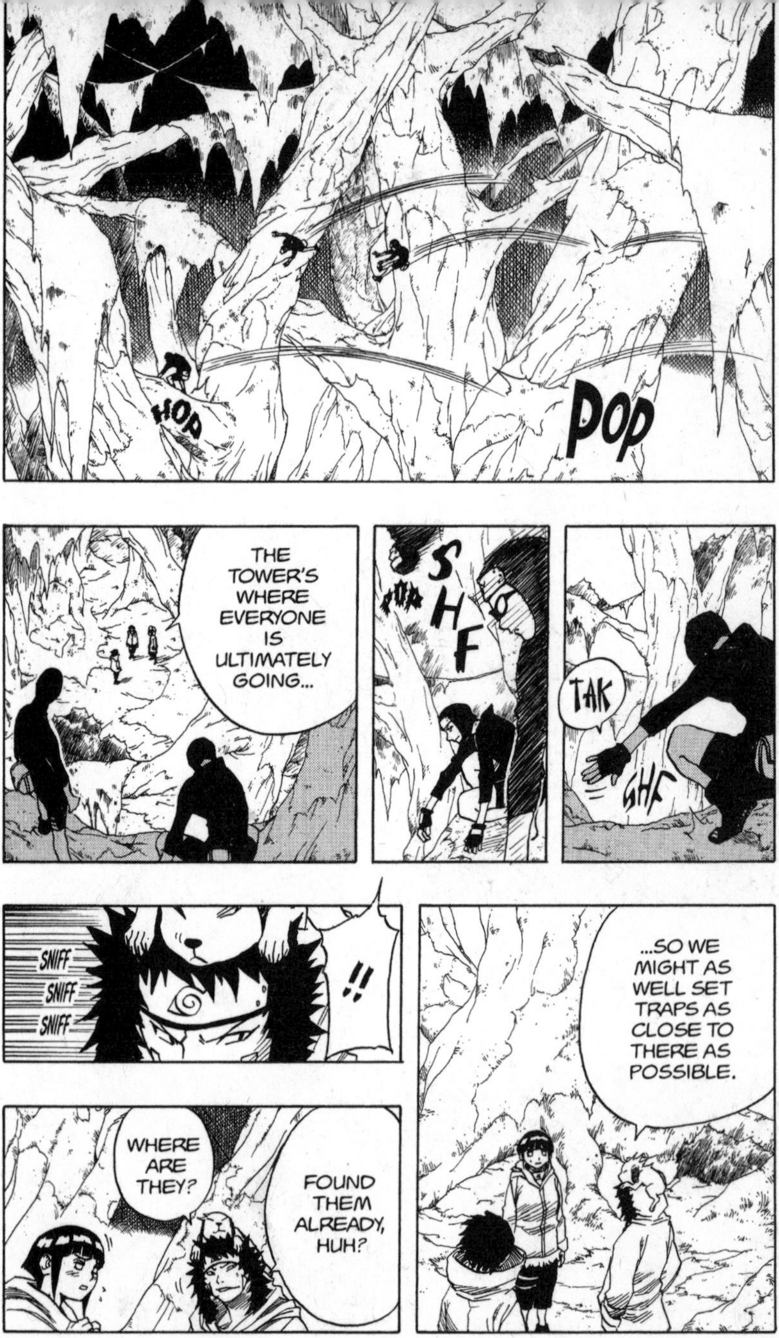
POP
HOP
TAK
SHF
SHF
POP
THE TOWER'S WHERE EVERYONE IS ULTIMATELY GOING...
...SO WE MIGHT AS WELL SET TRAPS AS CLOSE TO THERE AS POSSIBLE.
!!
SNIFF
SNIFF
SNIFF
FOUND THEM ALREADY, HUH?
WHERE ARE THEY?

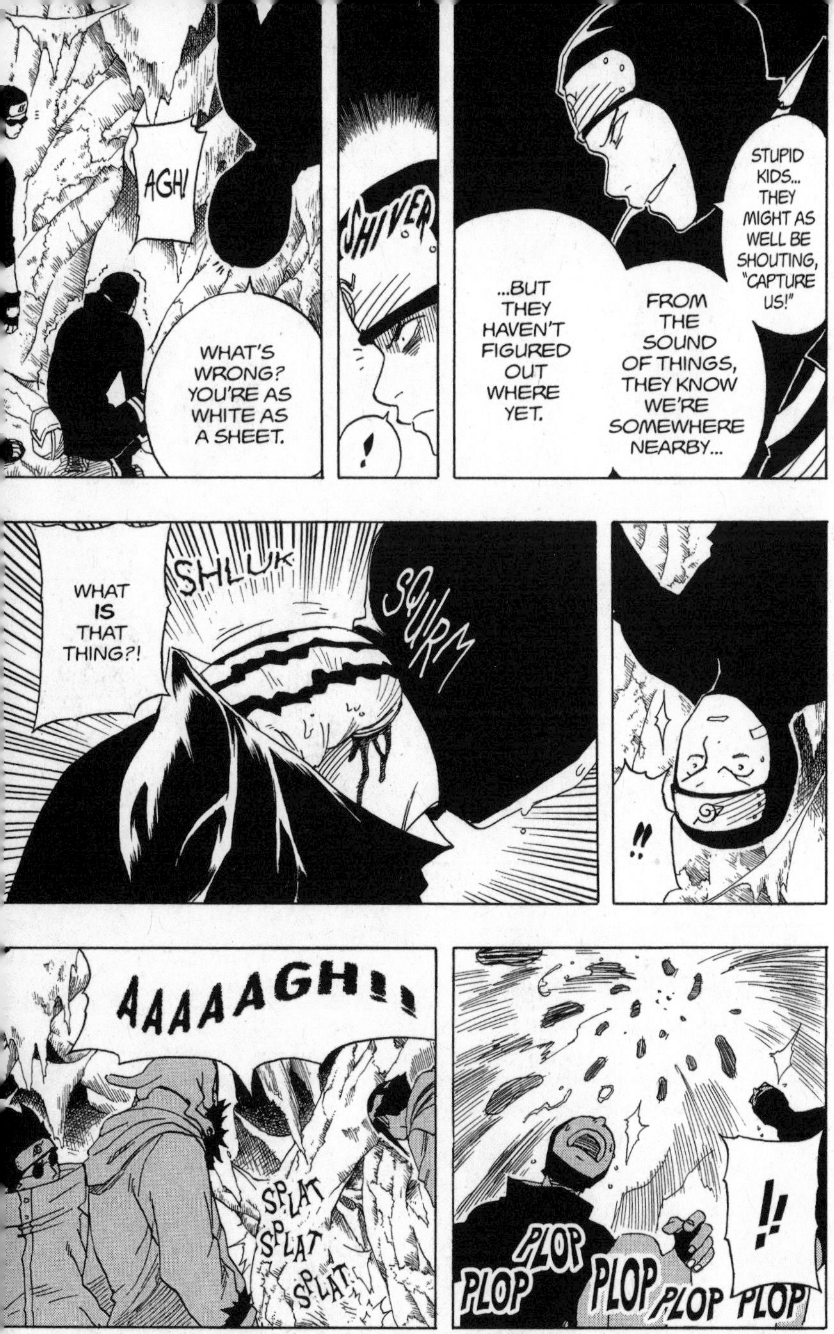
STUPID KIDS... THEY MIGHT AS WELL BE SHOUTING, "CAPTURE US!"
FROM THE SOUND OF THINGS, THEY KNOW WE'RE SOMEWHERE NEARBY...
...BUT THEY HAVEN'T FIGURED OUT WHERE YET.
SHIVER
!
AGH!
WHAT'S WRONG? YOU'RE AS WHITE AS A SHEET.
!!
SQUIRM
SHLUK
WHAT **IS** THAT THING?!
!!
PLOP
PLOP
PLOP
PLOP
PLOP
AAAAAGH!!
SPLAT
SPLAT
SPLAT

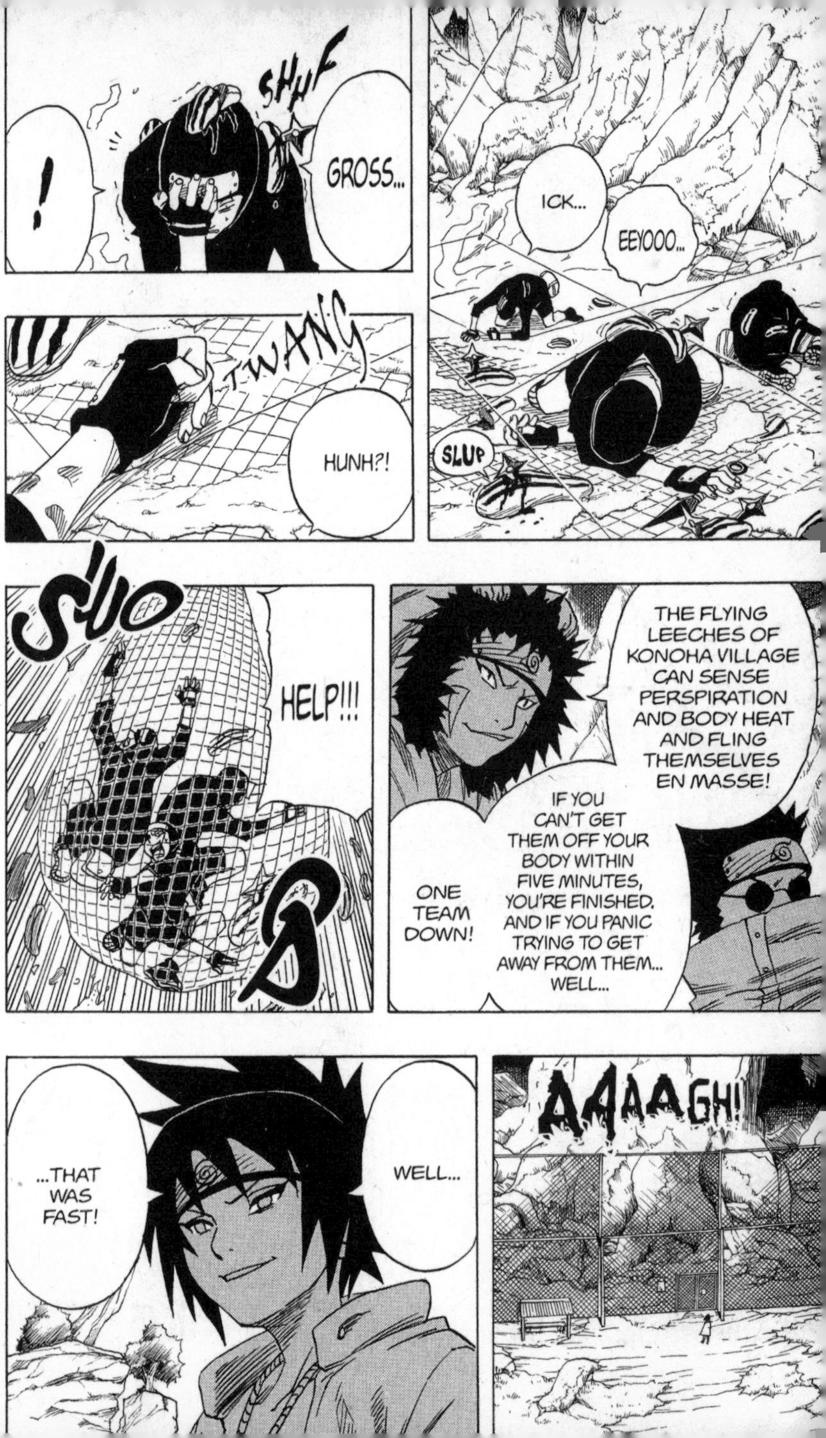
ICK...
EEYOOO...
SLUP
SHUF
GROSS...
!
TWANG
HUNH?!
THE FLYING LEECHES OF KONOHA VILLAGE CAN SENSE PERSPIRATION AND BODY HEAT AND FLING THEMSELVES EN MASSE!
IF YOU CAN'T GET THEM OFF YOUR BODY WITHIN FIVE MINUTES, YOU'RE FINISHED. AND IF YOU PANIC TRYING TO GET AWAY FROM THEM... WELL...
ONE TEAM DOWN!
HELP!!!
AAAAGH!
WELL...
...THAT WAS FAST!

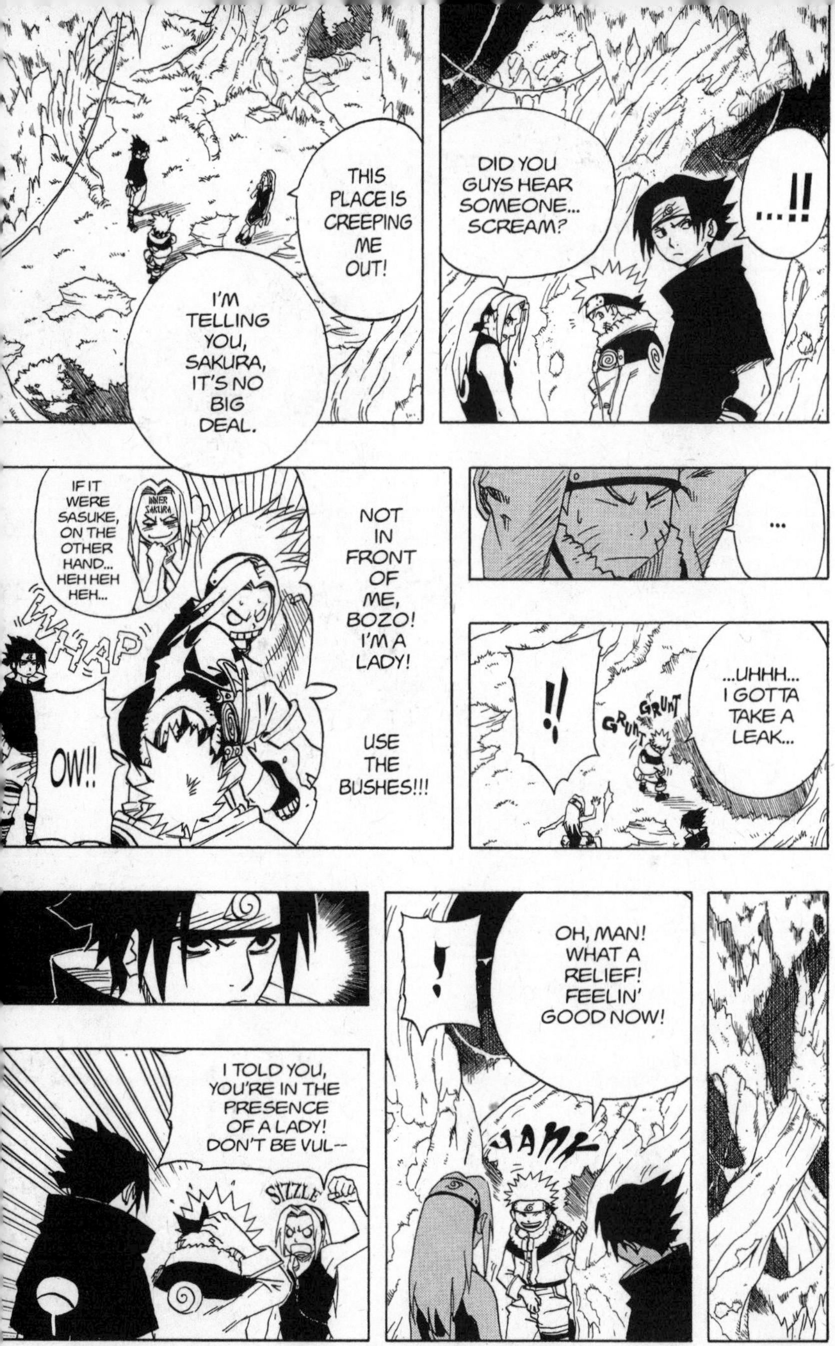
...!!
DID YOU GUYS HEAR SOMEONE... SCREAM?
THIS PLACE IS CREEPING ME OUT!
I'M TELLING YOU, SAKURA, IT'S NO BIG DEAL.
...
...UHHH... I GOTTA TAKE A LEAK...
!!
GRUNT GRUNT
NOT IN FRONT OF ME, BOZO! I'M A LADY!
USE THE BUSHES!!!
INNER SAKURA
IF IT WERE SASUKE, ON THE OTHER HAND... HEH HEH HEH...
WHAP
OW!!
OH, MAN! WHAT A RELIEF! FEELIN' GOOD NOW!
!
YANK
I TOLD YOU, YOU'RE IN THE PRESENCE OF A LADY! DON'T BE VUL--
SIZZLE

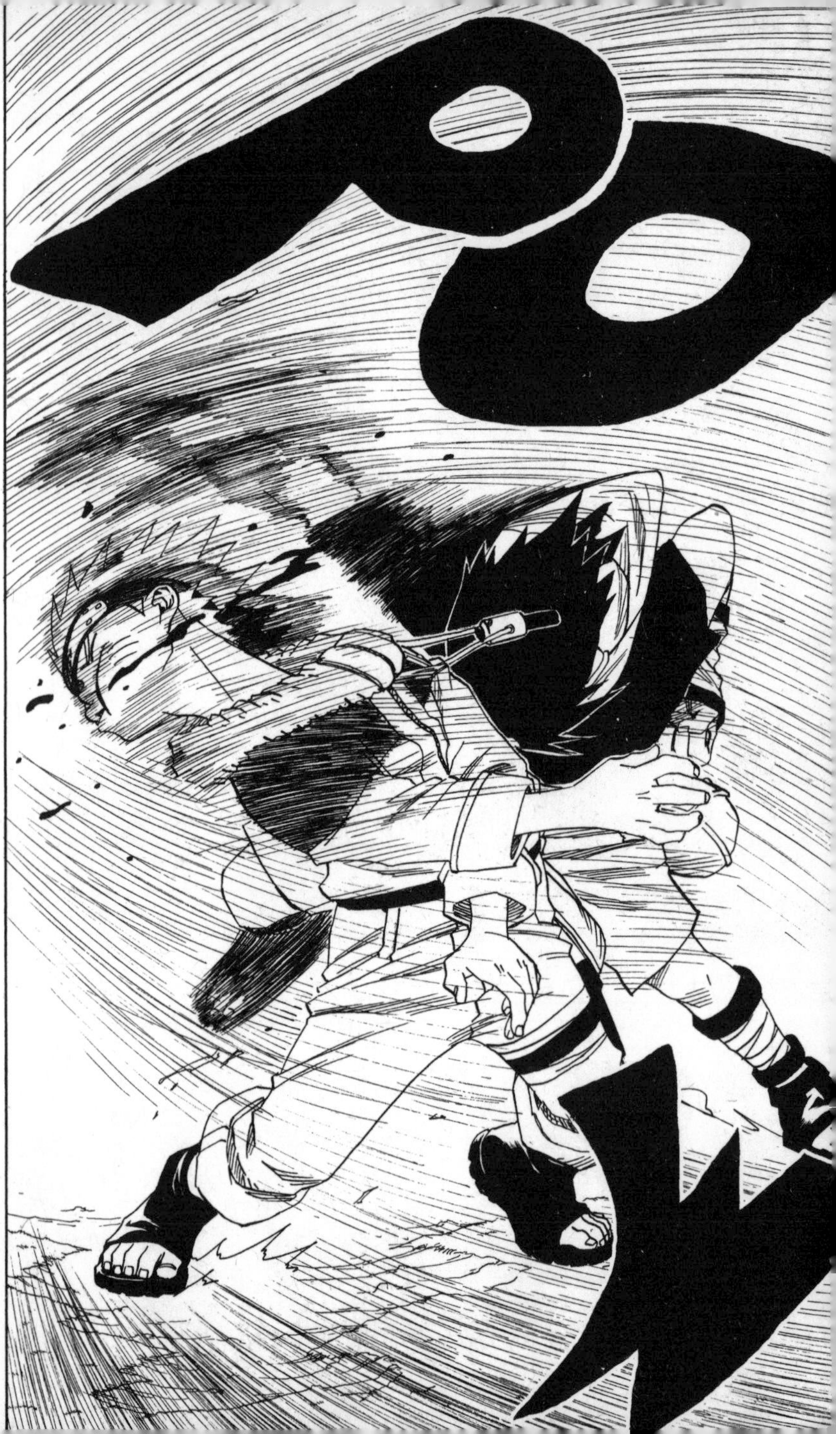

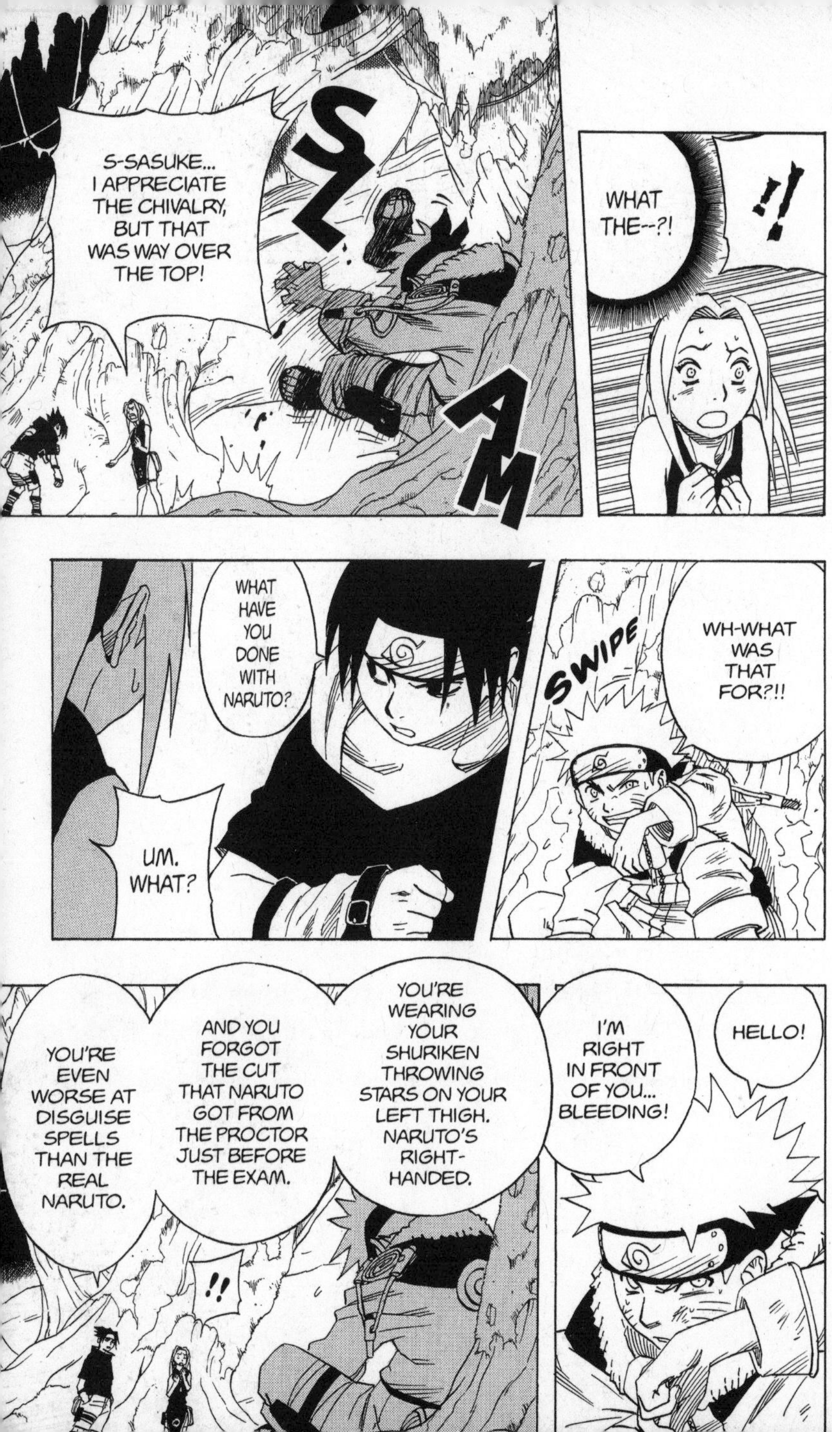
WHAT THE--?!
!!
SLAM
S-SASUKE... I APPRECIATE THE CHIVALRY, BUT THAT WAS WAY OVER THE TOP!
SWIPE
WH-WHAT WAS THAT FOR?!!
WHAT HAVE YOU DONE WITH NARUTO?
UM. WHAT?
HELLO!
I'M RIGHT IN FRONT OF YOU... BLEEDING!
YOU'RE WEARING YOUR SHURIKEN THROWING STARS ON YOUR LEFT THIGH. NARUTO'S RIGHT-HANDED.
AND YOU FORGOT THE CUT THAT NARUTO GOT FROM THE PROCTOR JUST BEFORE THE EXAM.
YOU'RE EVEN WORSE AT DISGUISE SPELLS THAN THE REAL NARUTO.
!!

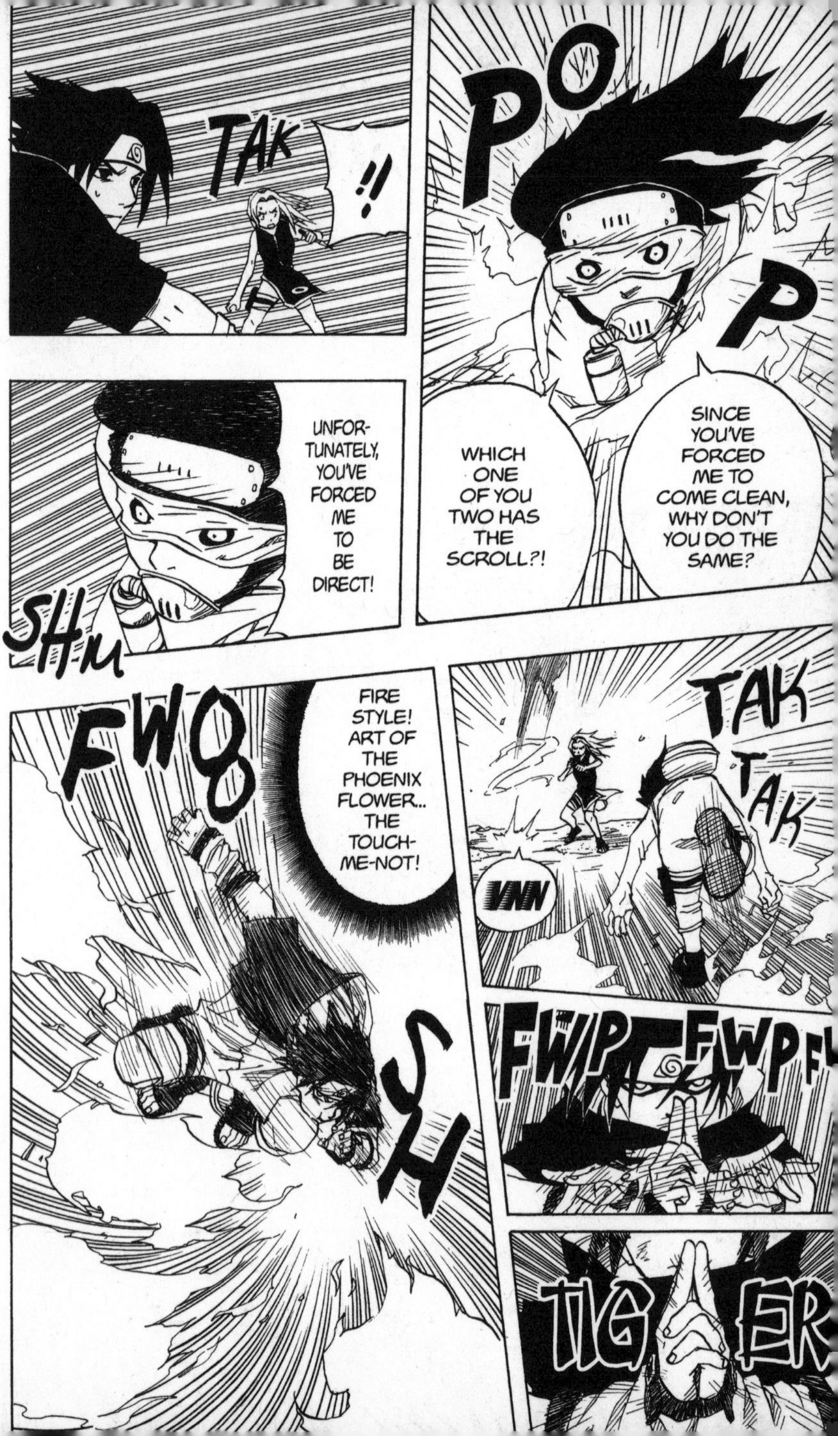

POP
P
SINCE YOU'VE FORCED ME TO COME CLEAN, WHY DON'T YOU DO THE SAME?
WHICH ONE OF YOU TWO HAS THE SCROLL?!
TAK
!!
UNFOR-TUNATELY, YOU'VE FORCED ME TO BE DIRECT!
SHM
TAK TAK
VNN
FWP FWPF
TIGER
FWOO
FIRE STYLE! ART OF THE PHOENIX FLOWER... THE TOUCH-ME-NOT!
SH

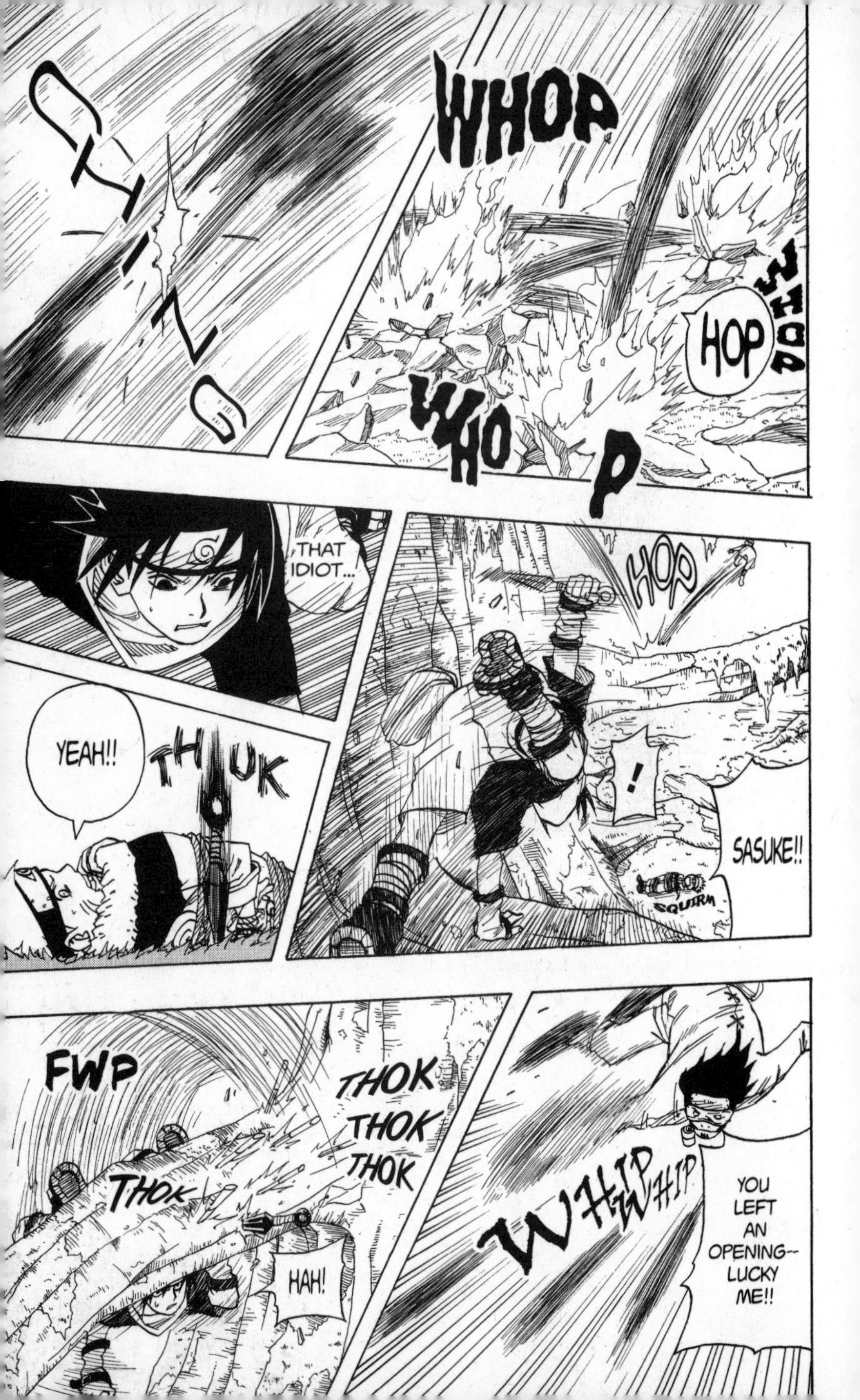

WHOP
HOP
WHOP
WHO P
CHING
HOP
!
SASUKE!!
SQUIRM
THAT IDIOT...
YEAH!!
THUK
YOU LEFT AN OPENING-- LUCKY ME!!
WHIP
WHIP
FWP
THOK
THOK
THOK
THOK
HAH!

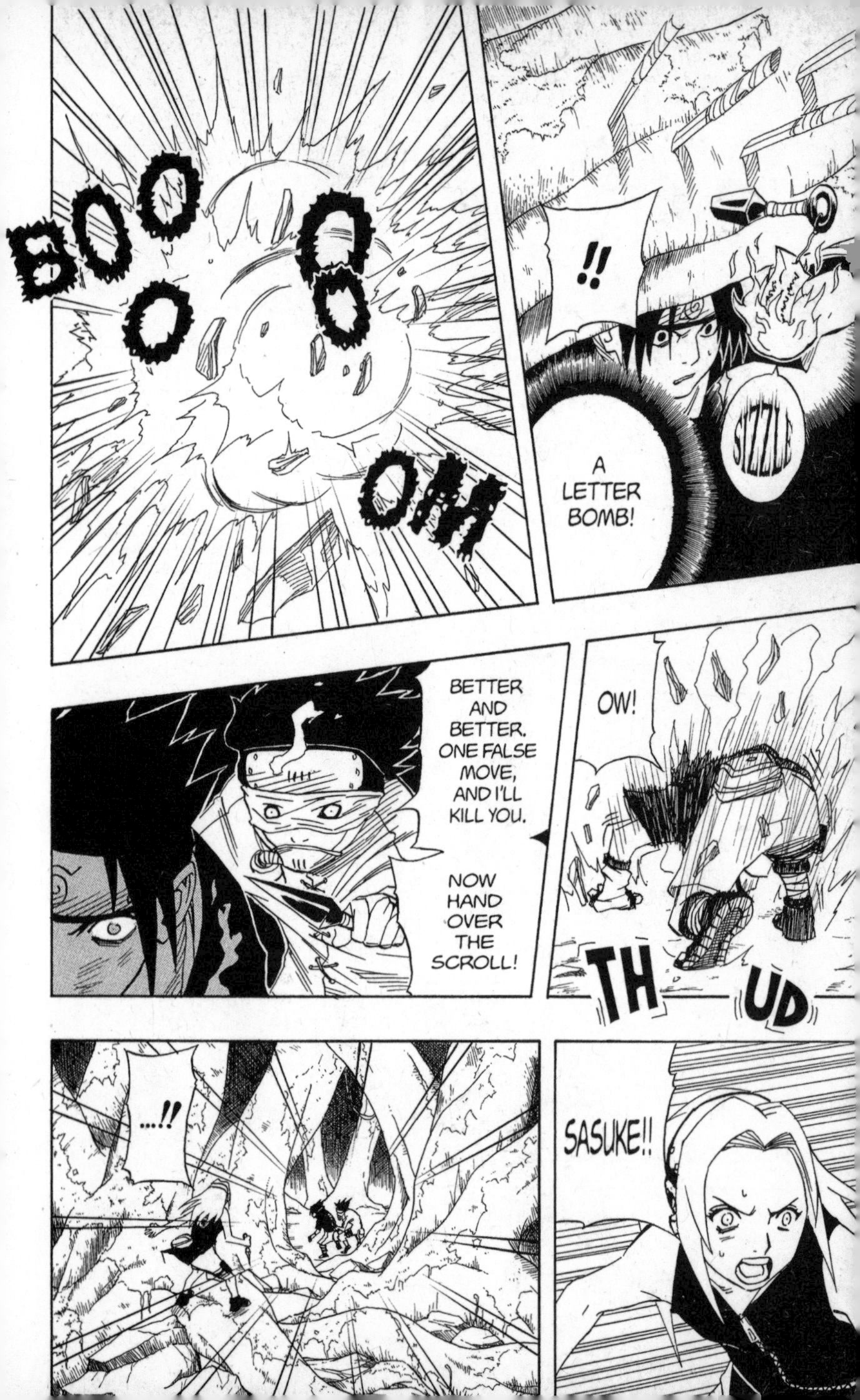
!!
SIZZLE
A LETTER BOMB!
BOOOOOOM
OW!
THUD
BETTER AND BETTER. ONE FALSE MOVE, AND I'LL KILL YOU.
NOW HAND OVER THE SCROLL!
SASUKE!!
...!!

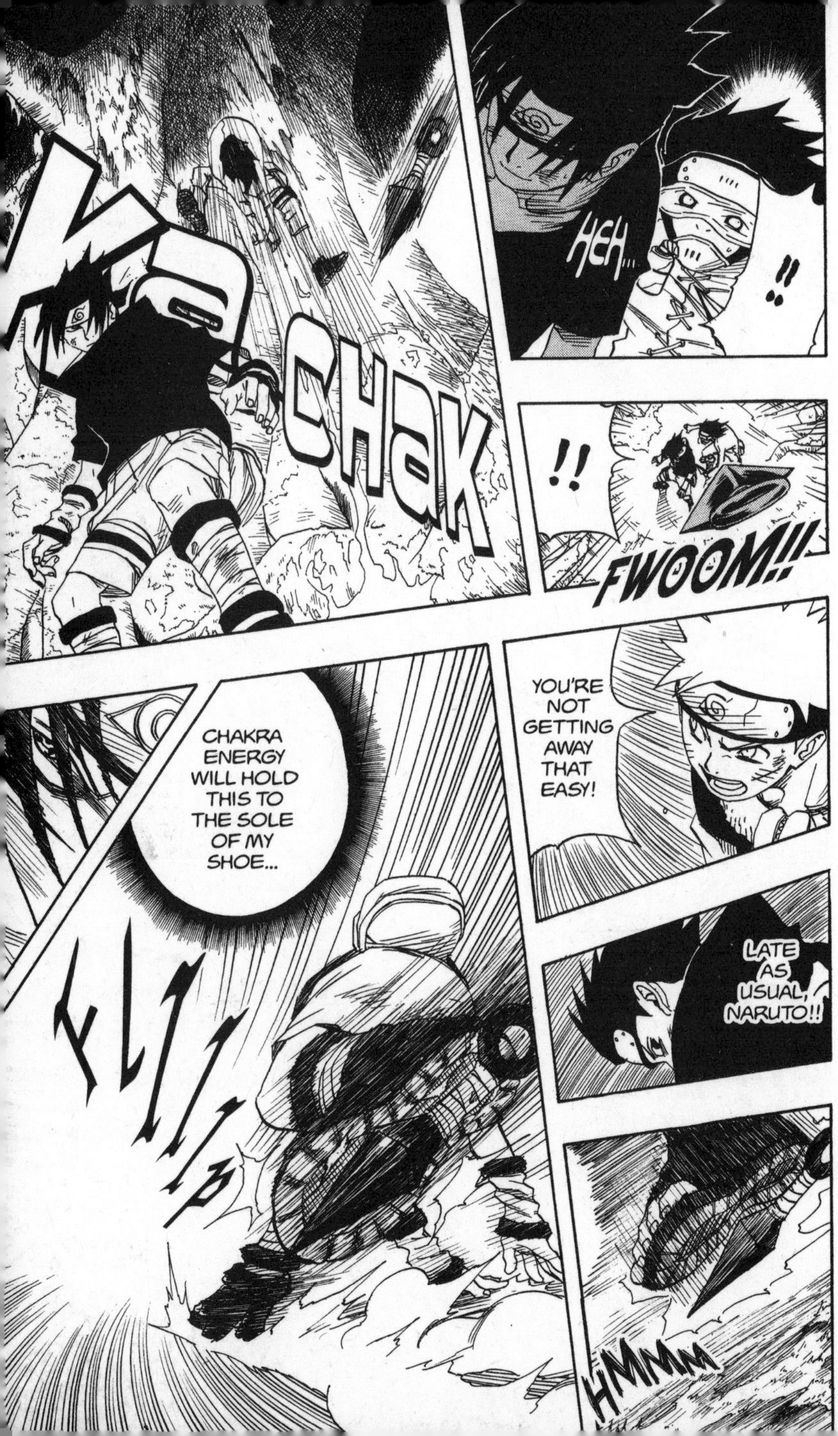
HEH...
!!
!!
FWOOM!!
CHAK
YOU'RE NOT GETTING AWAY THAT EASY!
LATE AS USUAL, NARUTO!!
HMMM
CHAKRA ENERGY WILL HOLD THIS TO THE SOLE OF MY SHOE...

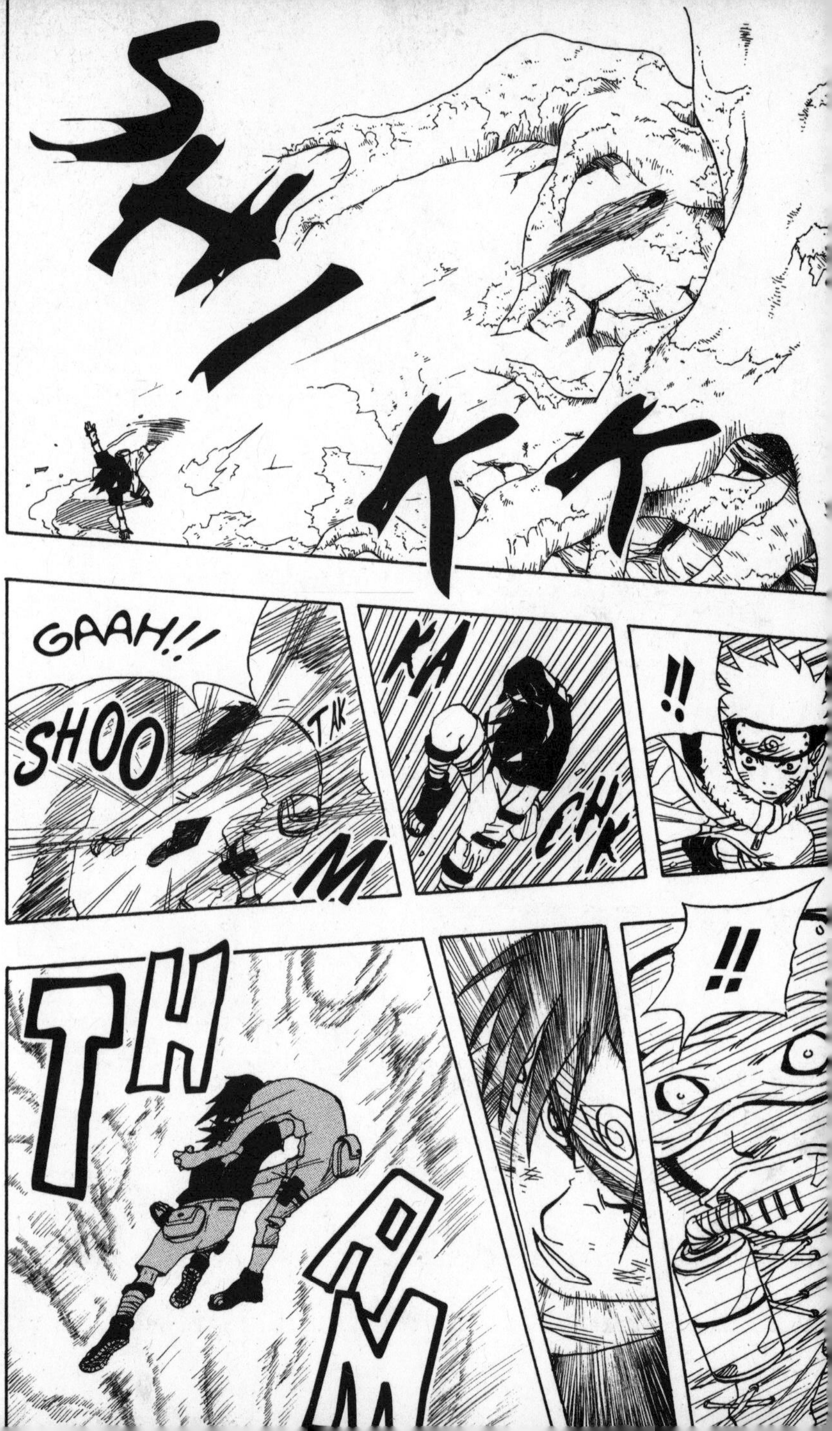
!!
KA
CHK
GAAH!!!
SHOOM
TAK
!!
THAM

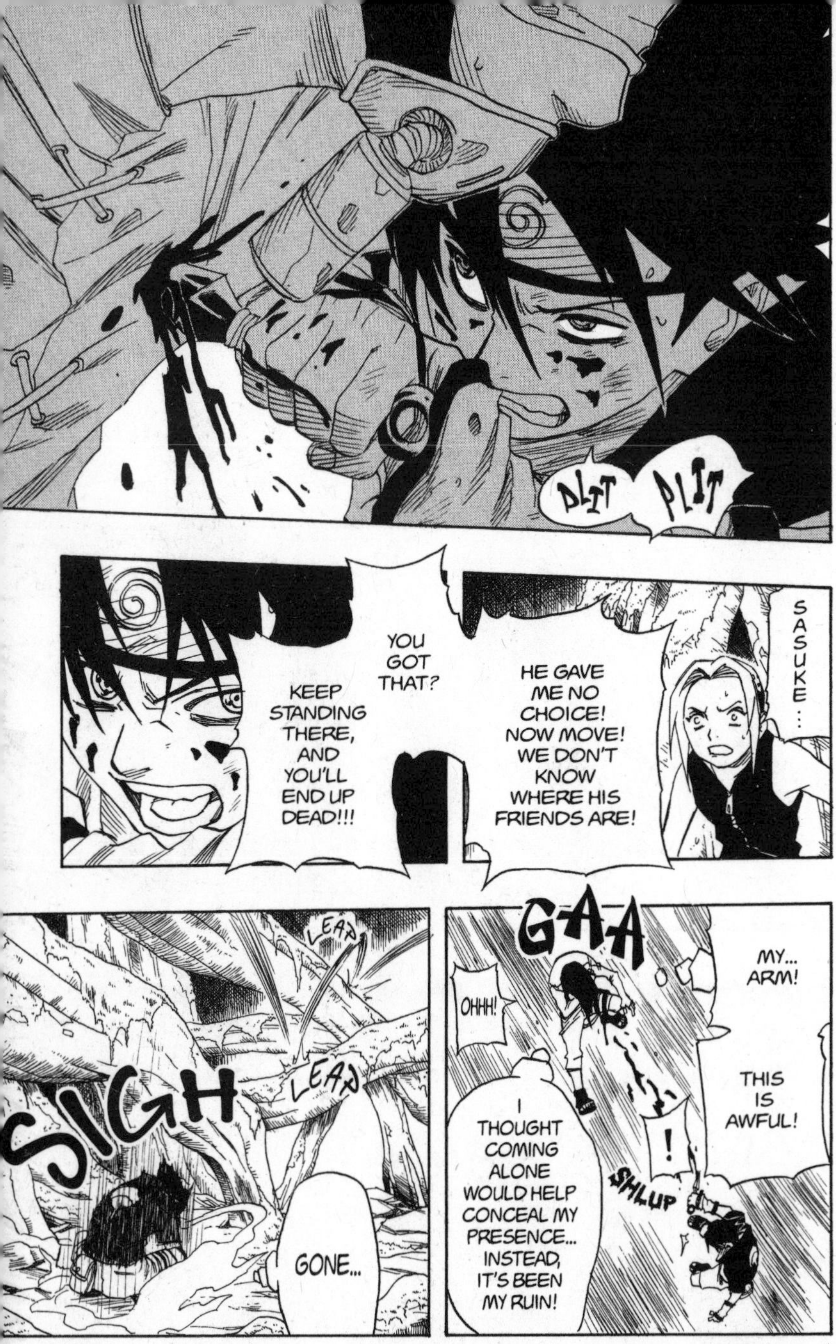
PLIT
PLIT
SASUKE...
HE GAVE ME NO CHOICE! NOW MOVE! WE DON'T KNOW WHERE HIS FRIENDS ARE!
YOU GOT THAT?
KEEP STANDING THERE, AND YOU'LL END UP DEAD!!!
GAA
MY... ARM!
OHHH!
THIS IS AWFUL!
!
SHLUP
I THOUGHT COMING ALONE WOULD HELP CONCEAL MY PRESENCE... INSTEAD, IT'S BEEN MY RUIN!
LEAP
LEAP
SIGH
GONE...

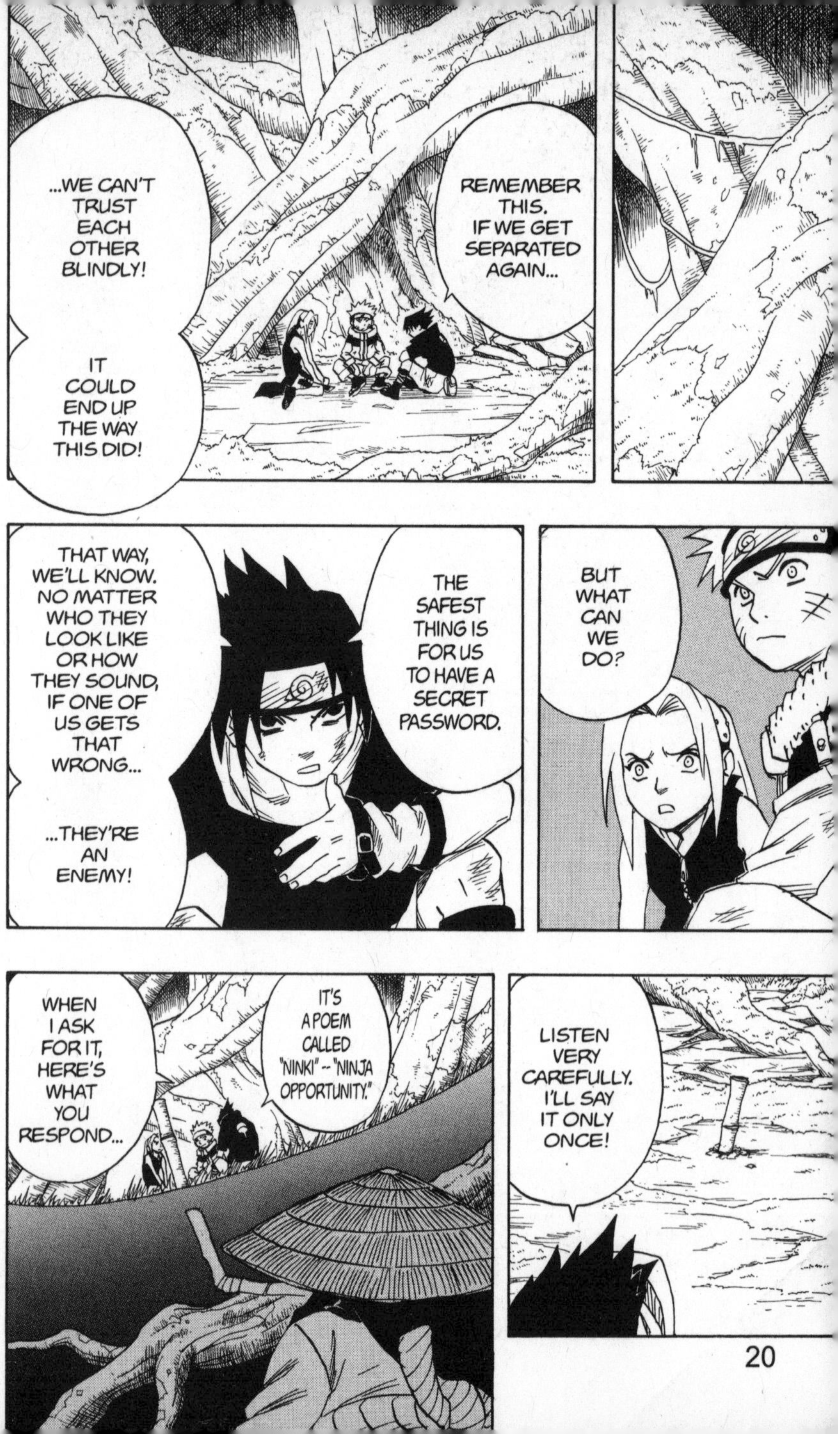
REMEMBER THIS. IF WE GET SEPARATED AGAIN...
...WE CAN'T TRUST EACH OTHER BLINDLY!
IT COULD END UP THE WAY THIS DID!
BUT WHAT CAN WE DO?
THE SAFEST THING IS FOR US TO HAVE A SECRET PASSWORD.
THAT WAY, WE'LL KNOW. NO MATTER WHO THEY LOOK LIKE OR HOW THEY SOUND, IF ONE OF US GETS THAT WRONG...
...THEY'RE AN ENEMY!
LISTEN VERY CAREFULLY. I'LL SAY IT ONLY ONCE!
IT'S A POEM CALLED "NINKI" -- "NINJA OPPORTUNITY."
WHEN I ASK FOR IT, HERE'S WHAT YOU RESPOND...

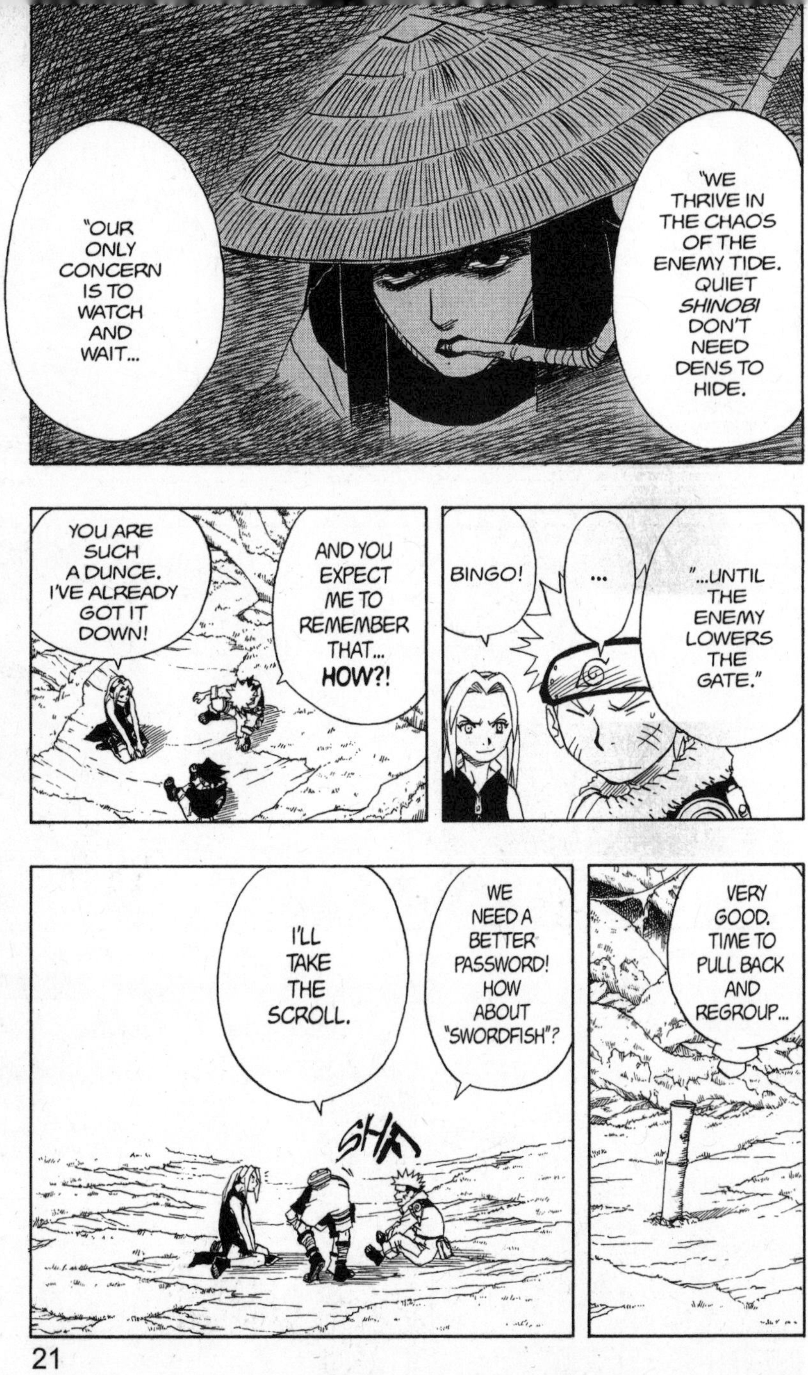
"WE THRIVE IN THE CHAOS OF THE ENEMY TIDE. QUIET *SHINOBI* DON'T NEED DENS TO HIDE.
"OUR ONLY CONCERN IS TO WATCH AND WAIT...
"...UNTIL THE ENEMY LOWERS THE GATE."
...
BINGO!
AND YOU EXPECT ME TO REMEMBER THAT... **HOW?!**
YOU ARE SUCH A DUNCE. I'VE ALREADY GOT IT DOWN!
VERY GOOD. TIME TO PULL BACK AND REGROUP...
WE NEED A BETTER PASSWORD! HOW ABOUT "SWORDFISH"?
I'LL TAKE THE SCROLL.
SHF

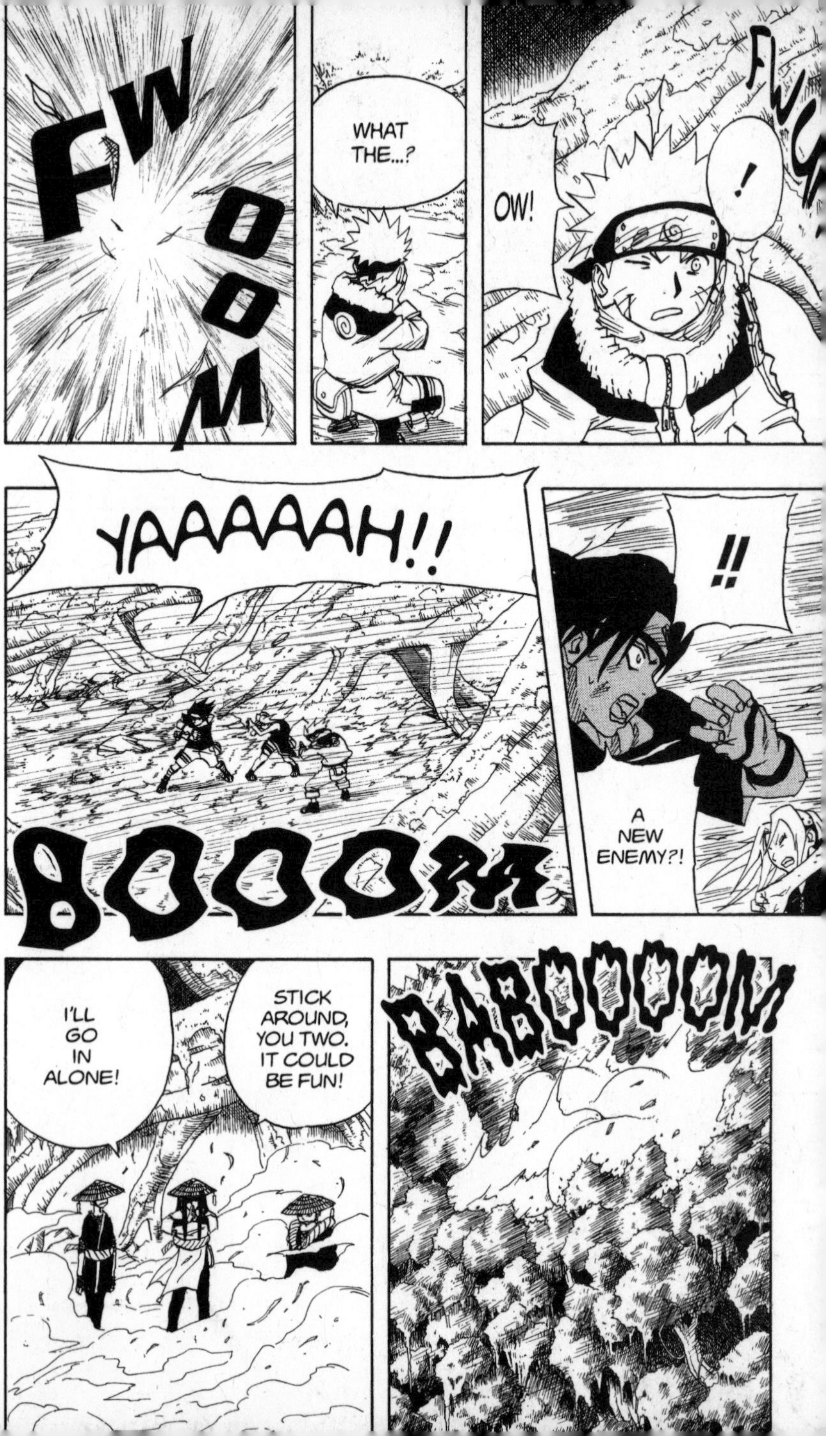
!
OW!
WHAT THE...?
FWOOM
!!
A NEW ENEMY?!
YAAAAAH!!
BOOOM
BABOOOOM
STICK AROUND, YOU TWO. IT COULD BE FUN!
I'LL GO IN ALONE!

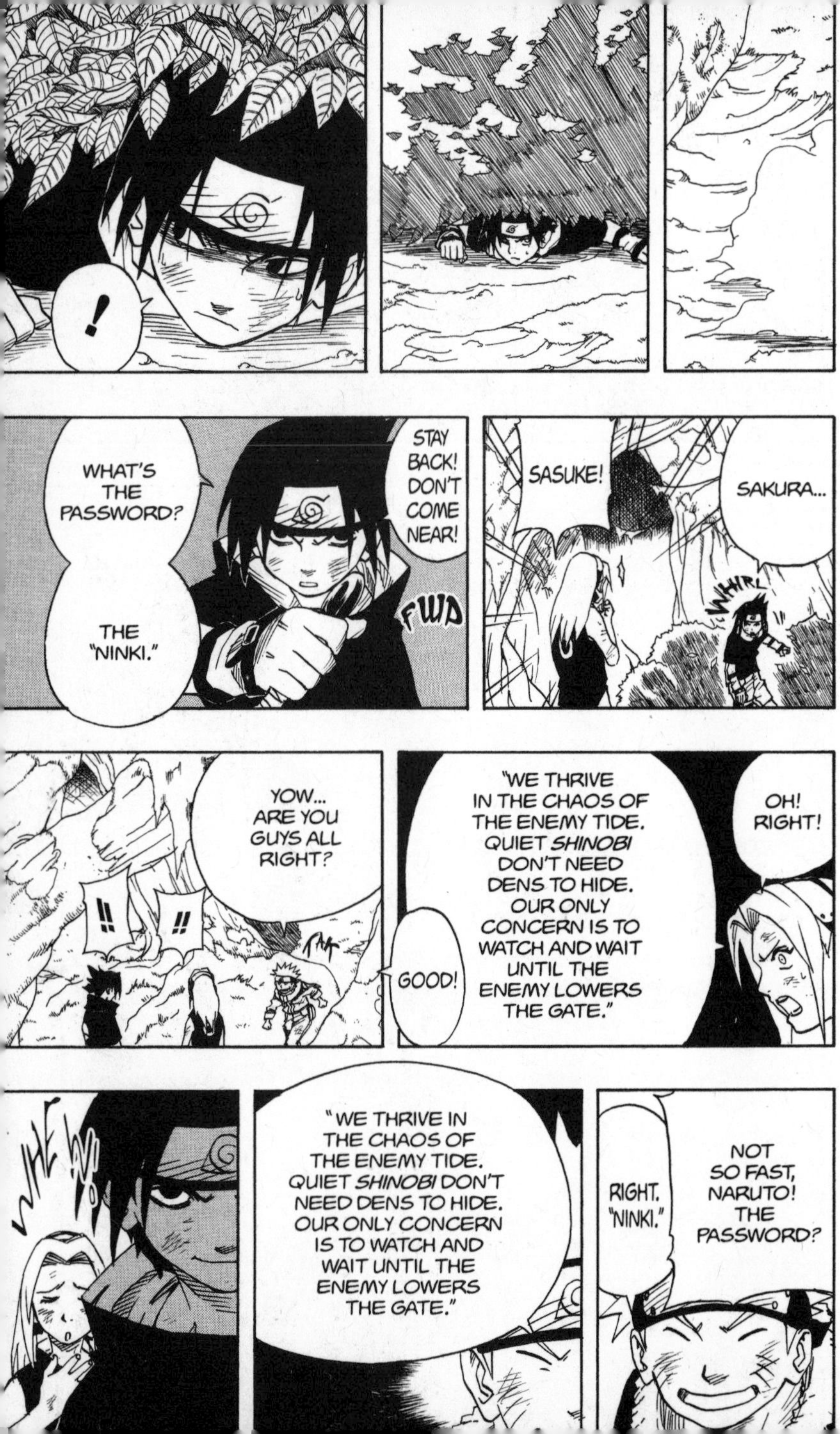
!
SAKURA...
SASUKE!
WHIRL
!!
STAY BACK! DON'T COME NEAR!
WHAT'S THE PASSWORD?
THE "NINKI."
OH! RIGHT!
"WE THRIVE IN THE CHAOS OF THE ENEMY TIDE. QUIET *SHINOBI* DON'T NEED DENS TO HIDE. OUR ONLY CONCERN IS TO WATCH AND WAIT UNTIL THE ENEMY LOWERS THE GATE."
GOOD!
YOW... ARE YOU GUYS ALL RIGHT?
!!
!!
NOT SO FAST, NARUTO! THE PASSWORD?
RIGHT. "NINKI."
"WE THRIVE IN THE CHAOS OF THE ENEMY TIDE. QUIET *SHINOBI* DON'T NEED DENS TO HIDE. OUR ONLY CONCERN IS TO WATCH AND WAIT UNTIL THE ENEMY LOWERS THE GATE."

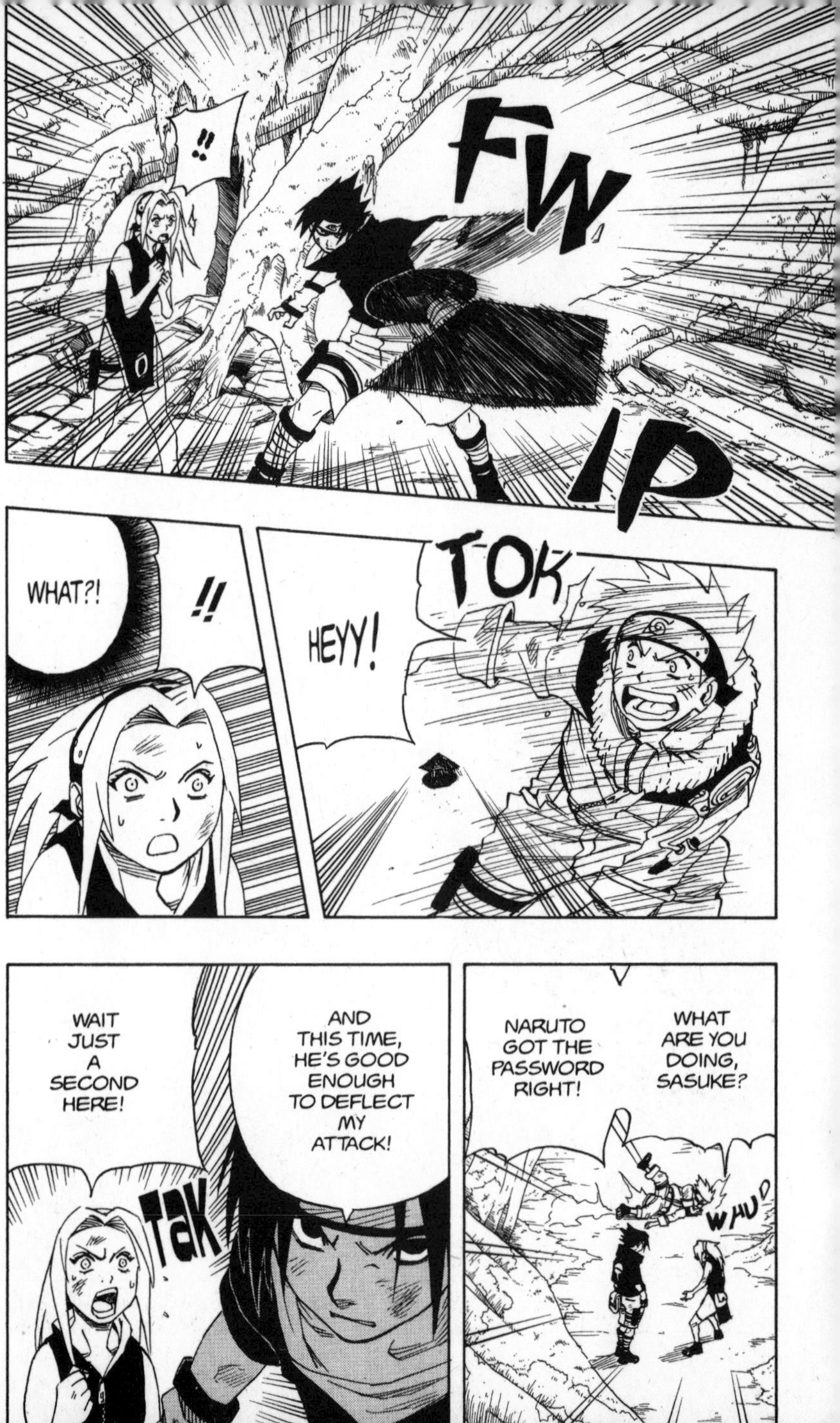
!!
FWIP
TOK
HEYY!
WHAT?!
!!
WHAT ARE YOU DOING, SASUKE?
NARUTO GOT THE PASSWORD RIGHT!
WHUD
AND THIS TIME, HE'S GOOD ENOUGH TO DEFLECT MY ATTACK!
WAIT JUST A SECOND HERE!
TAK

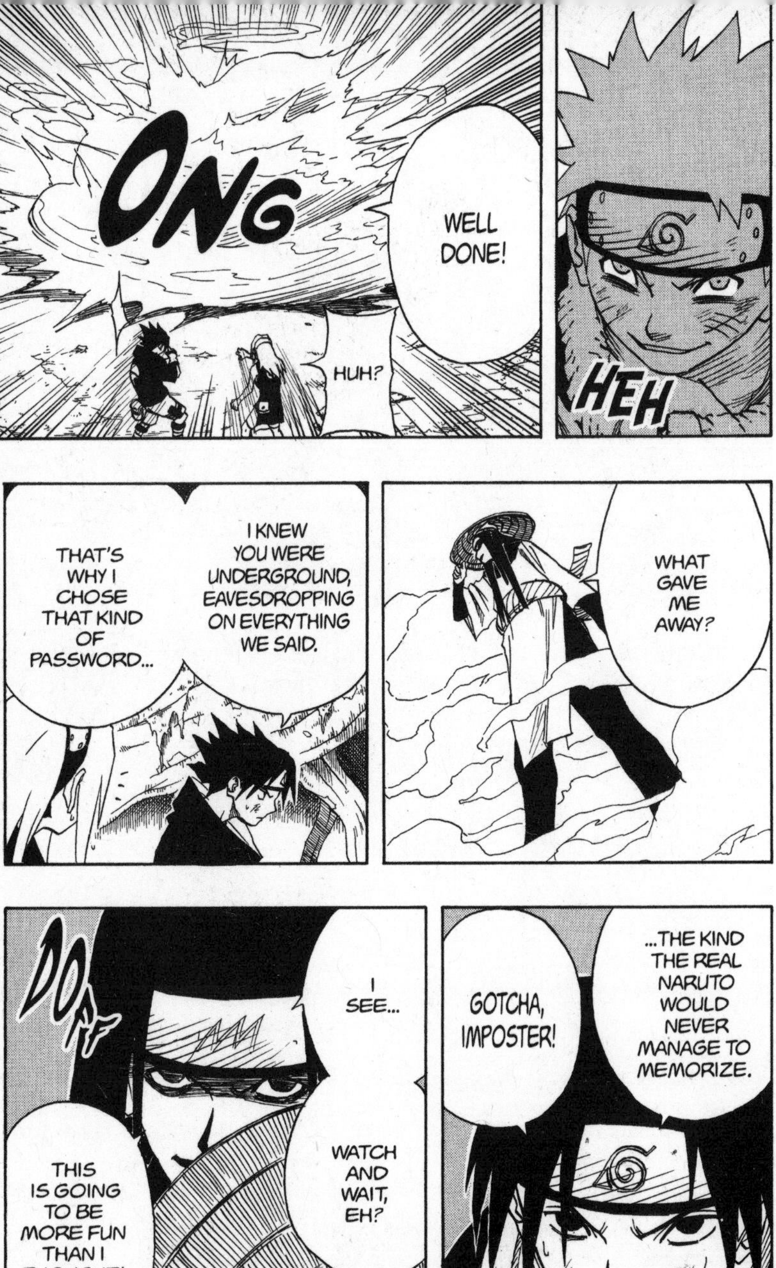
HEH
WELL DONE!
ONG
HUH?
WHAT GAVE ME AWAY?
I KNEW YOU WERE UNDERGROUND, EAVESDROPPING ON EVERYTHING WE SAID.
THAT'S WHY I CHOSE THAT KIND OF PASSWORD...
...THE KIND THE REAL NARUTO WOULD NEVER MANAGE TO MEMORIZE.
GOTCHA, IMPOSTER!
I SEE...
DOFF
WATCH AND WAIT, EH?
THIS IS GOING TO BE MORE FUN THAN I THOUGHT!

MEET KISHIMOTO MASASHI'S ASSISTANTS - PART ONE

◦ASSISTANT NO. 1: TAKAHASHI KAZUHIRO

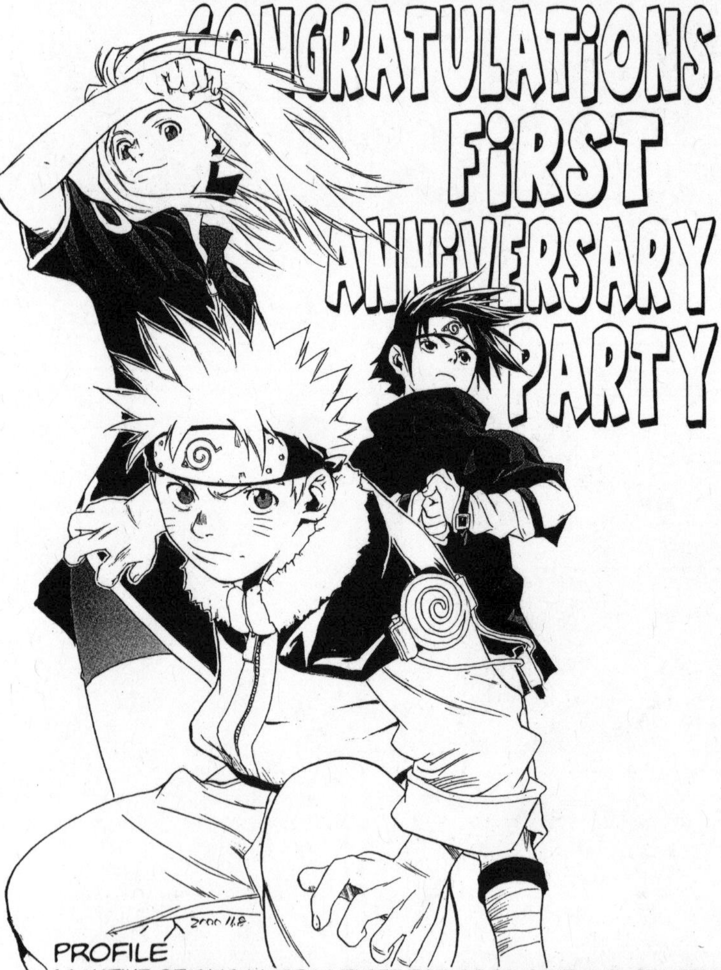
CONGRATULATIONS
FIRST
ANNIVERSARY
PARTY
2000.11.8

PROFILE

- A NATIVE OF KYUSHU WITH A TASTE FOR GOOD SAKE AND RED BEAN BUNS, HE COMES FROM THE BEAUTIFUL CITY OF BEPPU, ALSO KNOWN AS HELL (BECAUSE OF THE SULFUROUS FUMES THAT BILLOW FROM ITS FAMOUS HOT SPRINGS).
- LOVES TO EAT AND ALWAYS HAS HIS NOSE IN THE OFFICE REFRIGERATOR.
- LOTS OF TREASURES ARE SLEEPING IN HIS CLOSET AT HOME.
- HAS A TASTE FOR LEATHER AND WILD MOTORBIKE RIDES.
- HE'S A SUB-ZERO SUPER-COOL BAD BOY WHO LIKES TO PLAY DUMB. HE WORKS AS MY BETA -- THE ARTIST WHO SPOTS THE SOLID BLACKS IN HAIR AND CLOTHING, LAYS DOWN THE HALF-TONES, AND COMPLETES THE BACKGROUND ART -- AND LIVES LIKE A CHIEF.

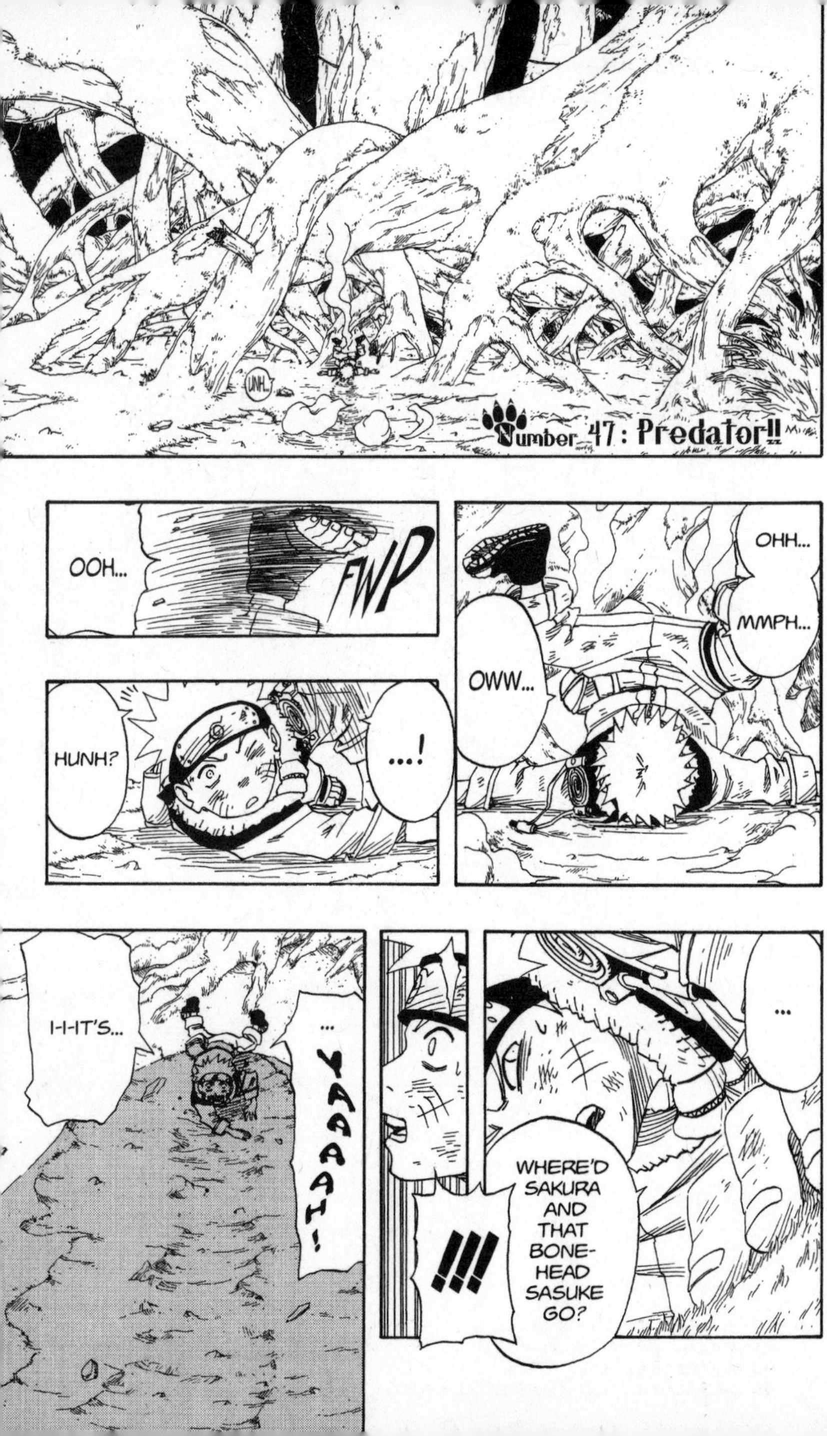
UNH...
Number 47 : Predator!!
OHH...
MMPH...
OWW...
FWP
OOH...
...!
HUNH?
...
WHERE'D SAKURA AND THAT BONE-HEAD SASUKE GO?
!!!
... YAAAAAH!
I-I-IT'S...

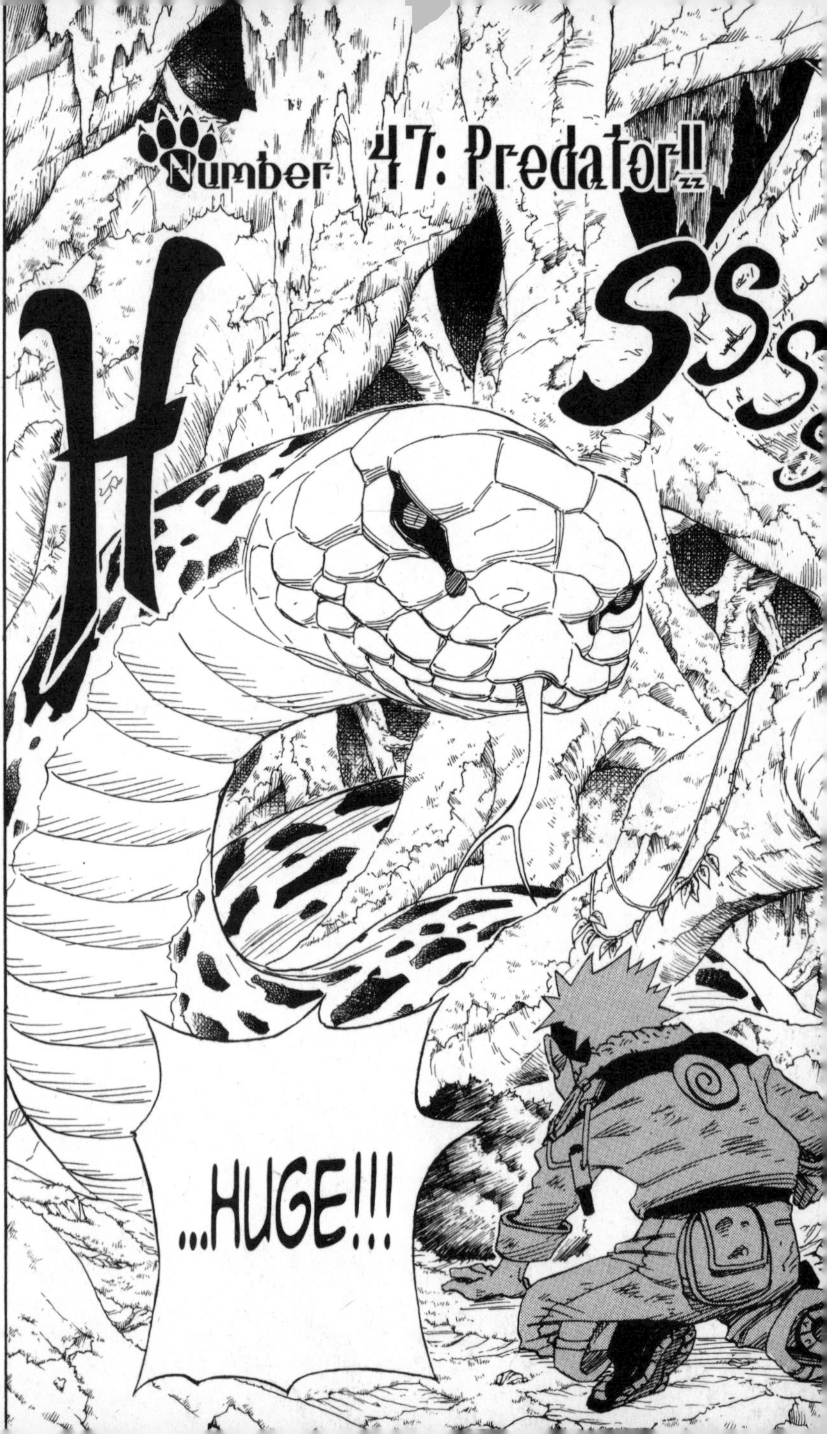
Number 47: Predator!!
SSS
H
...HUGE!!!

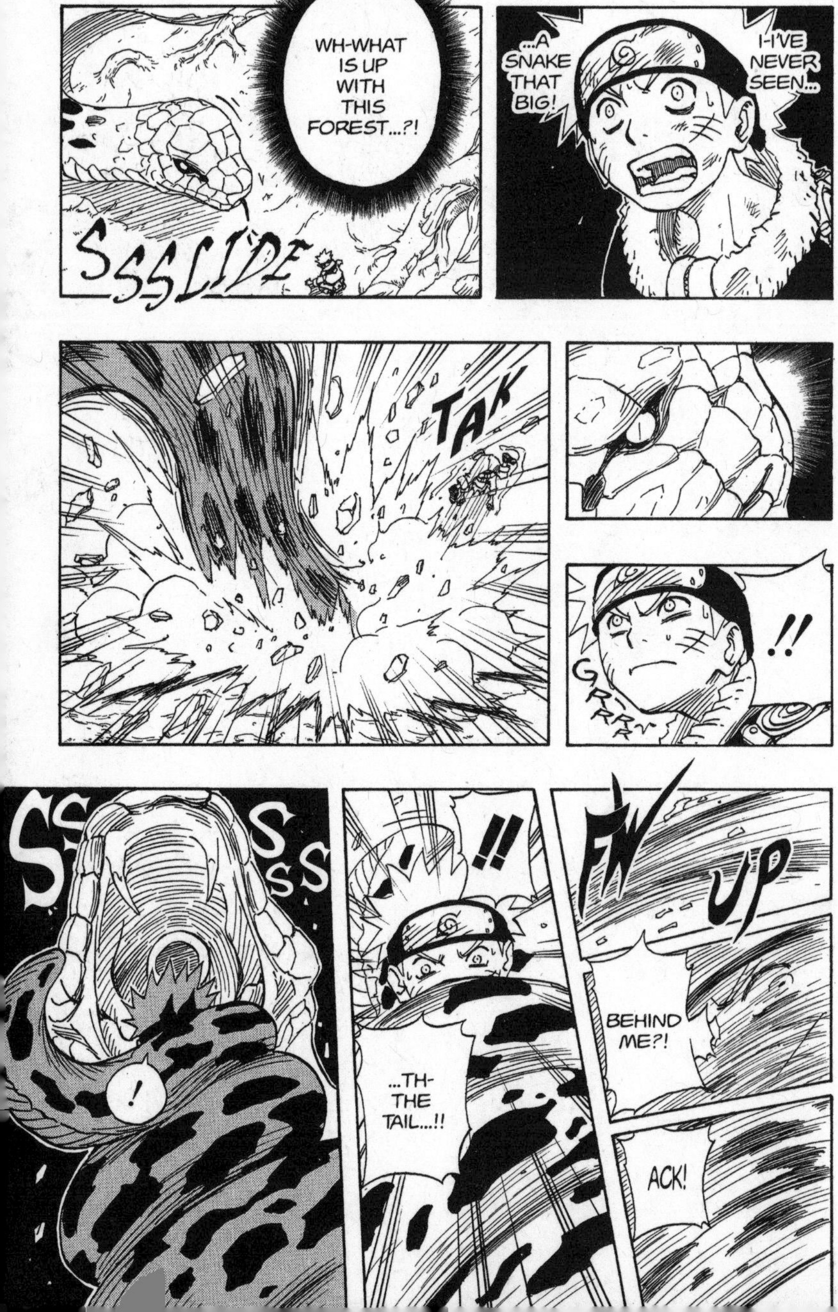
I-I'VE NEVER SEEN...
...A SNAKE THAT BIG!
WH-WHAT IS UP WITH THIS FOREST...?!
SSSLIDE
!!
GRRRR
TAK
FW
UP
BEHIND ME?!
ACK!
!!
...TH- THE TAIL...!!
SSSSS
!

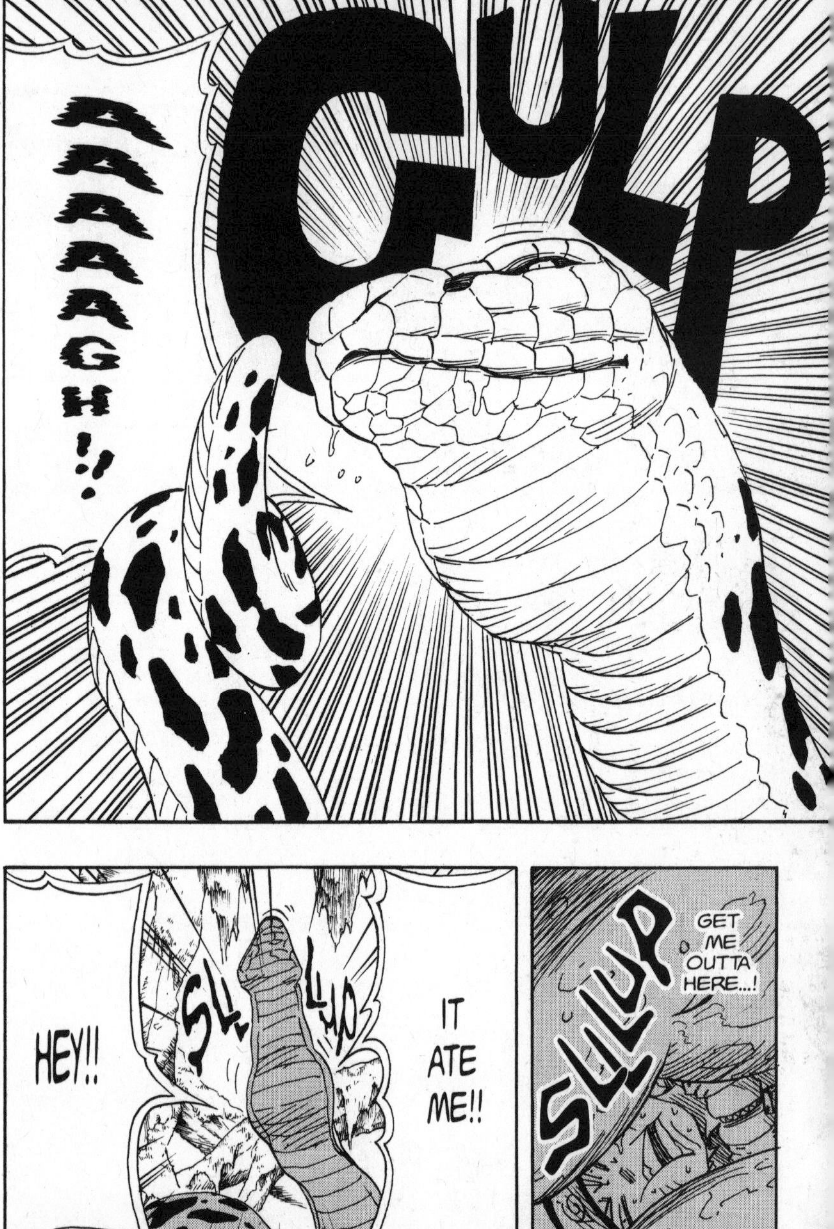
AAAAAGH!!
GULP
GET ME OUTTA HERE...!
SLLLUP
IT ATE ME!!
SLLLUP
HEY!!

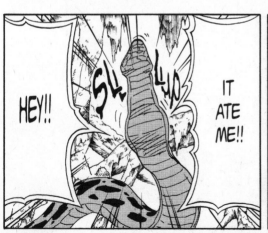

READ THIS WAY

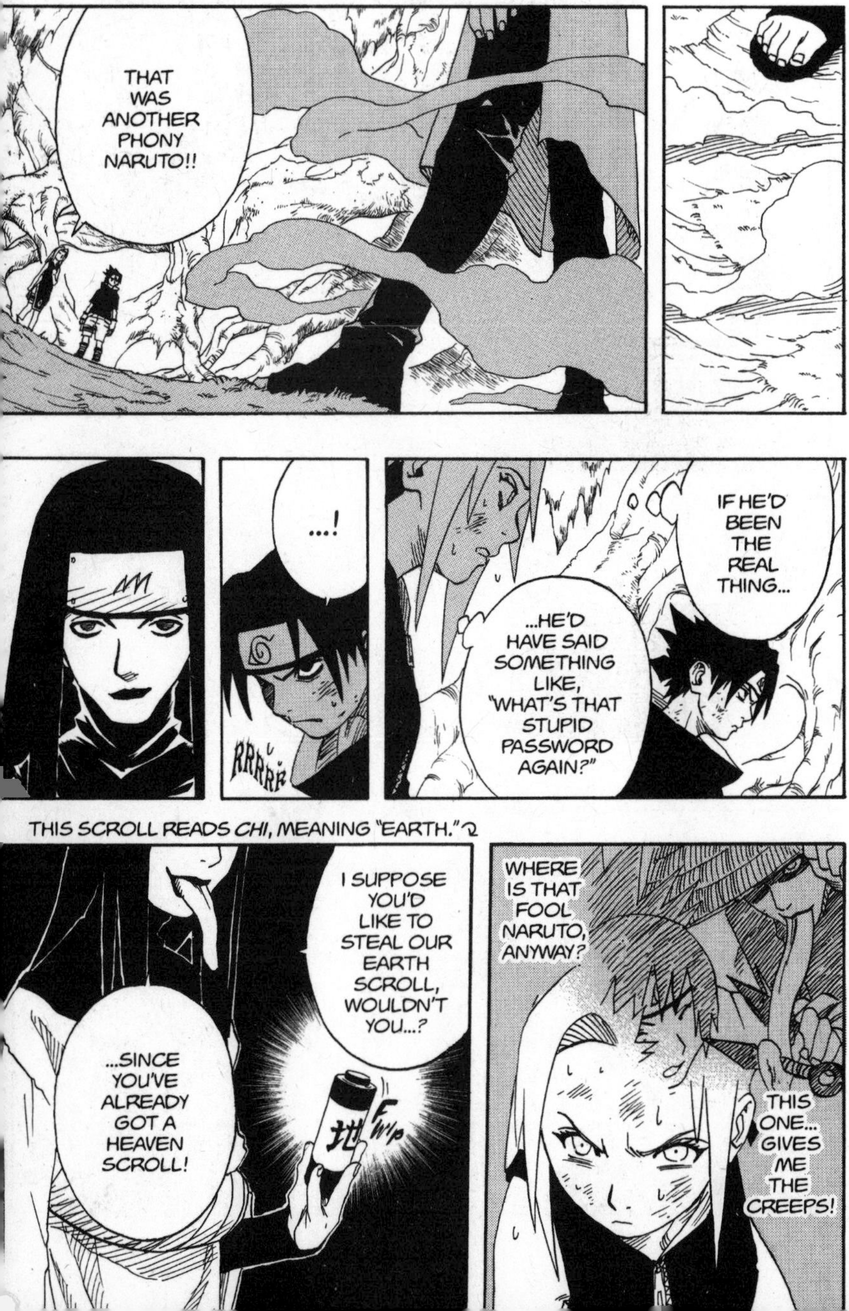
THAT WAS ANOTHER PHONY NARUTO!!
IF HE'D BEEN THE REAL THING...
...HE'D HAVE SAID SOMETHING LIKE, "WHAT'S THAT STUPID PASSWORD AGAIN?"
...!
RRRRR
THIS SCROLL READS CHI, MEANING "EARTH."
WHERE IS THAT FOOL NARUTO, ANYWAY?
THIS ONE... GIVES ME THE CREEPS!
I SUPPOSE YOU'D LIKE TO STEAL OUR EARTH SCROLL, WOULDN'T YOU...?
...SINCE YOU'VE ALREADY GOT A HEAVEN SCROLL!
地
FWIP

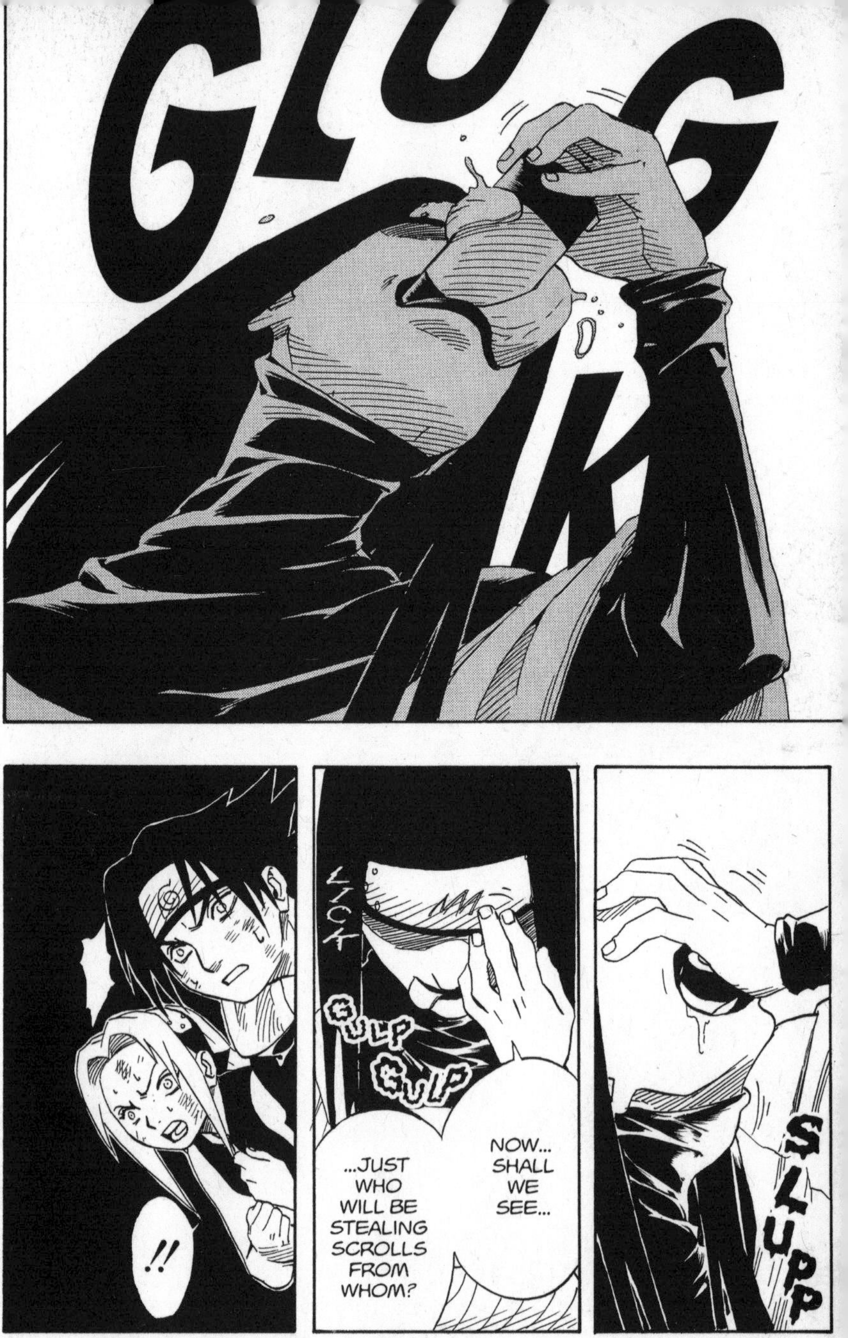
GLUG
GLUK
SLUPP
LICK
GULP GULP
NOW... SHALL WE SEE...
...JUST WHO WILL BE STEALING SCROLLS FROM WHOM?
!!

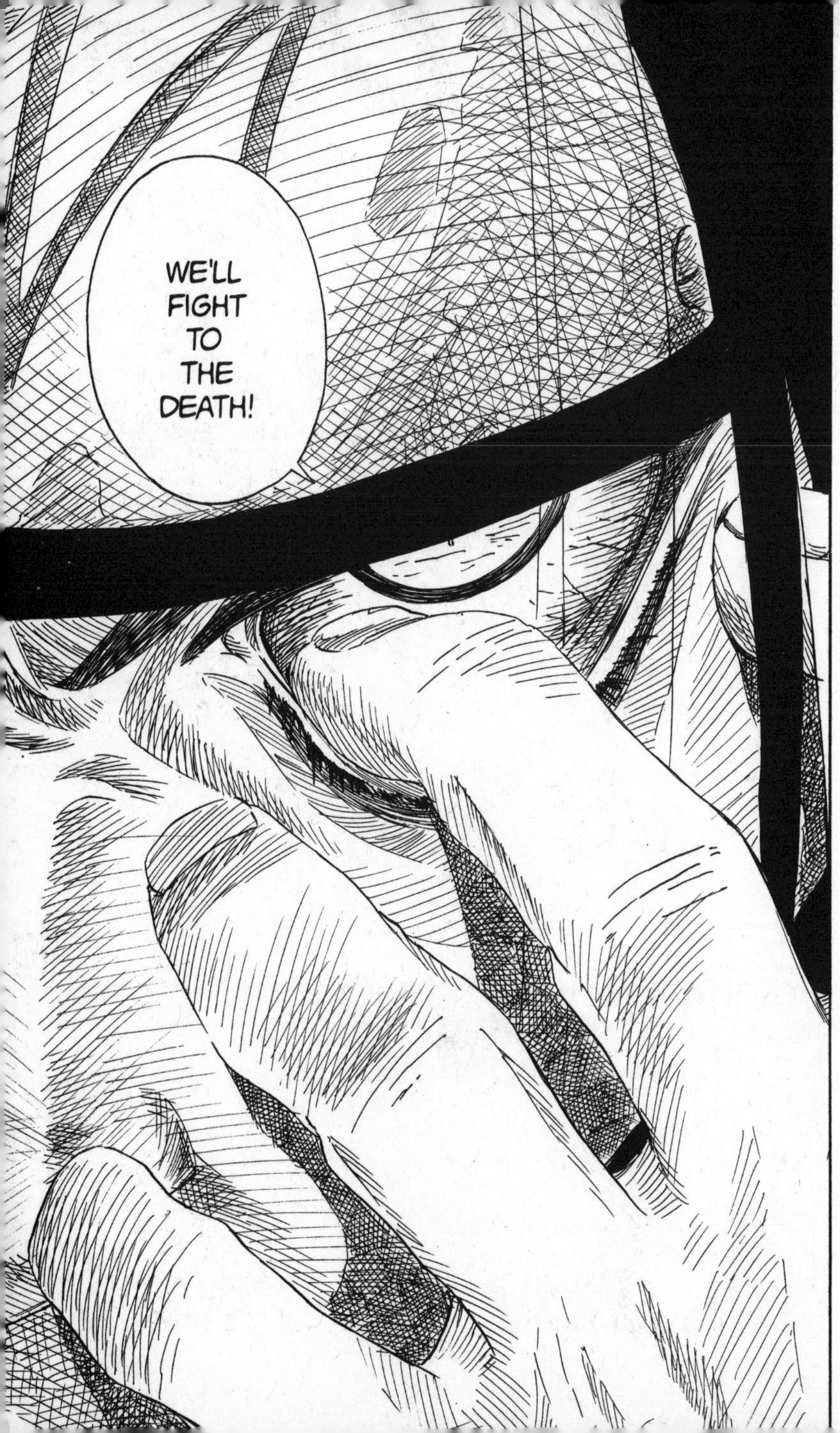
WE'LL FIGHT TO THE DEATH!

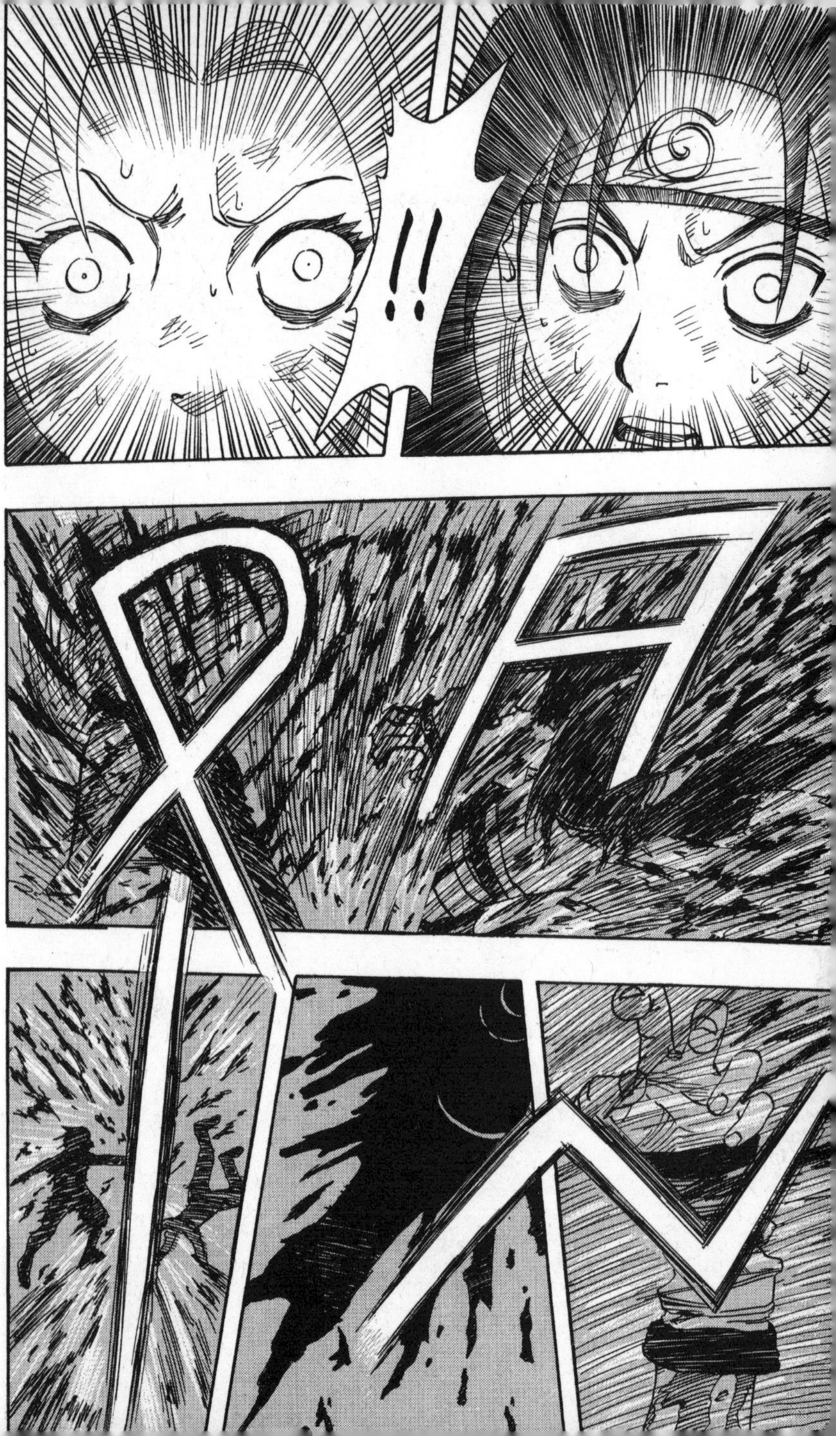
!!

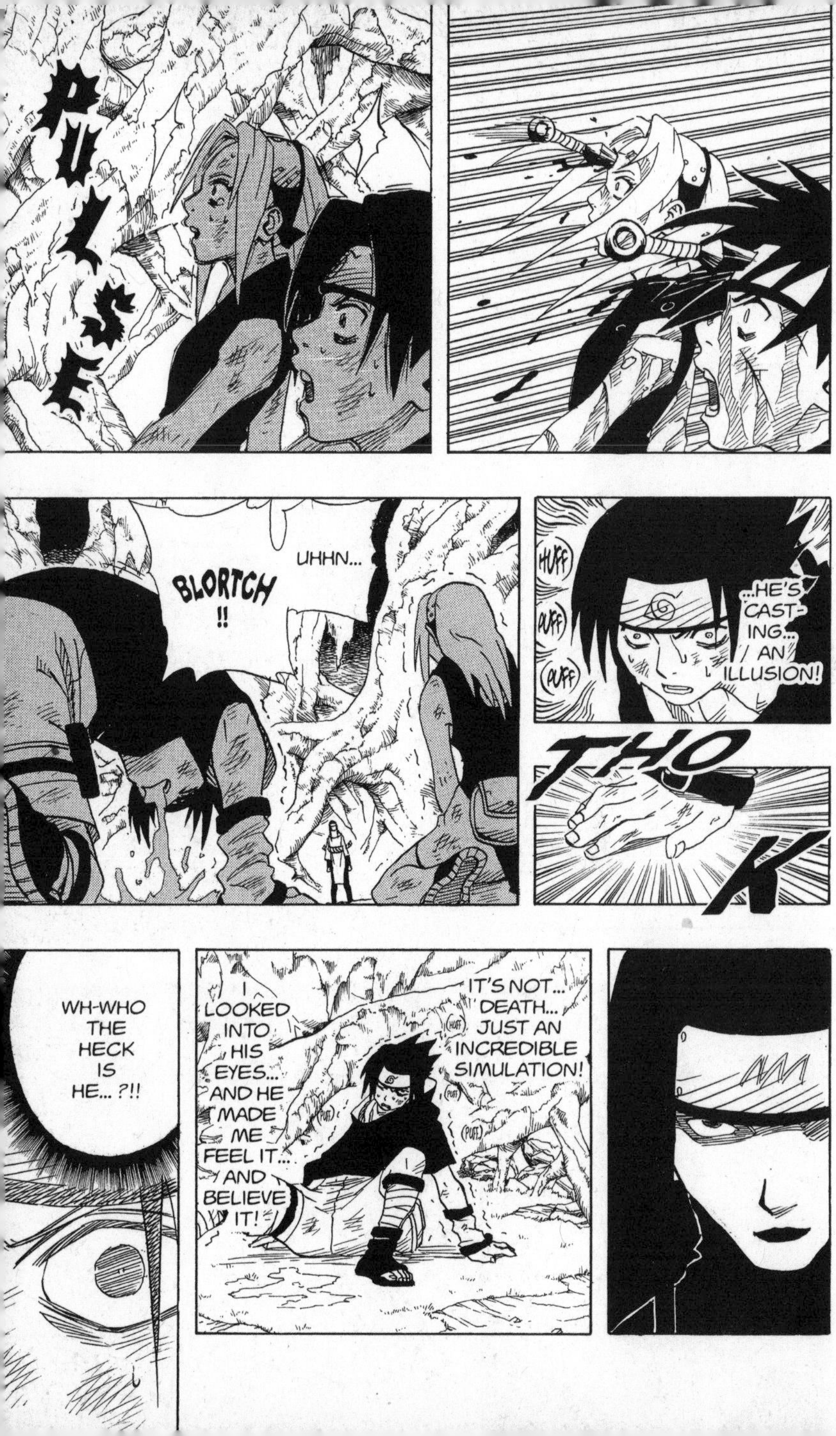
PULSE
HUFF
PUFF
PUFF
...HE'S CASTING... AN ILLUSION!
THOK
UHHN...
BLORTCH !!
IT'S NOT... DEATH... JUST AN INCREDIBLE SIMULATION!
HUFF
PUFF
PUFF
I LOOKED INTO HIS EYES... AND HE MADE ME FEEL IT... AND BELIEVE IT!
WH-WHO THE HECK IS HE... ?!!

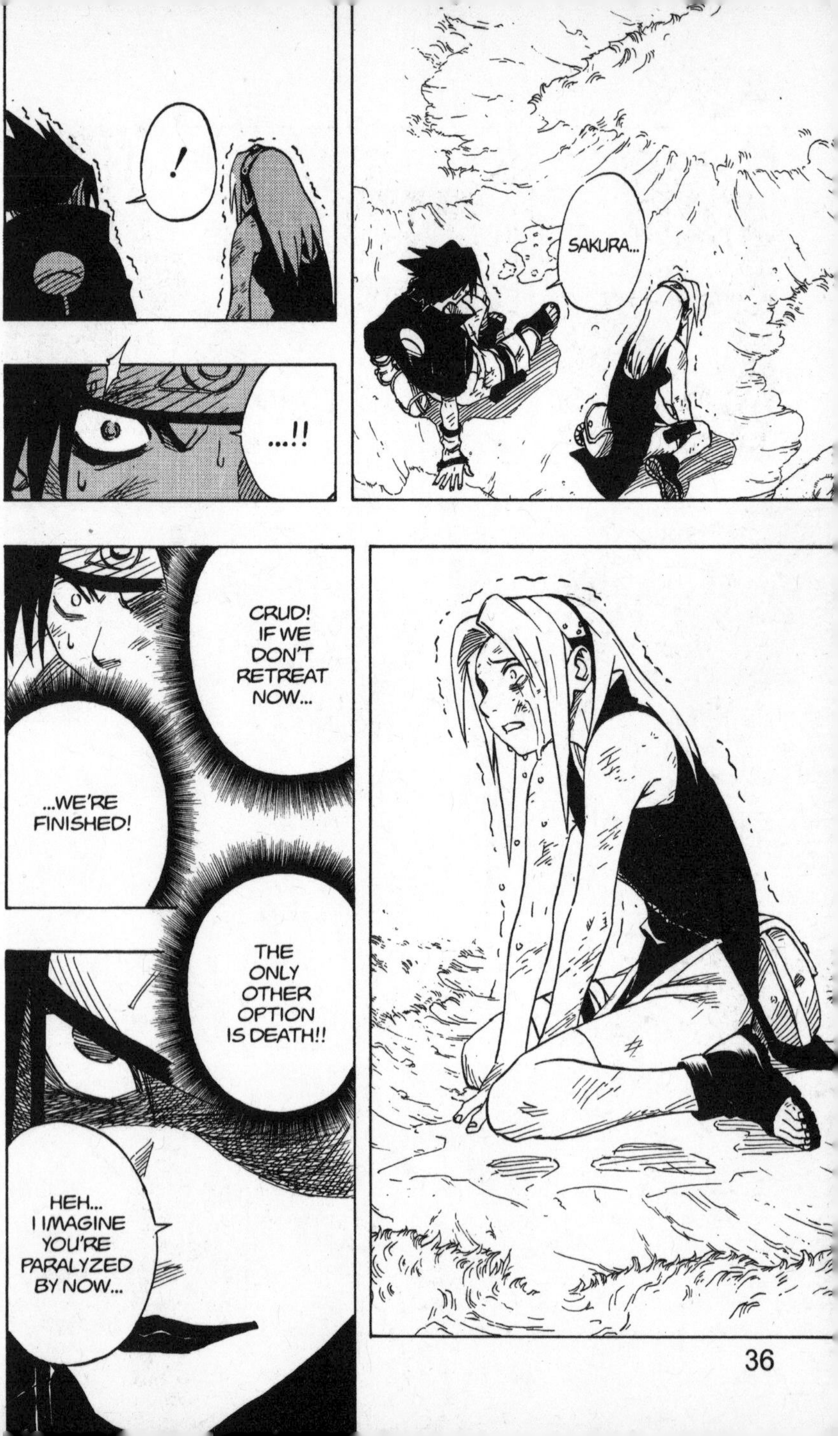
SAKURA...
!
...!!
CRUD! IF WE DON'T RETREAT NOW...
...WE'RE FINISHED!
THE ONLY OTHER OPTION IS DEATH!!
HEH... I IMAGINE YOU'RE PARALYZED BY NOW...

READ THIS WAY

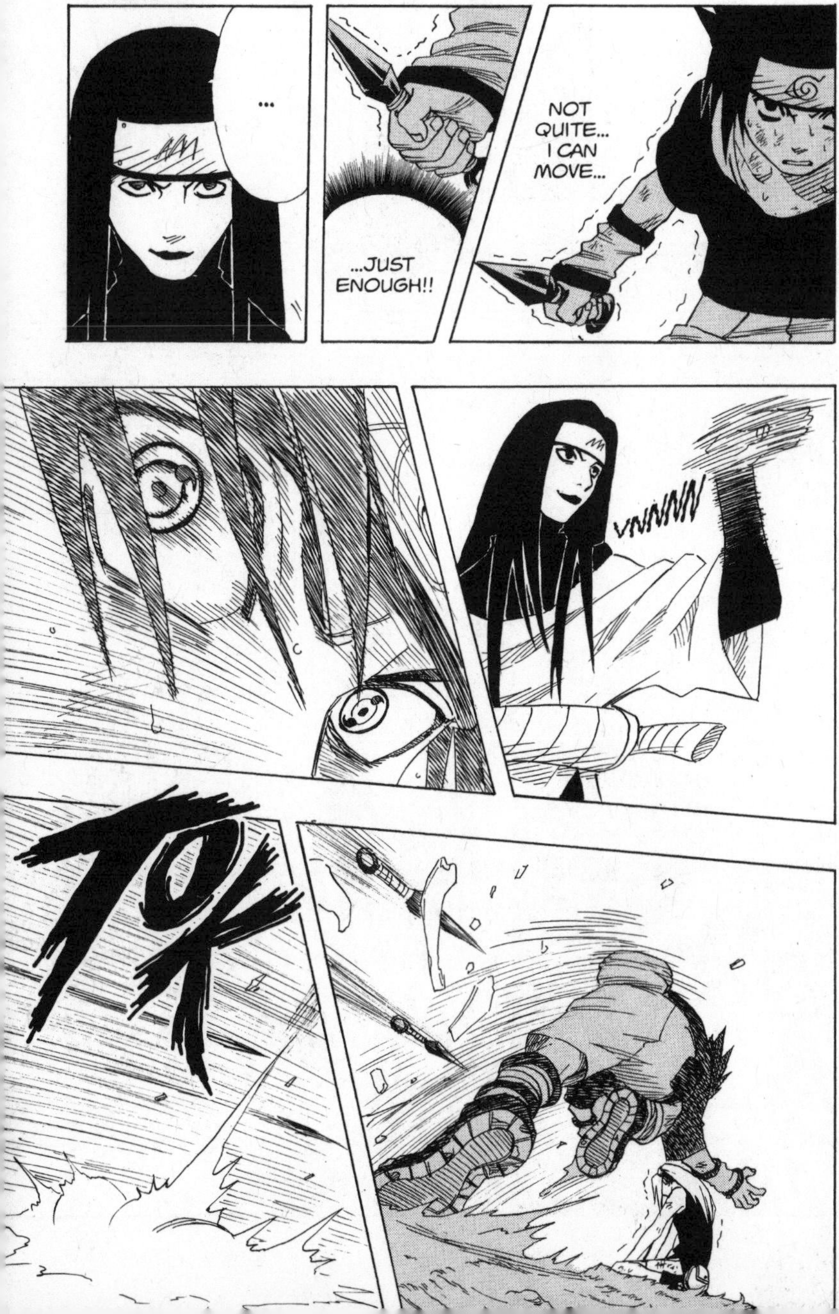
NOT QUITE... I CAN MOVE...
...JUST ENOUGH!!
...
VNNNNN
TOK

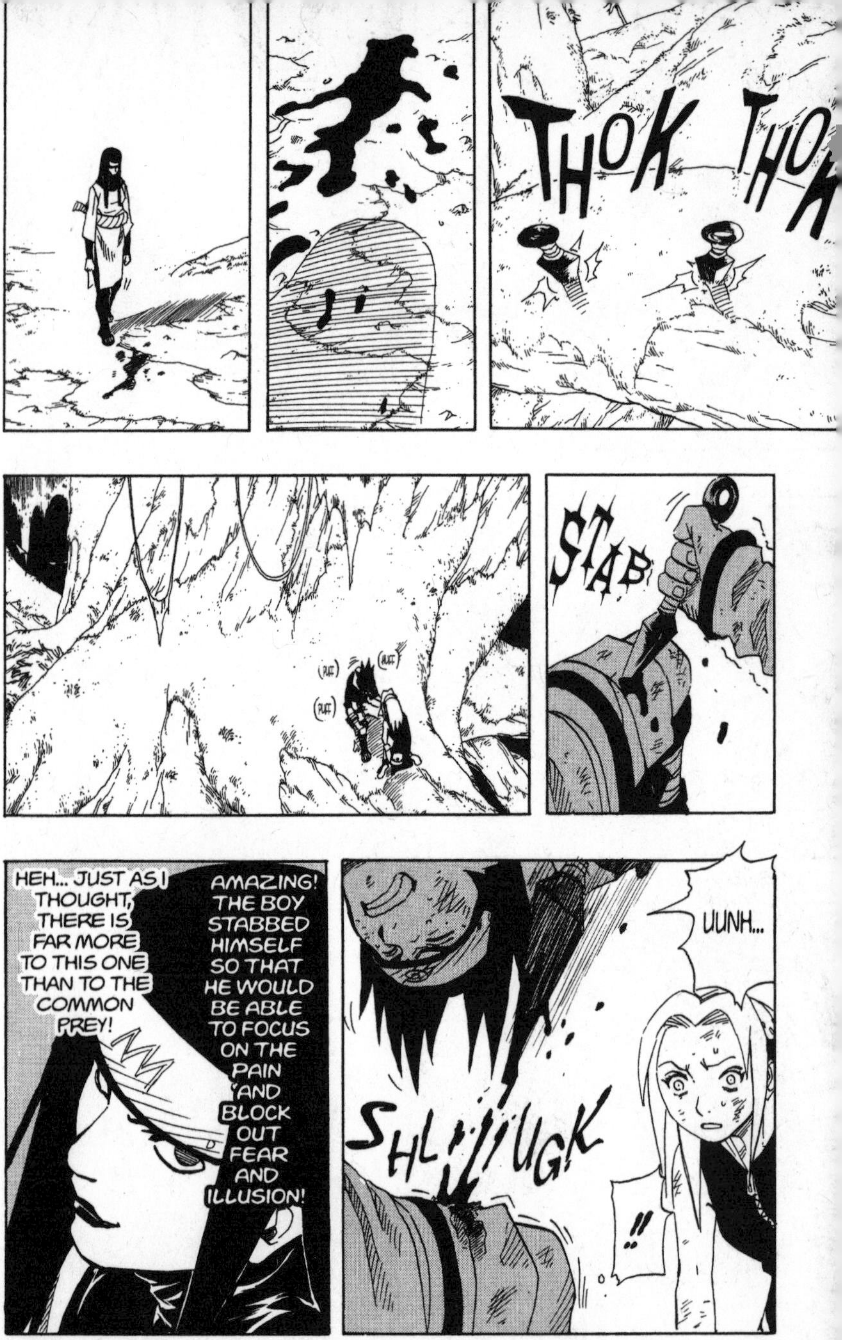
THOK THOK
STAB
(HUFF)
(PUFF)
(PUFF)
UUNH...
SHLUUGK
!!
AMAZING! THE BOY STABBED HIMSELF SO THAT HE WOULD BE ABLE TO FOCUS ON THE PAIN AND BLOCK OUT FEAR AND ILLUSION!
HEH... JUST AS I THOUGHT, THERE IS FAR MORE TO THIS ONE THAN TO THE COMMON PREY!

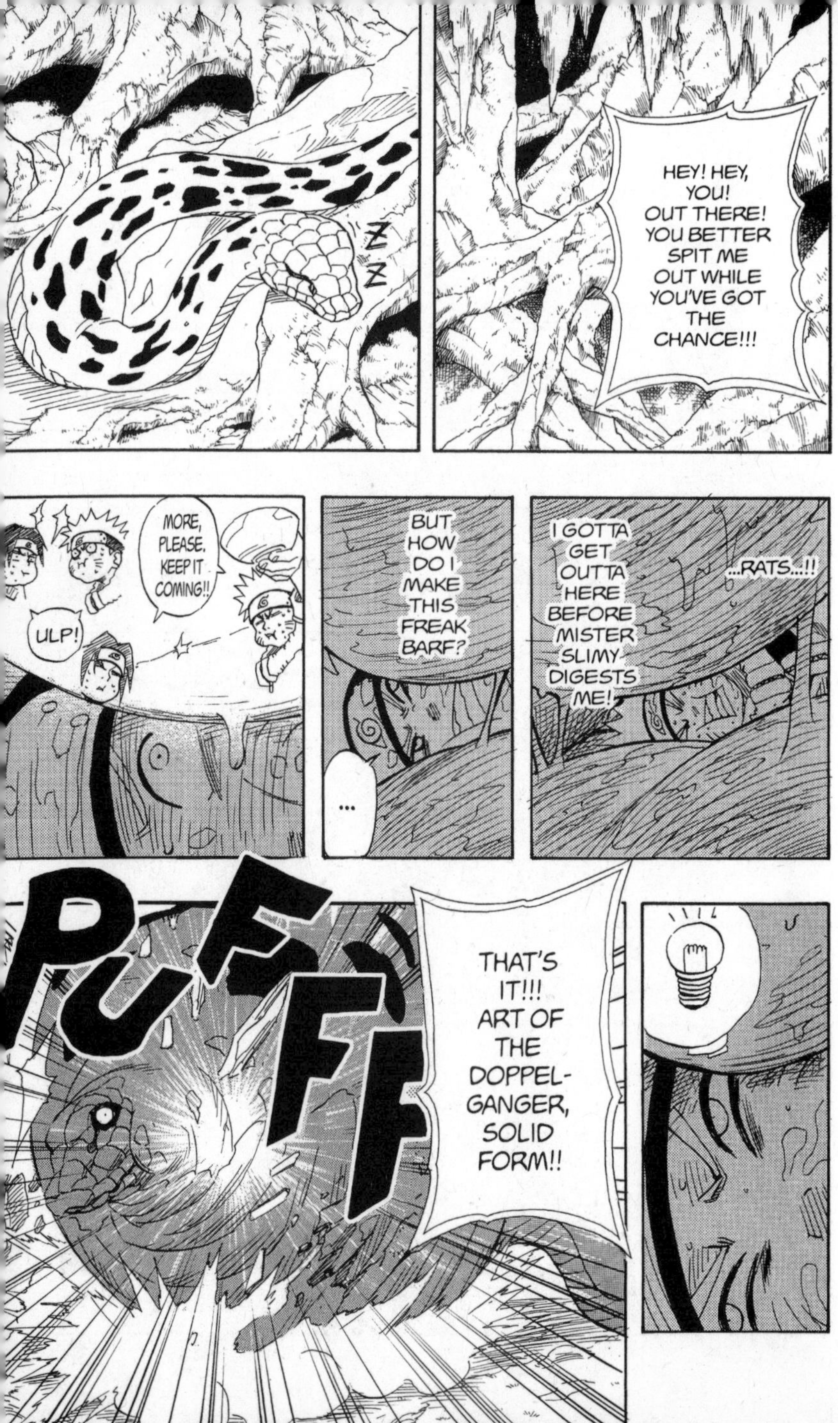
HEY! HEY, YOU! OUT THERE! YOU BETTER SPIT ME OUT WHILE YOU'VE GOT THE CHANCE!!!
Z Z
I GOTTA GET OUTTA HERE BEFORE MISTER SLIMY DIGESTS ME!
...RATS...!!
BUT HOW DO I MAKE THIS FREAK BARF?
...
MORE, PLEASE. KEEP IT COMING!!
ULP!
THAT'S IT!!! ART OF THE DOPPEL-GANGER, SOLID FORM!!
PUFFF

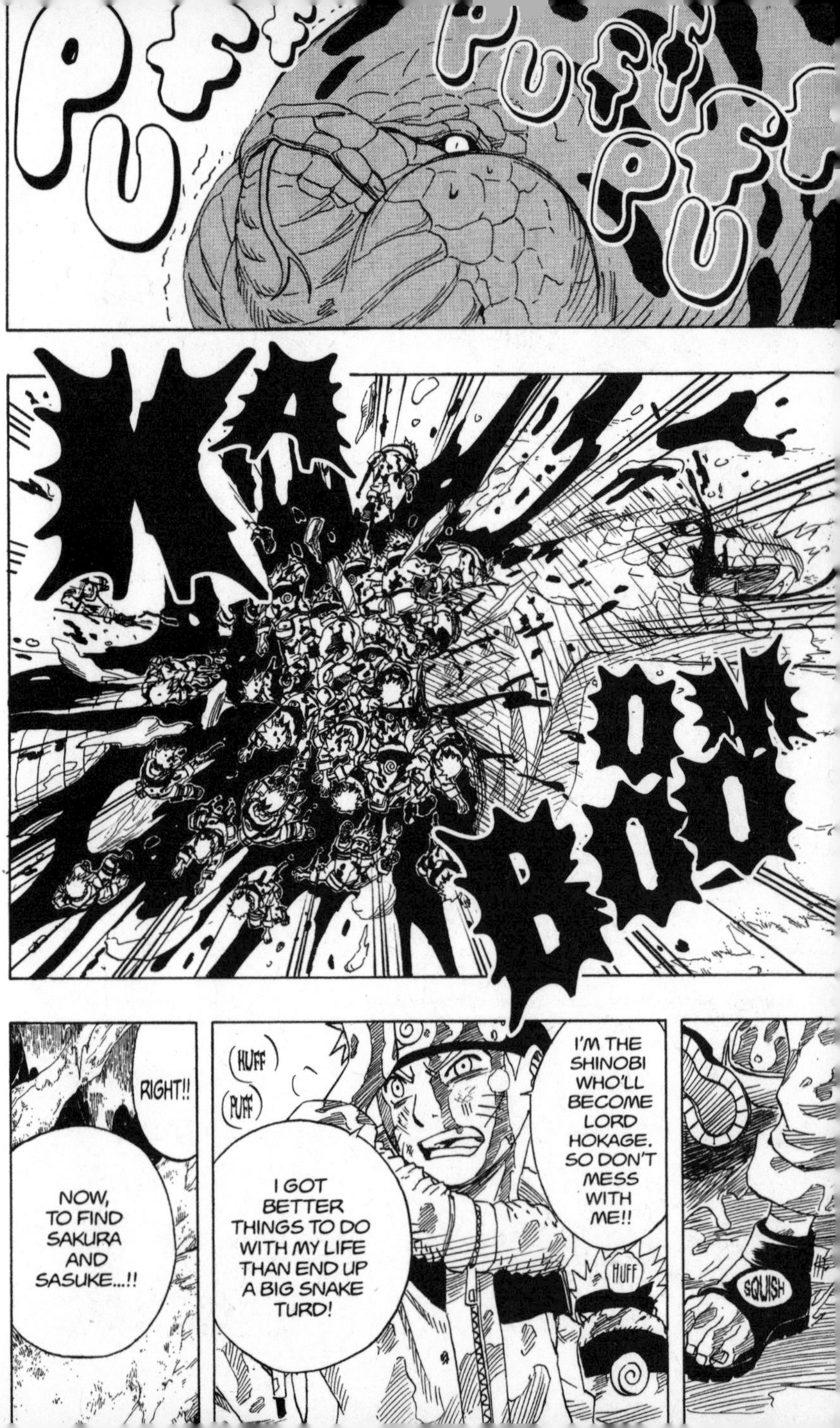
PUFF
PUFF
PU
PUFF
PU
KA
BOOM
SQUISH
I'M THE SHINOBI WHO'LL BECOME LORD HOKAGE. SO DON'T MESS WITH ME!!
HUFF
PUFF
I GOT BETTER THINGS TO DO WITH MY LIFE THAN END UP A BIG SNAKE TURD!
HUFF
RIGHT!!
NOW, TO FIND SAKURA AND SASUKE...!!

READ THIS WAY

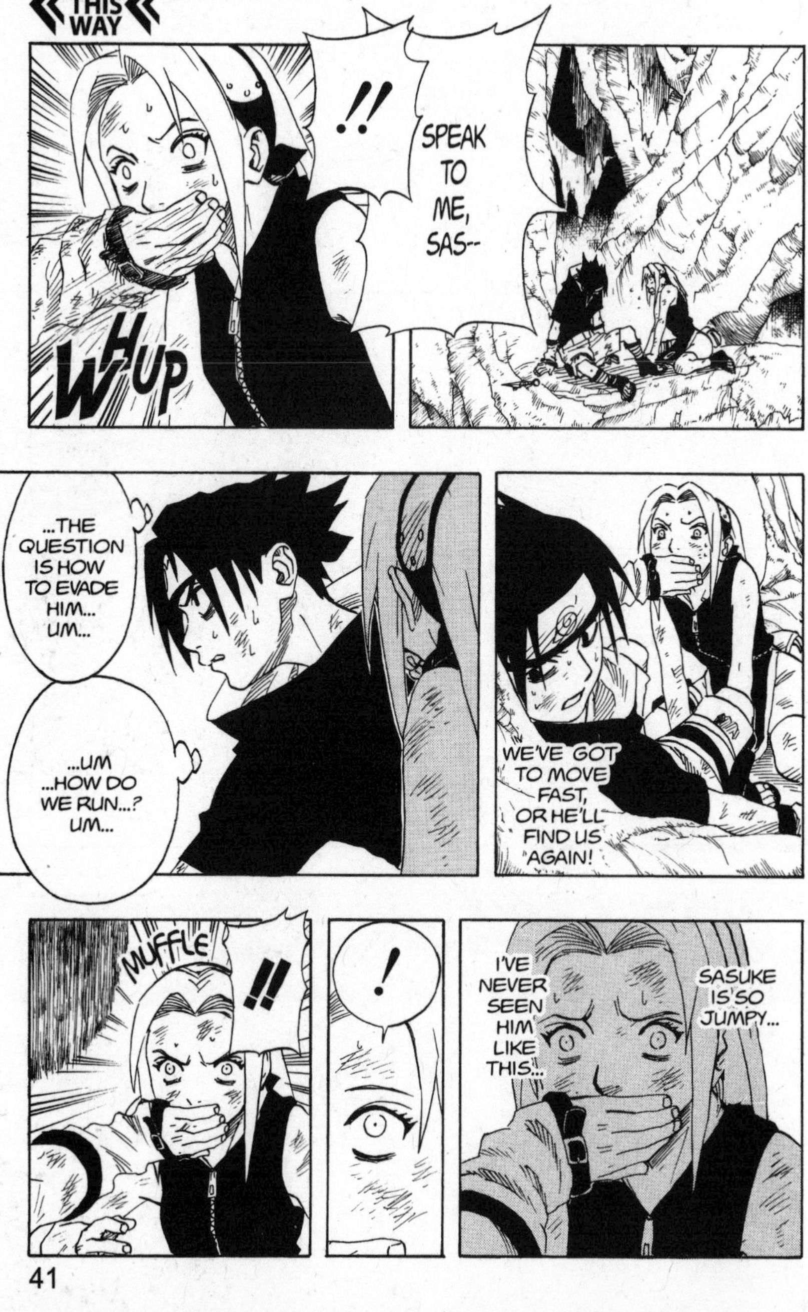
SPEAK TO ME, SAS--
!!
WHUP
WE'VE GOT TO MOVE FAST, OR HE'LL FIND US AGAIN!
...THE QUESTION IS HOW TO EVADE HIM... UM...
...UM ...HOW DO WE RUN...? UM...
SASUKE IS SO JUMPY...
I'VE NEVER SEEN HIM LIKE THIS...
!
MUFFLE
!!

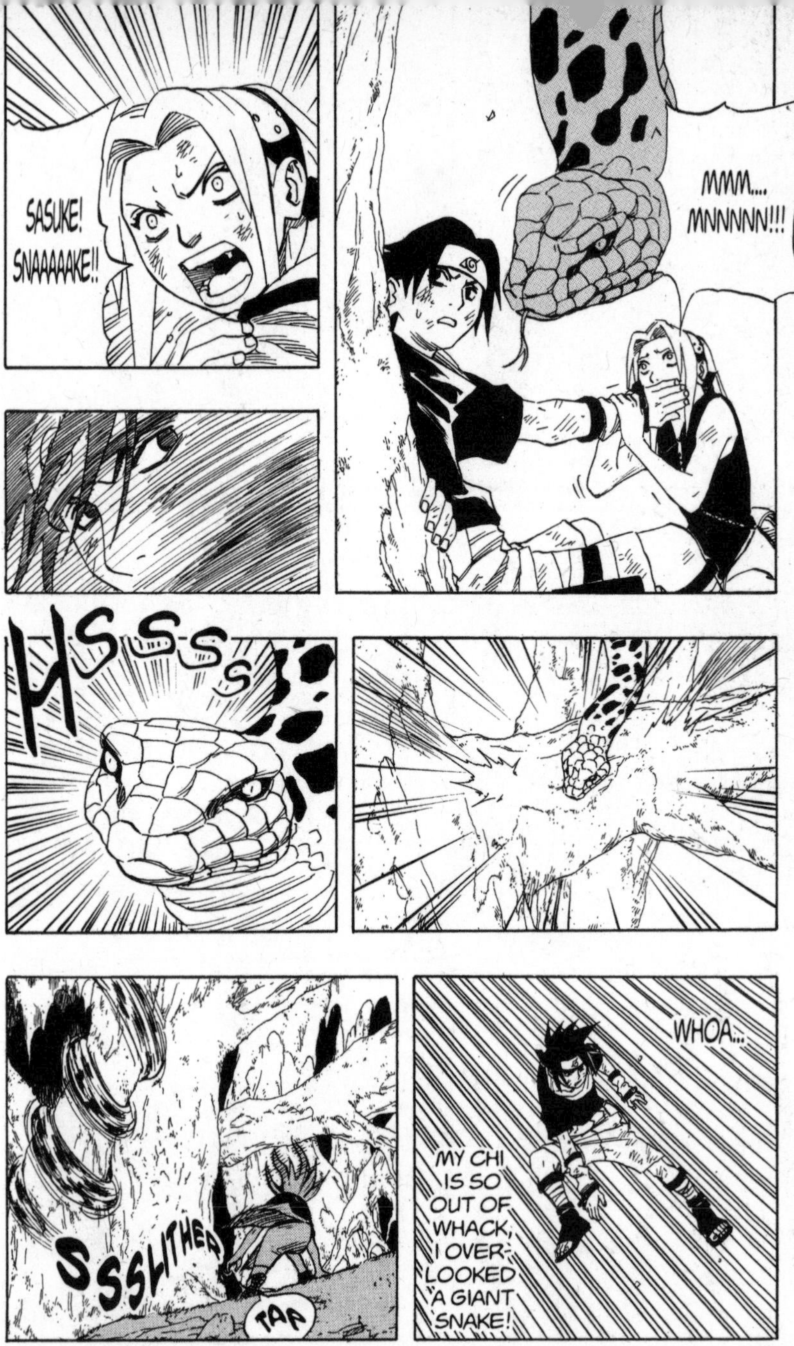
MMM... MNNNNN!!!
SASUKE! SNAAAAAKE!!
HSSSSS
WHOA...
MY CHI IS SO OUT OF WHACK, I OVER-LOOKED A GIANT SNAKE!
SSSLITHER
TAP

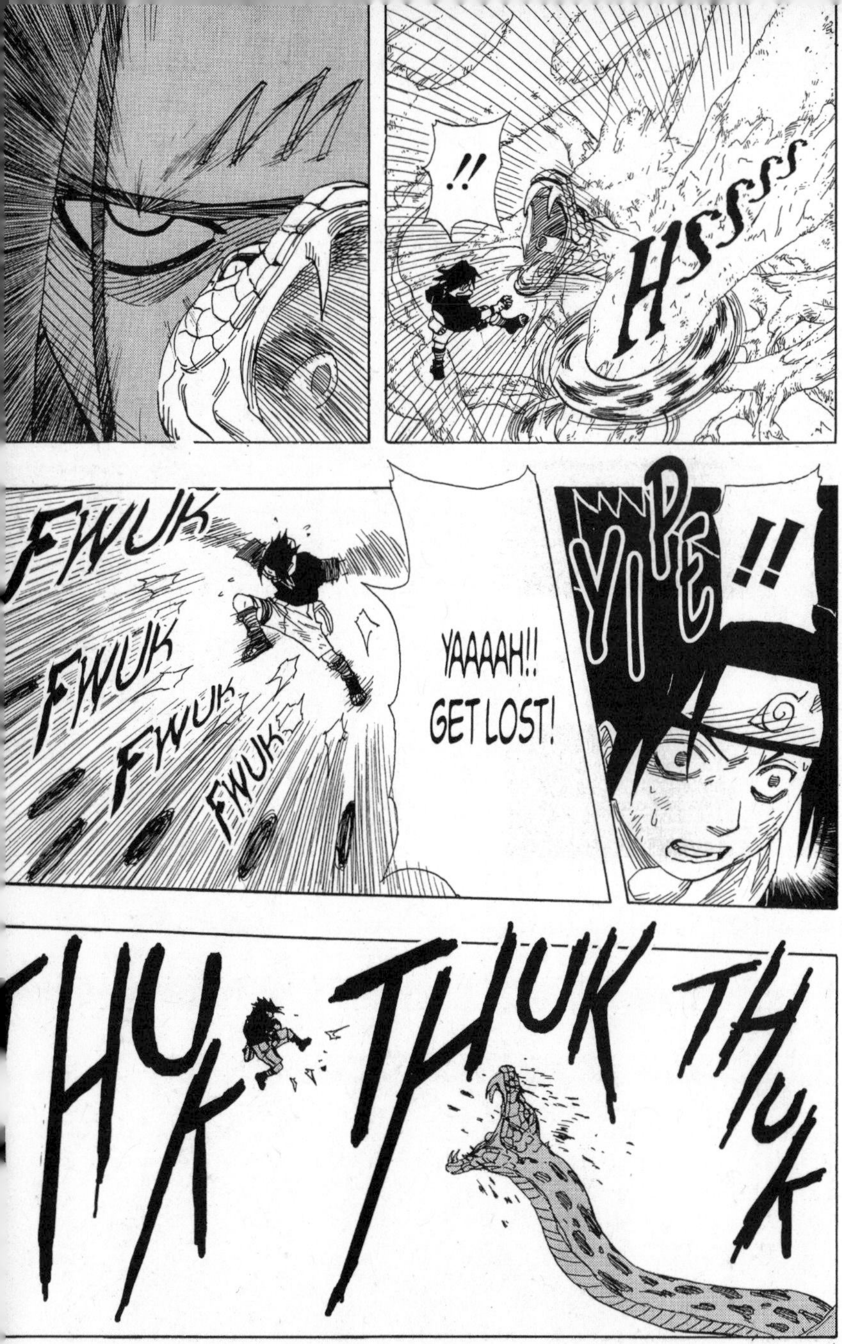
!!
HSSSS
YIPE!!
YAAAAH!! GET LOST!
FWUK FWUK FWUK FWUK
THUK
THUK
THUK

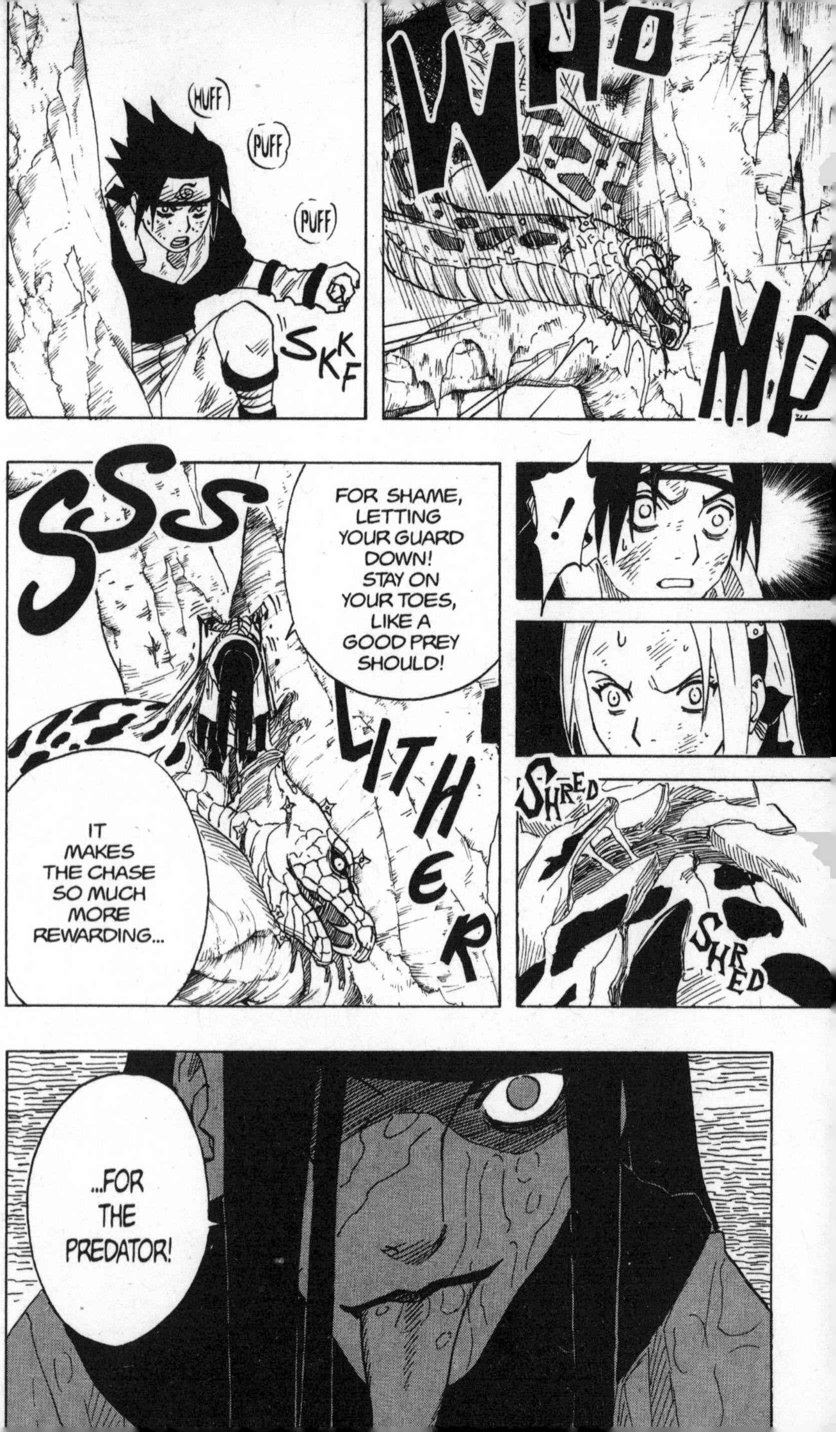
WHOMP
(HUFF)
(PUFF)
(PUFF)
SKKF
!
SHRED
SHRED
SSS
FOR SHAME, LETTING YOUR GUARD DOWN! STAY ON YOUR TOES, LIKE A GOOD PREY SHOULD!
SLITHER
IT MAKES THE CHASE SO MUCH MORE REWARDING...
...FOR THE PREDATOR!

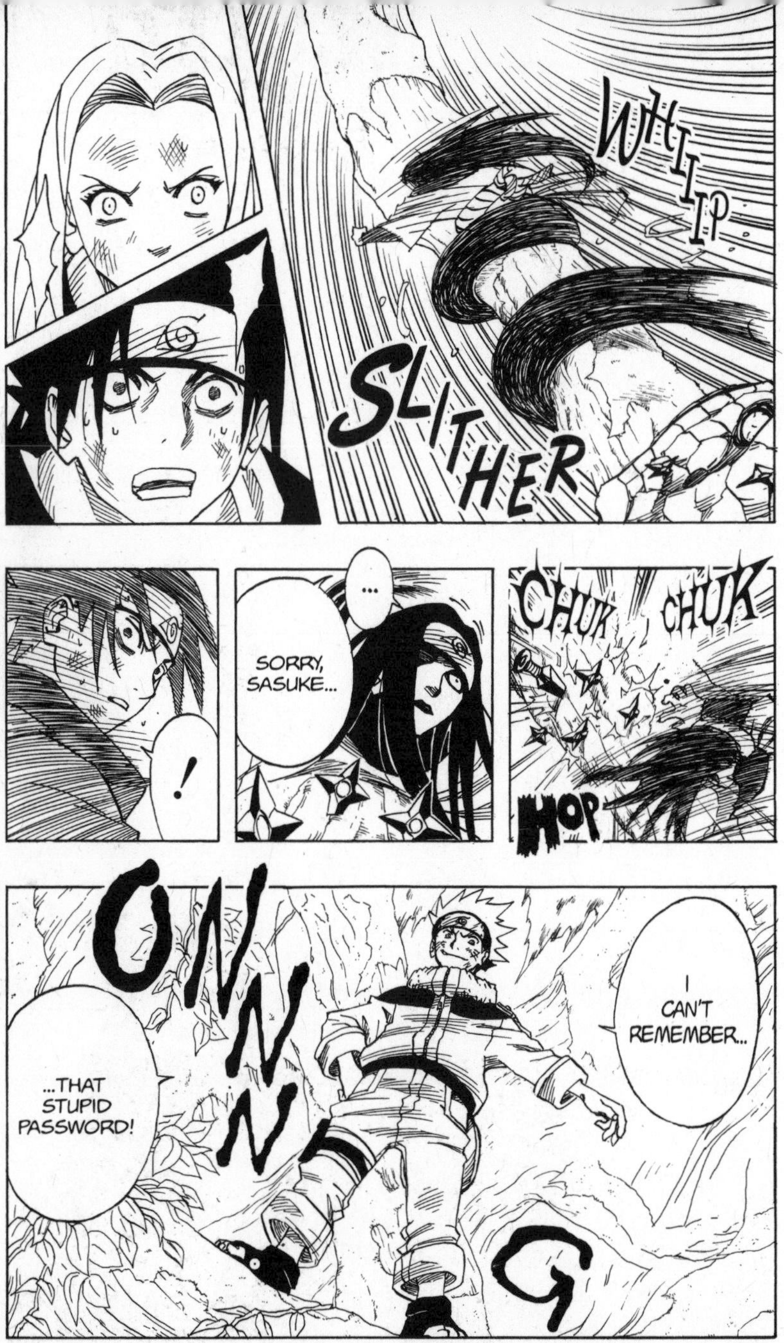
WHIIIP
SLITHER
CHUK CHUK
HOP
...
SORRY, SASUKE...
!
ONNNNG
I CAN'T REMEMBER...
...THAT STUPID PASSWORD!

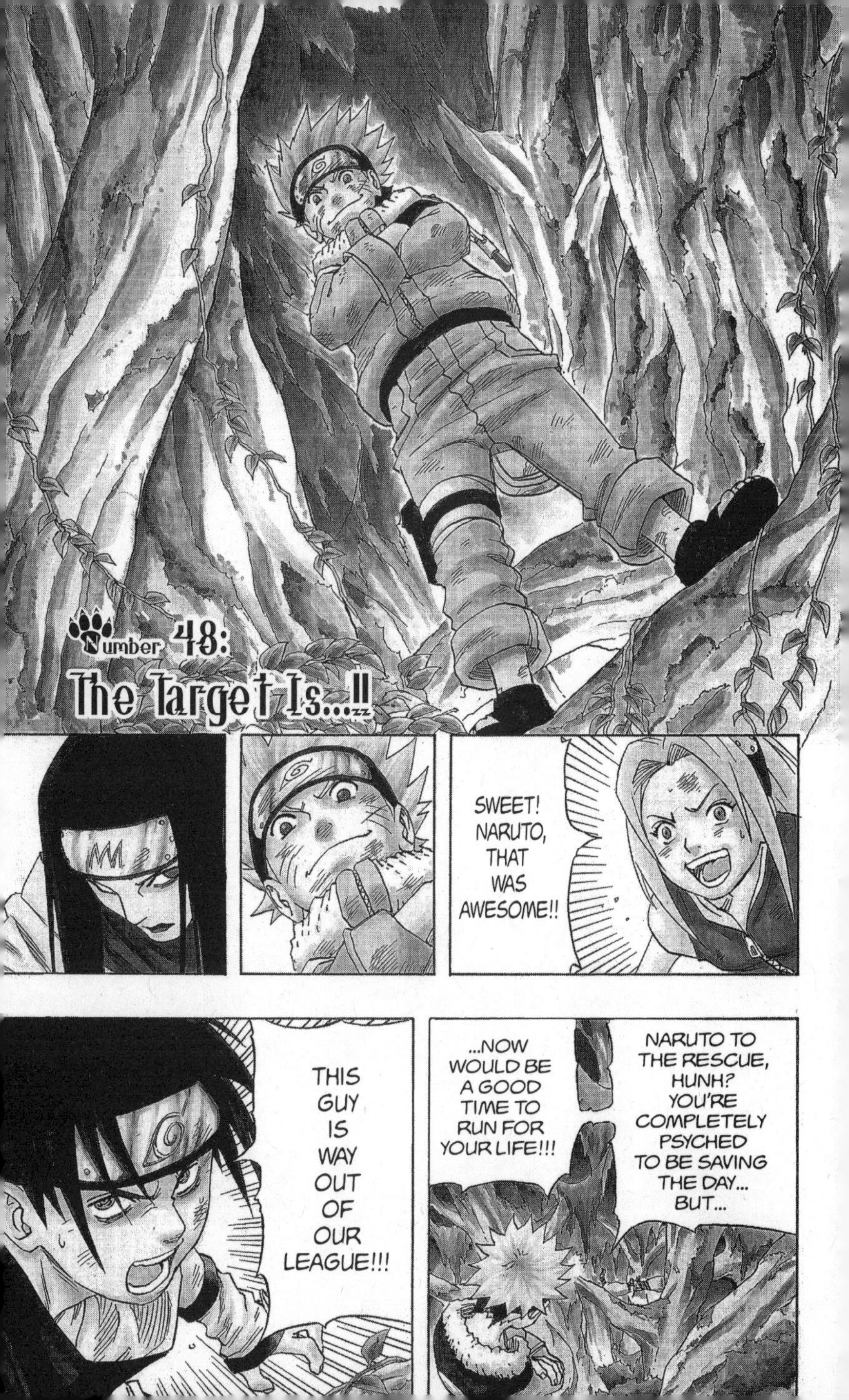
Number 48:
The Target Is...!!
SWEET! NARUTO, THAT WAS AWESOME!!
NARUTO TO THE RESCUE, HUNH? YOU'RE COMPLETELY PSYCHED TO BE SAVING THE DAY... BUT...
...NOW WOULD BE A GOOD TIME TO RUN FOR YOUR LIFE!!!
THIS GUY IS WAY OUT OF OUR LEAGUE!!!

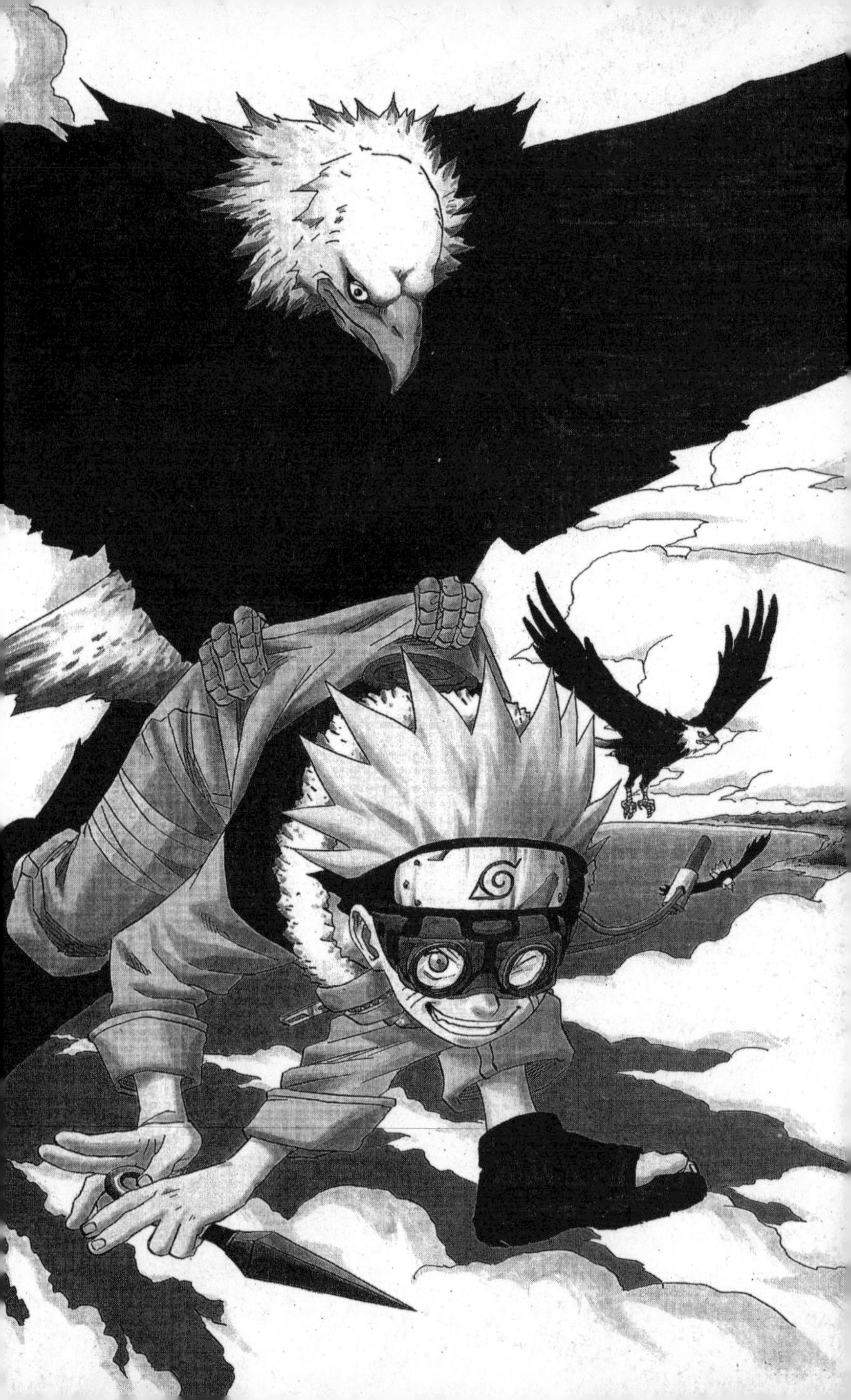

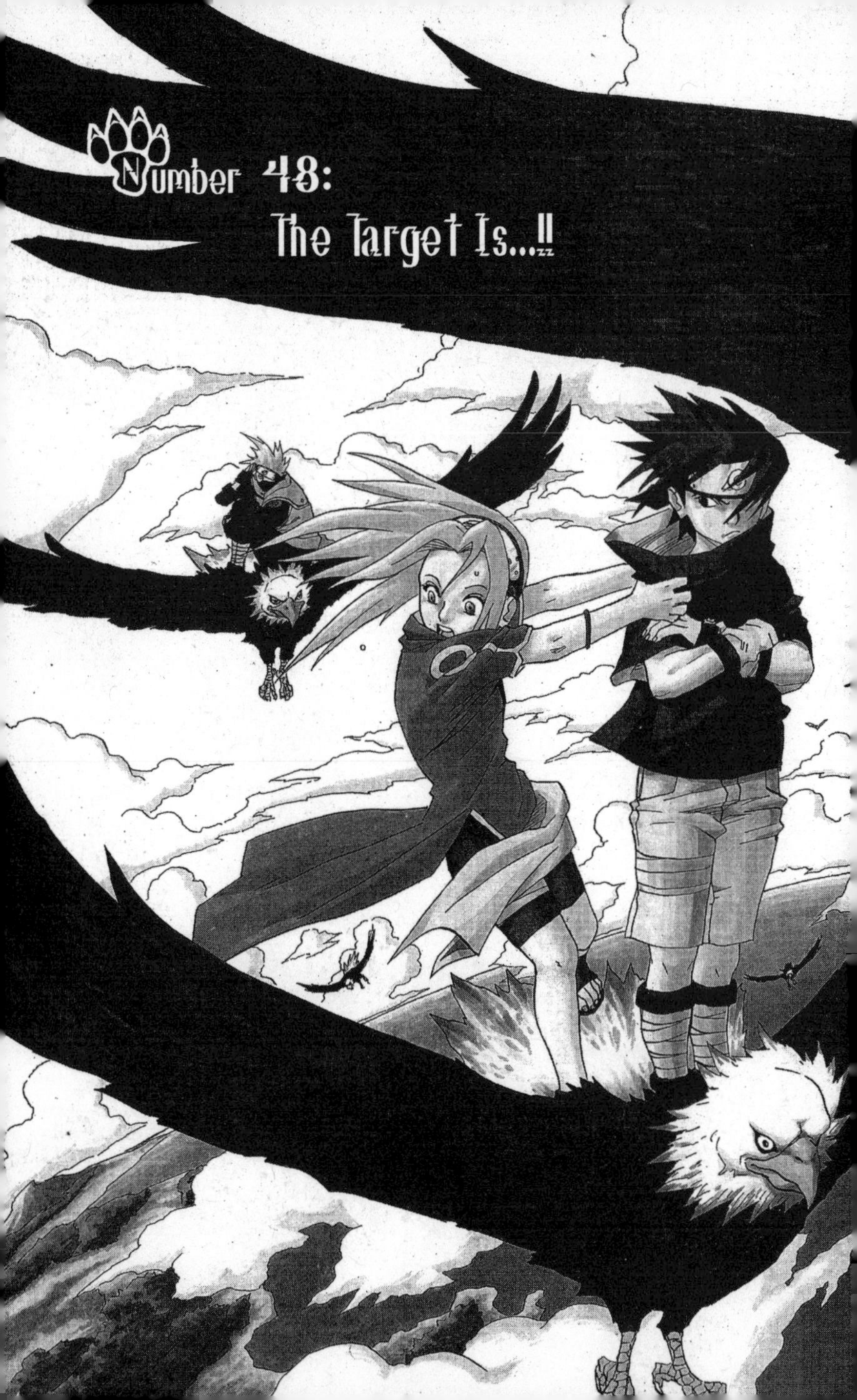
Number 48:
The Target Is...!!

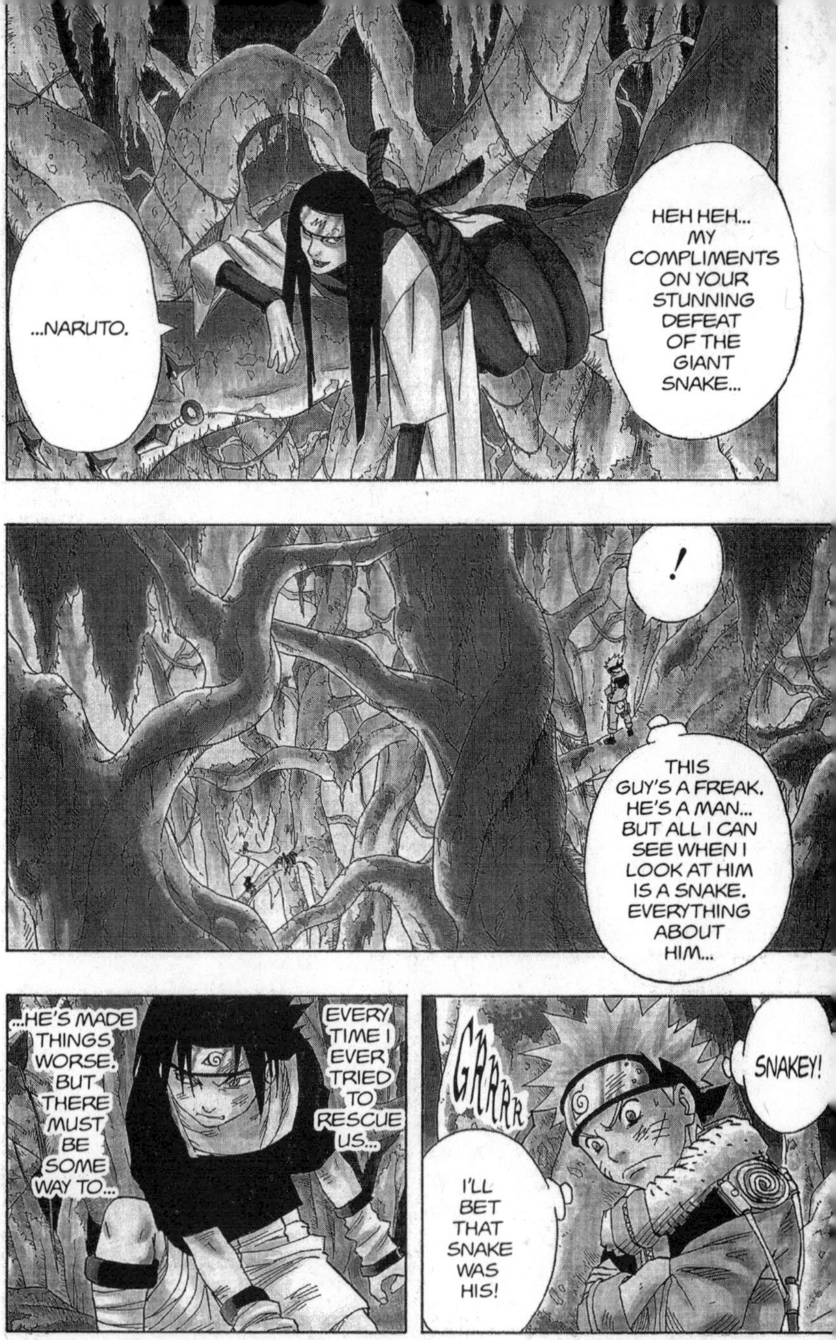
HEH HEH... MY COMPLIMENTS ON YOUR STUNNING DEFEAT OF THE GIANT SNAKE...
...NARUTO.
!
THIS GUY'S A FREAK. HE'S A MAN... BUT ALL I CAN SEE WHEN I LOOK AT HIM IS A SNAKE. EVERYTHING ABOUT HIM...
SNAKEY!
GRRRR
I'LL BET THAT SNAKE WAS HIS!
EVERY TIME I EVER TRIED TO RESCUE US...
...HE'S MADE THINGS WORSE. BUT THERE MUST BE SOME WAY TO...

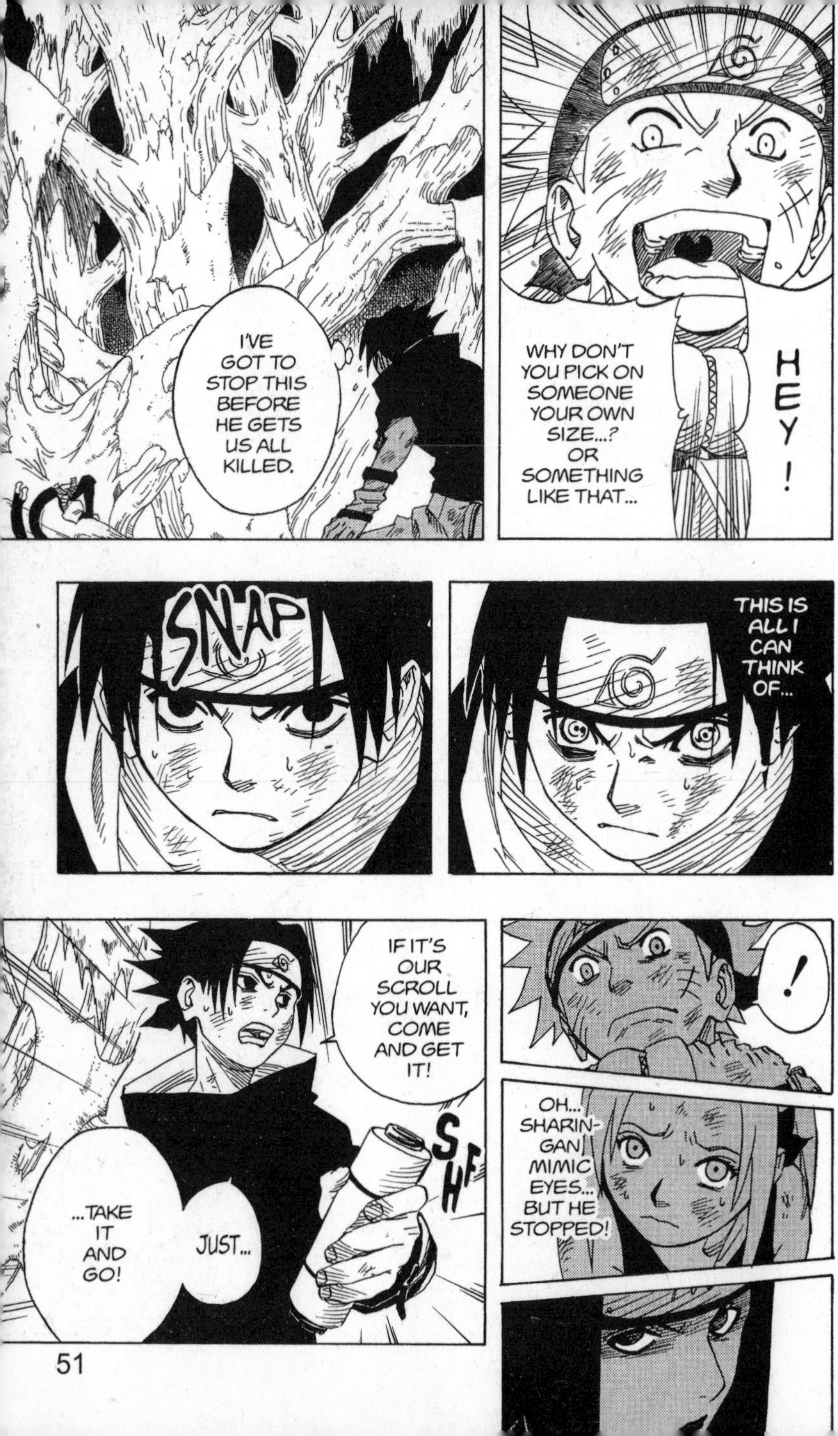
HEY!
WHY DON'T YOU PICK ON SOMEONE YOUR OWN SIZE...? OR SOMETHING LIKE THAT...
I'VE GOT TO STOP THIS BEFORE HE GETS US ALL KILLED.
THIS IS ALL I CAN THINK OF...
SNAP
!
OH... SHARIN-GAN, MIMIC EYES... BUT HE STOPPED!
IF IT'S OUR SCROLL YOU WANT, COME AND GET IT!
SHF
JUST...
...TAKE IT AND GO!

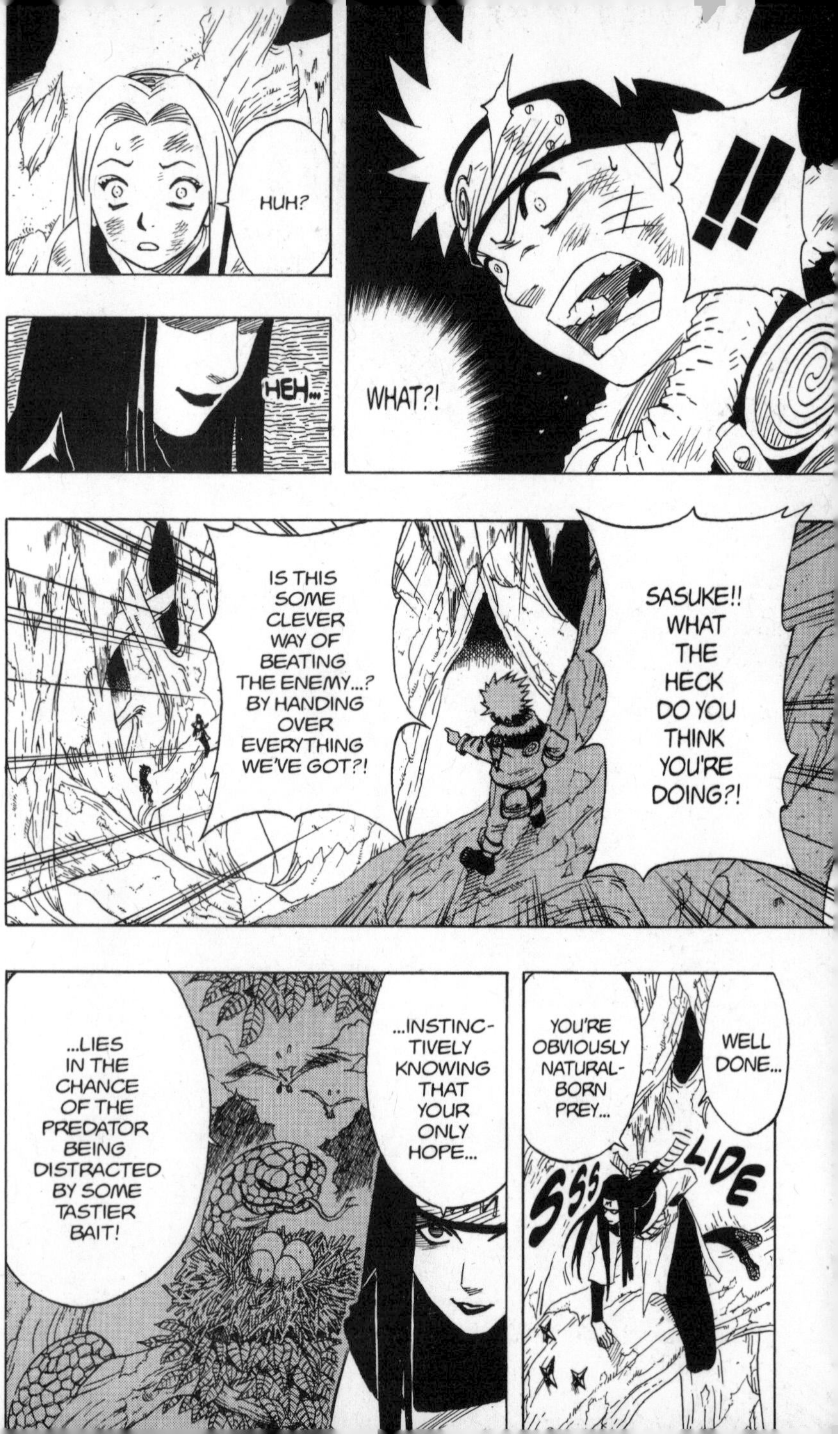
!!
WHAT?!
HUH?
HEH...
SASUKE!! WHAT THE HECK DO YOU THINK YOU'RE DOING?!
IS THIS SOME CLEVER WAY OF BEATING THE ENEMY...? BY HANDING OVER EVERYTHING WE'VE GOT?!
WELL DONE...
SSSLIDE
YOU'RE OBVIOUSLY NATURAL-BORN PREY...
...INSTINCTIVELY KNOWING THAT YOUR ONLY HOPE...
...LIES IN THE CHANCE OF THE PREDATOR BEING DISTRACTED BY SOME TASTIER BAIT!

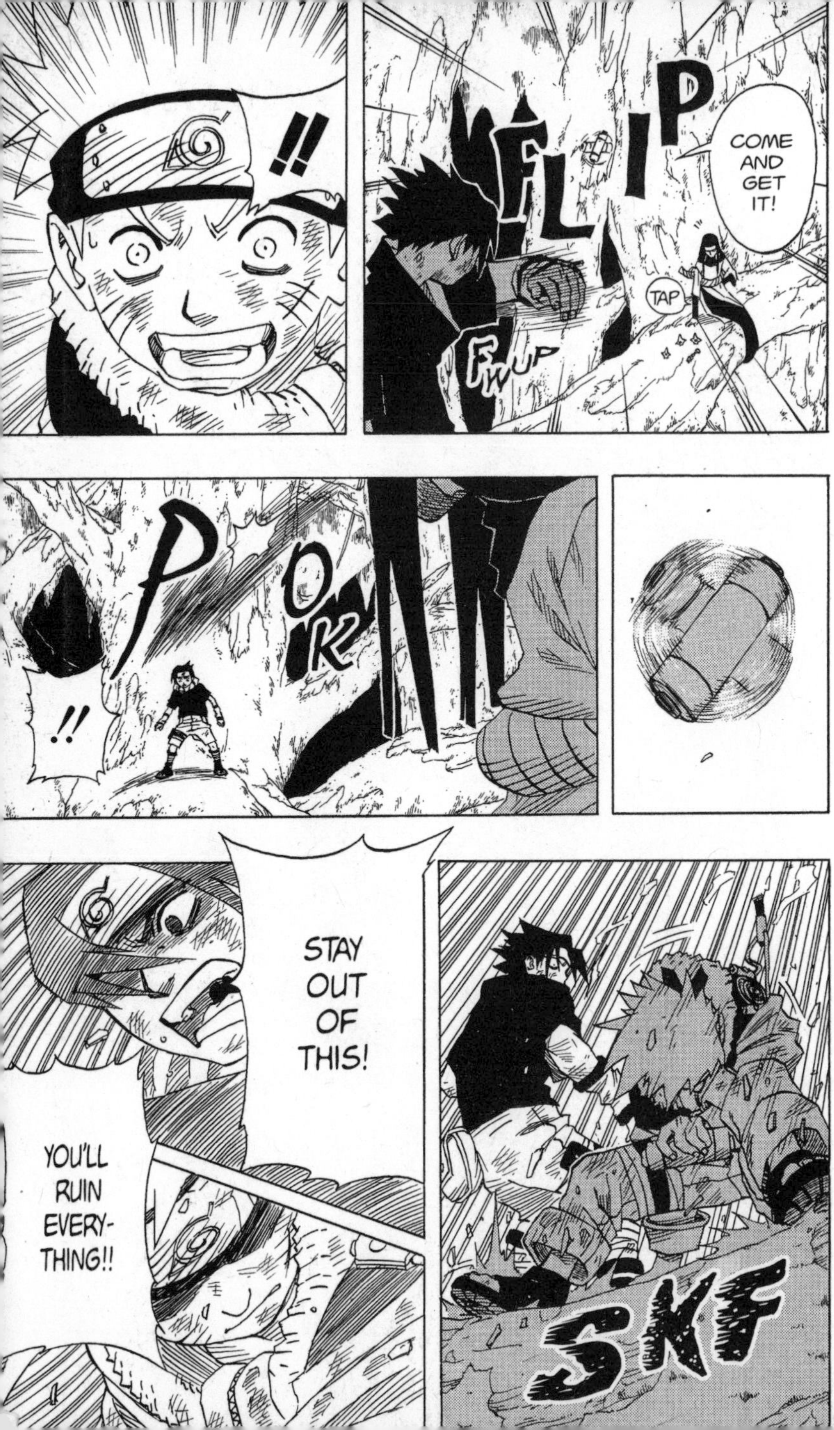
FLIP
COME AND GET IT!
TAP
FWUP
!!
POK
!!
SKF
STAY OUT OF THIS!
YOU'LL RUIN EVERY-THING!!

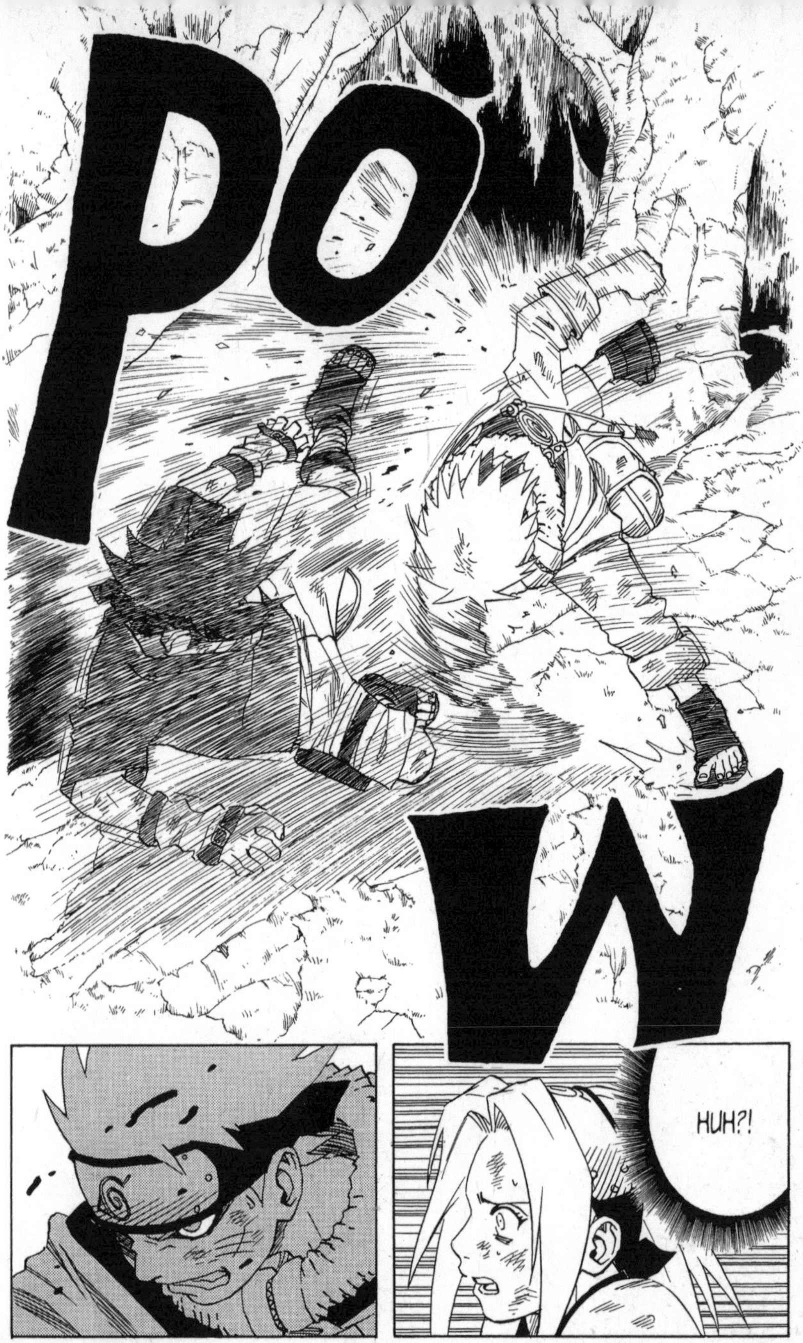
POW
HUH?!

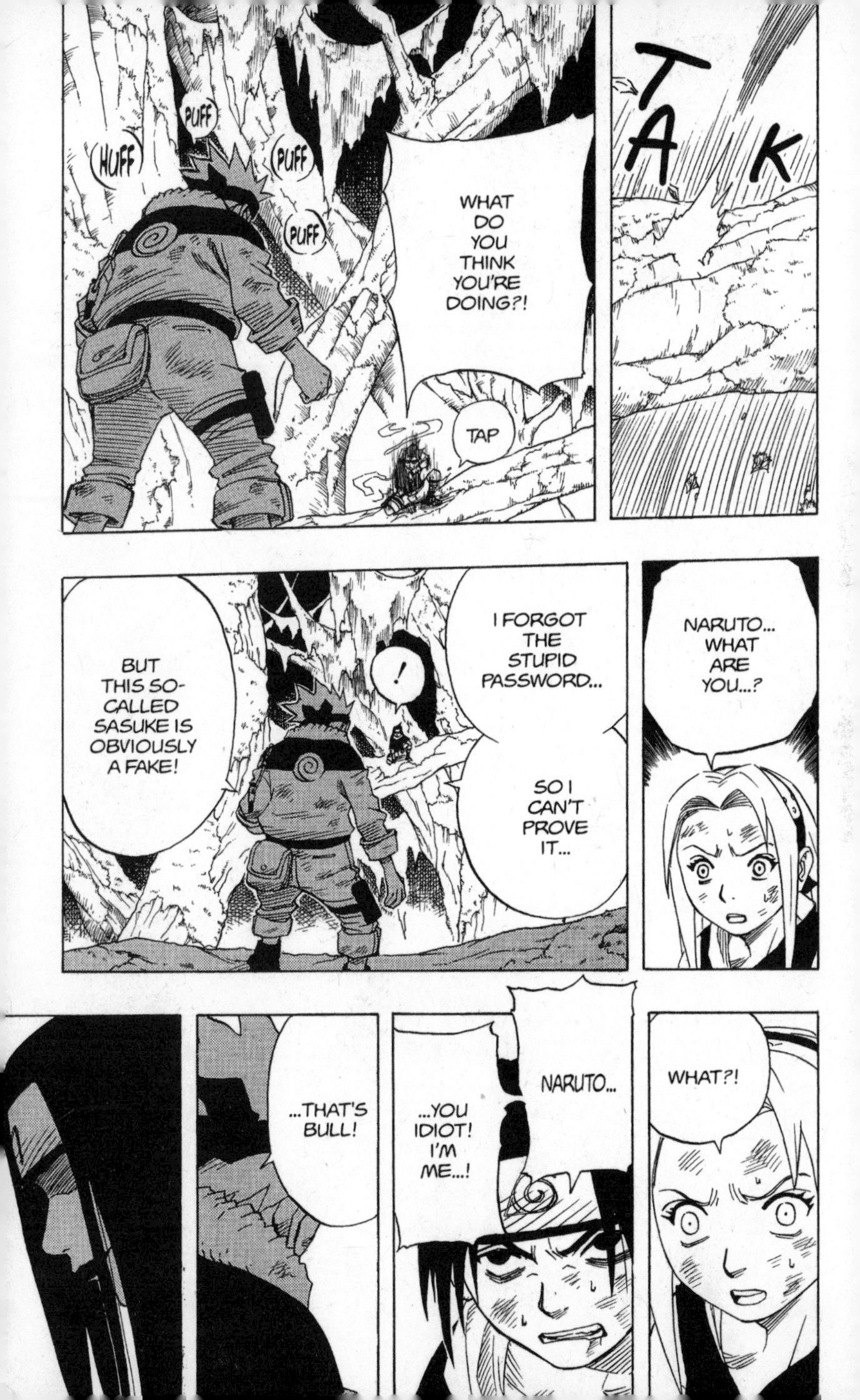

TAK
WHAT DO YOU THINK YOU'RE DOING?!
PUFF
PUFF
HUFF
PUFF
TAP
NARUTO... WHAT ARE YOU...?
I FORGOT THE STUPID PASSWORD...
SO I CAN'T PROVE IT...
!
BUT THIS SO-CALLED SASUKE IS OBVIOUSLY A FAKE!
WHAT?!
NARUTO...
...YOU IDIOT! I'M ME...!
...THAT'S BULL!

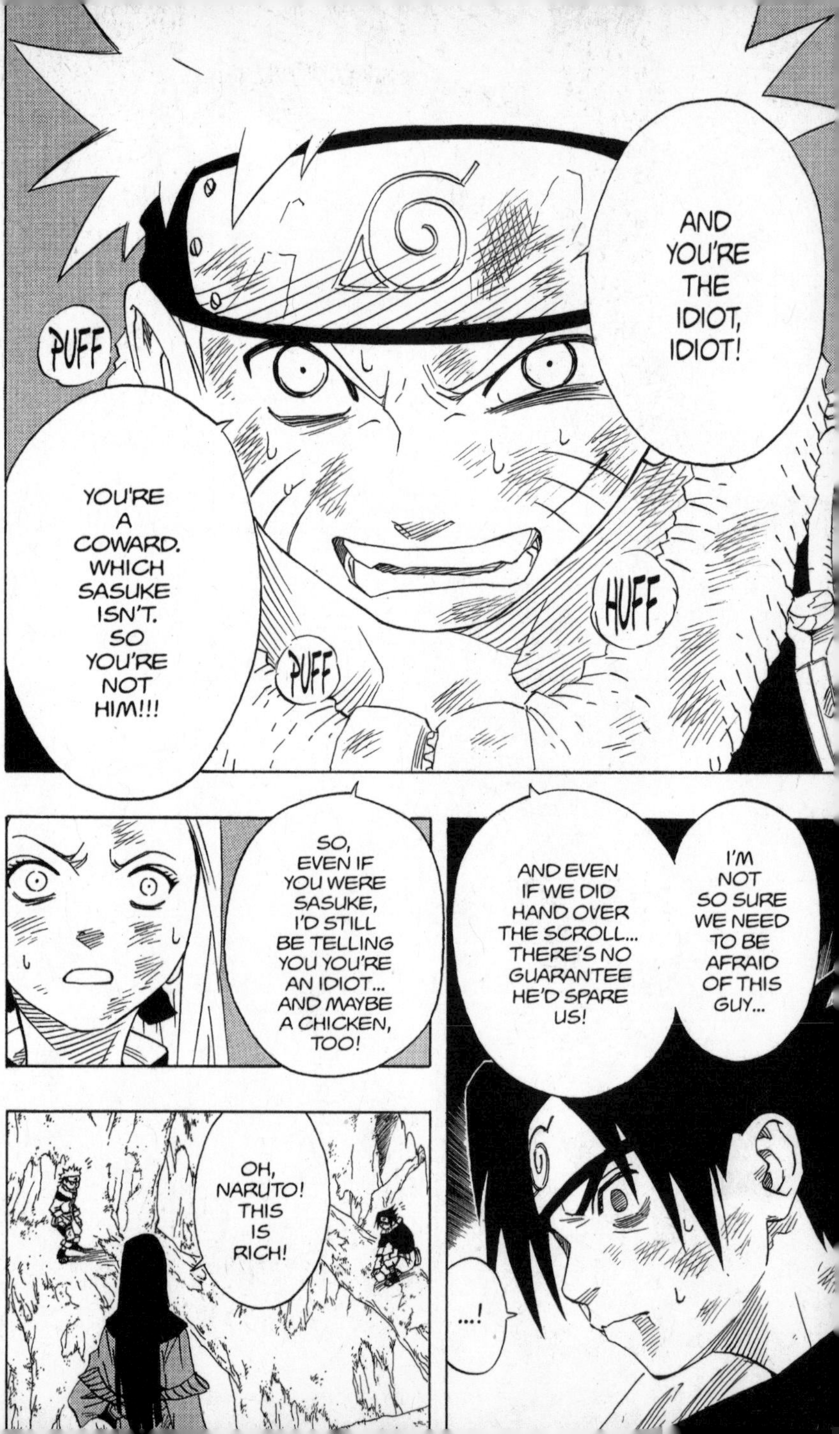
AND YOU'RE THE IDIOT, IDIOT!
PUFF
YOU'RE A COWARD. WHICH SASUKE ISN'T. SO YOU'RE NOT HIM!!!
HUFF
PUFF
I'M NOT SO SURE WE NEED TO BE AFRAID OF THIS GUY...
AND EVEN IF WE DID HAND OVER THE SCROLL... THERE'S NO GUARANTEE HE'D SPARE US!
...!
SO, EVEN IF YOU WERE SASUKE, I'D STILL BE TELLING YOU YOU'RE AN IDIOT... AND MAYBE A CHICKEN, TOO!
OH, NARUTO! THIS IS RICH!

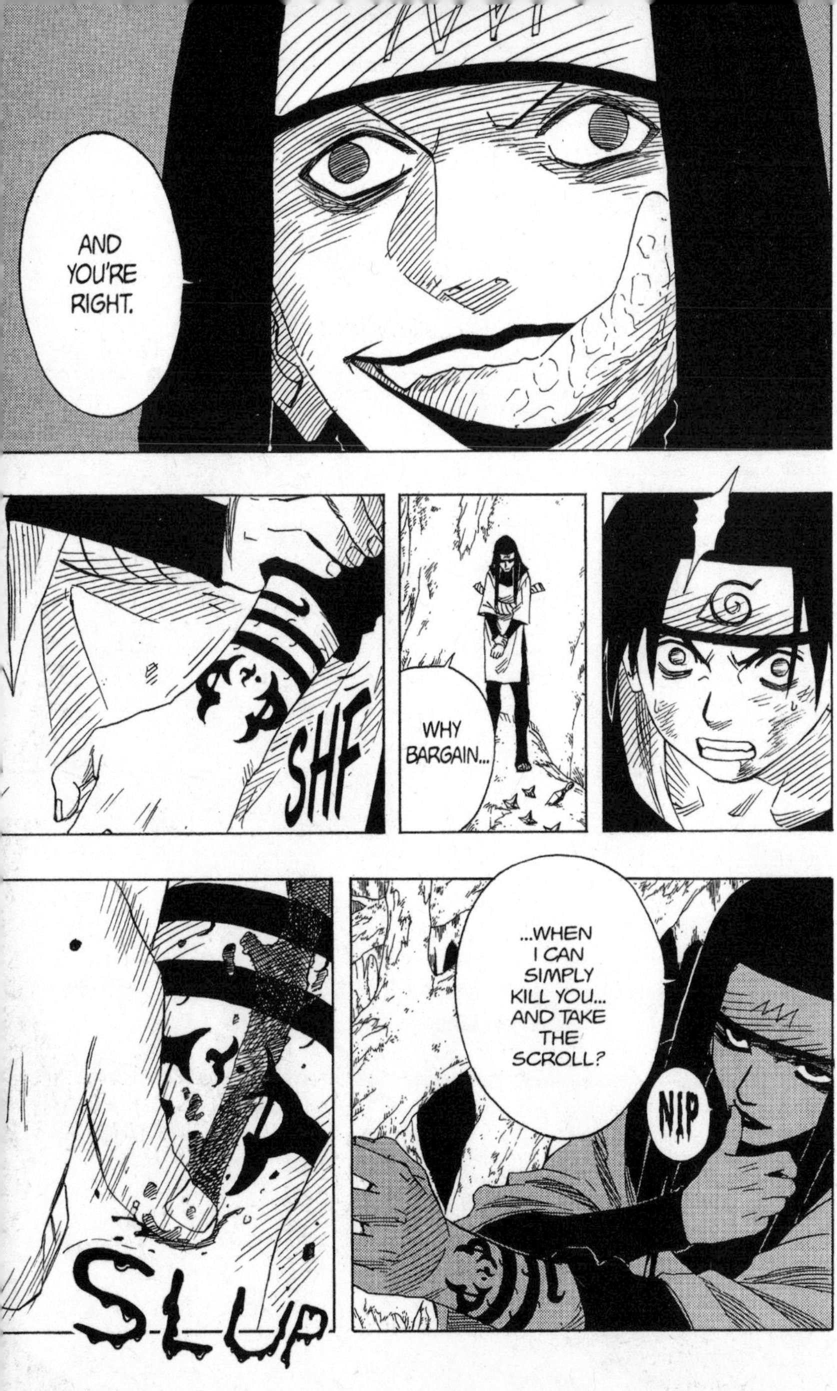
AND YOU'RE RIGHT.
WHY BARGAIN...
SHF
...WHEN I CAN SIMPLY KILL YOU... AND TAKE THE SCROLL?
NIP
SLUP

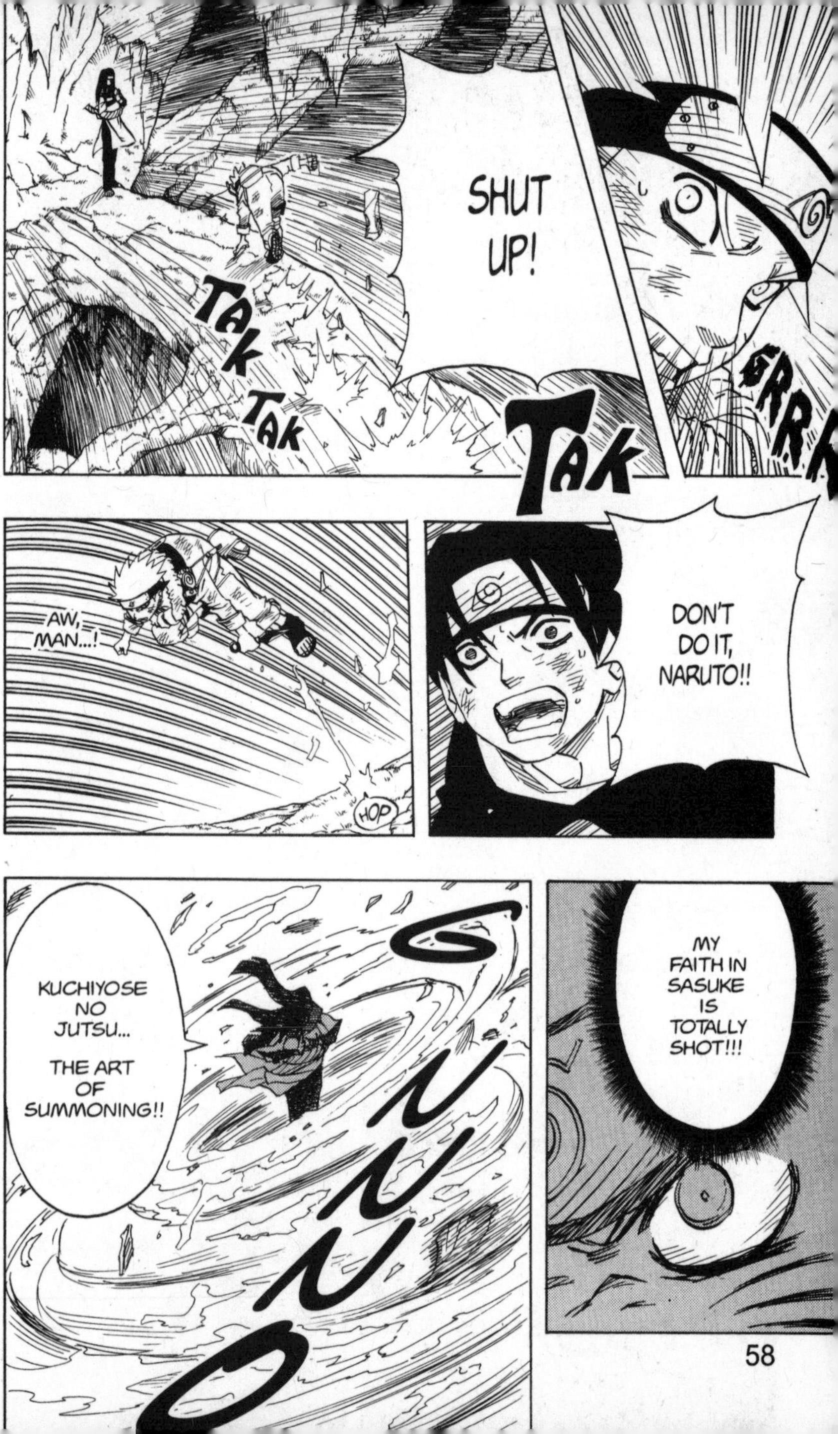
SHUT UP!
GRRRK
TAK
TAK TAK TAK
DON'T DO IT, NARUTO!!
AW, MAN...!
HOP
MY FAITH IN SASUKE IS TOTALLY SHOT!!!
KUCHIYOSE NO JUTSU...
THE ART OF SUMMONING!!
GNNNO

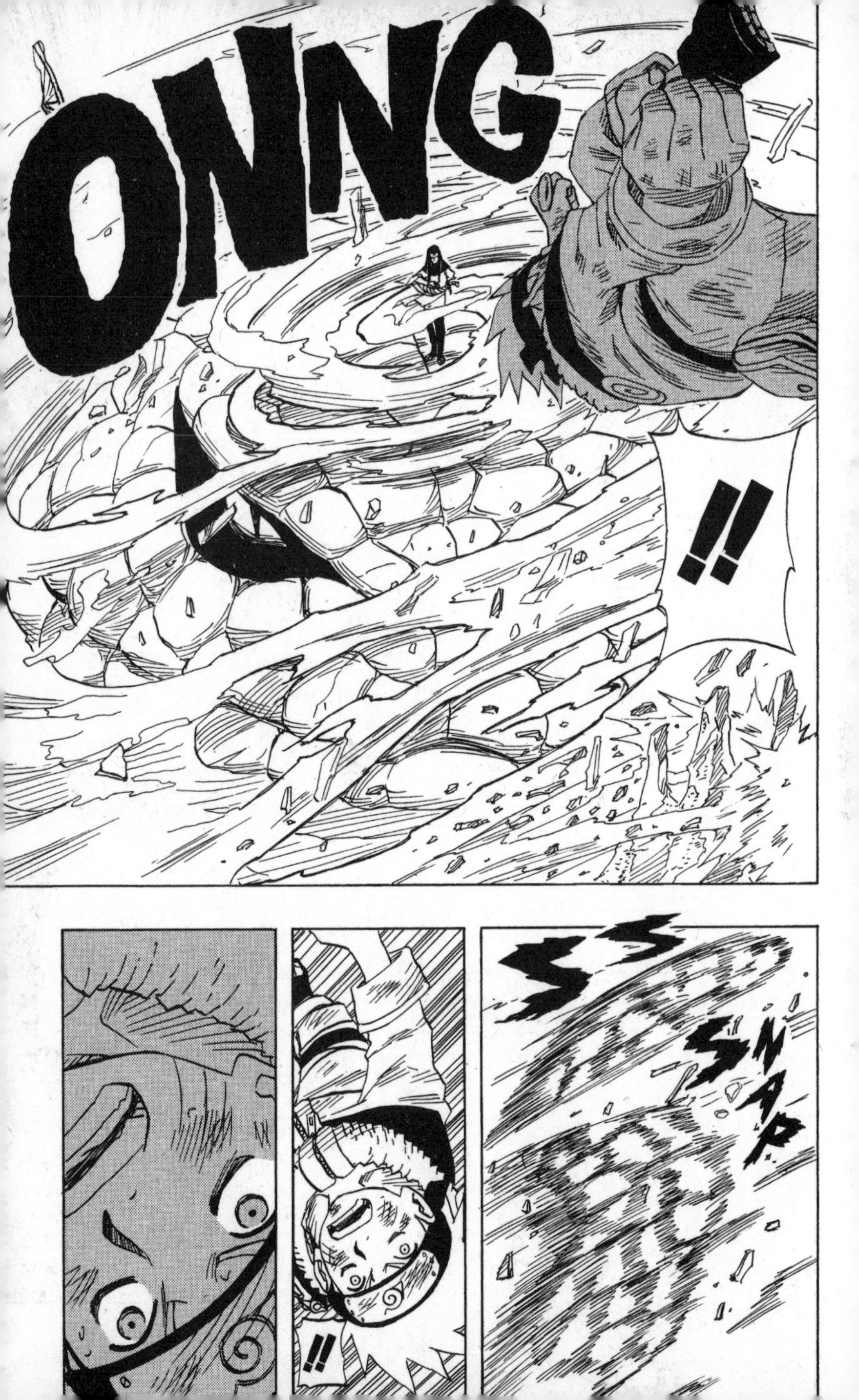
ONNG
!!
SS
SNAP
!!

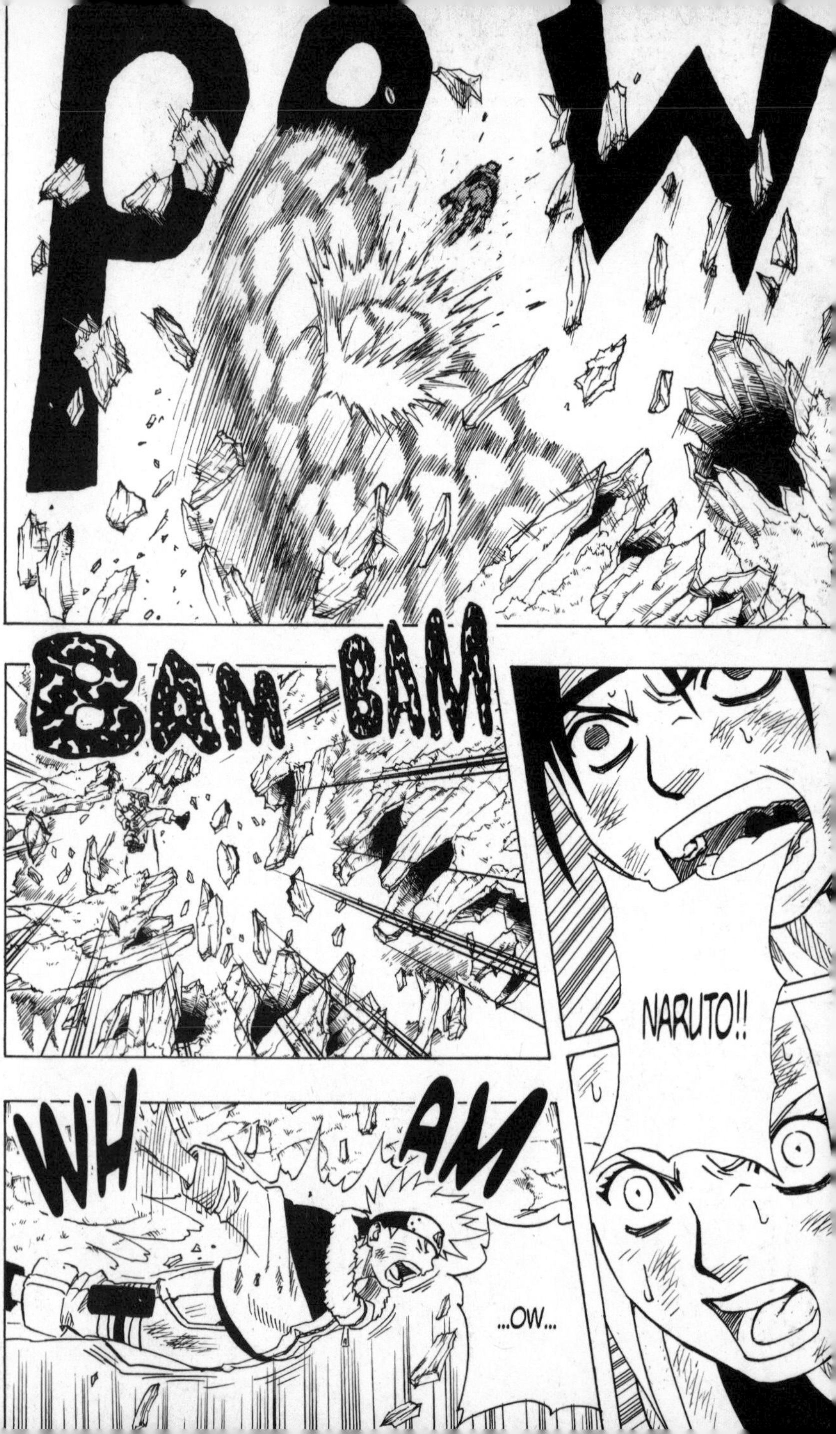
POW
NARUTO!!
BAM BAM
WHAM
...OW...

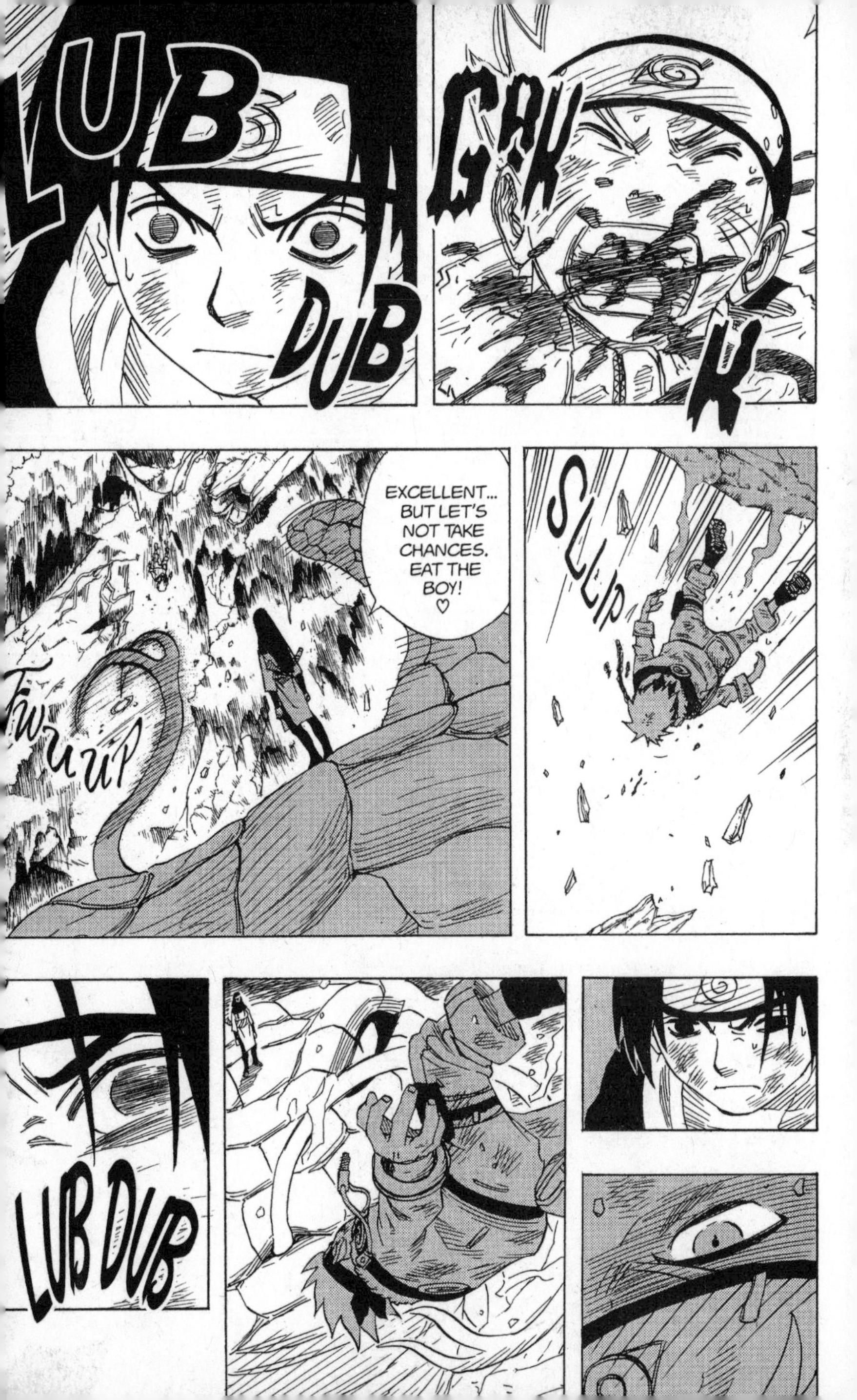

GAH
K
LUB
DUB
SLLIP
EXCELLENT... BUT LET'S NOT TAKE CHANCES. EAT THE BOY! ♡
FWUUUP
LUB DUB

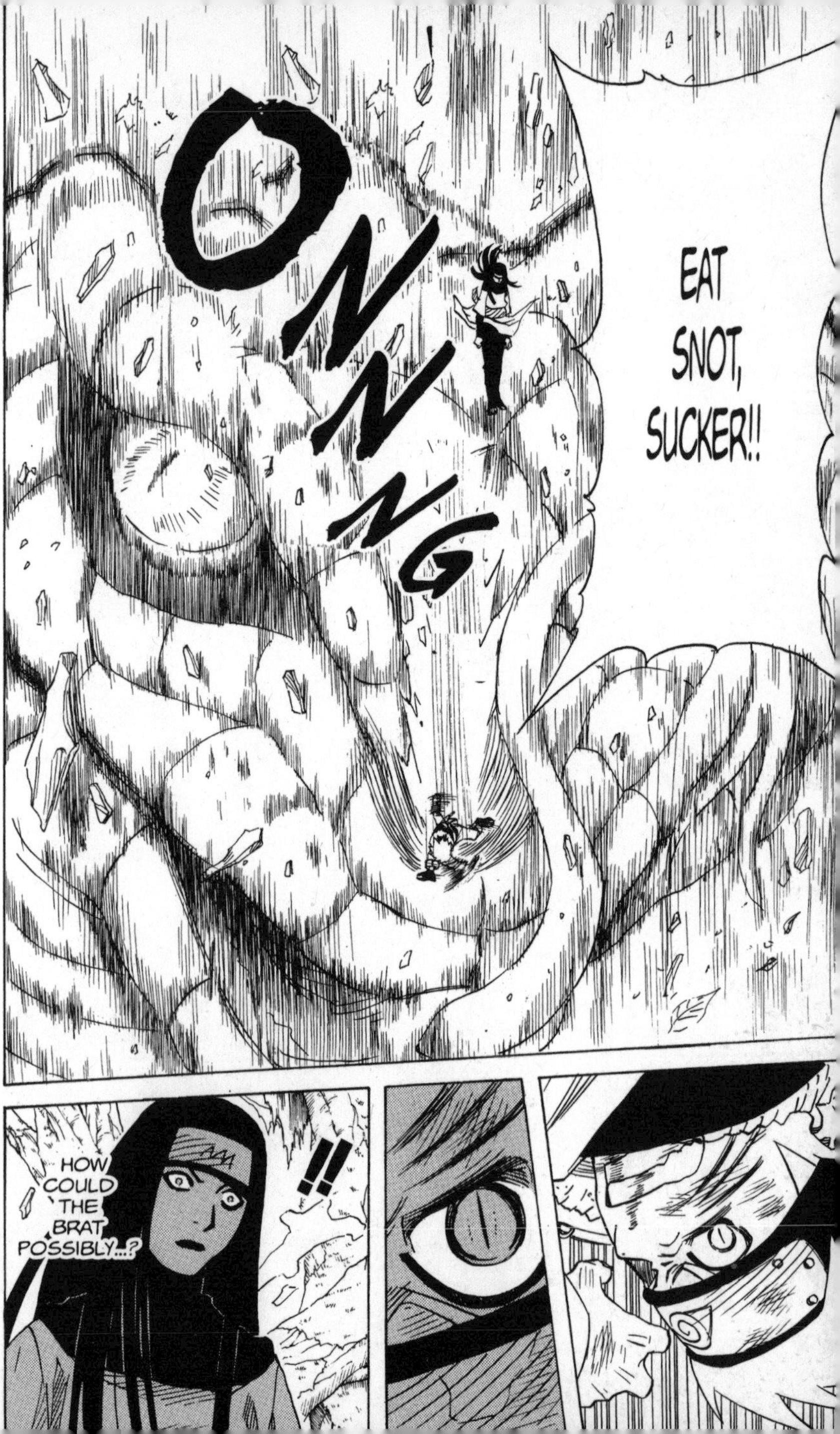
EAT SNOT, SUCKER!!
ONNNG
!!
HOW COULD THE BRAT POSSIBLY...?

READ THIS WAY

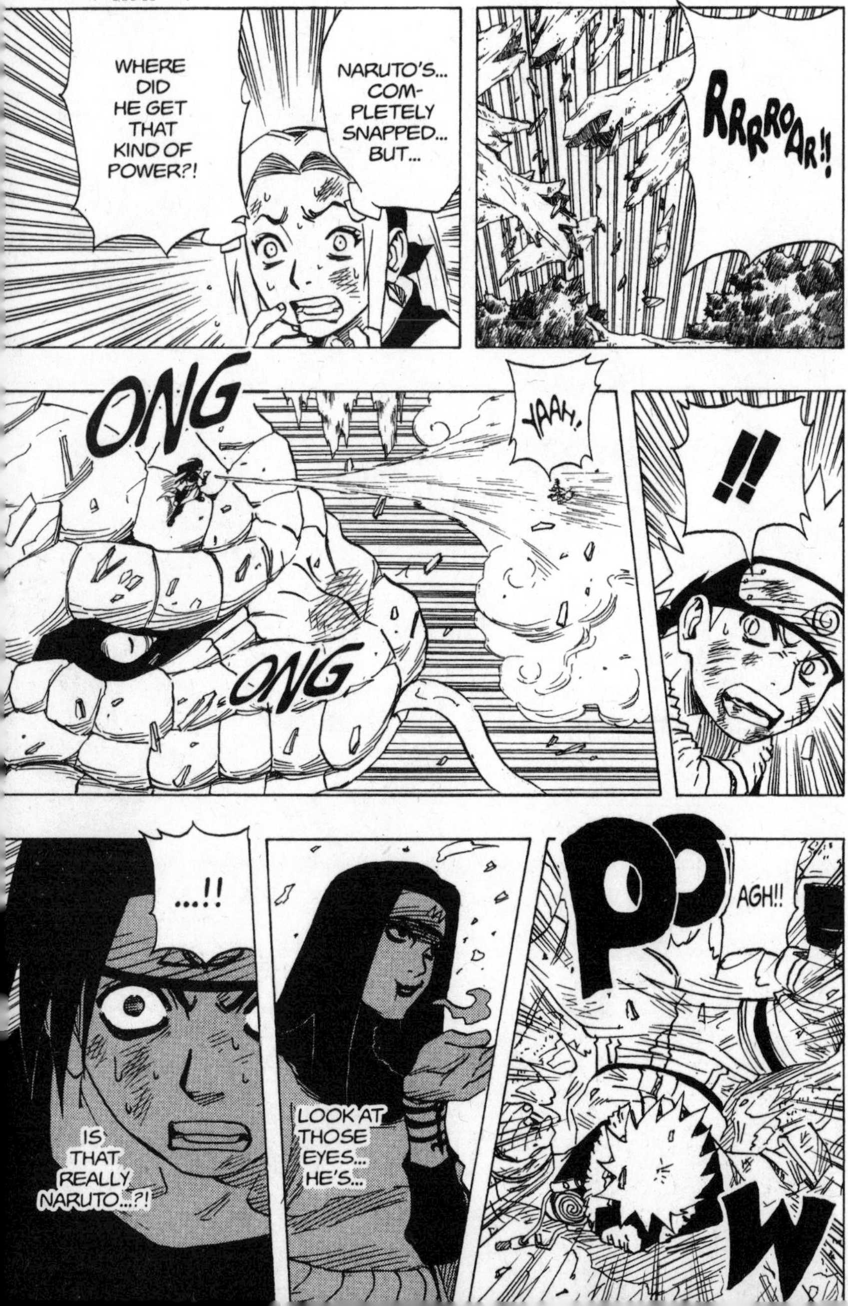
RRRROAR!!
NARUTO'S... COM-PLETELY SNAPPED... BUT...
WHERE DID HE GET THAT KIND OF POWER?!
!!
YAAAH!
ONG
ONG
PO
AGH!!
W
LOOK AT THOSE EYES... HE'S...
...!!
IS THAT REALLY NARUTO...?!

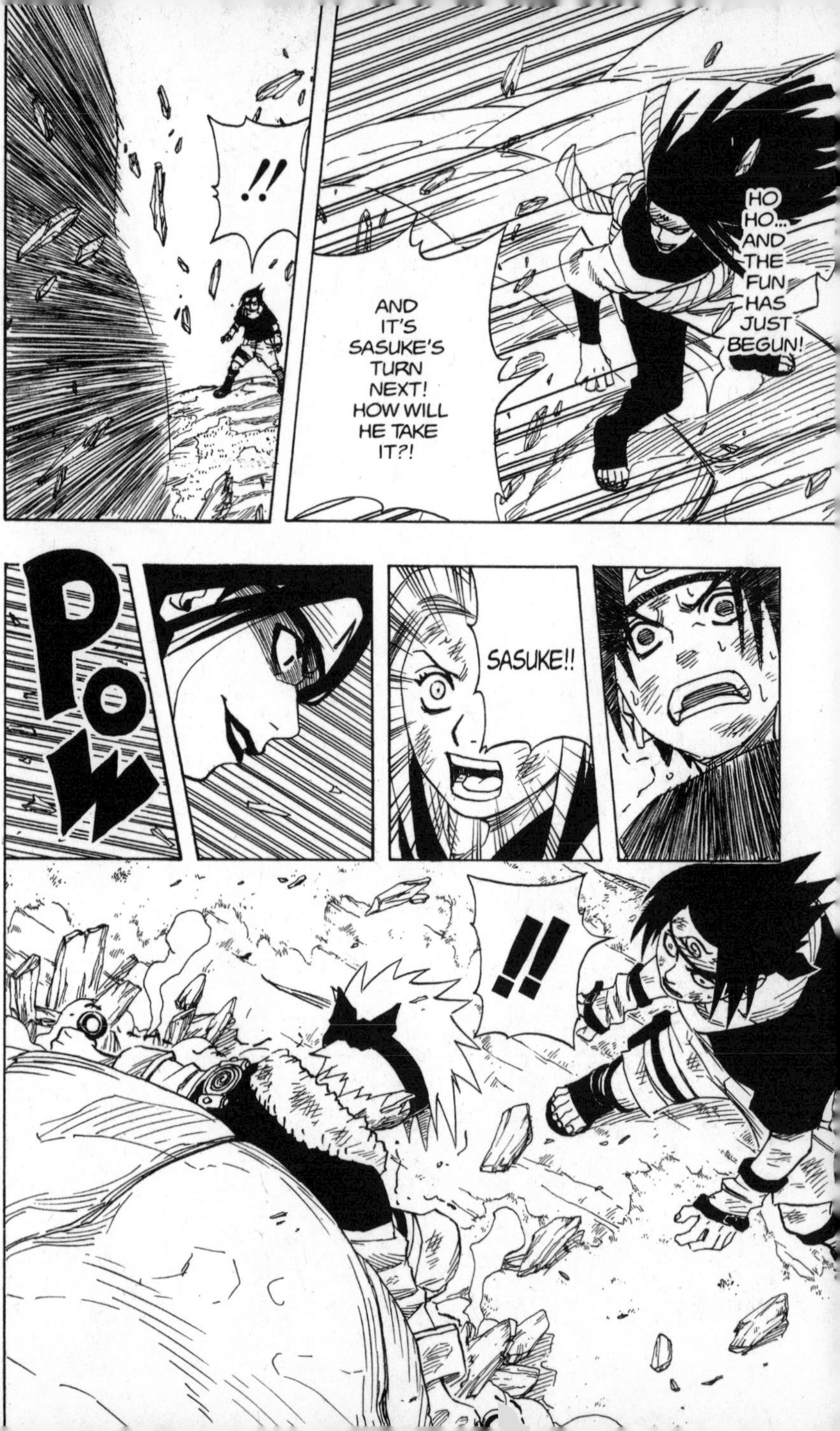
HO HO... AND THE FUN HAS JUST BEGUN!
AND IT'S SASUKE'S TURN NEXT! HOW WILL HE TAKE IT?!
!!
SASUKE!!
POW
!!

...HEY, ARE YOU OKAY...?

PUFF

HUFF

...!

PUFF

...

LUB DUB

HUFF

...YOU BIG CHICKEN?!

PUFF

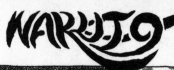

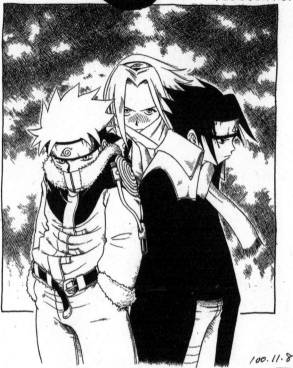

NARUTO

MEET KISHIMOTO MASASHI'S ASSISTANTS PART TWO
ASSISTANT NO. 2: KAZISA OSAMU

'00.11.8

KAZISA

HAPPY FIRST ANNIVERSARY!

PROFILE

- USUALLY WEARS GLASSES, BUT WHEN HE TAKES THEM OFF AND PUTS ON HIS CONTACTS HE BECOMES THE HANDSOME OFFICE HEARTTHROB. NO, REALLY!
- HE FALLS ASLEEP WITH THE SPEED OF NOBITA FROM DORAEMON! IN ABOUT TWO SECONDS FLAT!
- LOVES TO TRAVEL THE WORLD. HE'S BEEN TO PRAGUE AND CHINA.
- PIERCES THOSE AROUND HIM WITH THE SHARPNESS OF HIS QUESTIONS.
- IN AN ARGUMENT, HIS WORDS ARE AS MERCILESS AND COLD AS ICE!
- ALWAYS THE FIRST ONE TO BUY THE LATEST TOYS...LIKE "THE CHALLENGER"! HE WORKS AS MY BETA--THE ARTIST WHO SPOTS THE SOLID BLACKS IN HAIR AND CLOTHING, LAYS DOWN THE HALF-TONES, COMPLETES THE BACKGROUND ART... AND IS A WHIZ AT SPEED LINES AND SPECIAL EFFECTS. HAS A WAY WITH PLANT LIFE...ON THE PAGE.

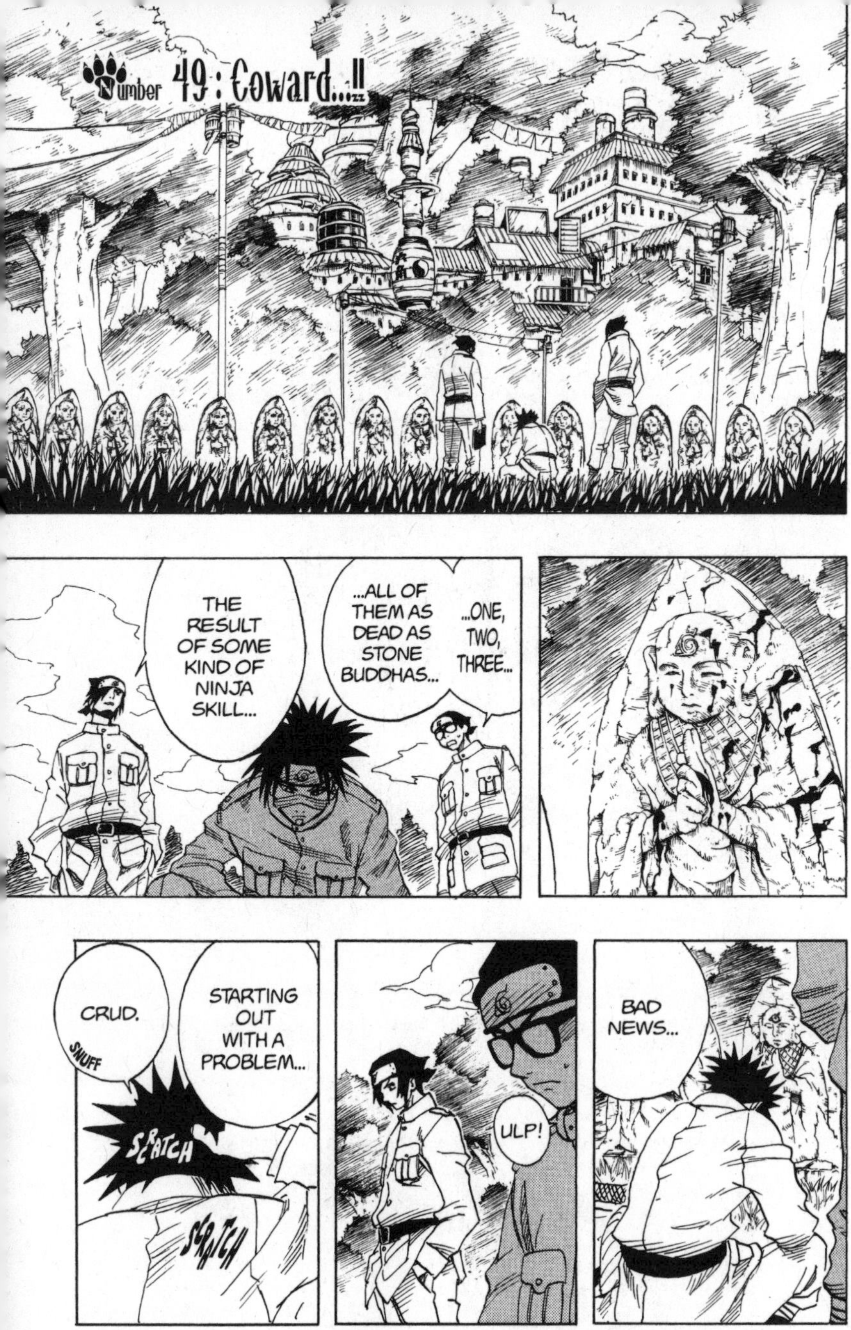
Number 49: Coward...!!
...ONE, TWO, THREE...
...ALL OF THEM AS DEAD AS STONE BUDDHAS...
THE RESULT OF SOME KIND OF NINJA SKILL...
BAD NEWS...
ULP!
STARTING OUT WITH A PROBLEM...
CRUD.
SNUFF
SCRATCH
SCRATCH

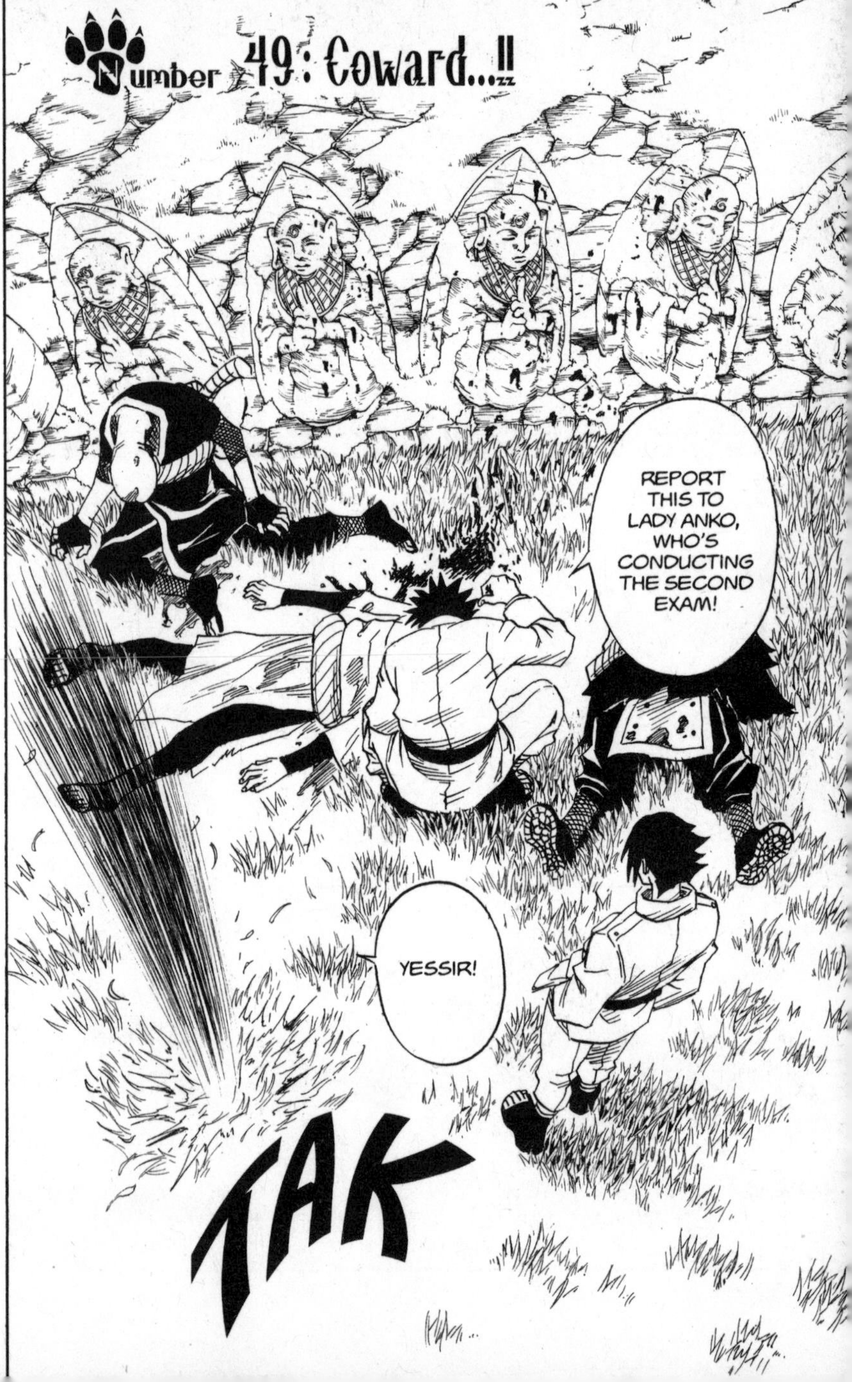
Number 49: Coward...!!
REPORT THIS TO LADY ANKO, WHO'S CONDUCTING THE SECOND EXAM!
YESSIR!
TAK

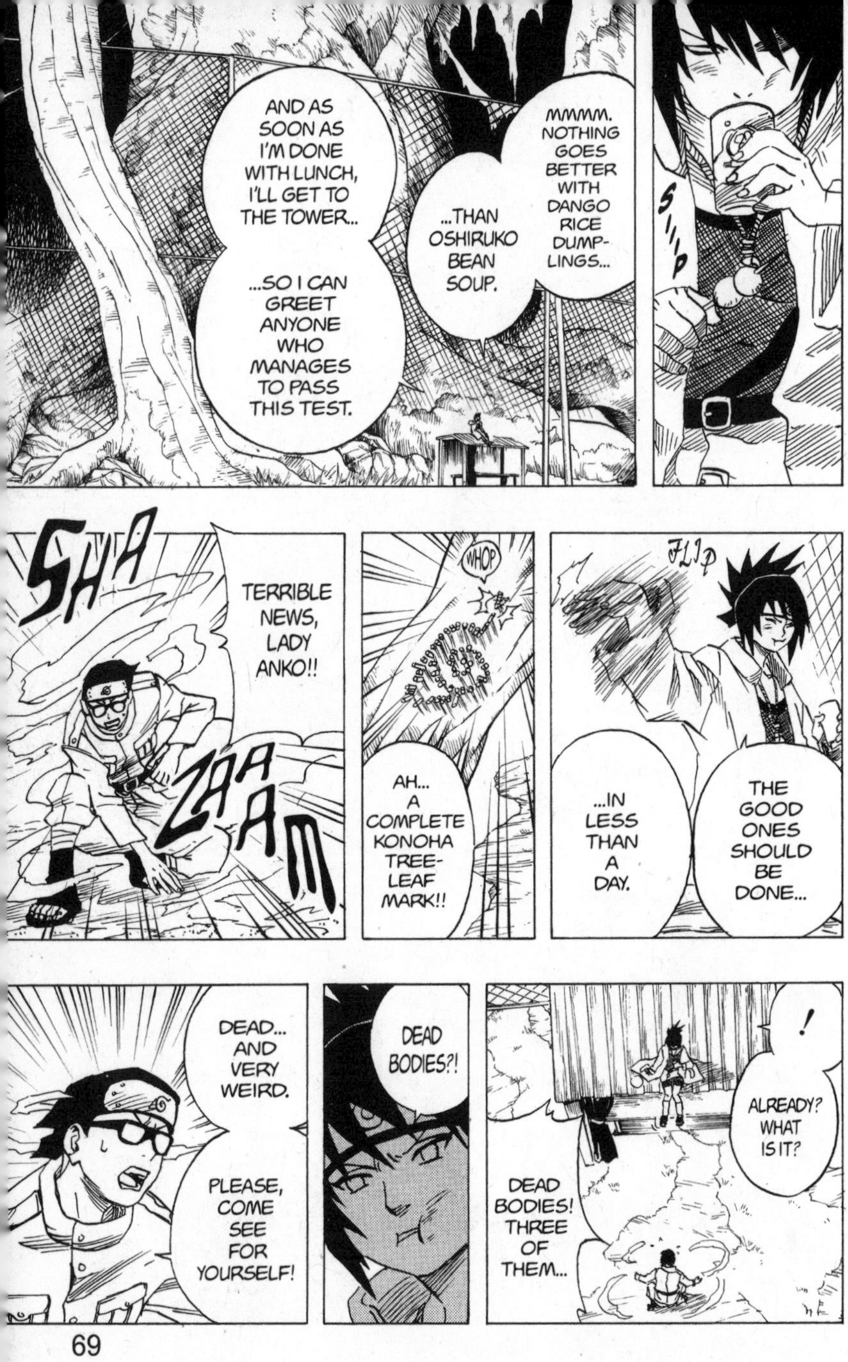
SIIIP
MMMM. NOTHING GOES BETTER WITH DANGO RICE DUMPLINGS...
...THAN OSHIRUKO BEAN SOUP.
AND AS SOON AS I'M DONE WITH LUNCH, I'LL GET TO THE TOWER...
...SO I CAN GREET ANYONE WHO MANAGES TO PASS THIS TEST.
FLIP
THE GOOD ONES SHOULD BE DONE...
...IN LESS THAN A DAY.
WHOP
AH... A COMPLETE KONOHA TREE-LEAF MARK!!
SHA
TERRIBLE NEWS, LADY ANKO!!
ZAAAM
!
ALREADY? WHAT IS IT?
DEAD BODIES! THREE OF THEM...
DEAD BODIES?!
DEAD... AND VERY WEIRD.
PLEASE, COME SEE FOR YOURSELF!

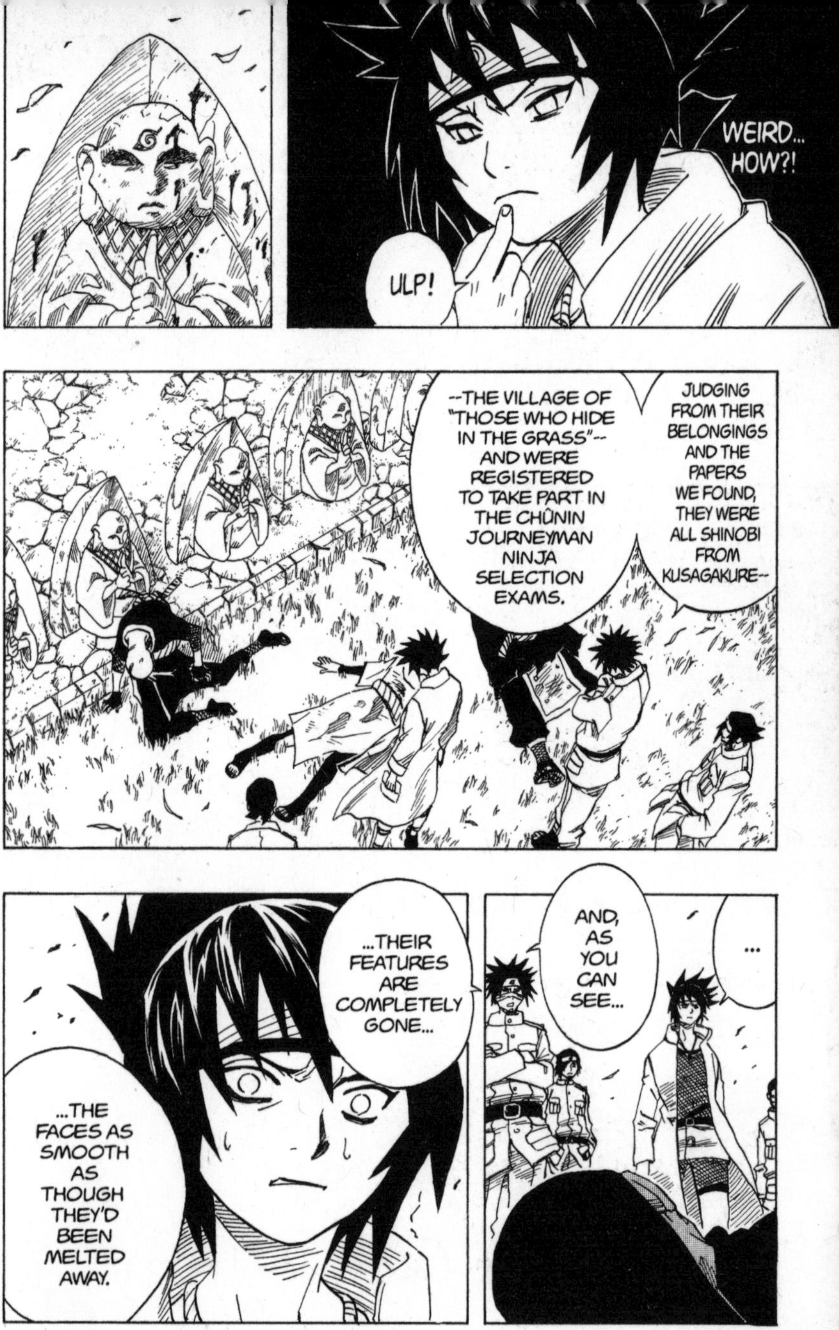
WEIRD... HOW?!
ULP!
JUDGING FROM THEIR BELONGINGS AND THE PAPERS WE FOUND, THEY WERE ALL SHINOBI FROM KUSAGAKURE--
--THE VILLAGE OF "THOSE WHO HIDE IN THE GRASS"-- AND WERE REGISTERED TO TAKE PART IN THE CHÛNIN JOURNEYMAN NINJA SELECTION EXAMS.
...
AND, AS YOU CAN SEE...
...THEIR FEATURES ARE COMPLETELY GONE...
...THE FACES AS SMOOTH AS THOUGH THEY'D BEEN MELTED AWAY.

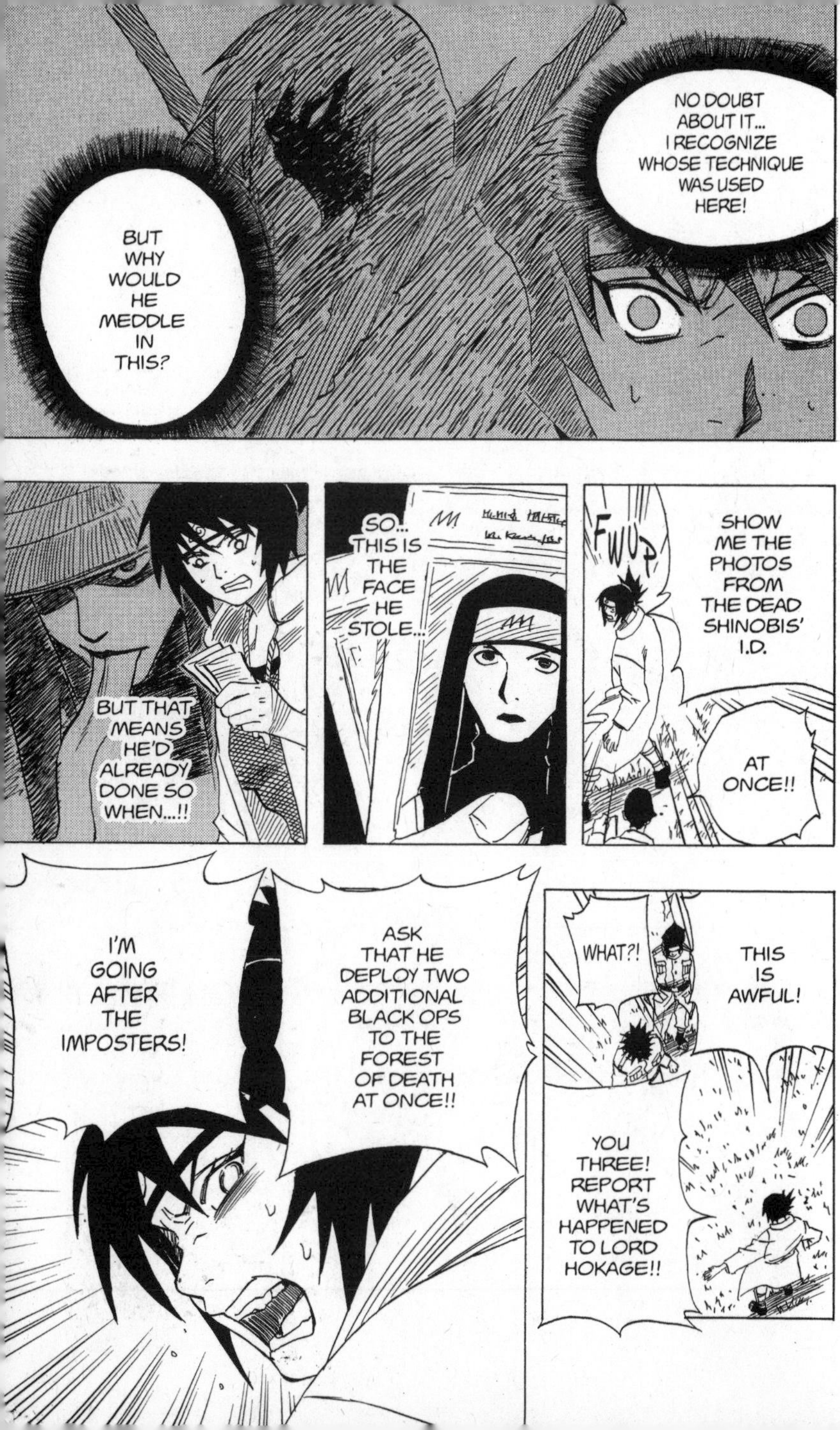
NO DOUBT ABOUT IT... I RECOGNIZE WHOSE TECHNIQUE WAS USED HERE!
BUT WHY WOULD HE MEDDLE IN THIS?
FWUP
SHOW ME THE PHOTOS FROM THE DEAD SHINOBIS' I.D.
AT ONCE!!
SO... THIS IS THE FACE HE STOLE...
BUT THAT MEANS HE'D ALREADY DONE SO WHEN...!!
THIS IS AWFUL!
WHAT?!
YOU THREE! REPORT WHAT'S HAPPENED TO LORD HOKAGE!!
ASK THAT HE DEPLOY TWO ADDITIONAL BLACK OPS TO THE FOREST OF DEATH AT ONCE!!
I'M GOING AFTER THE IMPOSTERS!

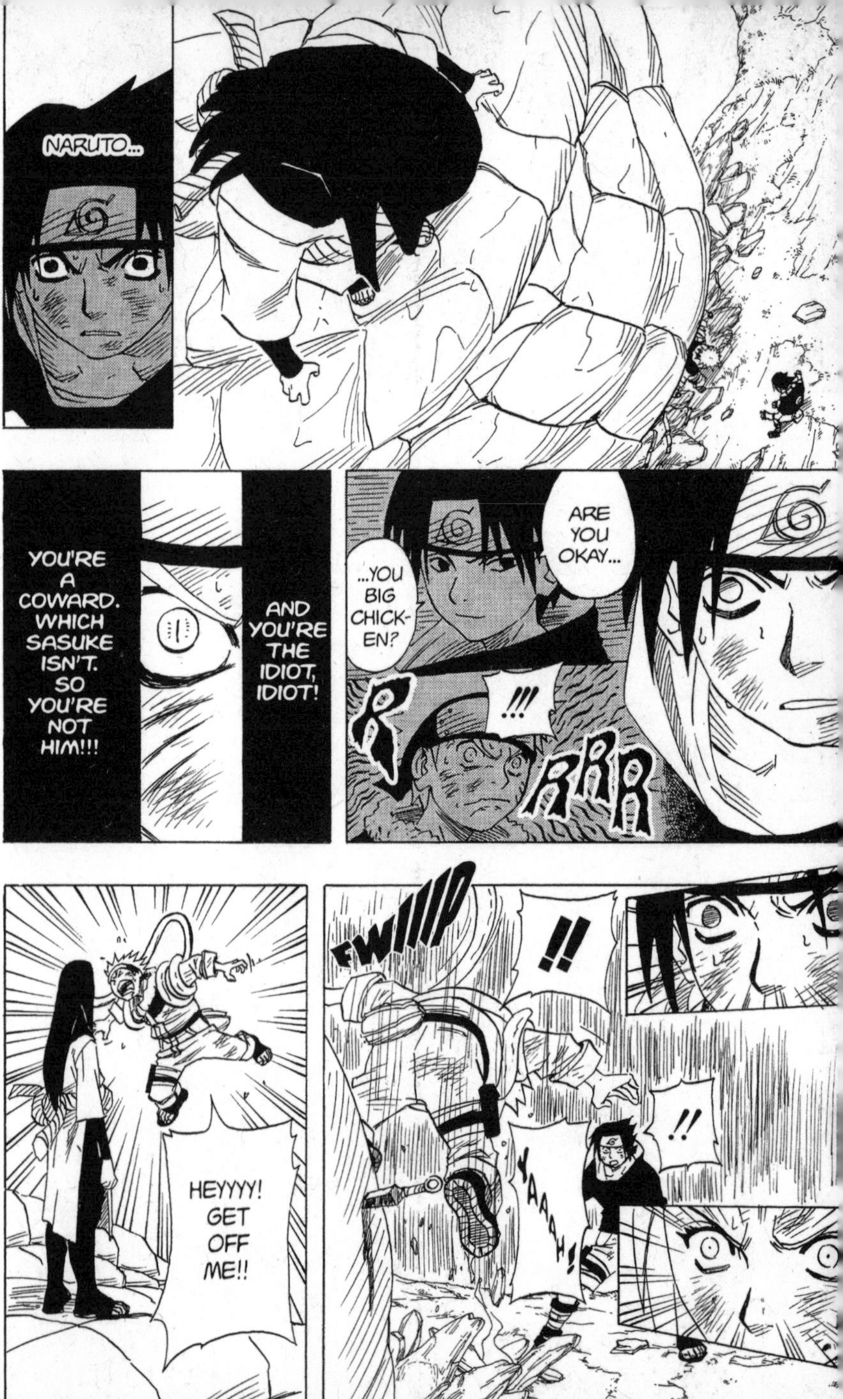
NARUTO...
ARE YOU OKAY...
...YOU BIG CHICK-EN?
!!!
RRRR
YOU'RE A COWARD. WHICH SASUKE ISN'T. SO YOU'RE NOT HIM!!!
AND YOU'RE THE IDIOT, IDIOT!
!!
FWIIIP
!!
YAAAH!
HEYYYY! GET OFF ME!!

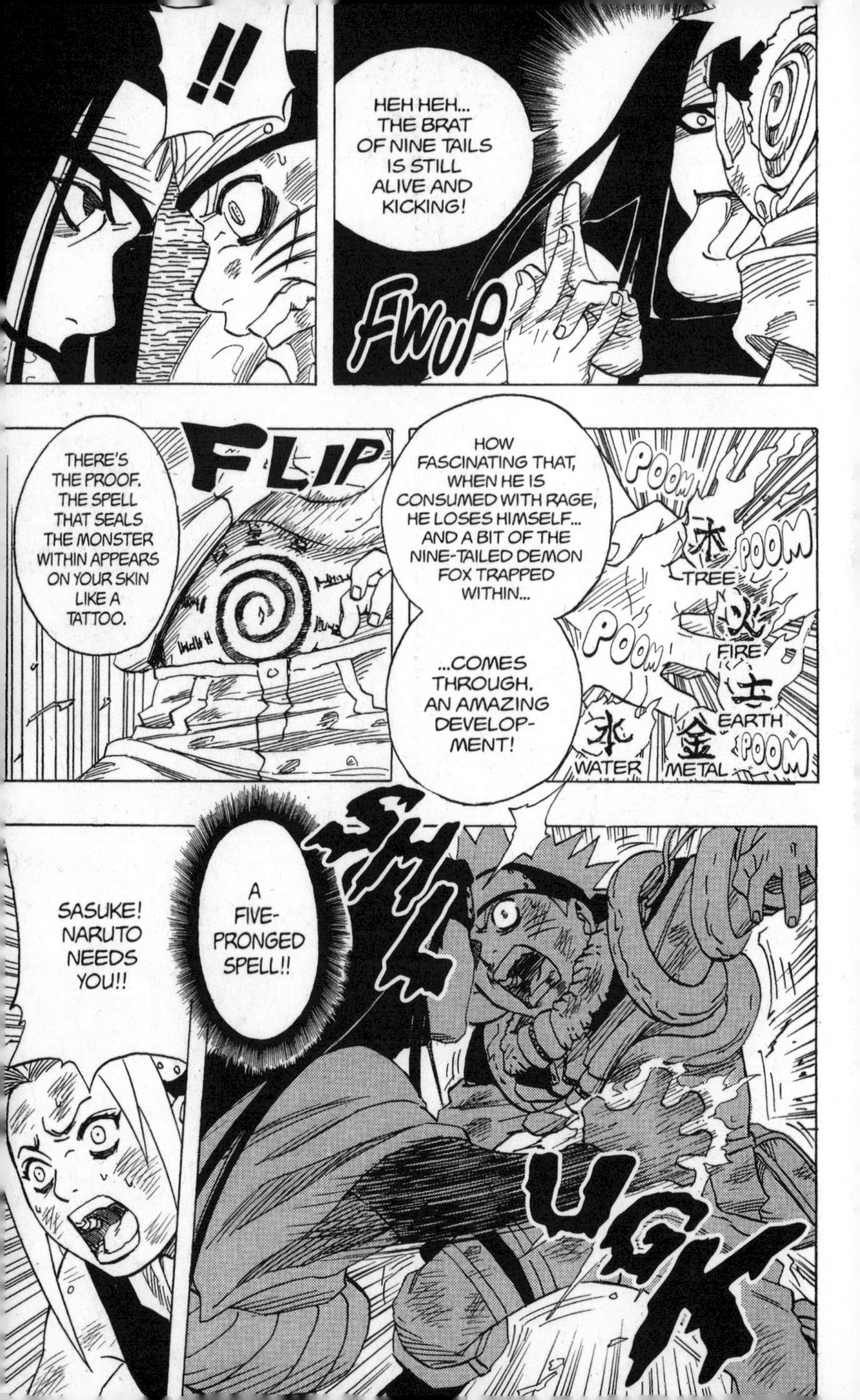

HEH HEH... THE BRAT OF NINE TAILS IS STILL ALIVE AND KICKING!
FWUP
!!
HOW FASCINATING THAT, WHEN HE IS CONSUMED WITH RAGE, HE LOSES HIMSELF... AND A BIT OF THE NINE-TAILED DEMON FOX TRAPPED WITHIN...
...COMES THROUGH. AN AMAZING DEVELOP-MENT!
POOM
POOM
POOM
POOM
木 TREE
火 FIRE
土 EARTH
金 METAL
水 WATER
FLIP
THERE'S THE PROOF. THE SPELL THAT SEALS THE MONSTER WITHIN APPEARS ON YOUR SKIN LIKE A TATTOO.
A FIVE-PRONGED SPELL!!
UGK
SASUKE! NARUTO NEEDS YOU!!

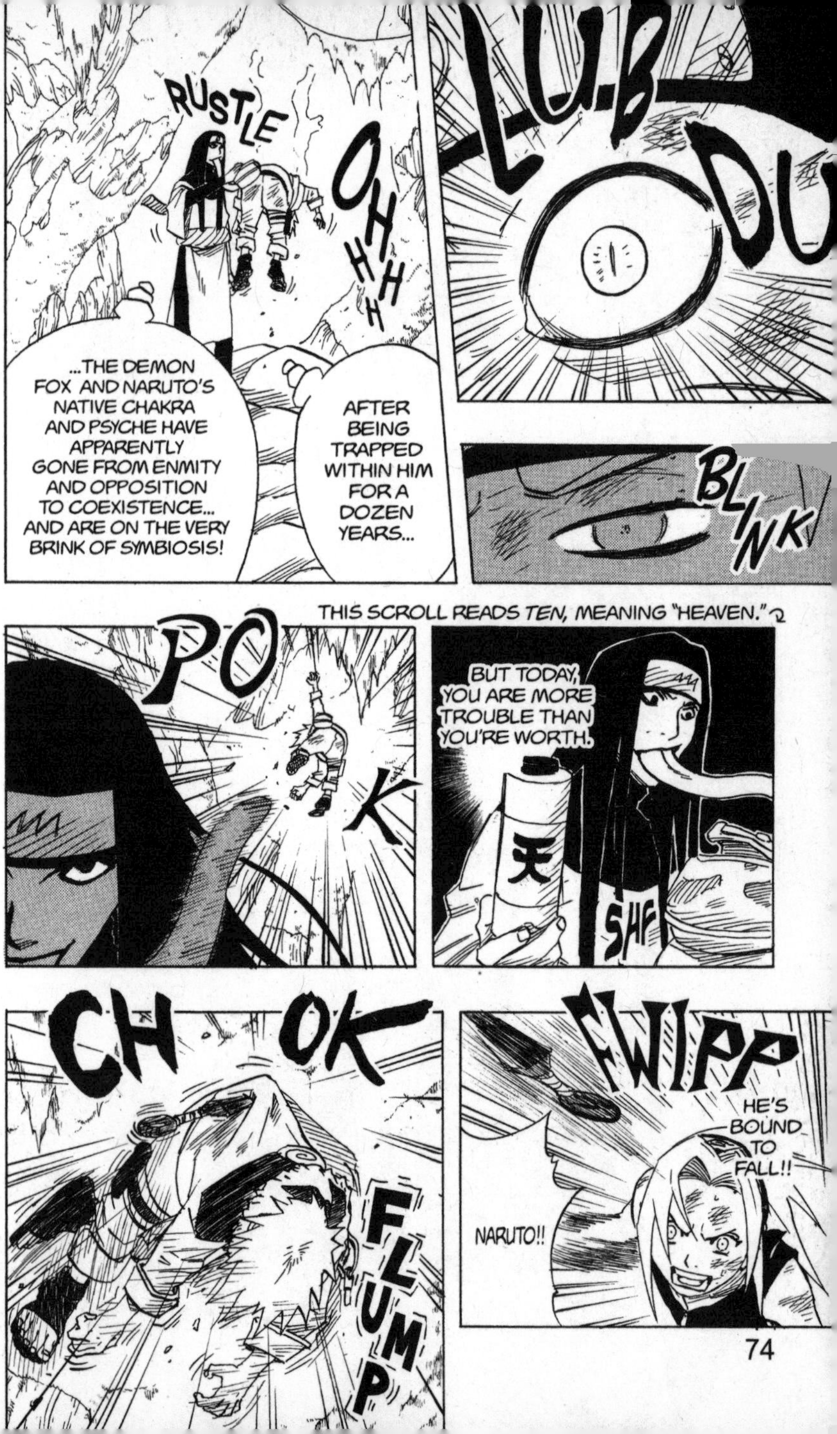

DU
LU.B
BLINK
RUSTLE
OHHHH
AFTER BEING TRAPPED WITHIN HIM FOR A DOZEN YEARS...
...THE DEMON FOX AND NARUTO'S NATIVE CHAKRA AND PSYCHE HAVE APPARENTLY GONE FROM ENMITY AND OPPOSITION TO COEXISTENCE... AND ARE ON THE VERY BRINK OF SYMBIOSIS!
THIS SCROLL READS *TEN*, MEANING "HEAVEN."
BUT TODAY, YOU ARE MORE TROUBLE THAN YOU'RE WORTH.
天
SHF
POK
FWIPP
HE'S BOUND TO FALL!!
NARUTO!!
CHOK
FLUMP

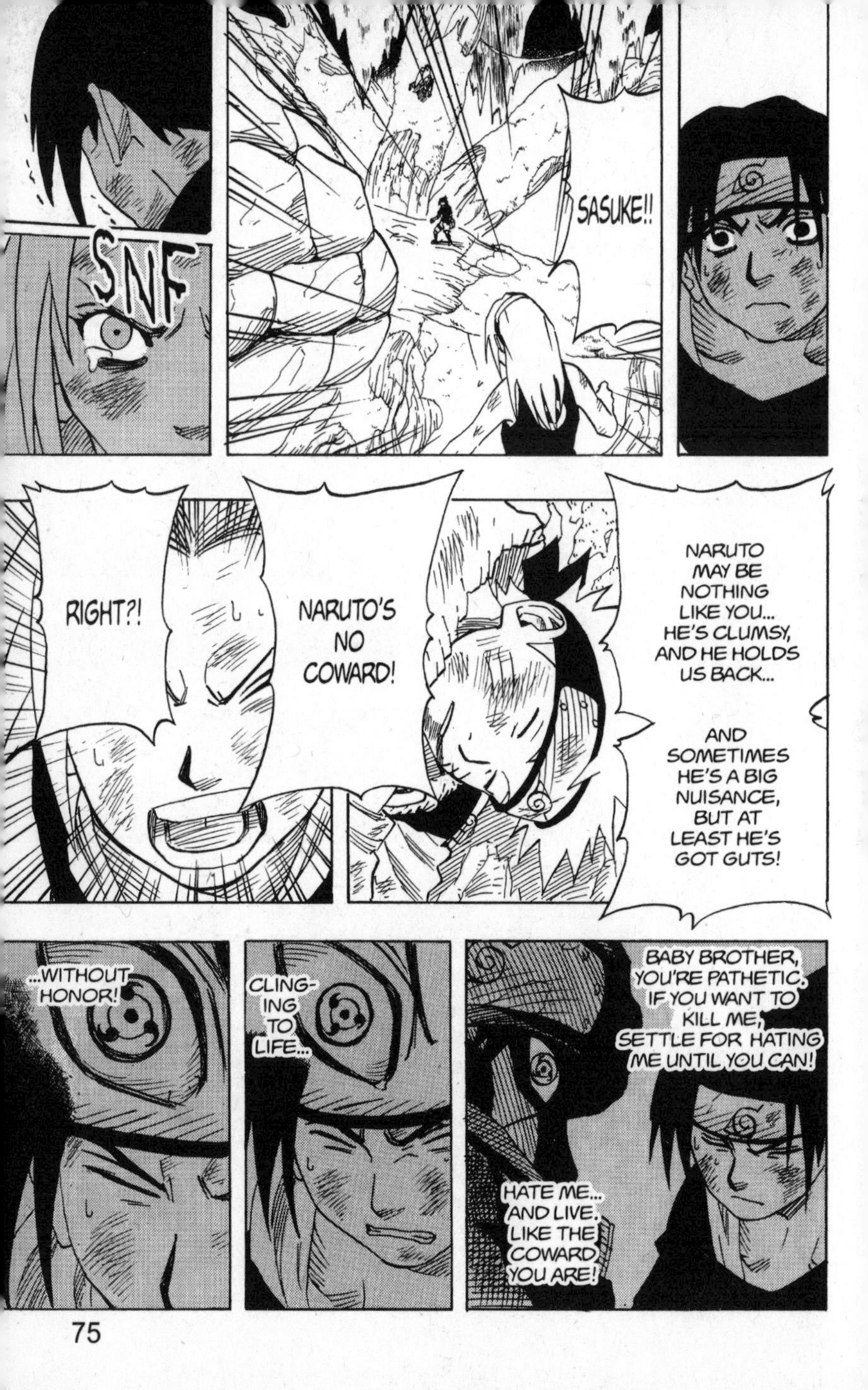
SASUKE!!
SNF
NARUTO MAY BE NOTHING LIKE YOU... HE'S CLUMSY, AND HE HOLDS US BACK...
AND SOMETIMES HE'S A BIG NUISANCE, BUT AT LEAST HE'S GOT GUTS!
NARUTO'S NO COWARD!
RIGHT?!
BABY BROTHER, YOU'RE PATHETIC. IF YOU WANT TO KILL ME, SETTLE FOR HATING ME UNTIL YOU CAN!
HATE ME... AND LIVE. LIKE THE COWARD YOU ARE!
CLING-ING TO LIFE...
...WITHOUT HONOR!

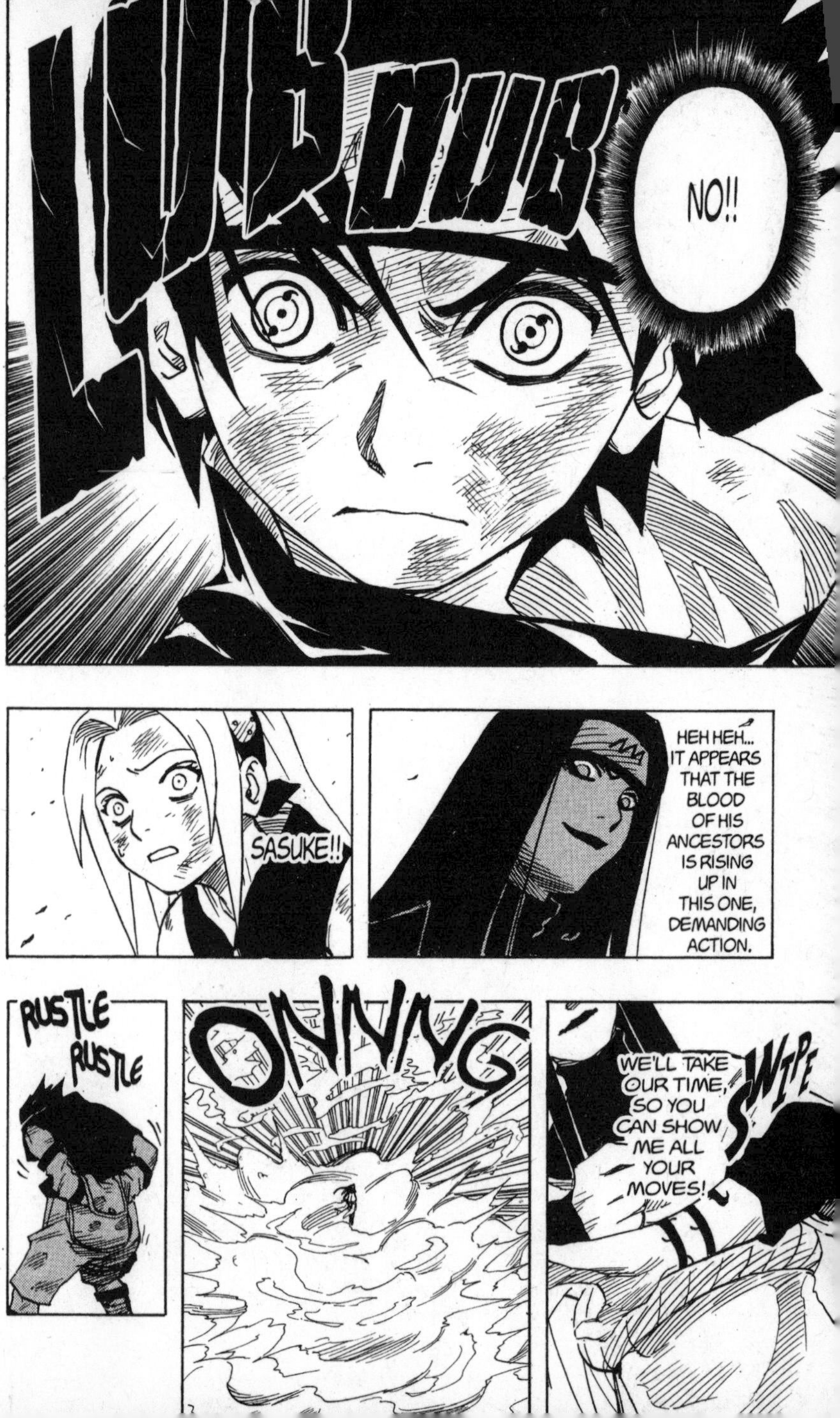
LUB DUB
NO!!
HEH HEH... IT APPEARS THAT THE BLOOD OF HIS ANCESTORS IS RISING UP IN THIS ONE, DEMANDING ACTION.
SASUKE!!
WE'LL TAKE OUR TIME, SO YOU CAN SHOW ME ALL YOUR MOVES!
SWIPE
ONNNG
RUSTLE RUSTLE

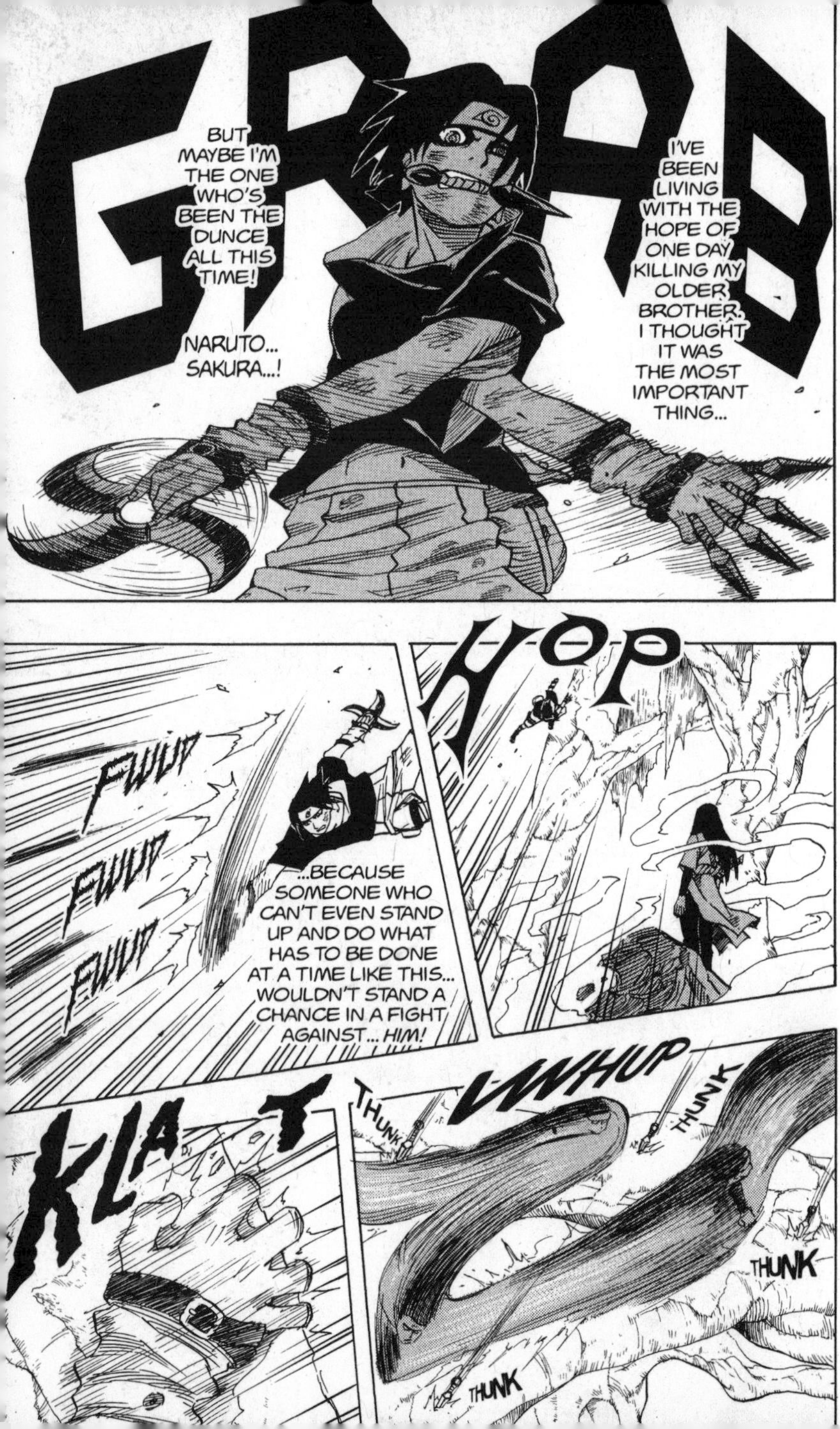
GRAB
I'VE BEEN LIVING WITH THE HOPE OF ONE DAY KILLING MY OLDER BROTHER. I THOUGHT IT WAS THE MOST IMPORTANT THING...
BUT MAYBE I'M THE ONE WHO'S BEEN THE DUNCE ALL THIS TIME!
NARUTO... SAKURA...!
HOP
FWUP
FWUP
FWUP
...BECAUSE SOMEONE WHO CAN'T EVEN STAND UP AND DO WHAT HAS TO BE DONE AT A TIME LIKE THIS... WOULDN'T STAND A CHANCE IN A FIGHT AGAINST... *HIM!*
THUNK
WHUP
THUNK
THUNK
THUNK
KLAT

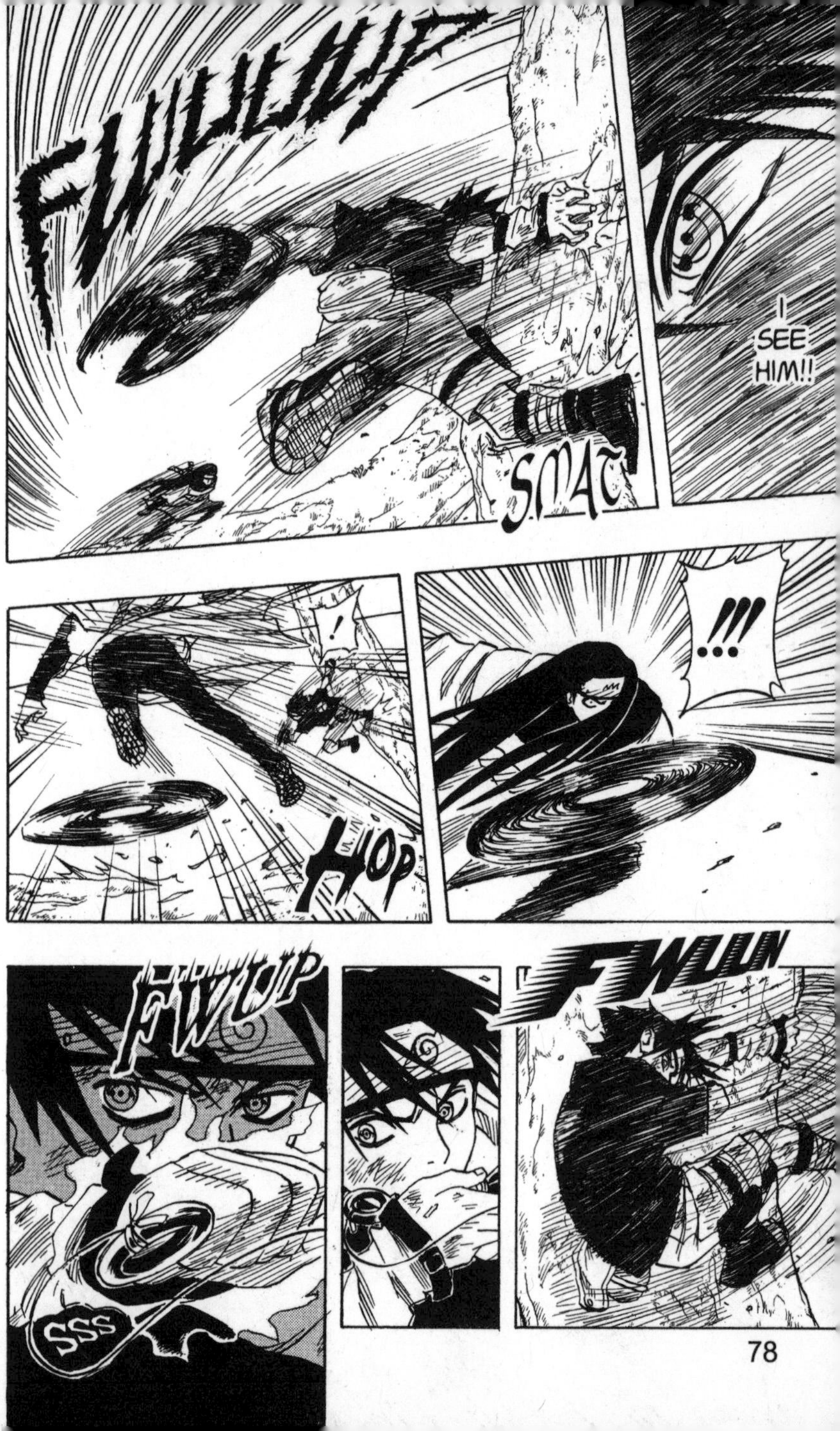
I SEE HIM!!
SMAT
!!!
!
HOP
FWUN
FWUP
SSS

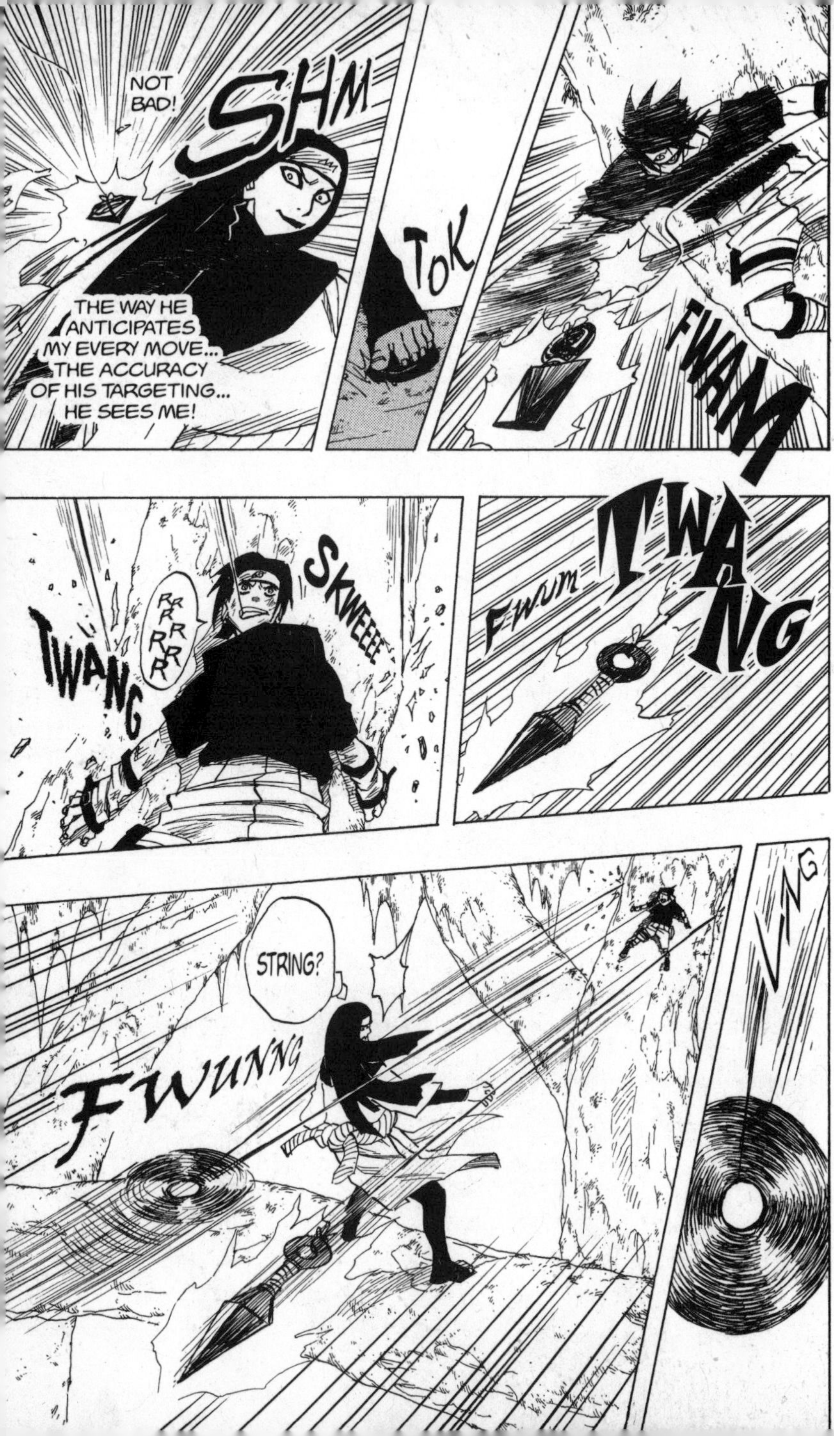
FWAM
TOK
NOT BAD!
SHM
THE WAY HE ANTICIPATES MY EVERY MOVE... THE ACCURACY OF HIS TARGETING... HE SEES ME!
Fwum
TWANG
SKWEEEE
RRRRRR
TWANG
STRING?
FWUNNG

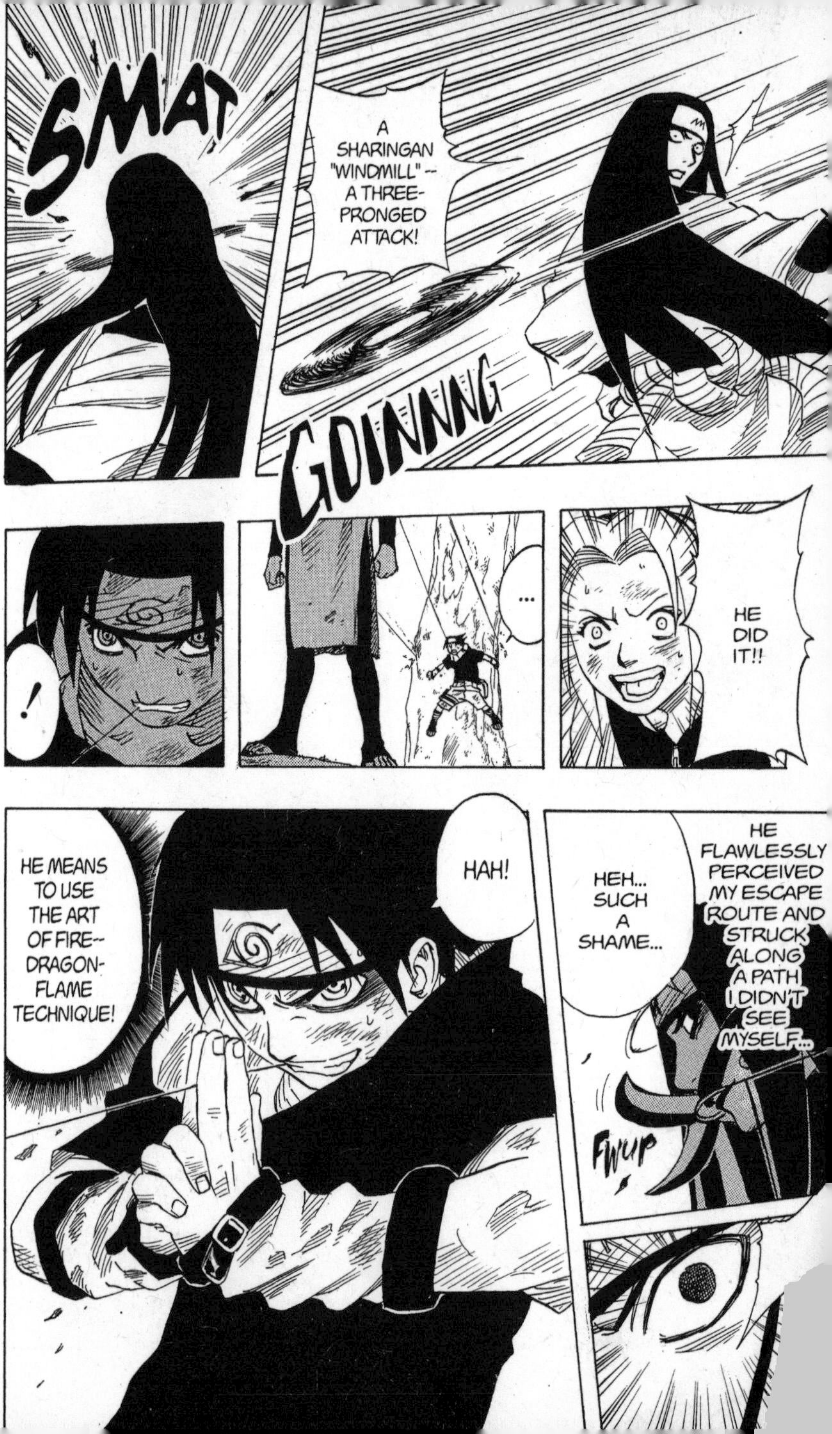
A SHARINGAN "WINDMILL" -- A THREE-PRONGED ATTACK!
GDINNNG
SMAT
HE DID IT!!
...
!
HE FLAWLESSLY PERCEIVED MY ESCAPE ROUTE AND STRUCK ALONG A PATH I DIDN'T SEE MYSELF...
HEH... SUCH A SHAME...
FWUP
HAH!
HE MEANS TO USE THE ART OF FIRE--DRAGON-FLAME TECHNIQUE!

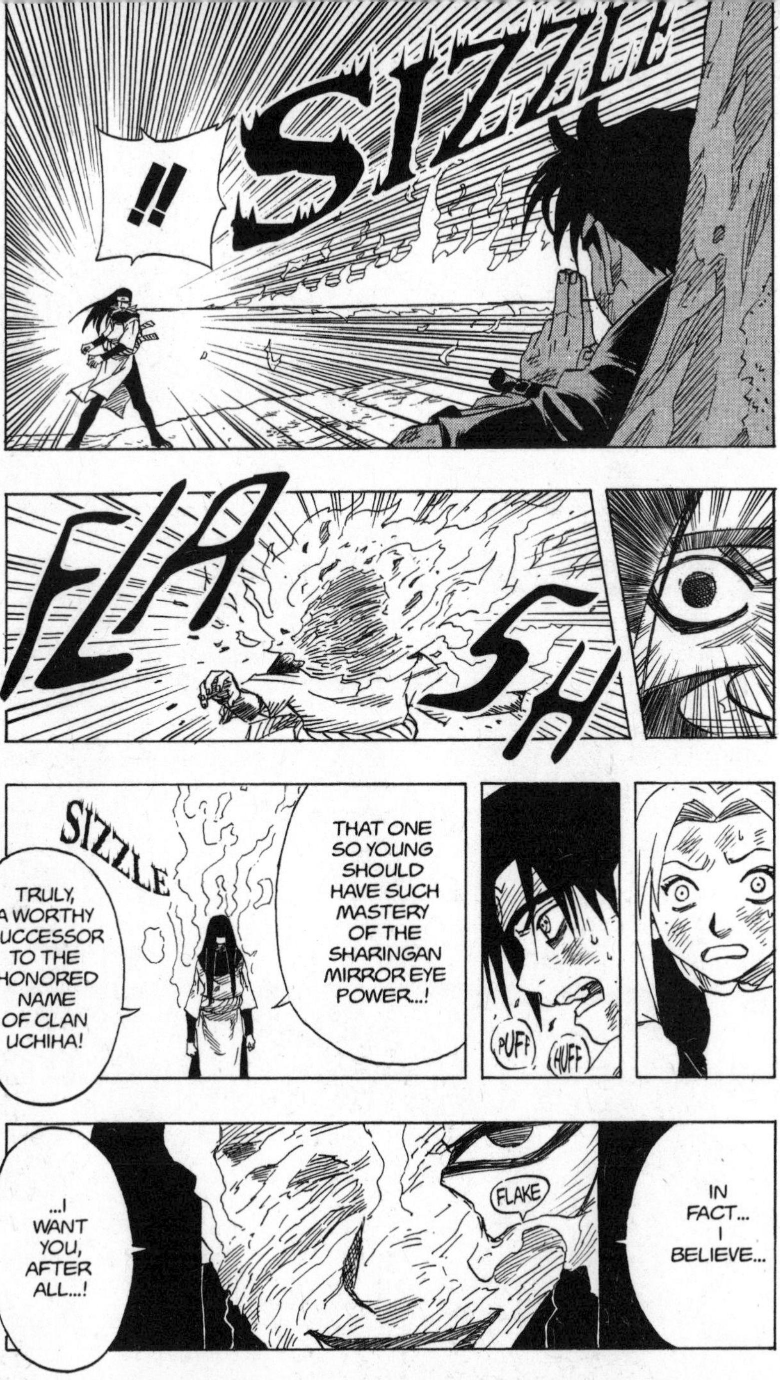
SIZZLE
!!
FLASH
PUFF
HUFF
THAT ONE SO YOUNG SHOULD HAVE SUCH MASTERY OF THE SHARINGAN MIRROR EYE POWER...!
SIZZLE
TRULY, A WORTHY SUCCESSOR TO THE HONORED NAME OF CLAN UCHIHA!
IN FACT... I BELIEVE...
FLAKE
...I WANT YOU, AFTER ALL...!

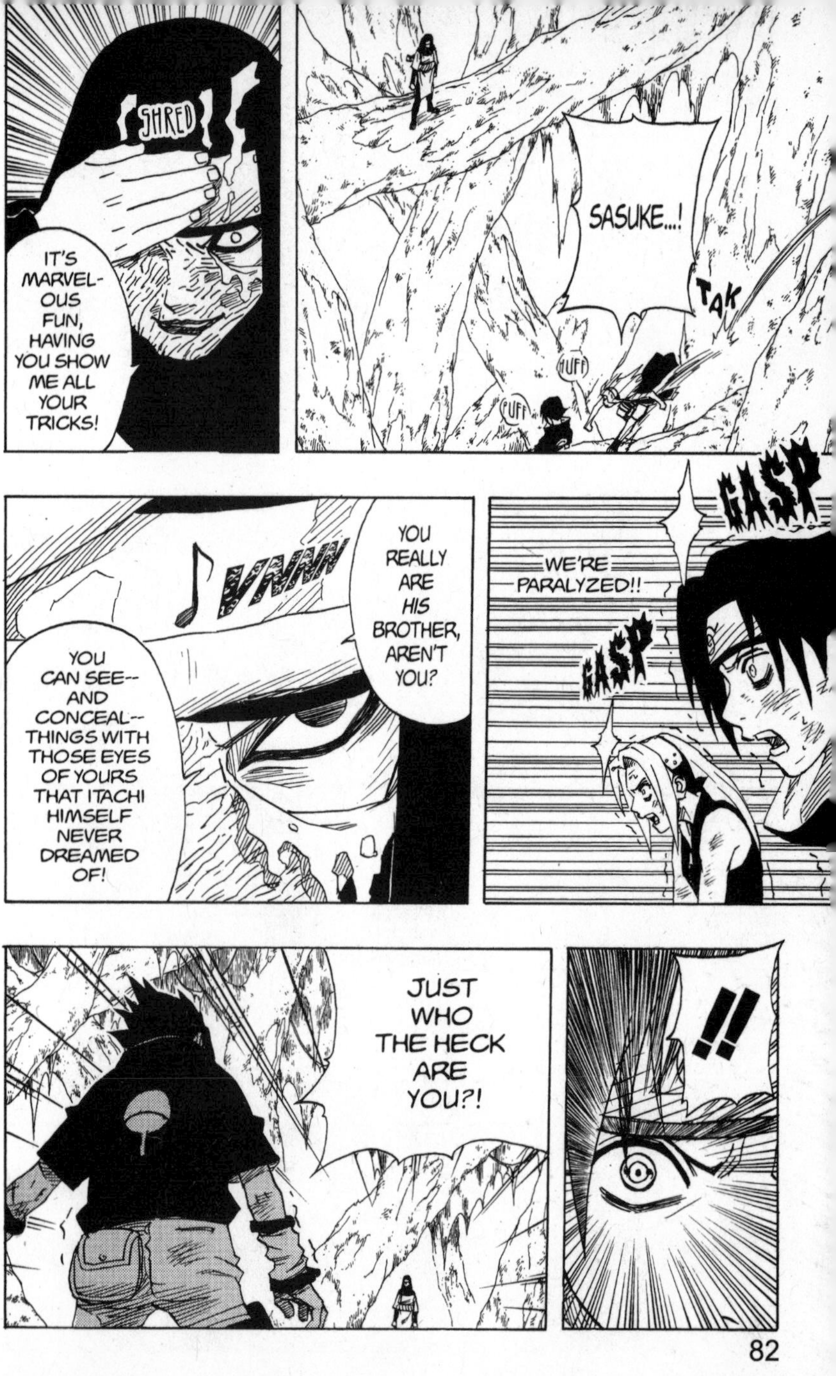
SASUKE...!
TAK
HUFF
PUFF
SHRED
IT'S MARVELOUS FUN, HAVING YOU SHOW ME ALL YOUR TRICKS!
GASP
WE'RE PARALYZED!!
GASP
YOU REALLY ARE HIS BROTHER, AREN'T YOU?
VNNN
YOU CAN SEE--AND CONCEAL--THINGS WITH THOSE EYES OF YOURS THAT ITACHI HIMSELF NEVER DREAMED OF!
!!
JUST WHO THE HECK ARE YOU?!

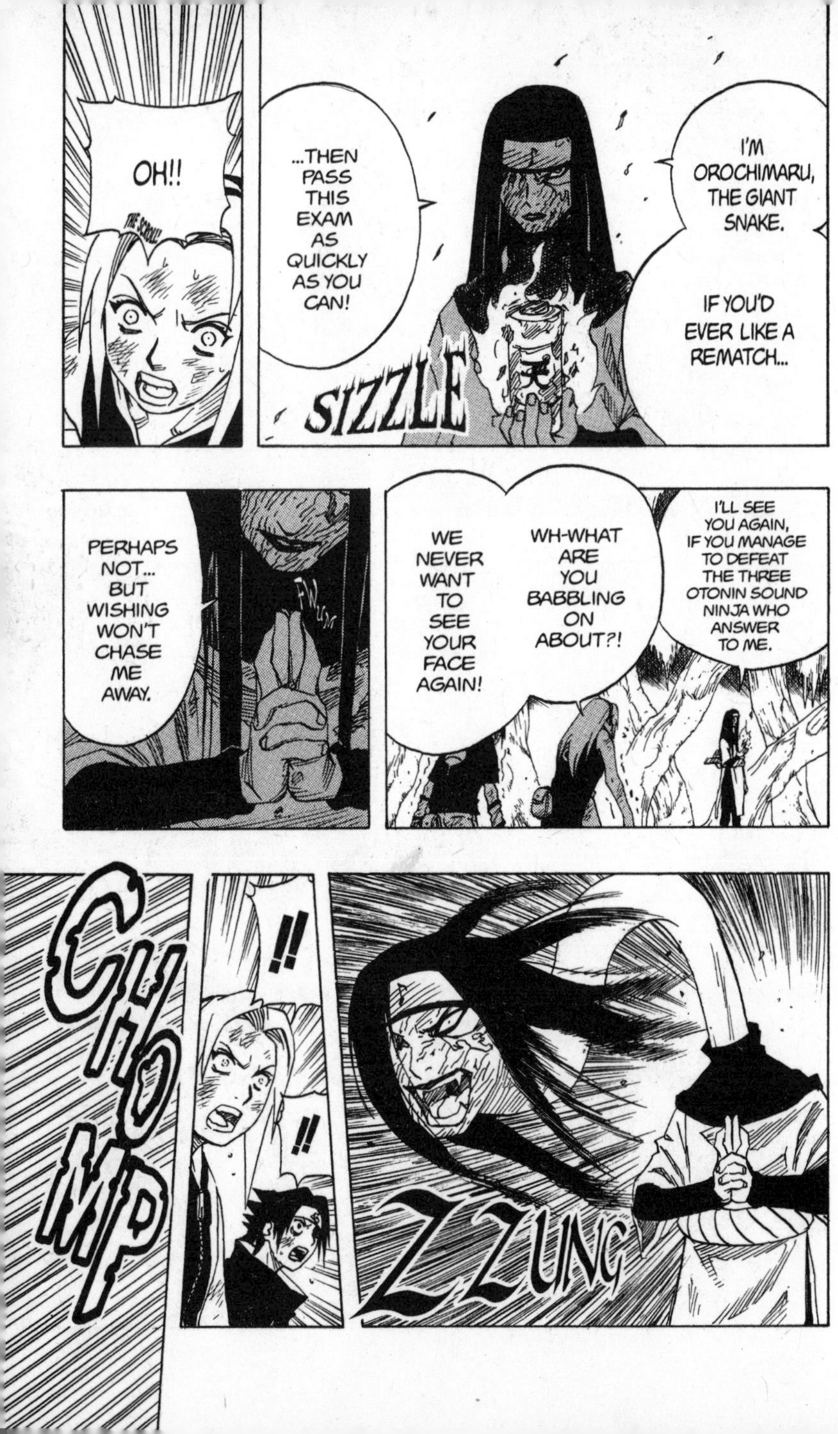
I'M OROCHIMARU, THE GIANT SNAKE.
IF YOU'D EVER LIKE A REMATCH...
...THEN PASS THIS EXAM AS QUICKLY AS YOU CAN!
SIZZLE
OH!!
THE SCROLL!
I'LL SEE YOU AGAIN, IF YOU MANAGE TO DEFEAT THE THREE OTONIN SOUND NINJA WHO ANSWER TO ME.
WH-WHAT ARE YOU BABBLING ON ABOUT?!
WE NEVER WANT TO SEE YOUR FACE AGAIN!
PERHAPS NOT... BUT WISHING WON'T CHASE ME AWAY.
FWUM
ZZUNG
!!
!!
CHOMP

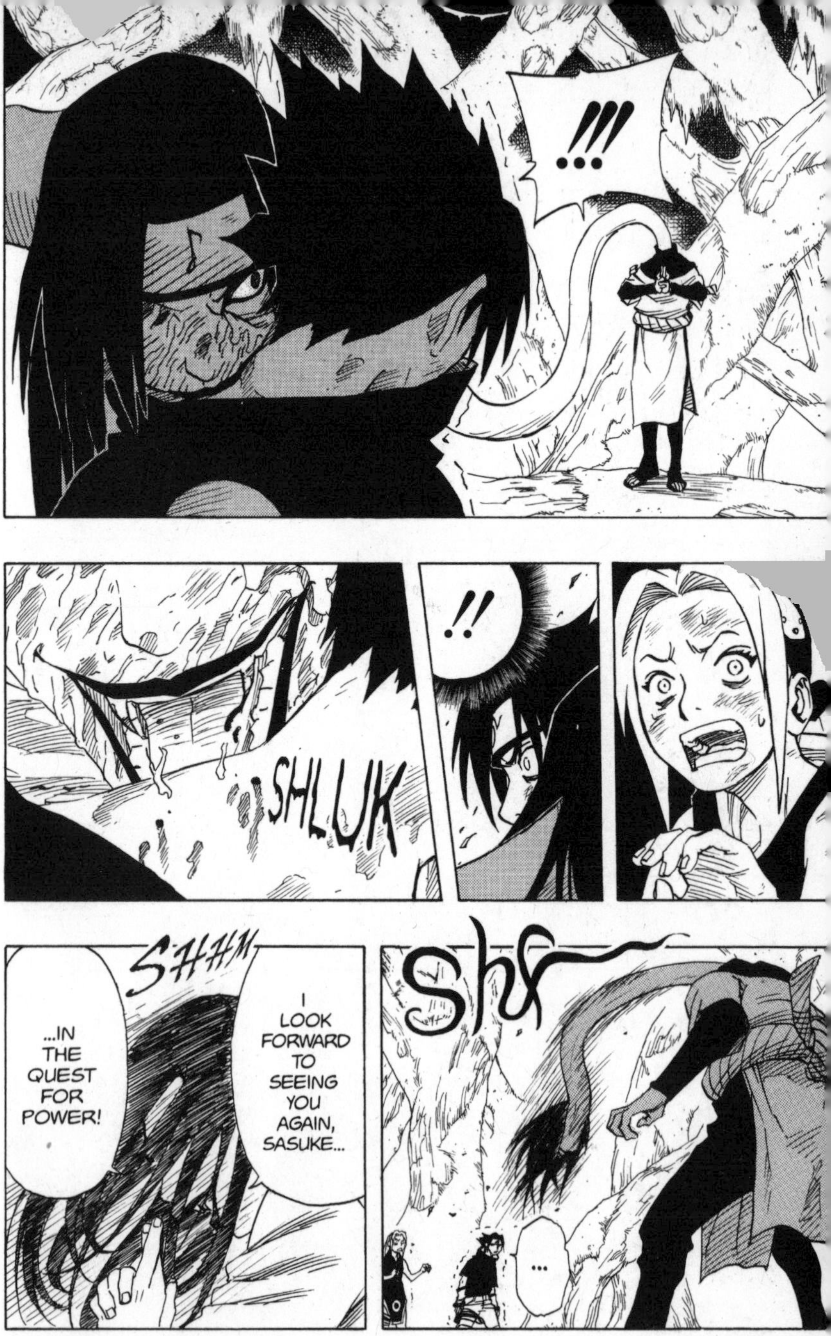

...!!!
!!
SHLUK
Shf
...
SHHM
I LOOK FORWARD TO SEEING YOU AGAIN, SASUKE...
...IN THE QUEST FOR POWER!

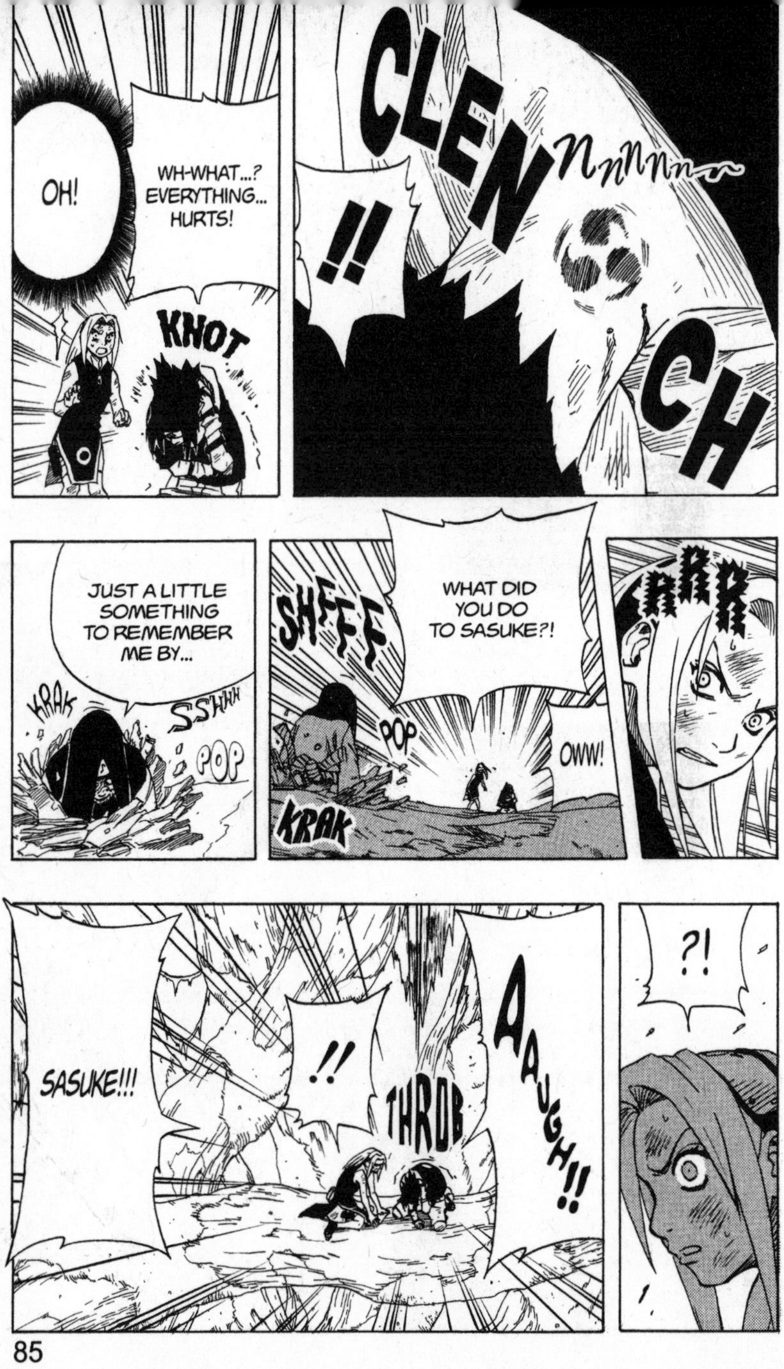

CLENCH
Nnnnnnn
!!
WH-WHAT...? EVERYTHING... HURTS!
OH!
KNOT
RRR
WHAT DID YOU DO TO SASUKE?!
SHFFF
POP
OWW!
KRAK
JUST A LITTLE SOMETHING TO REMEMBER ME BY...
KRAK
SSHHH
POP
?!
AAUGH!!
THROB
!!
SASUKE!!!

Number 50: I've Got to...!!

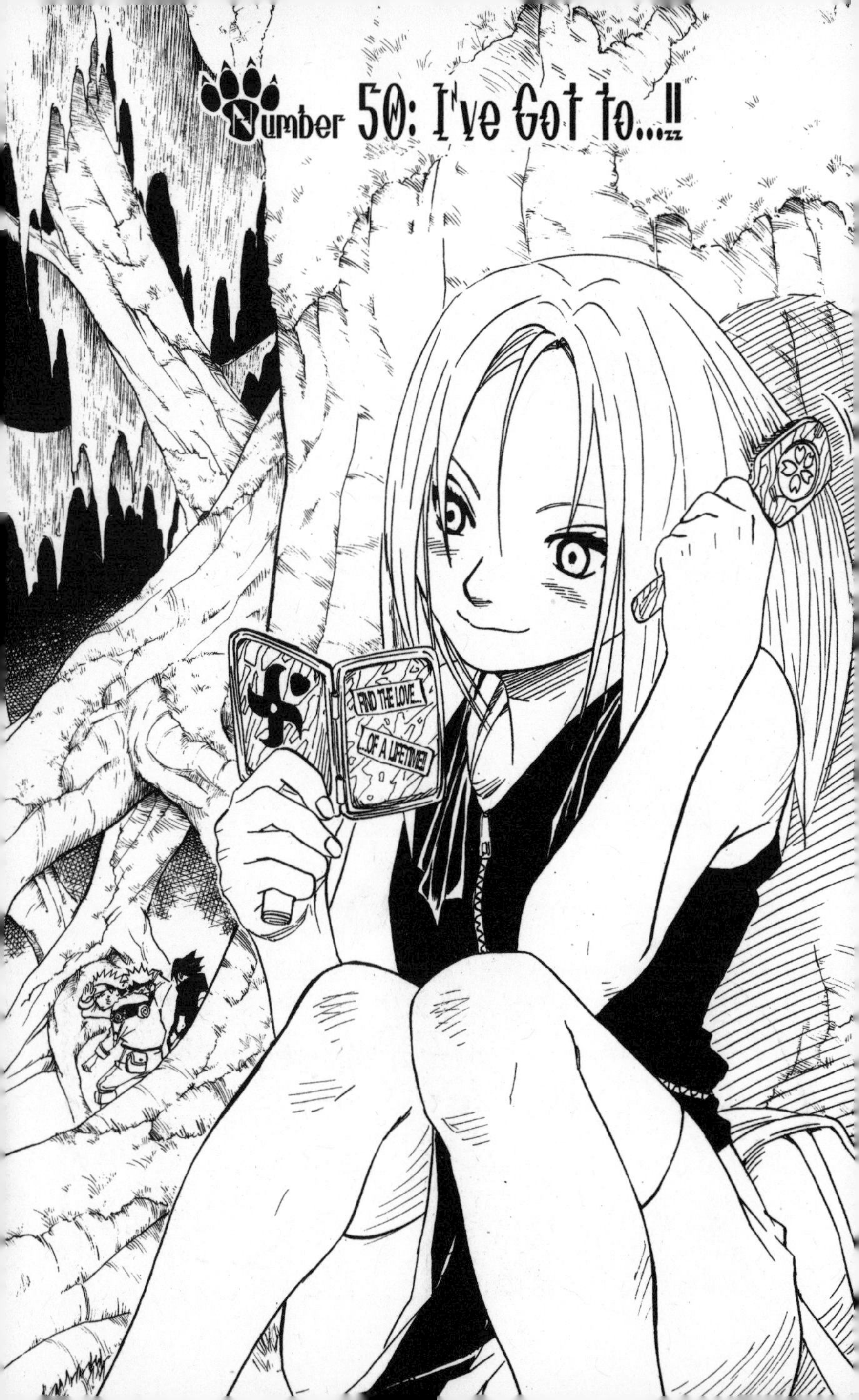
FIND THE LOVE...
...OF A LIFETIME!!

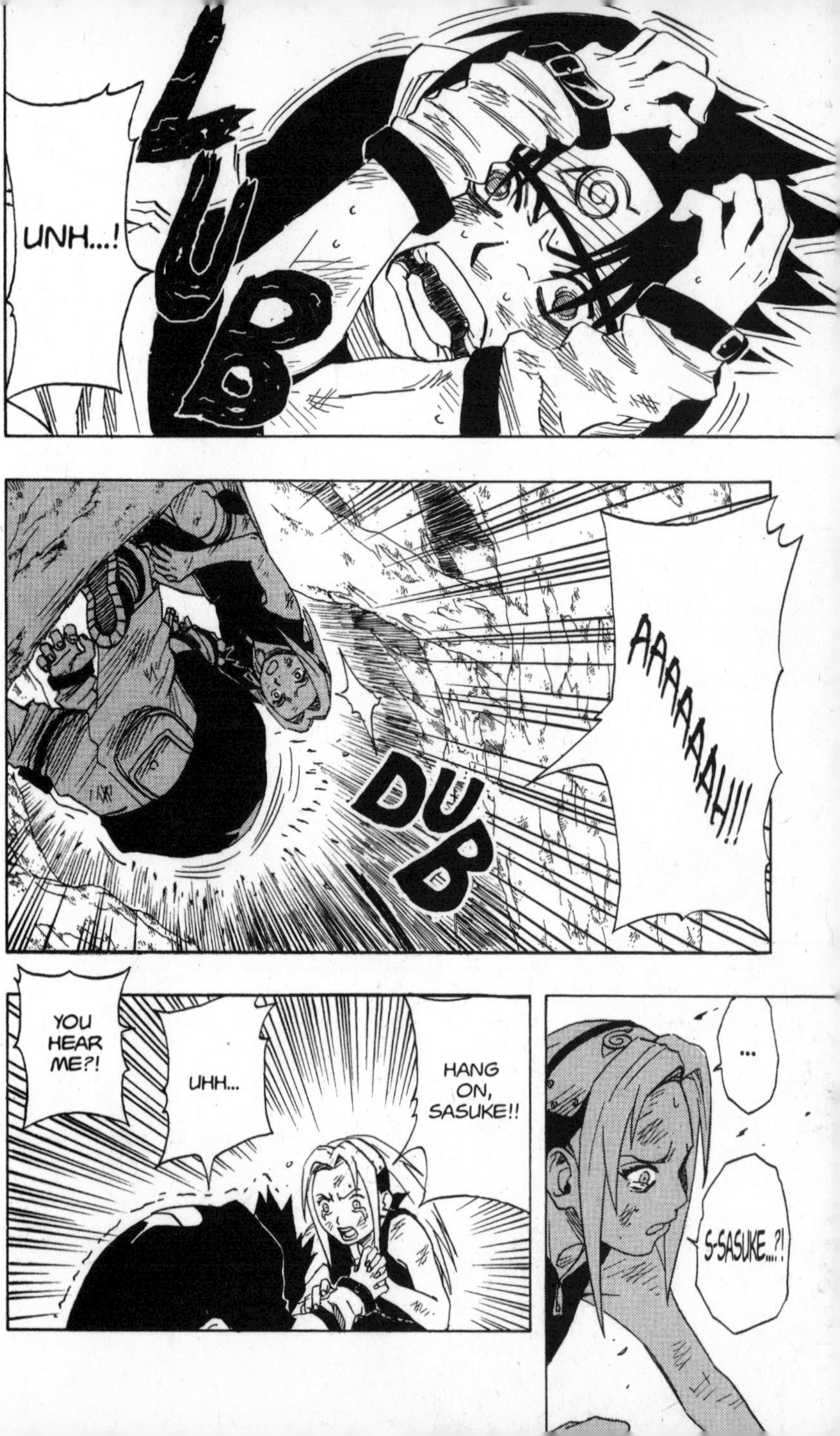
DUB
UNH...!
AAAAAAH!!
DUB
...
S-SASUKE...?!
HANG ON, SASUKE!!
UHH...
YOU HEAR ME?!

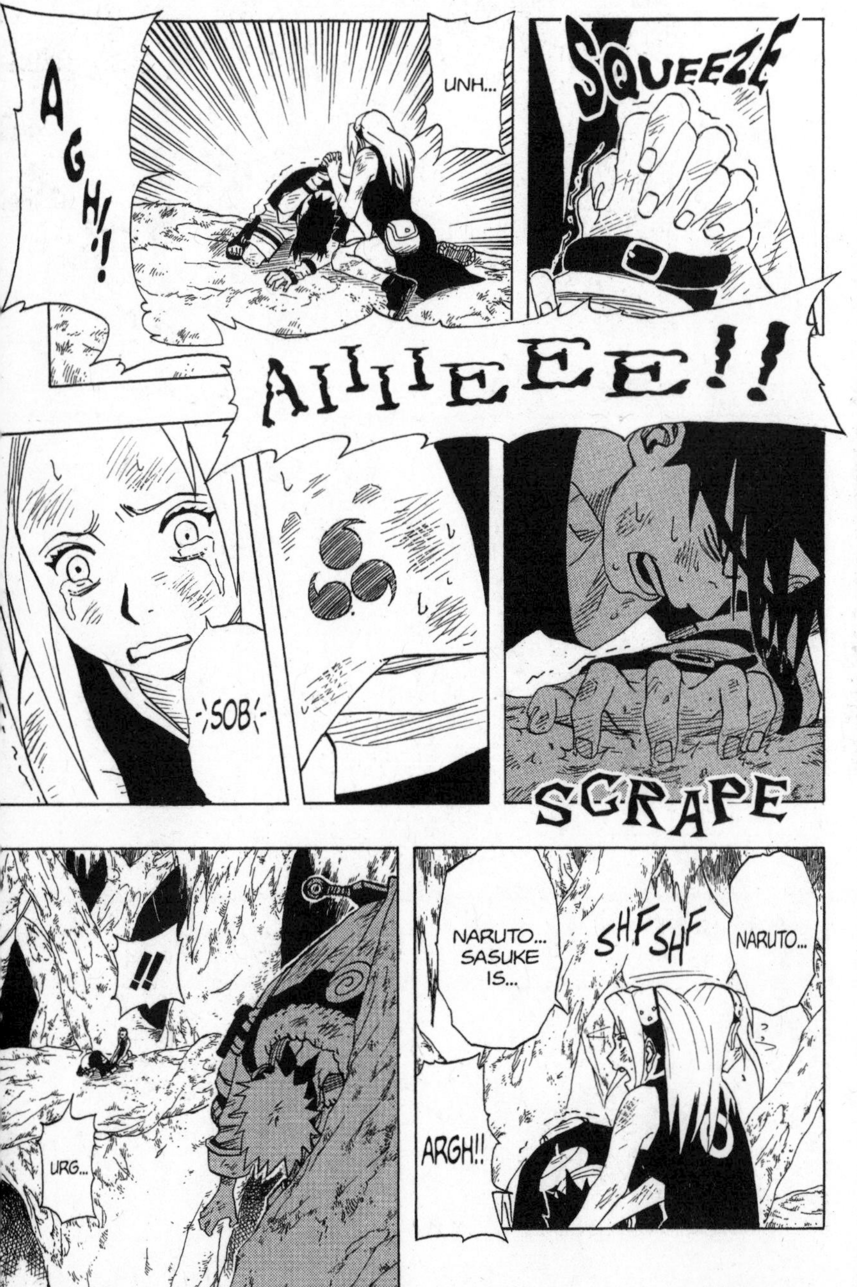
SQUEEZE
UNH...
AGH!!
AIIIEEE!!
SCRAPE
SOB
NARUTO...
SHF SHF
NARUTO... SASUKE IS...
ARGH!!
!!
URG...

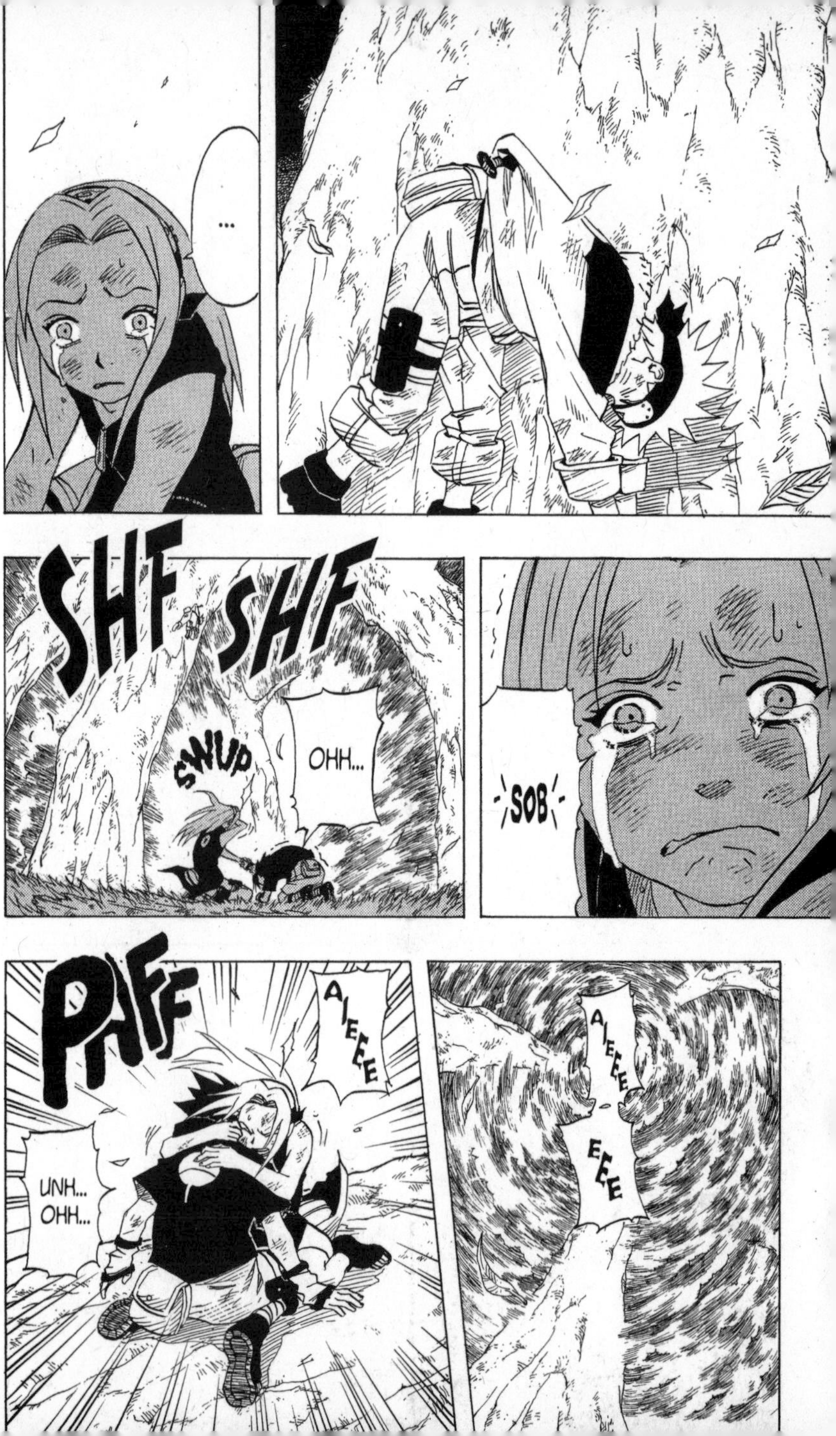
...
SOB
SHF SHF
SWUP
OHH...
AIEEE EEE
PAFF
AIEEE
UNH... OHH...

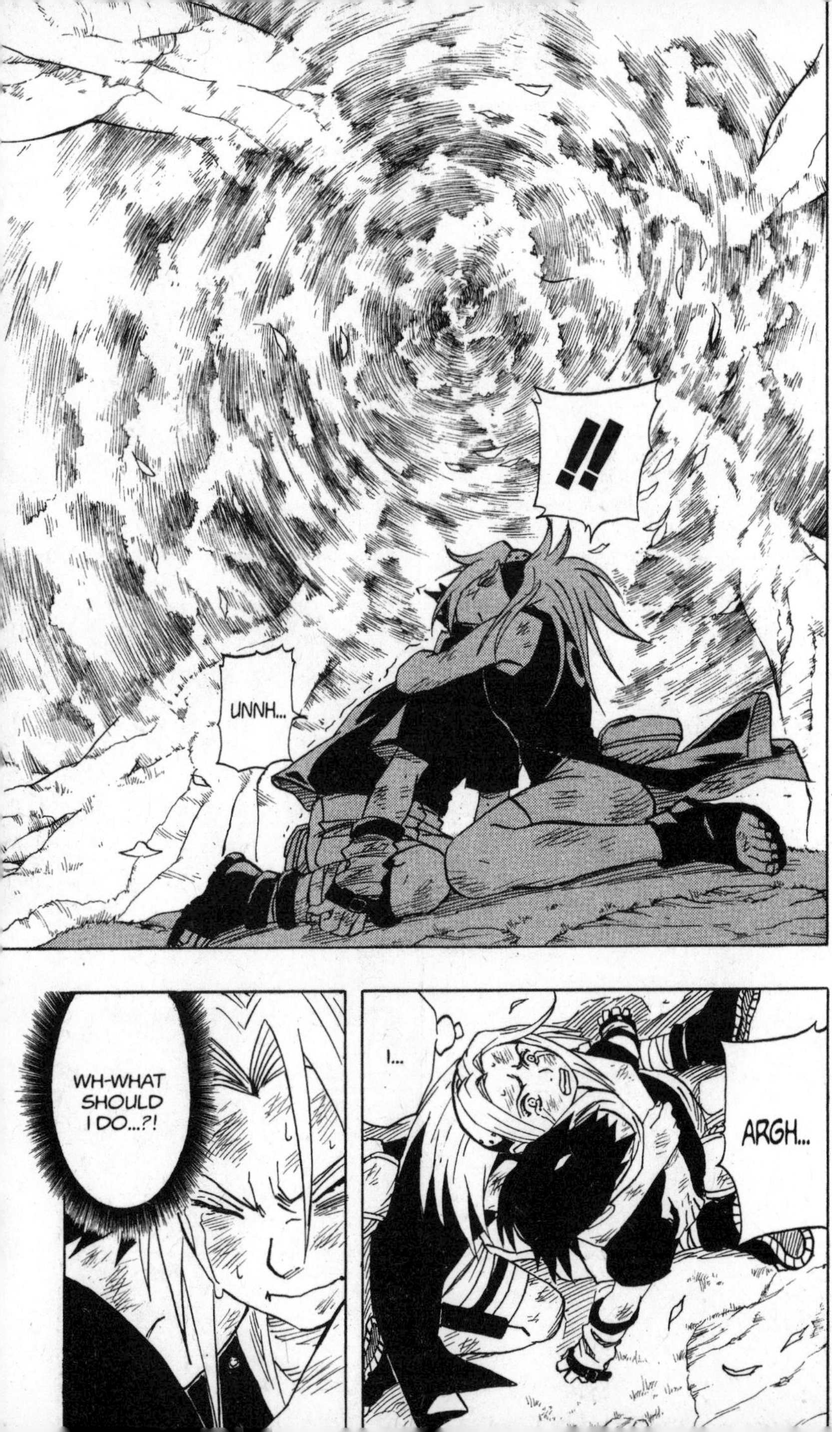
!!
UNNH...
I...
ARGH...
WH-WHAT SHOULD I DO...?!

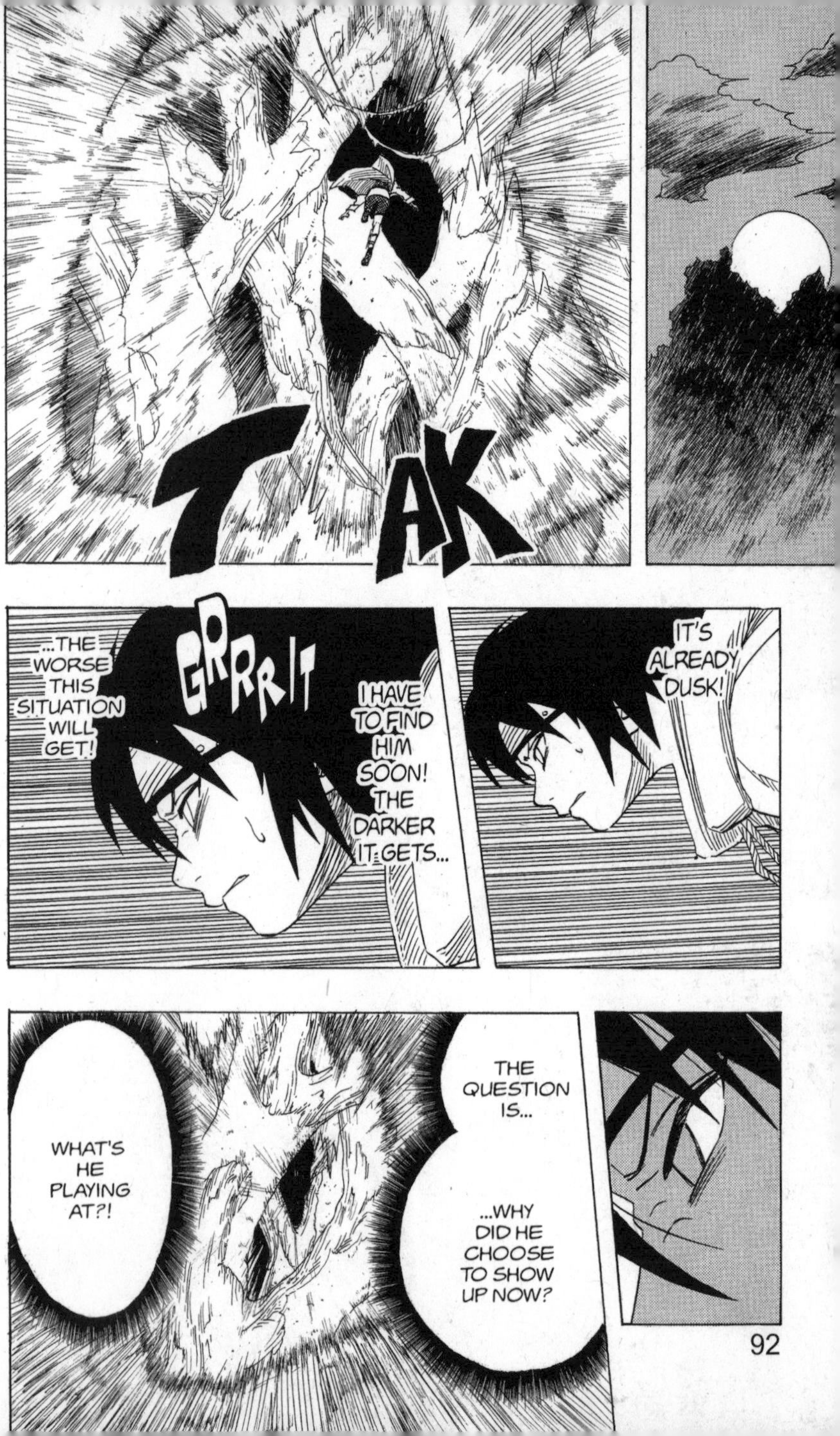
TAK
IT'S ALREADY DUSK!
GRRRIT
I HAVE TO FIND HIM SOON! THE DARKER IT GETS...
...THE WORSE THIS SITUATION WILL GET!
THE QUESTION IS...
...WHY DID HE CHOOSE TO SHOW UP NOW?
WHAT'S HE PLAYING AT?!

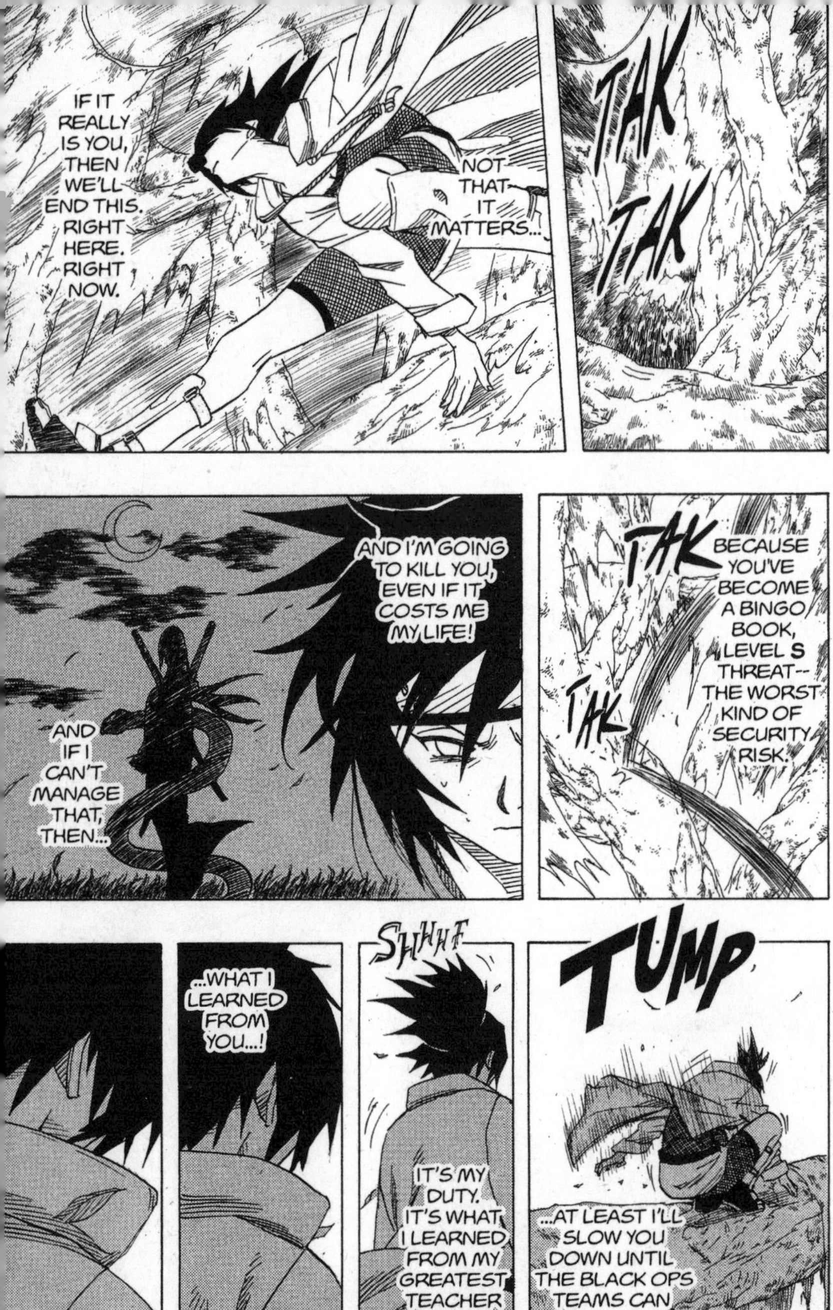
TAK
TAK
NOT THAT IT MATTERS...
IF IT REALLY IS YOU, THEN WE'LL END THIS. RIGHT HERE. RIGHT NOW.
TAK
BECAUSE YOU'VE BECOME A BINGO BOOK, LEVEL S THREAT-- THE WORST KIND OF SECURITY RISK.
TAK
AND I'M GOING TO KILL YOU, EVEN IF IT COSTS ME MY LIFE!
AND IF I CAN'T MANAGE THAT, THEN...
TUMP
...AT LEAST I'LL SLOW YOU DOWN UNTIL THE BLACK OPS TEAMS CAN GET HERE.
SHHHF
IT'S MY DUTY. IT'S WHAT I LEARNED FROM MY GREATEST TEACHER EVER...
...WHAT I LEARNED FROM YOU...!

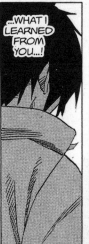

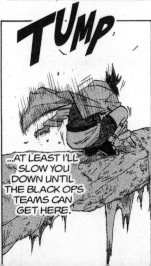

...ISN'T IT, OROCHIMARU?

IMPOSSIBLE...!

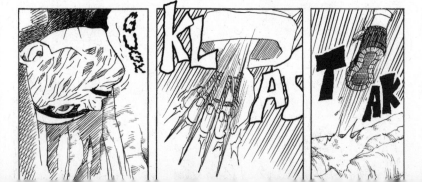

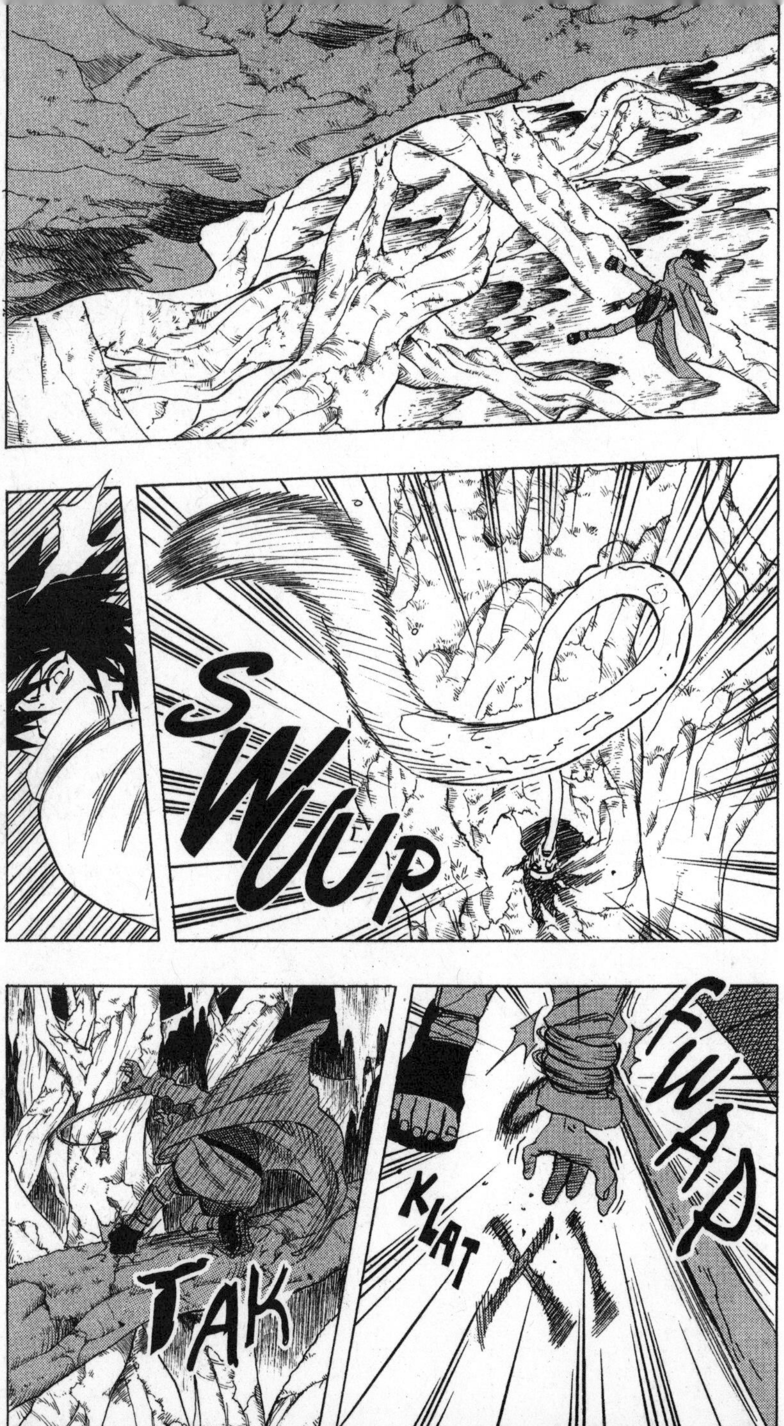
SWUUP
FWAP
KLAT
TAK

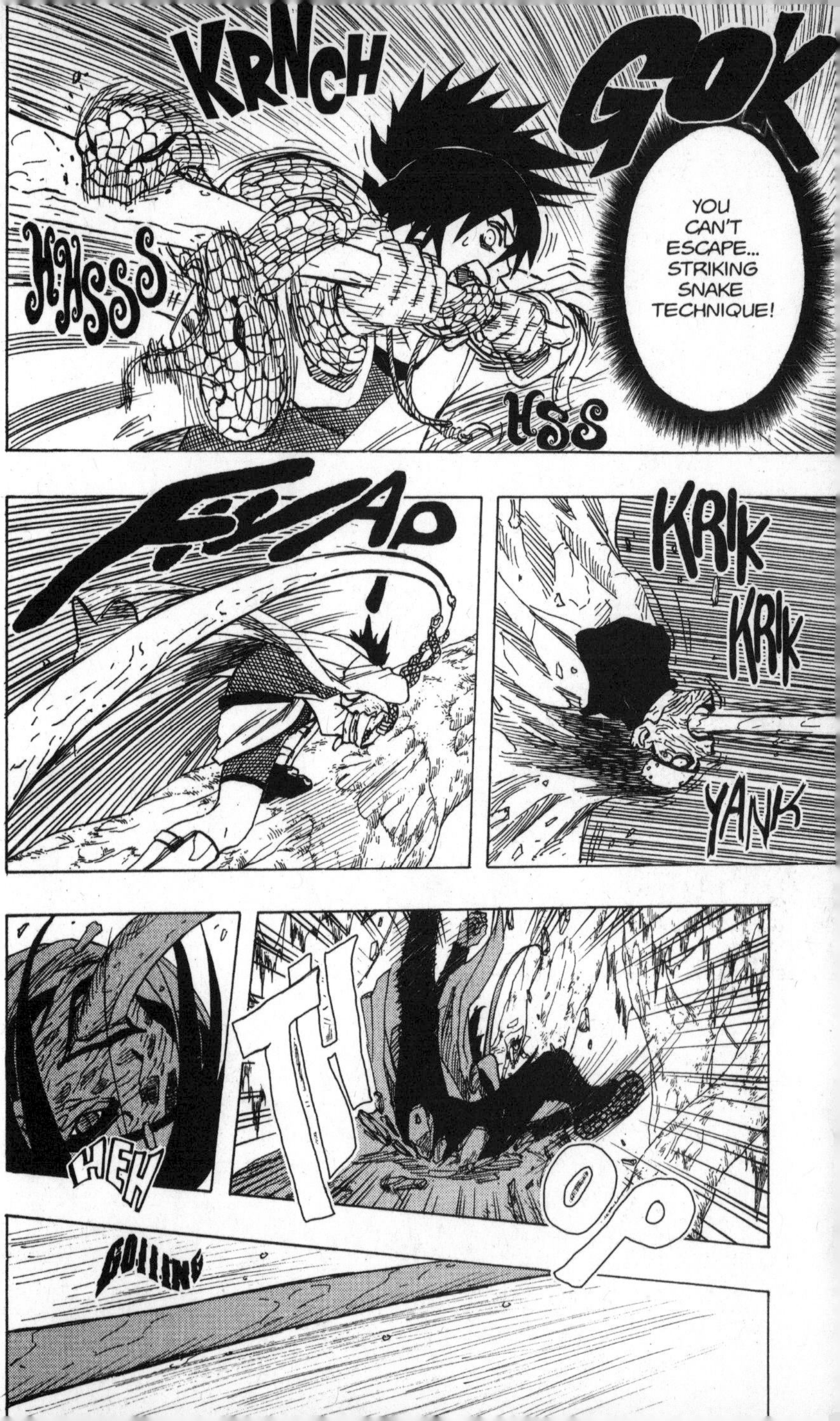
GOK
YOU CAN'T ESCAPE... STRIKING SNAKE TECHNIQUE!
KRNCH
HSS
KRIK
KRIK
YANK
HEH

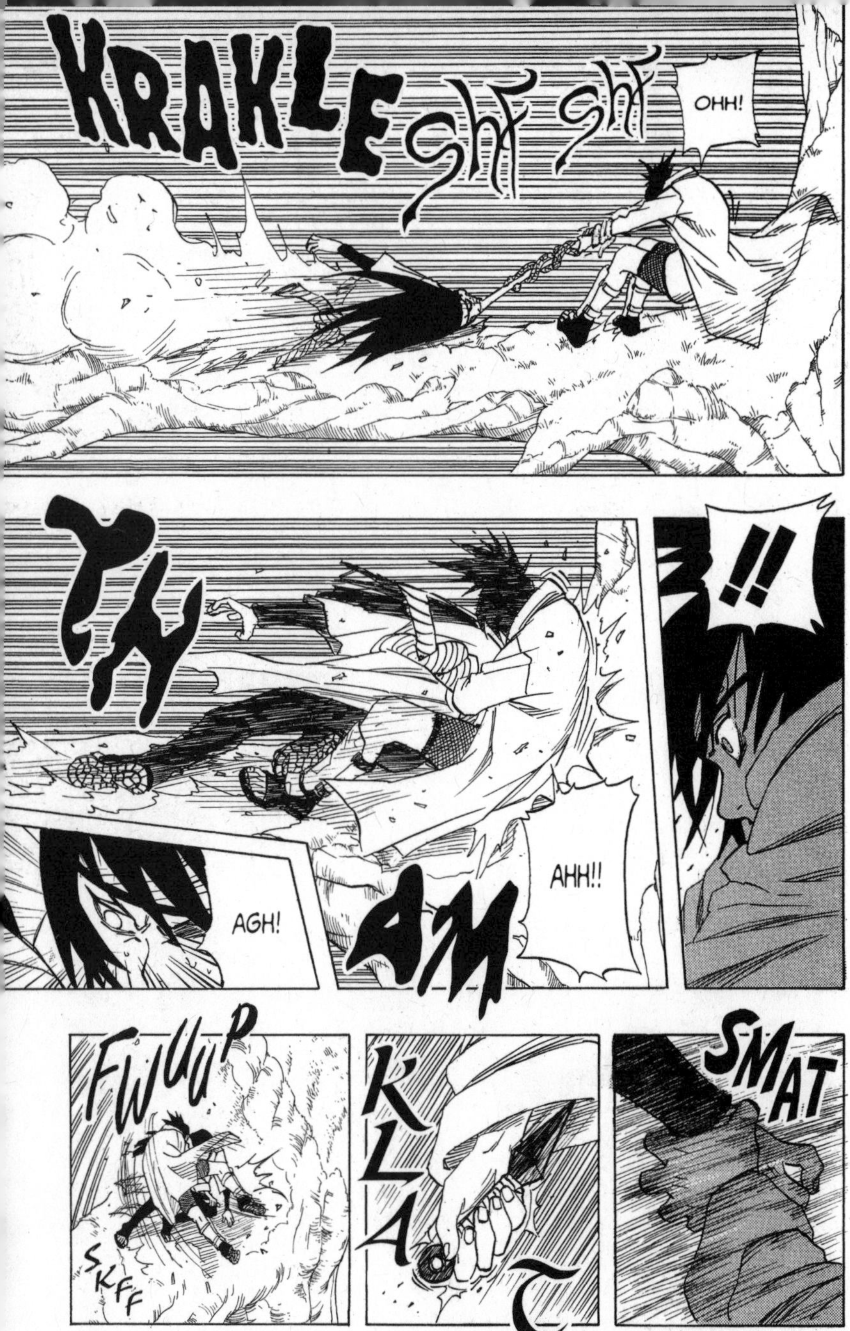
OHH!
SHF SHF
KRAKLE
!!
TCH
AHH!!
AM
AGH!
SMAT
KLAT
FWUUP
SKFF

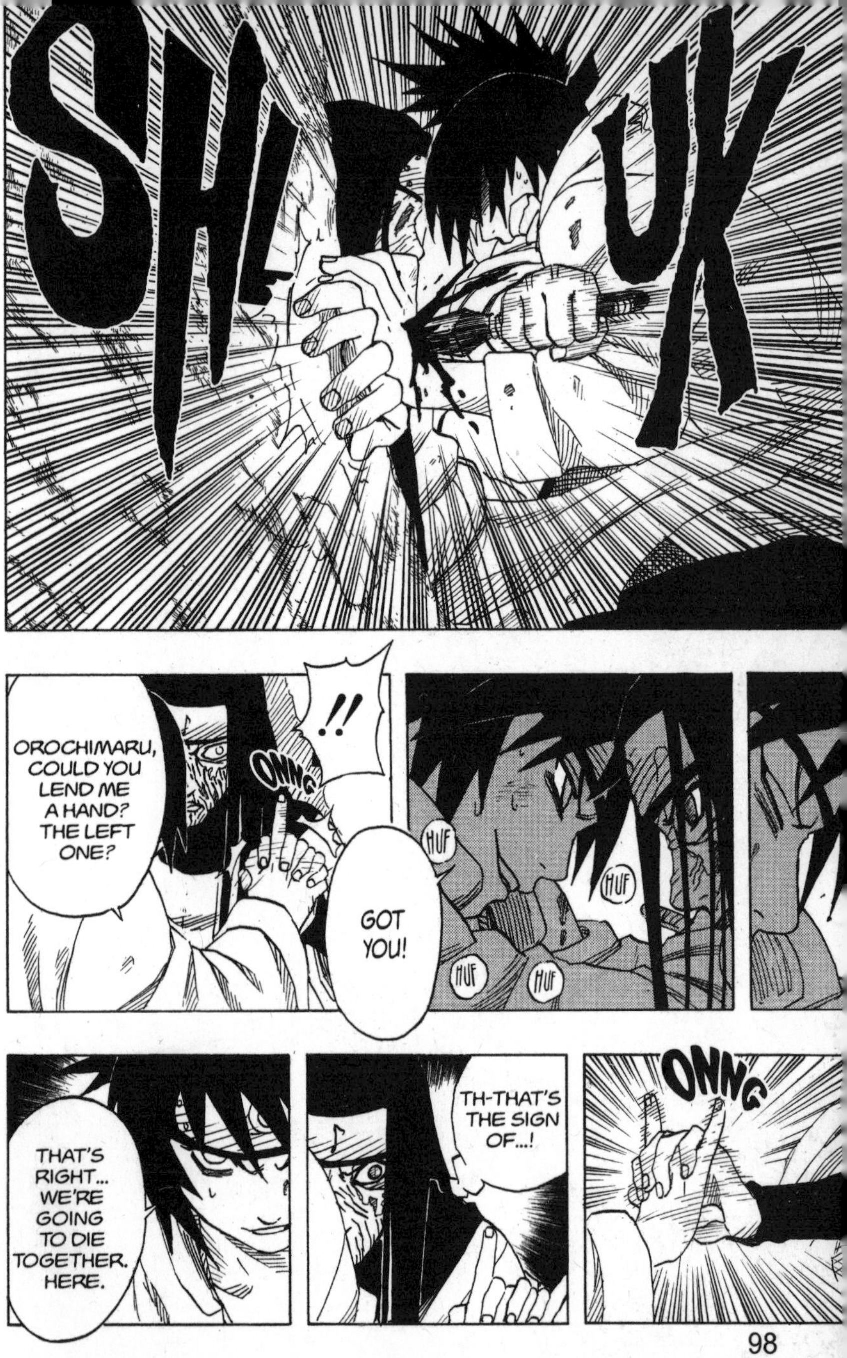
SH
UK
HUF
HUF
HUF
HUF
!!
ONNG
OROCHIMARU, COULD YOU LEND ME A HAND? THE LEFT ONE?
GOT YOU!
ONNG
TH-THAT'S THE SIGN OF...!
THAT'S RIGHT... WE'RE GOING TO DIE TOGETHER. HERE.

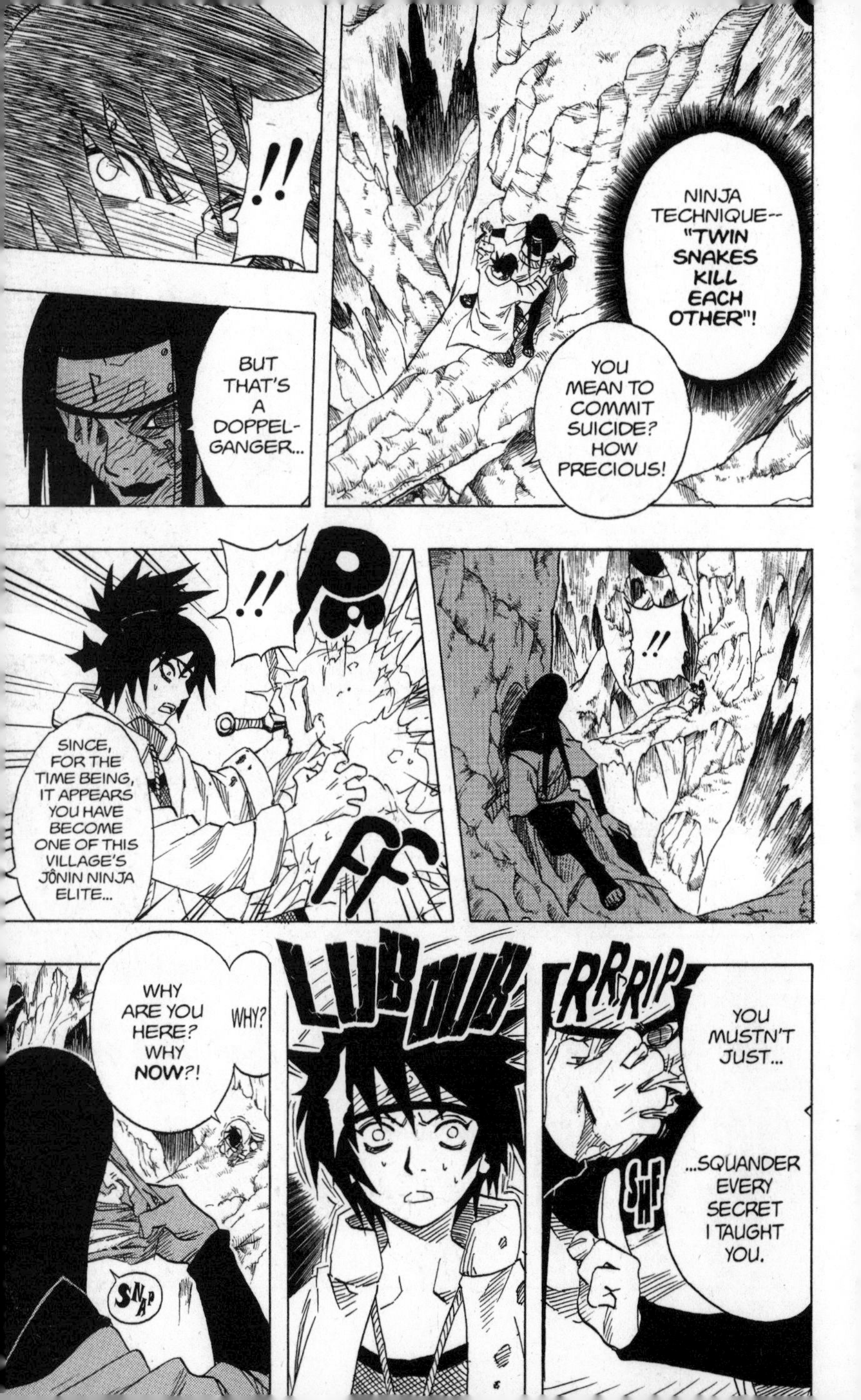
NINJA TECHNIQUE-- "TWIN SNAKES KILL EACH OTHER"!
YOU MEAN TO COMMIT SUICIDE? HOW PRECIOUS!
!!
BUT THAT'S A DOPPEL-GANGER...
!!
!!
POFF
SINCE, FOR THE TIME BEING, IT APPEARS YOU HAVE BECOME ONE OF THIS VILLAGE'S JÔNIN NINJA ELITE...
RRRIP
YOU MUSTN'T JUST...
SHF
...SQUANDER EVERY SECRET I TAUGHT YOU.
LUB DUB
WHY?
WHY ARE YOU HERE? WHY NOW?!
SNAP

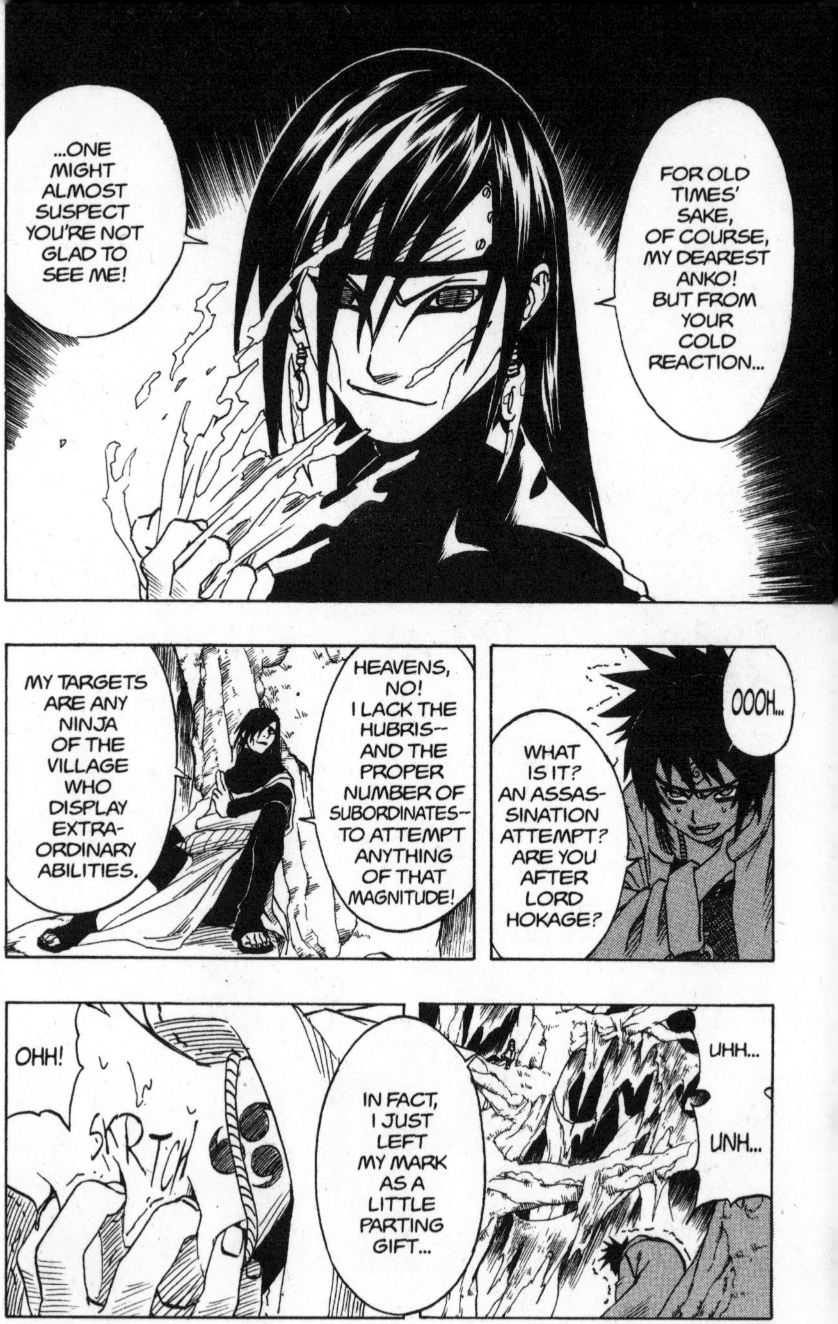
FOR OLD TIMES' SAKE, OF COURSE, MY DEAREST ANKO! BUT FROM YOUR COLD REACTION...
...ONE MIGHT ALMOST SUSPECT YOU'RE NOT GLAD TO SEE ME!
OOOH...
WHAT IS IT? AN ASSAS-SINATION ATTEMPT? ARE YOU AFTER LORD HOKAGE?
HEAVENS, NO! I LACK THE HUBRIS-- AND THE PROPER NUMBER OF SUBORDINATES-- TO ATTEMPT ANYTHING OF THAT MAGNITUDE!
MY TARGETS ARE ANY NINJA OF THE VILLAGE WHO DISPLAY EXTRA-ORDINARY ABILITIES.
UHH...
UNH...
IN FACT, I JUST LEFT MY MARK AS A LITTLE PARTING GIFT...
OHH!
SKRTCH

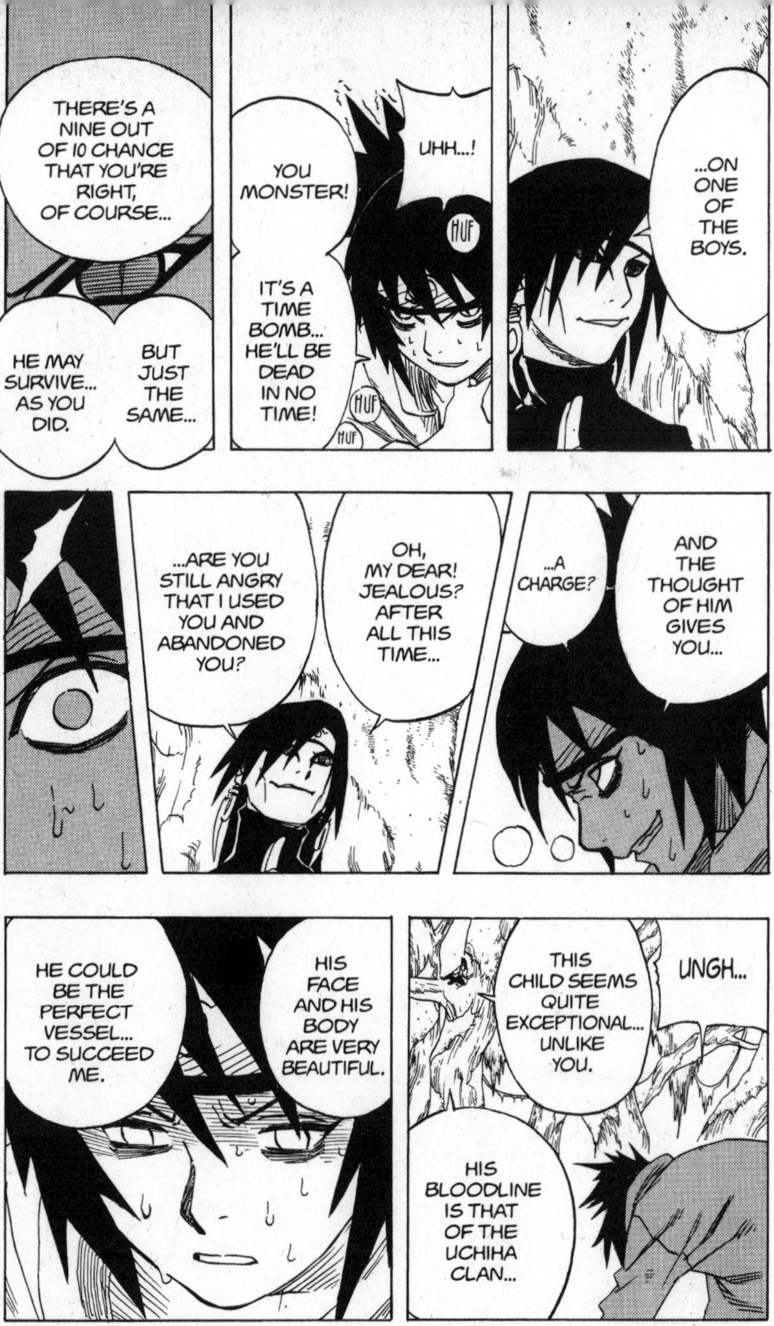
...ON ONE OF THE BOYS.
UHH...!
YOU MONSTER!
HUF
IT'S A TIME BOMB... HE'LL BE DEAD IN NO TIME!
HUF
HUF
THERE'S A NINE OUT OF 10 CHANCE THAT YOU'RE RIGHT, OF COURSE...
BUT JUST THE SAME...
HE MAY SURVIVE... AS YOU DID.
AND THE THOUGHT OF HIM GIVES YOU...
...A CHARGE?
OH, MY DEAR! JEALOUS? AFTER ALL THIS TIME...
...ARE YOU STILL ANGRY THAT I USED YOU AND ABANDONED YOU?
UNGH...
THIS CHILD SEEMS QUITE EXCEPTIONAL... UNLIKE YOU.
HIS BLOODLINE IS THAT OF THE UCHIHA CLAN...
HIS FACE AND HIS BODY ARE VERY BEAUTIFUL.
HE COULD BE THE PERFECT VESSEL... TO SUCCEED ME.

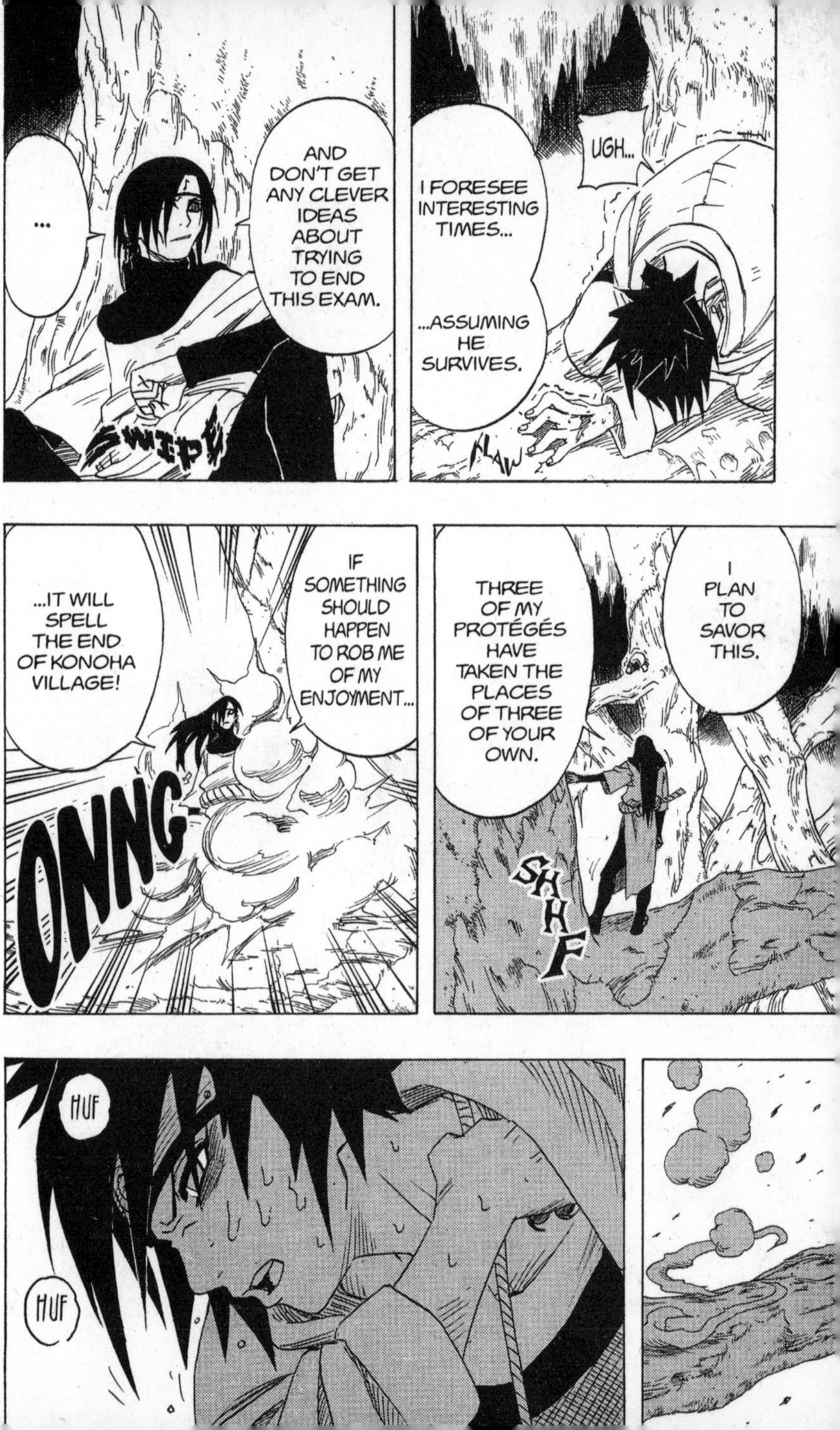
UGH...
I FORESEE INTERESTING TIMES...
...ASSUMING HE SURVIVES.
KLAW
AND DON'T GET ANY CLEVER IDEAS ABOUT TRYING TO END THIS EXAM.
...
SWIPE
I PLAN TO SAVOR THIS.
THREE OF MY PROTÉGÉS HAVE TAKEN THE PLACES OF THREE OF YOUR OWN.
SHHF
IF SOMETHING SHOULD HAPPEN TO ROB ME OF MY ENJOYMENT...
...IT WILL SPELL THE END OF KONOHA VILLAGE!
ONNG
HUF
HUF

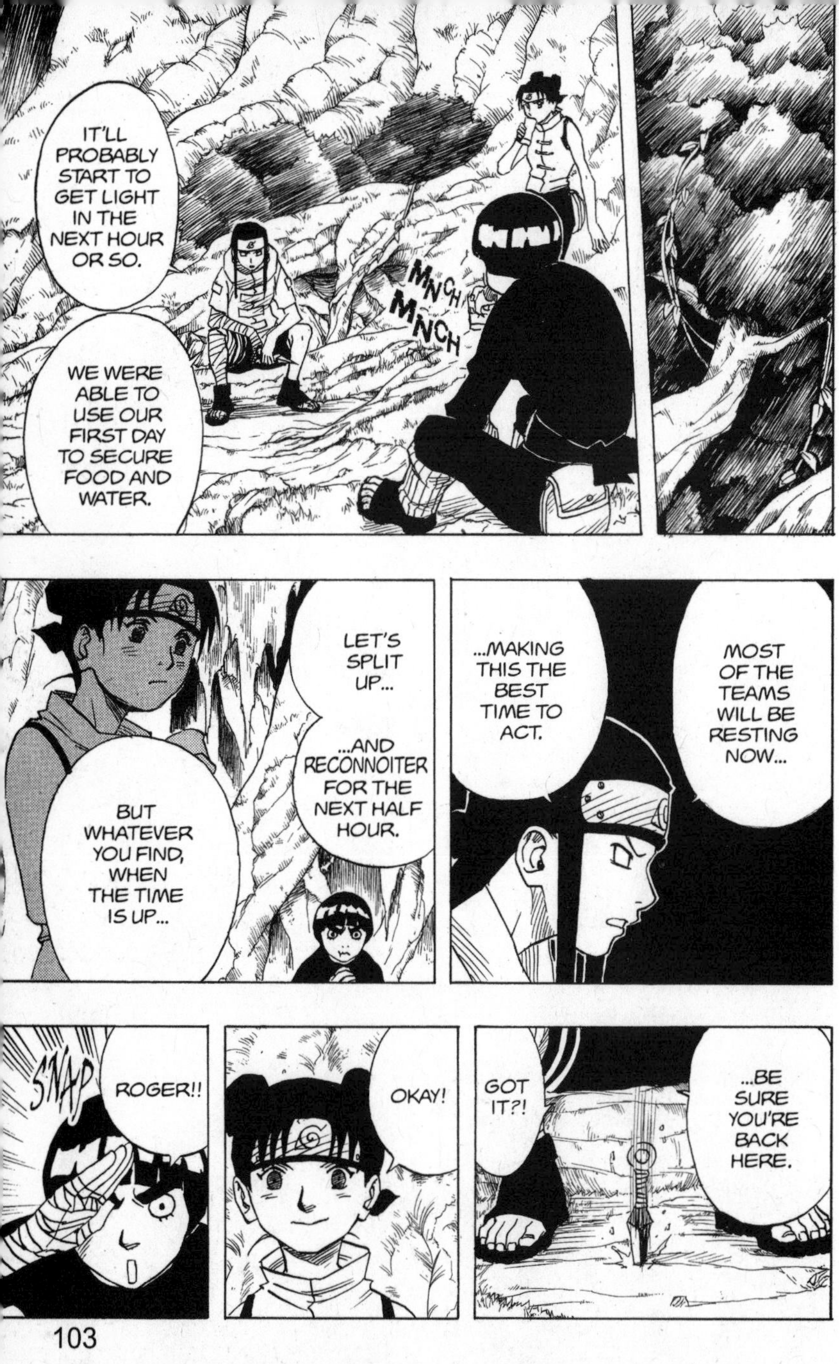
IT'LL PROBABLY START TO GET LIGHT IN THE NEXT HOUR OR SO.
WE WERE ABLE TO USE OUR FIRST DAY TO SECURE FOOD AND WATER.
MNCH MNCH
MOST OF THE TEAMS WILL BE RESTING NOW...
...MAKING THIS THE BEST TIME TO ACT.
LET'S SPLIT UP...
...AND RECONNOITER FOR THE NEXT HALF HOUR.
BUT WHATEVER YOU FIND, WHEN THE TIME IS UP...
...BE SURE YOU'RE BACK HERE.
GOT IT?!
OKAY!
ROGER!!
SNAP

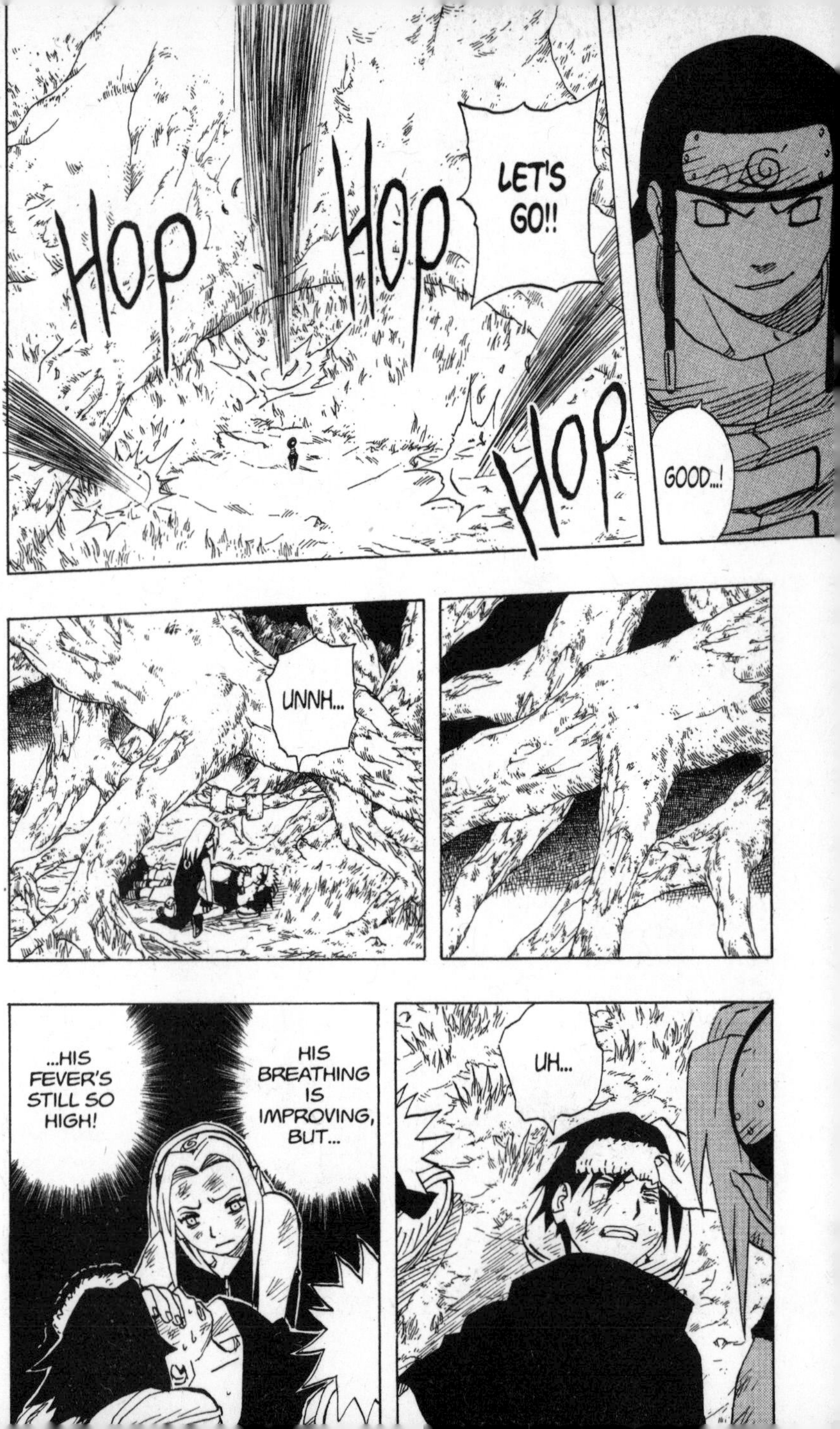
GOOD...!
LET'S GO!!
HOP
HOP
HOP
UNNH...
UH...
HIS BREATHING IS IMPROVING, BUT...
...HIS FEVER'S STILL SO HIGH!

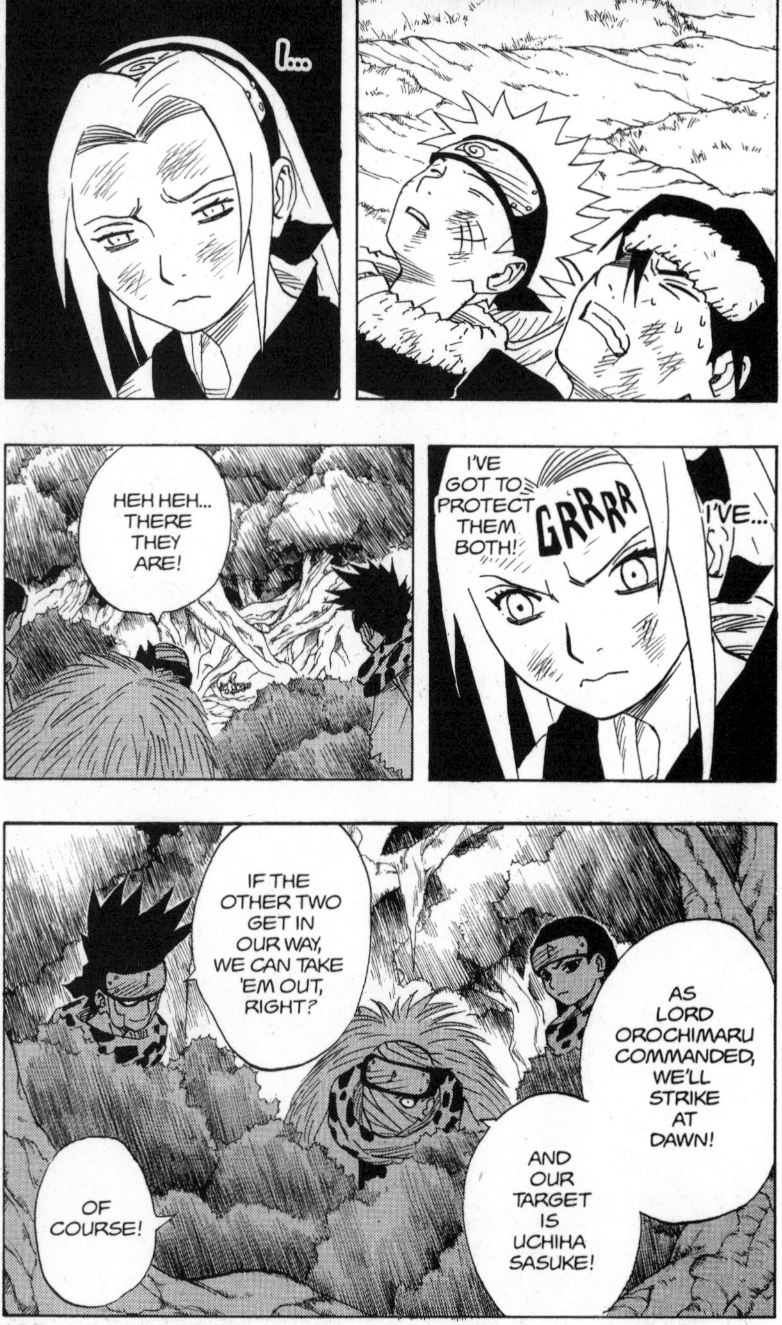
I...
I'VE...
I'VE GOT TO PROTECT THEM BOTH!
GRRRR
HEH HEH... THERE THEY ARE!
AS LORD OROCHIMARU COMMANDED, WE'LL STRIKE AT DAWN!
AND OUR TARGET IS UCHIHA SASUKE!
IF THE OTHER TWO GET IN OUR WAY, WE CAN TAKE 'EM OUT, RIGHT?
OF COURSE!

MEET KISHIMOTO MASASHI'S ASSISTANTS--PART THREE
ASSISTANT NO. 3: IKEMOTO MIKIO

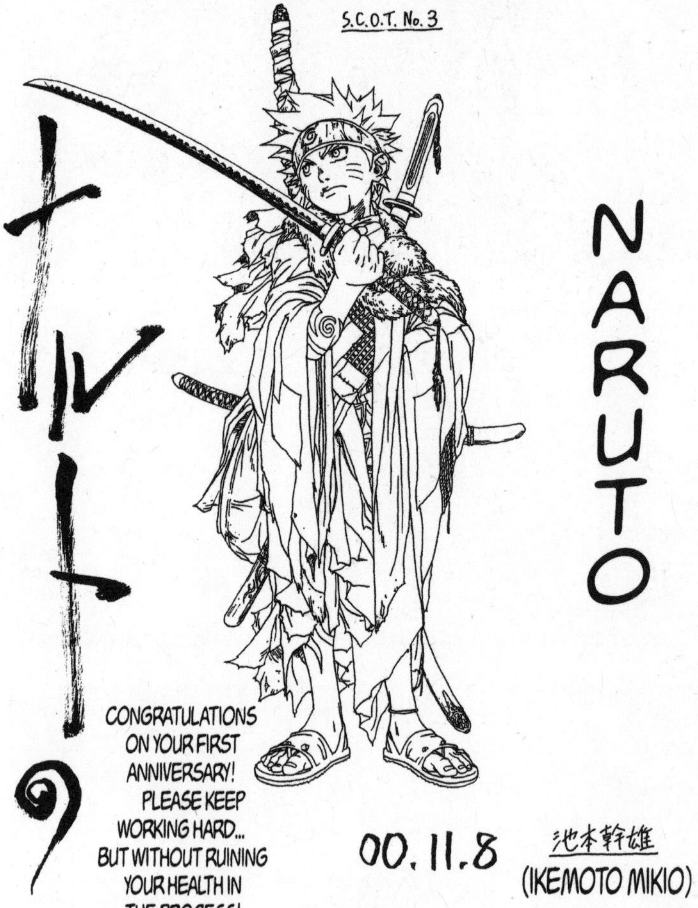
S.C.O.T. No. 3
NARUTO
ナルト
CONGRATULATIONS ON YOUR FIRST ANNIVERSARY! PLEASE KEEP WORKING HARD... BUT WITHOUT RUINING YOUR HEALTH IN THE PROCESS!
00.11.8
池本幹雄
(IKEMOTO MIKIO)

PROFILE

- LIKES SNACK STICKS AND COOKIES, AND EATS NATTÔ BEAN PASTE EVERY DAY.
- ADORES COFFEE. AT THE OFFICE, HE'S THE ONE WHO POURS.
- MASTER TINKERER.
- SHARP DRESSER.
- TALLEST ONE IN THE OFFICE.
- YOUNGEST ONE IN THE OFFICE.

} WE'RE SICK WITH ENVY!

WORKS AS A "MOB," DRAWING CROWDS AND BACKGROUND FIGURES, ADDING THE WHITE TO SPEED LINES, HIGHLIGHTS, AND CHARACTERS' EYES, AND WHITING OUT ANY ART THAT GOES OUT OF THE PANEL AND INTO THE GUTTER, AS WELL AS PUTTING STARS IN THE NIGHT SKY, AND ADDING IN HALF-TONES.

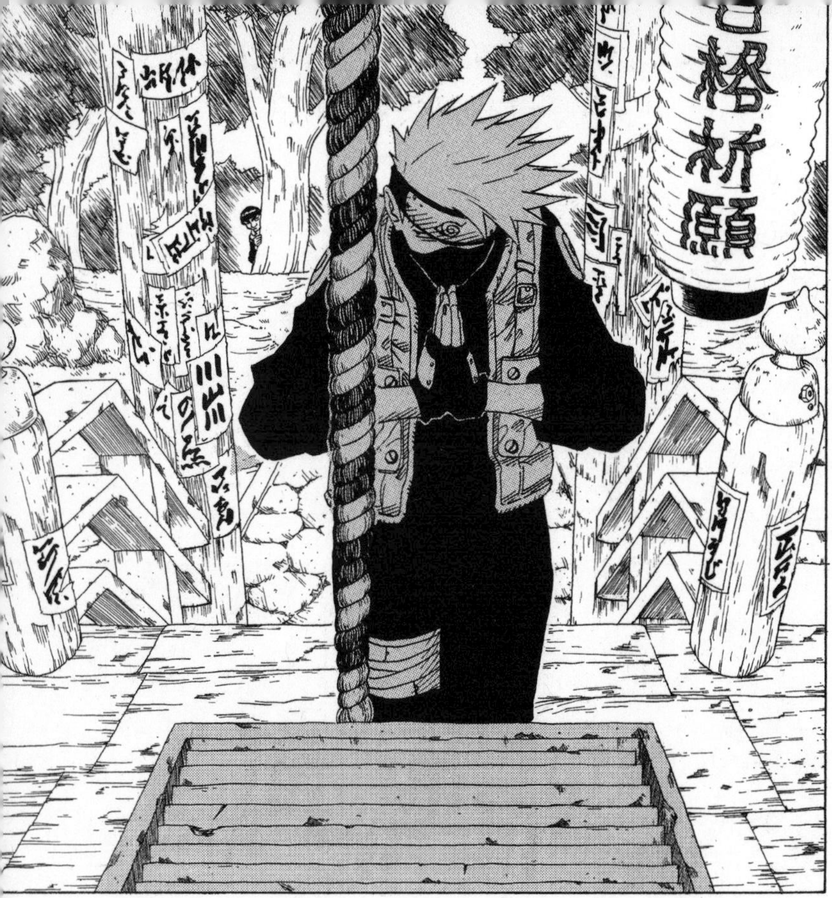
格祈願

Number 51: Beauty Is the Beast!!

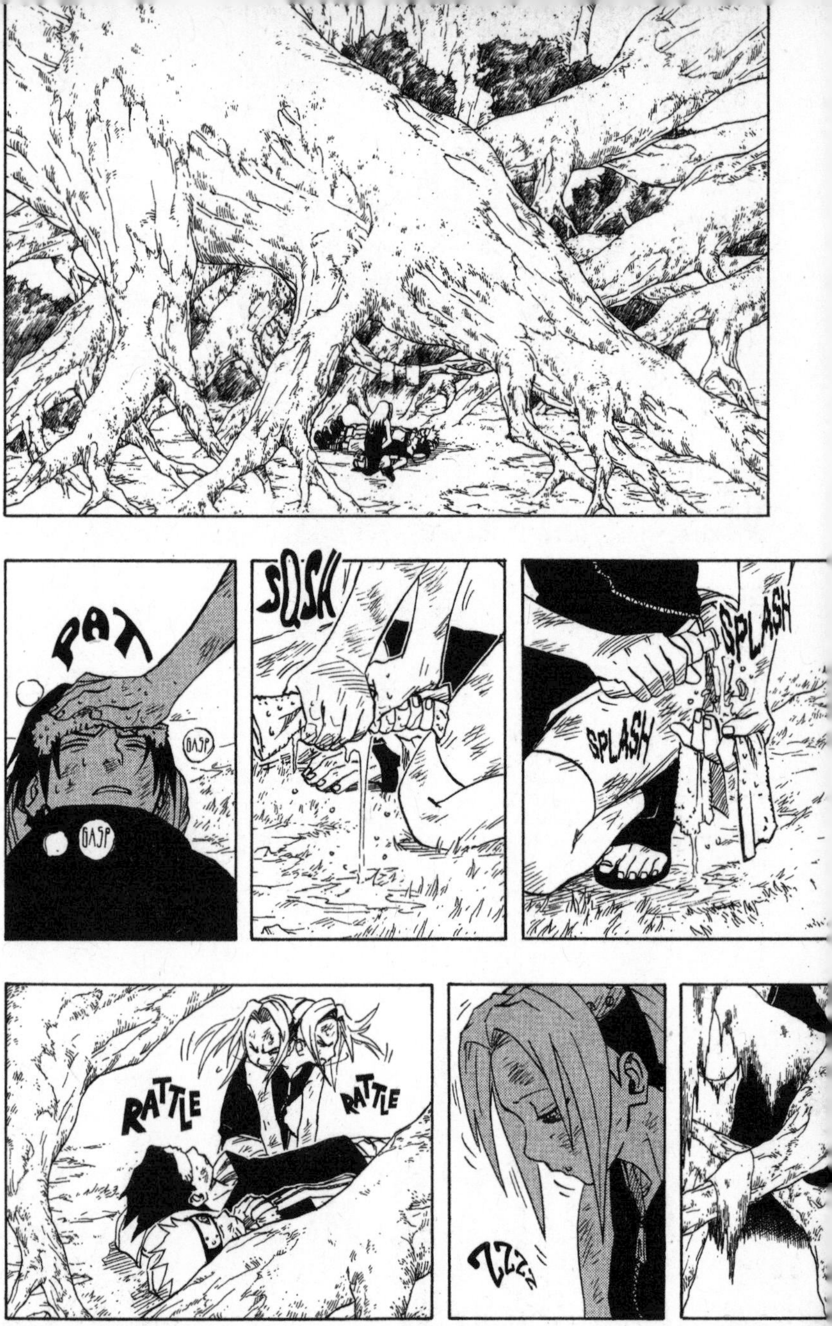
SPLASH
SPLASH
SQSK
PAT
GASP
GASP
ZZZZ
RATTLE
RATTLE

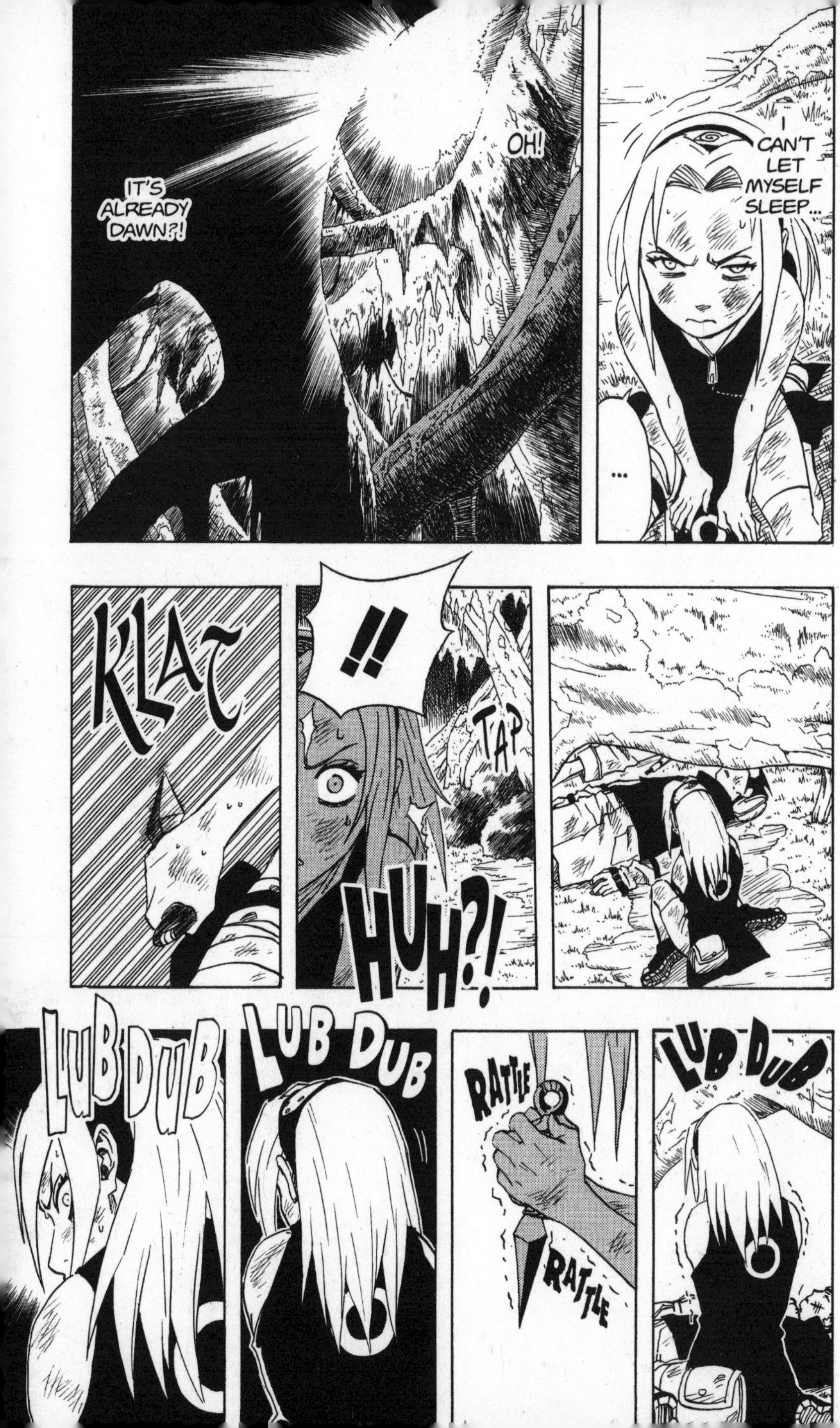
I CAN'T LET MYSELF SLEEP...
...
OH!
IT'S ALREADY DAWN?!
TAP
!!
HUH?!
KLAT
LUB DUB
RATTLE
RATTLE
LUB DUB
LUB DUB

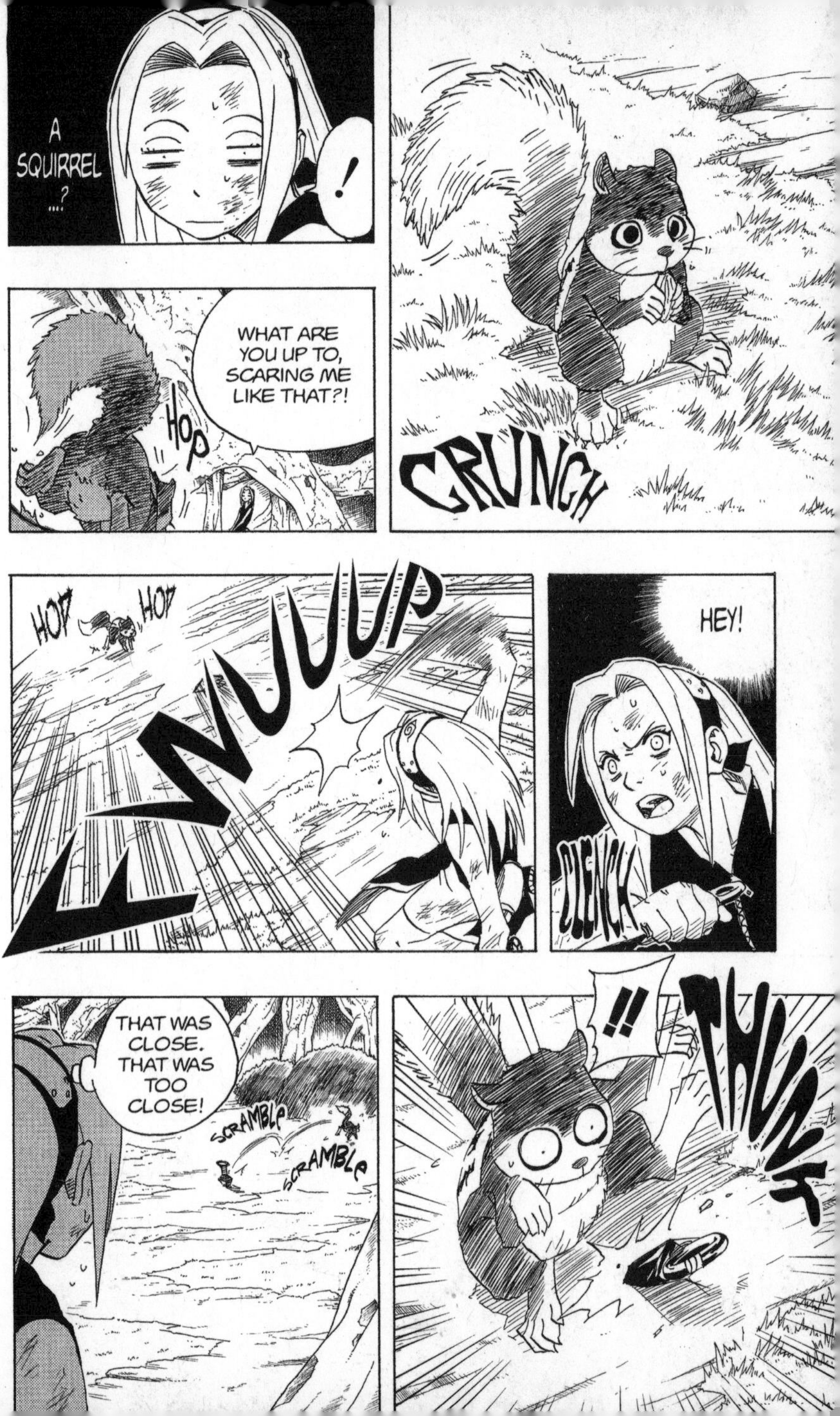
CRUNCH
A SQUIRREL ...?
!
WHAT ARE YOU UP TO, SCARING ME LIKE THAT?!
HOP
HEY!
CLENCH
FWUUUP
HOP HOP
!!
THUNK
THAT WAS CLOSE. THAT WAS TOO CLOSE!
SCRAMBLE
SCRAMBLE

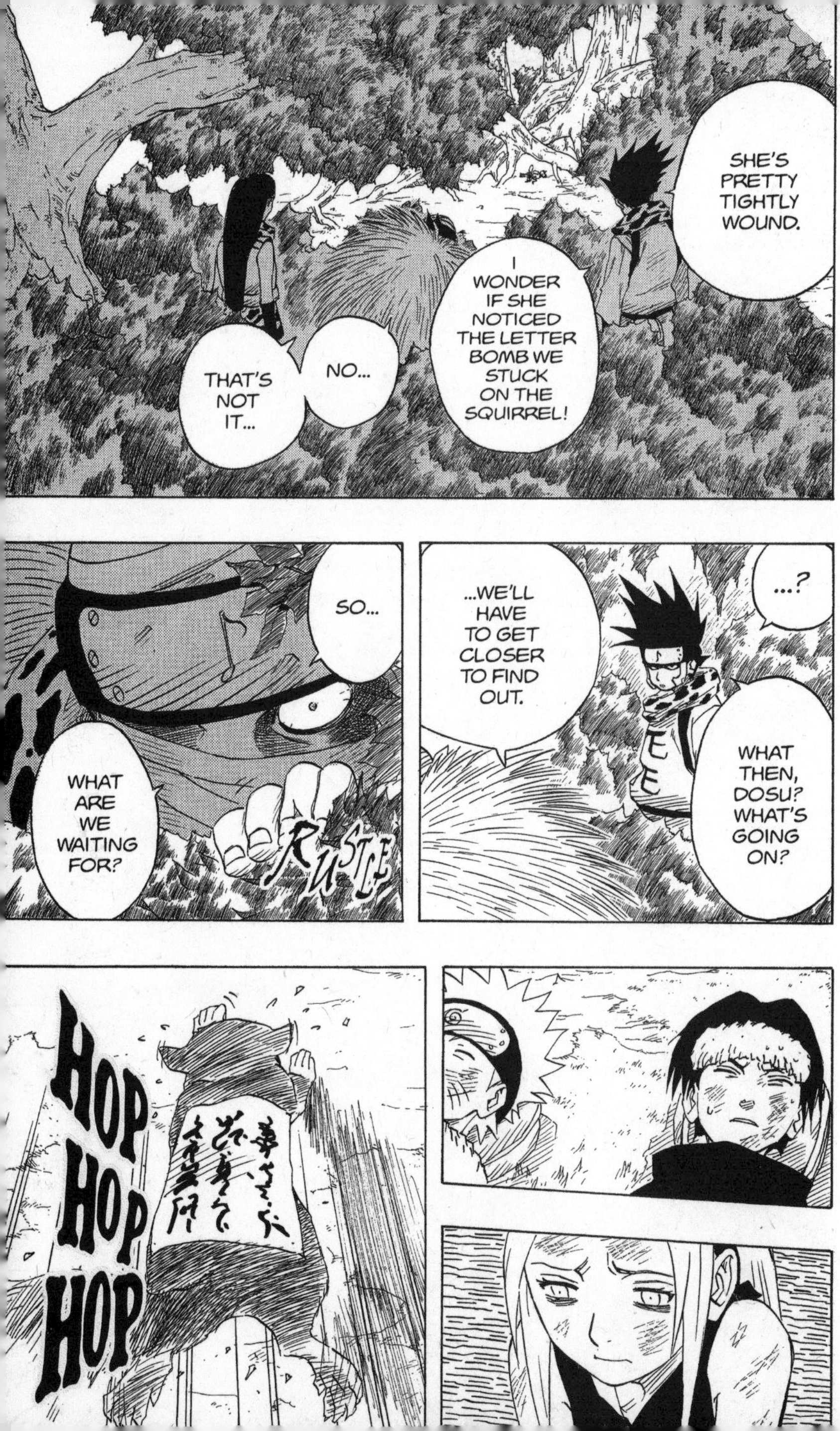
SHE'S PRETTY TIGHTLY WOUND.
I WONDER IF SHE NOTICED THE LETTER BOMB WE STUCK ON THE SQUIRREL!
NO...
THAT'S NOT IT...
...?
WHAT THEN, DOSU? WHAT'S GOING ON?
...WE'LL HAVE TO GET CLOSER TO FIND OUT.
SO...
WHAT ARE WE WAITING FOR?
RUSTLE
HOP HOP HOP

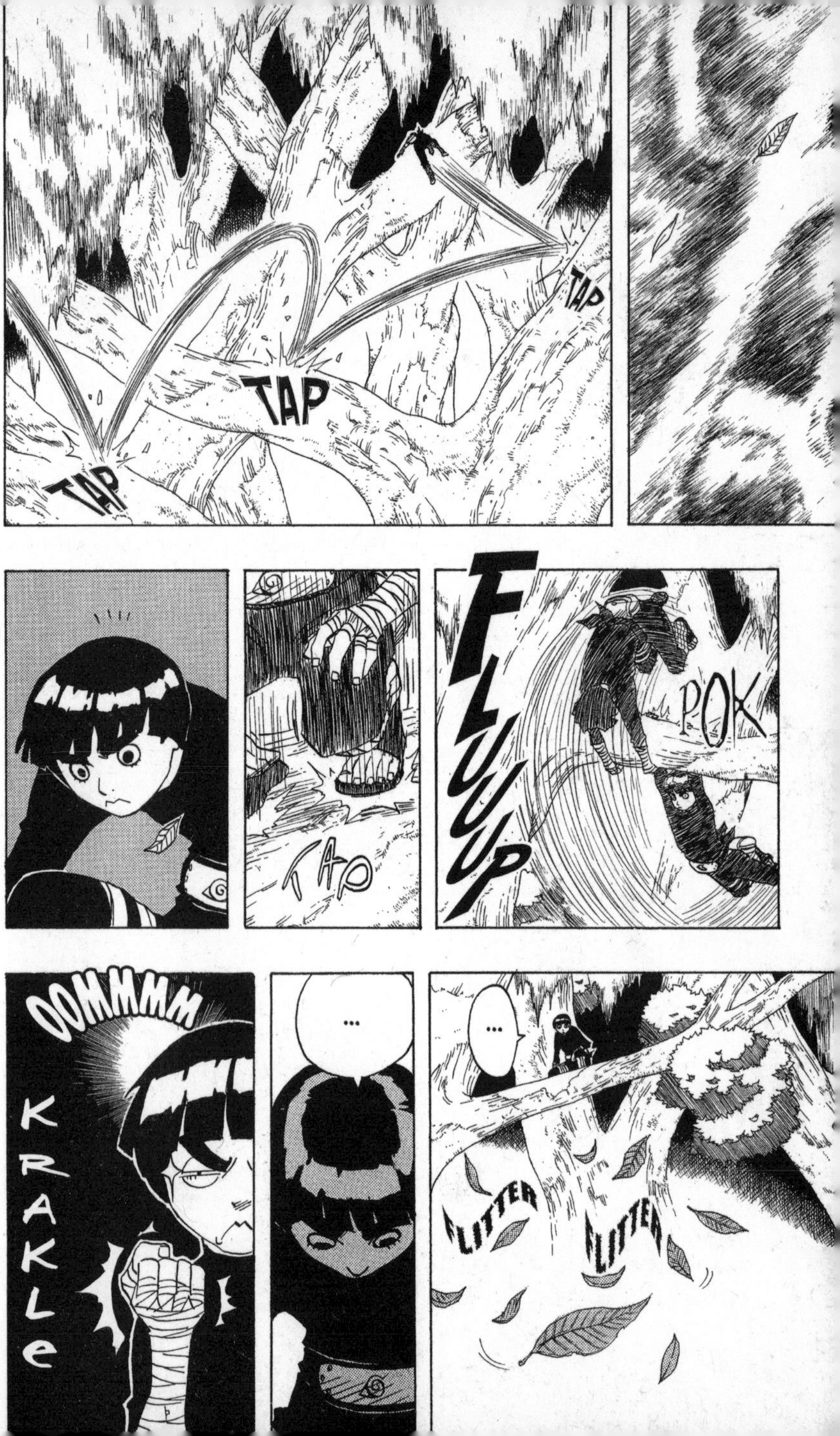
TAP
TAP
TAP
FLUUUP
POK
TAP
...
...
FLITTER
FLITTER
OOMMMM
KRAKLE

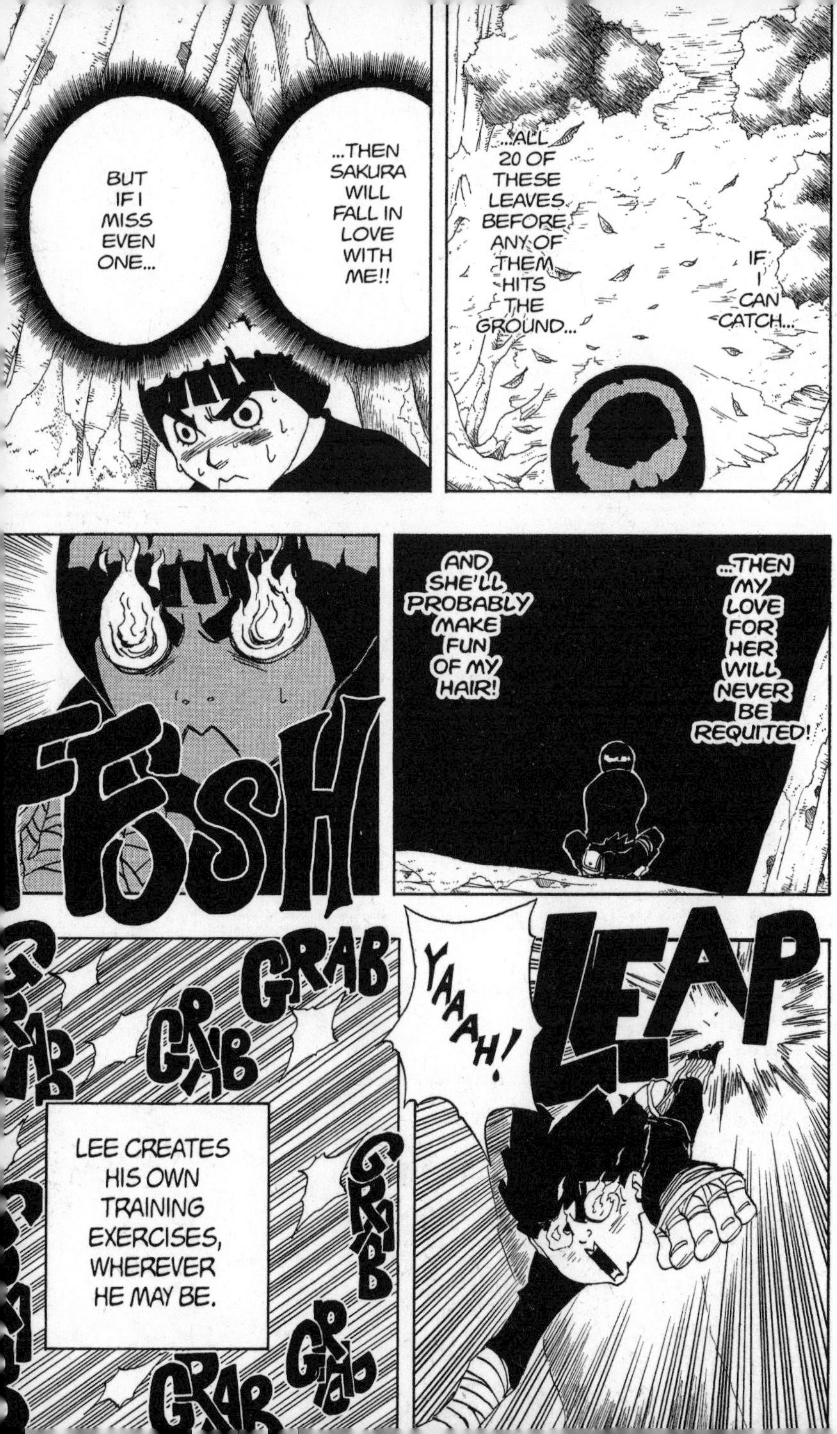
IF I CAN CATCH...
...ALL 20 OF THESE LEAVES BEFORE ANY OF THEM HITS THE GROUND...
...THEN SAKURA WILL FALL IN LOVE WITH ME!!
BUT IF I MISS EVEN ONE...
...THEN MY LOVE FOR HER WILL NEVER BE REQUITED!
AND SHE'LL PROBABLY MAKE FUN OF MY HAIR!
FOSH
LEAP
YAAAH!
GRAB
GRAB
GRAB
LEE CREATES HIS OWN TRAINING EXERCISES, WHEREVER HE MAY BE.
GRAB
GRAB
GRAB

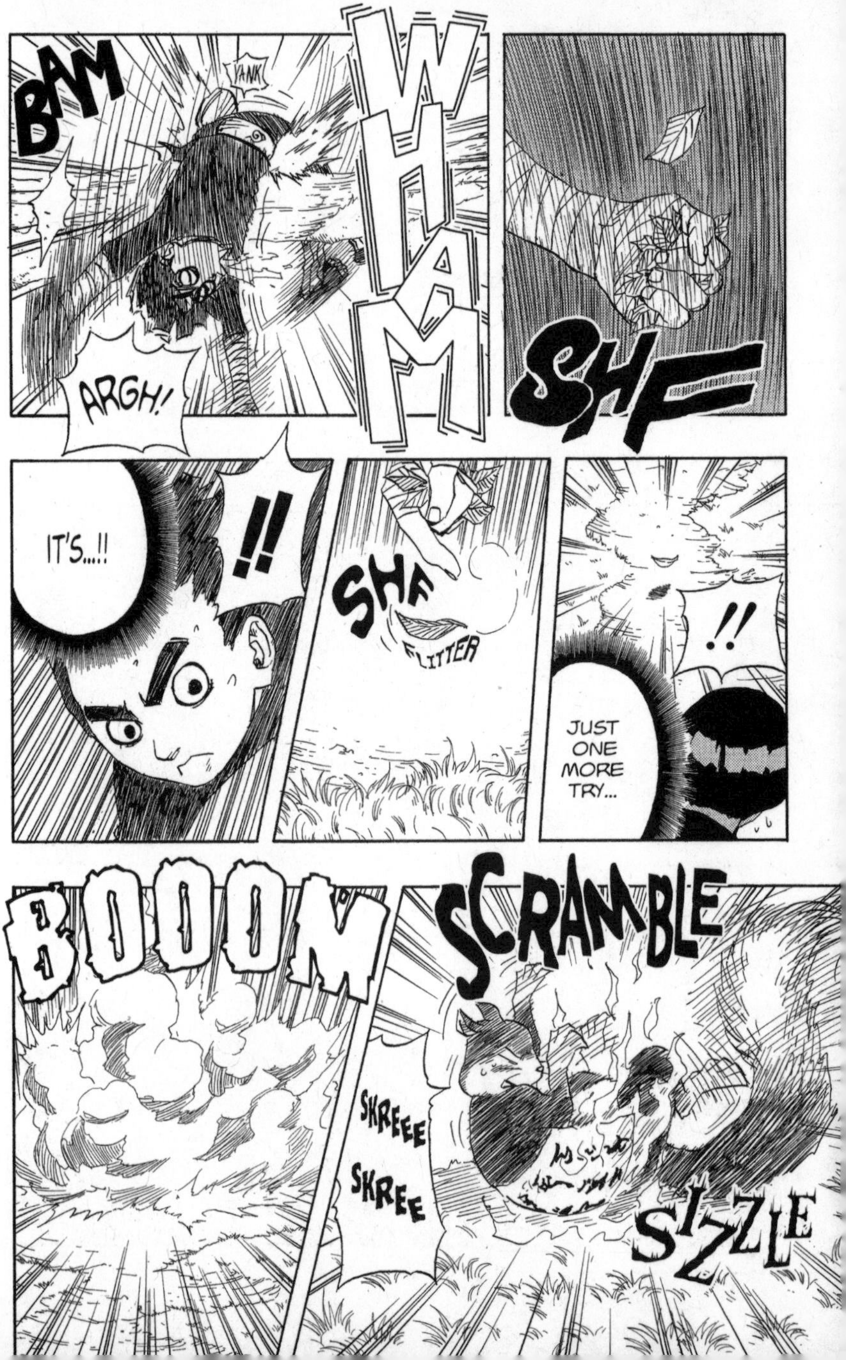
SHF
WHAM
YANK
BAM
ARGH!
!!
JUST ONE MORE TRY...
SHF
FLITTER
!!
IT'S...!!
SCRAMBLE
SIZZLE
SKREEE
SKREE
BOOOM

READ THIS WAY

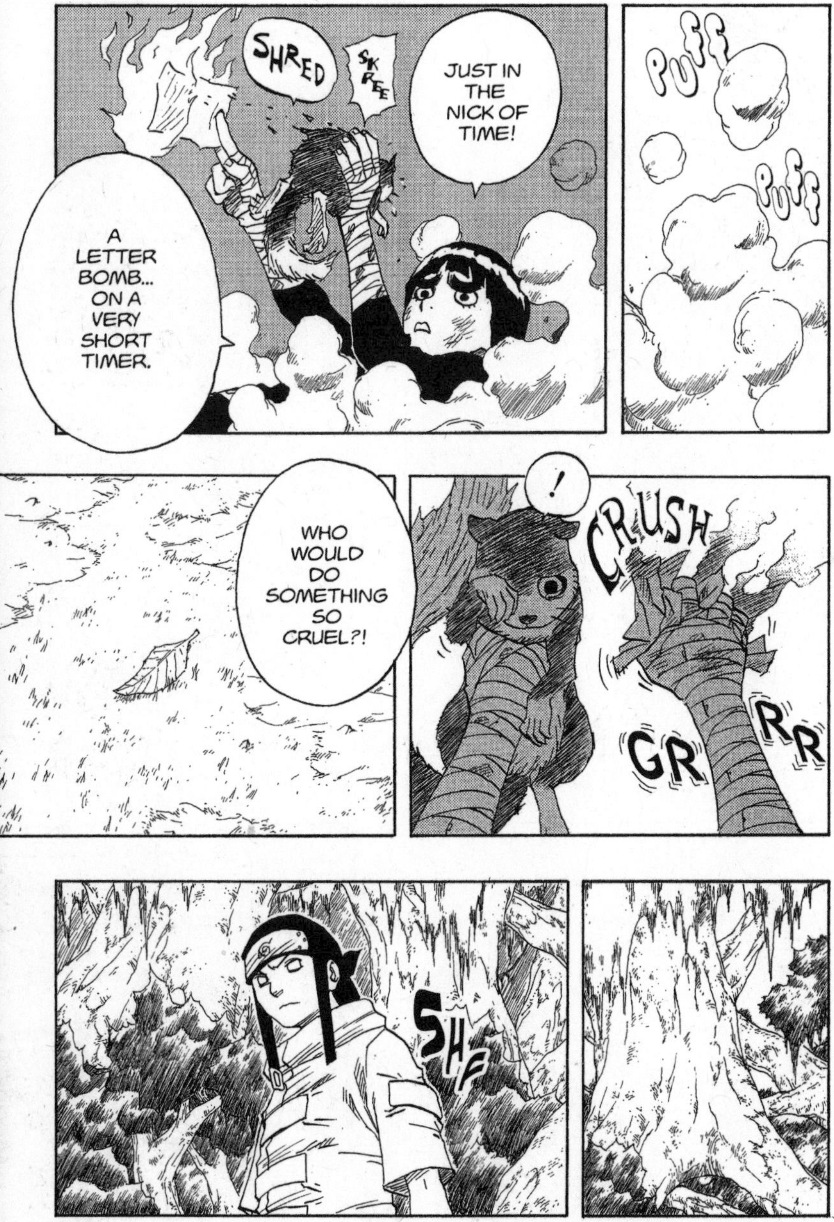
PUFF
PUFF
JUST IN THE NICK OF TIME!
SKREE
SHRED
A LETTER BOMB... ON A VERY SHORT TIMER.
!
CRUSH
GRRR
WHO WOULD DO SOMETHING SO CRUEL?!
SHF

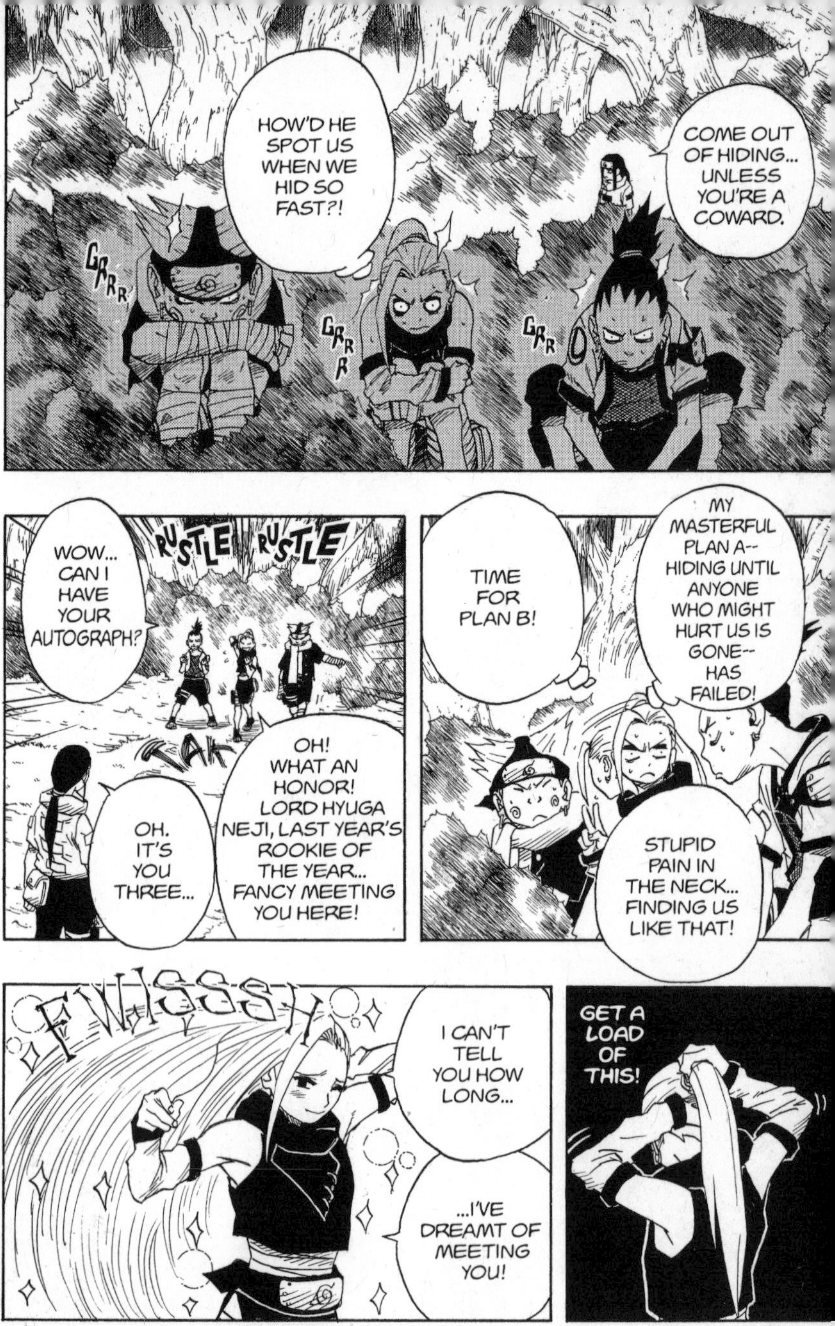
COME OUT OF HIDING... UNLESS YOU'RE A COWARD.
HOW'D HE SPOT US WHEN WE HID SO FAST?!
GRR
GRRR
GRRR
MY MASTERFUL PLAN A-- HIDING UNTIL ANYONE WHO MIGHT HURT US IS GONE-- HAS FAILED!
TIME FOR PLAN B!
STUPID PAIN IN THE NECK... FINDING US LIKE THAT!
RUSTLE RUSTLE
WOW... CAN I HAVE YOUR AUTOGRAPH?
OH! WHAT AN HONOR! LORD HYUGA NEJI, LAST YEAR'S ROOKIE OF THE YEAR... FANCY MEETING YOU HERE!
OH. IT'S YOU THREE...
GET A LOAD OF THIS!
FWISSSH
I CAN'T TELL YOU HOW LONG...
...I'VE DREAMT OF MEETING YOU!

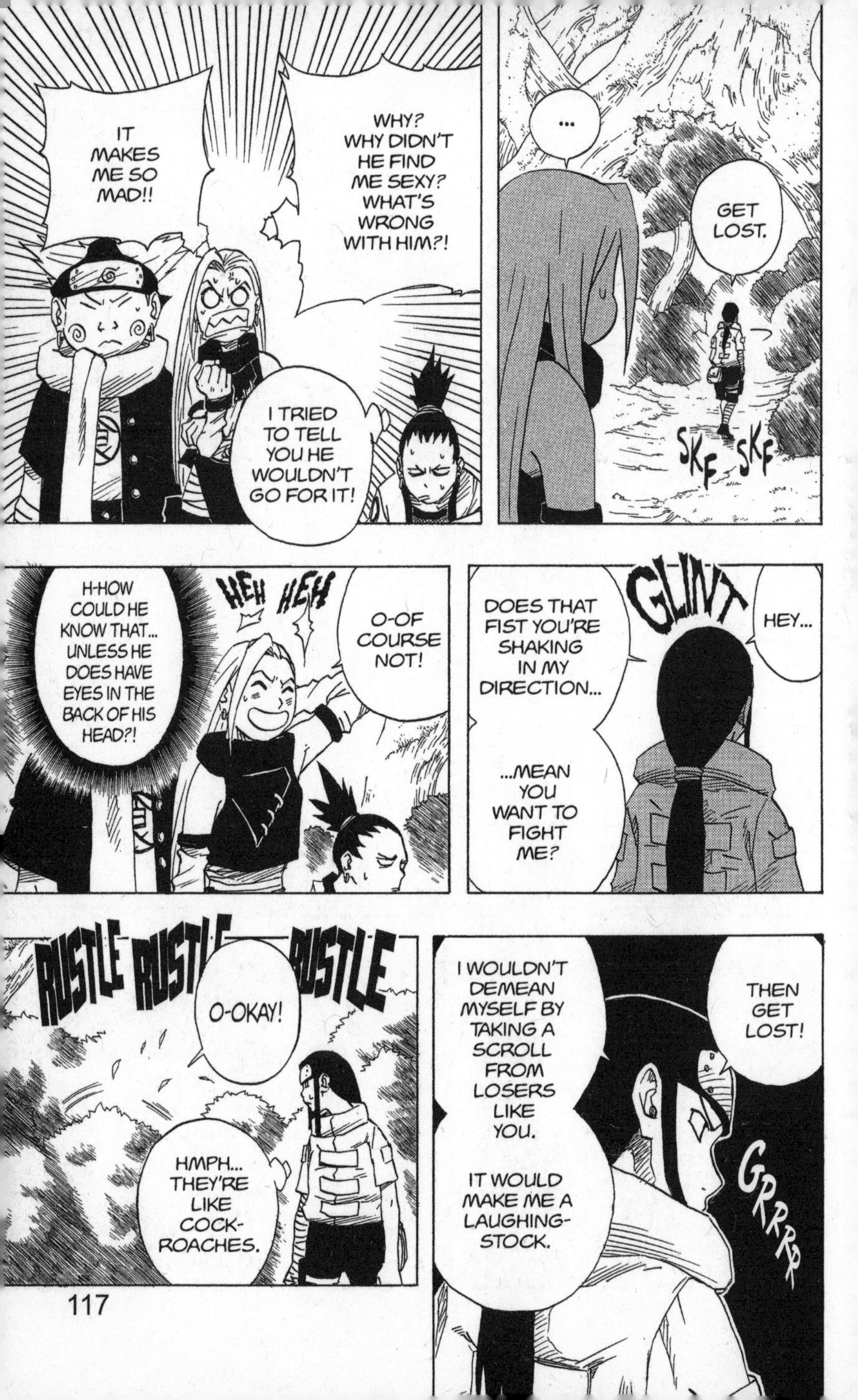

...
GET LOST.
SKF SKF
WHY? WHY DIDN'T HE FIND ME SEXY? WHAT'S WRONG WITH HIM?!
IT MAKES ME SO MAD!!
I TRIED TO TELL YOU HE WOULDN'T GO FOR IT!
GLINT
HEY...
DOES THAT FIST YOU'RE SHAKING IN MY DIRECTION...
...MEAN YOU WANT TO FIGHT ME?
O-OF COURSE NOT!
HEH HEH
H-HOW COULD HE KNOW THAT... UNLESS HE DOES HAVE EYES IN THE BACK OF HIS HEAD?!
THEN GET LOST!
I WOULDN'T DEMEAN MYSELF BY TAKING A SCROLL FROM LOSERS LIKE YOU.
IT WOULD MAKE ME A LAUGHING-STOCK.
GRRRR
RUSTLE RUSTLE RUSTLE
O-OKAY!
HMPH... THEY'RE LIKE COCK-ROACHES.

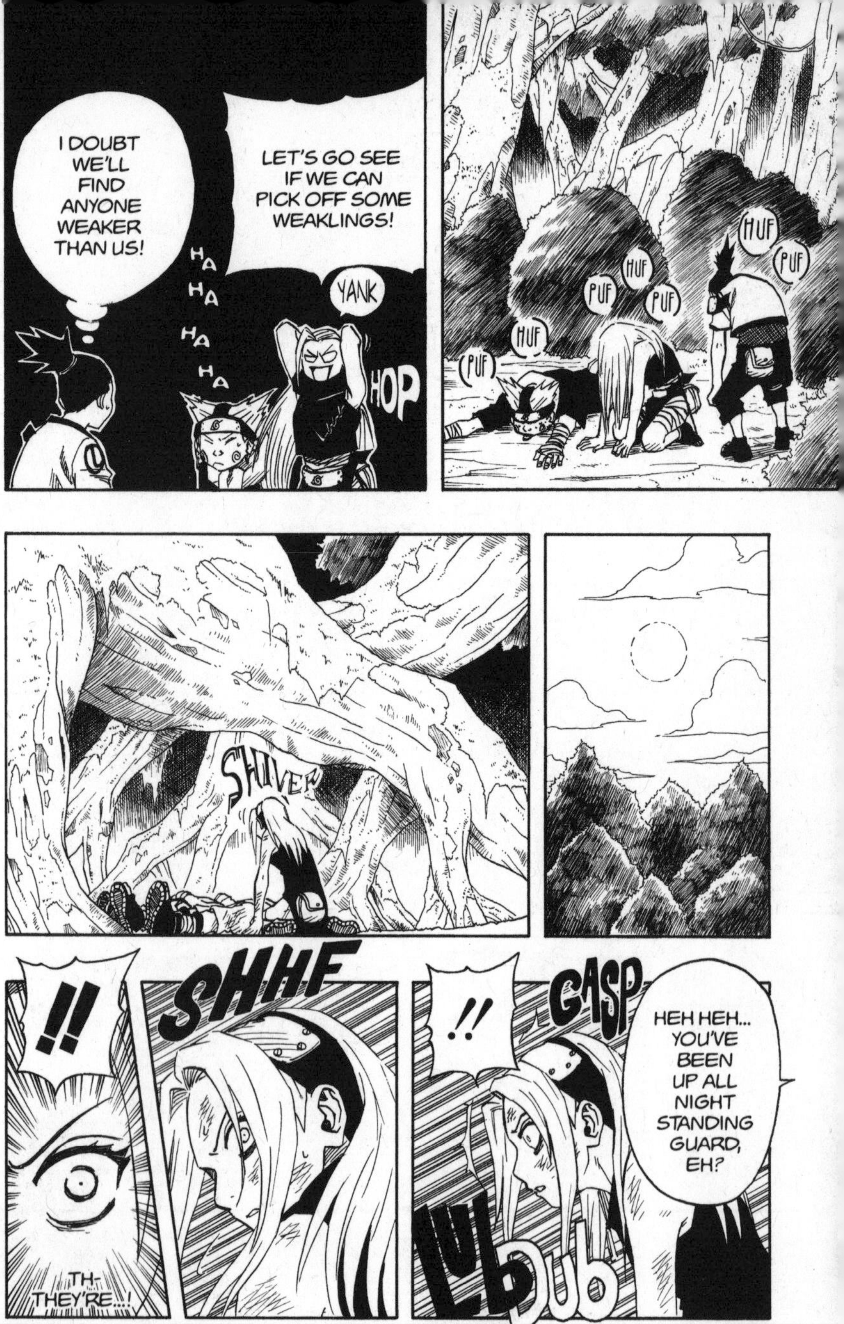
HUF
PUF
HUF
PUF
PUF
HUF
PUF
LET'S GO SEE IF WE CAN PICK OFF SOME WEAKLINGS!
YANK
HOP
I DOUBT WE'LL FIND ANYONE WEAKER THAN US!
HA HA HA HA HA
SHIVER
GASP
HEH HEH... YOU'VE BEEN UP ALL NIGHT STANDING GUARD, EH?
!!
LUB DUB
SHHF
!!
TH- THEY'RE...!

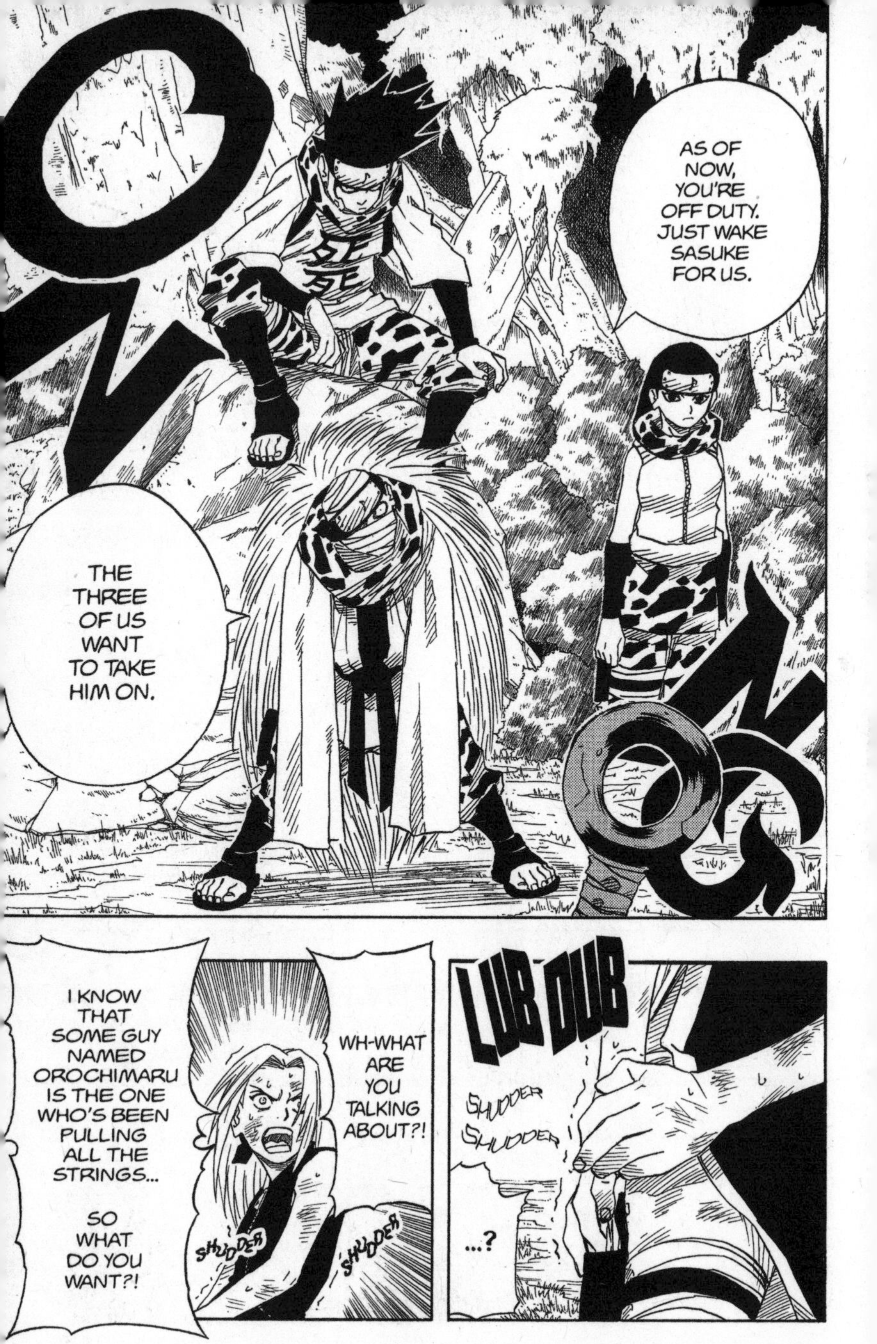
AS OF NOW, YOU'RE OFF DUTY. JUST WAKE SASUKE FOR US.
THE THREE OF US WANT TO TAKE HIM ON.
LUB DUB
SHUDDER SHUDDER
...?
WH-WHAT ARE YOU TALKING ABOUT?!
SHUDDER SHUDDER
I KNOW THAT SOME GUY NAMED OROCHIMARU IS THE ONE WHO'S BEEN PULLING ALL THE STRINGS...
SO WHAT DO YOU WANT?!

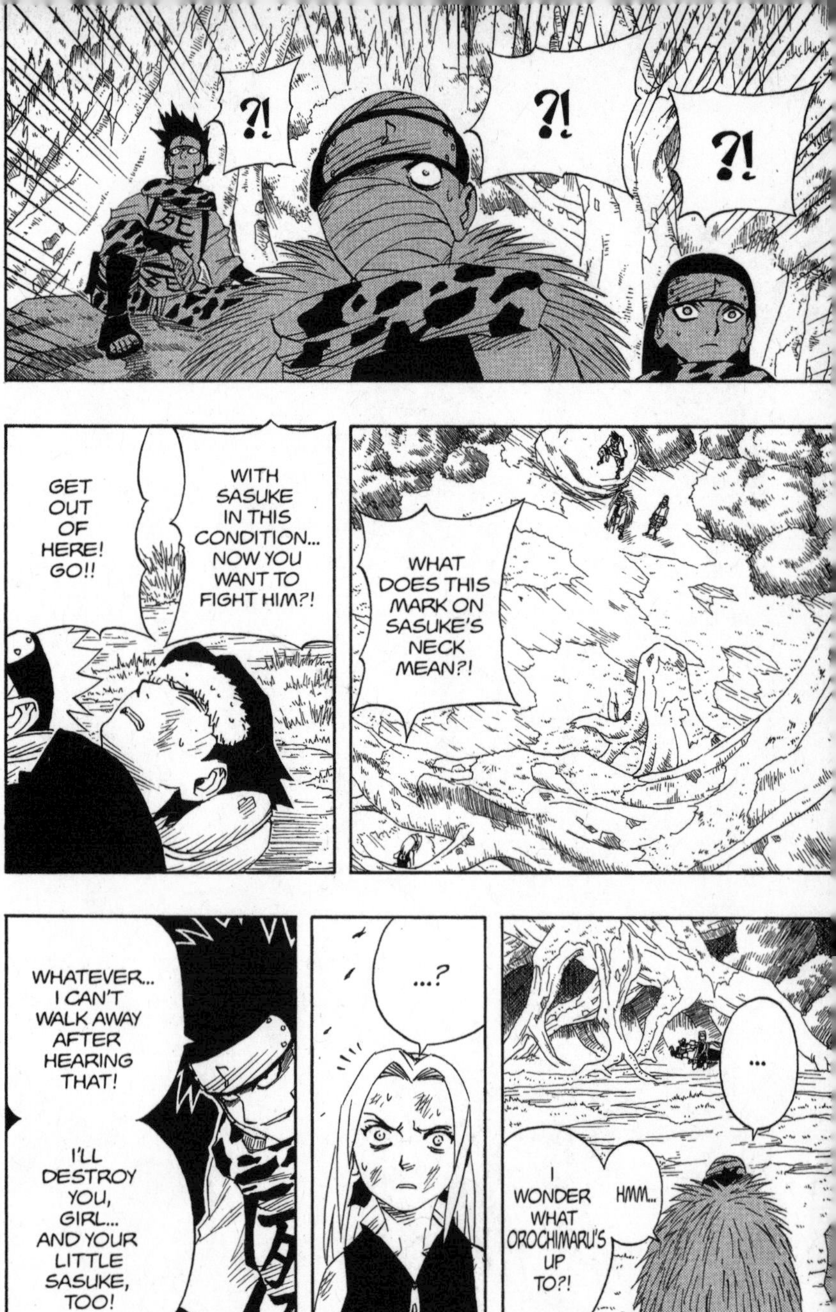
?!
?!
?!
WHAT DOES THIS MARK ON SASUKE'S NECK MEAN?!
WITH SASUKE IN THIS CONDITION... NOW YOU WANT TO FIGHT HIM?!
GET OUT OF HERE! GO!!
...
HMM...
I WONDER WHAT OROCHIMARU'S UP TO?!
...?
WHATEVER... I CAN'T WALK AWAY AFTER HEARING THAT!
I'LL DESTROY YOU, GIRL... AND YOUR LITTLE SASUKE, TOO!

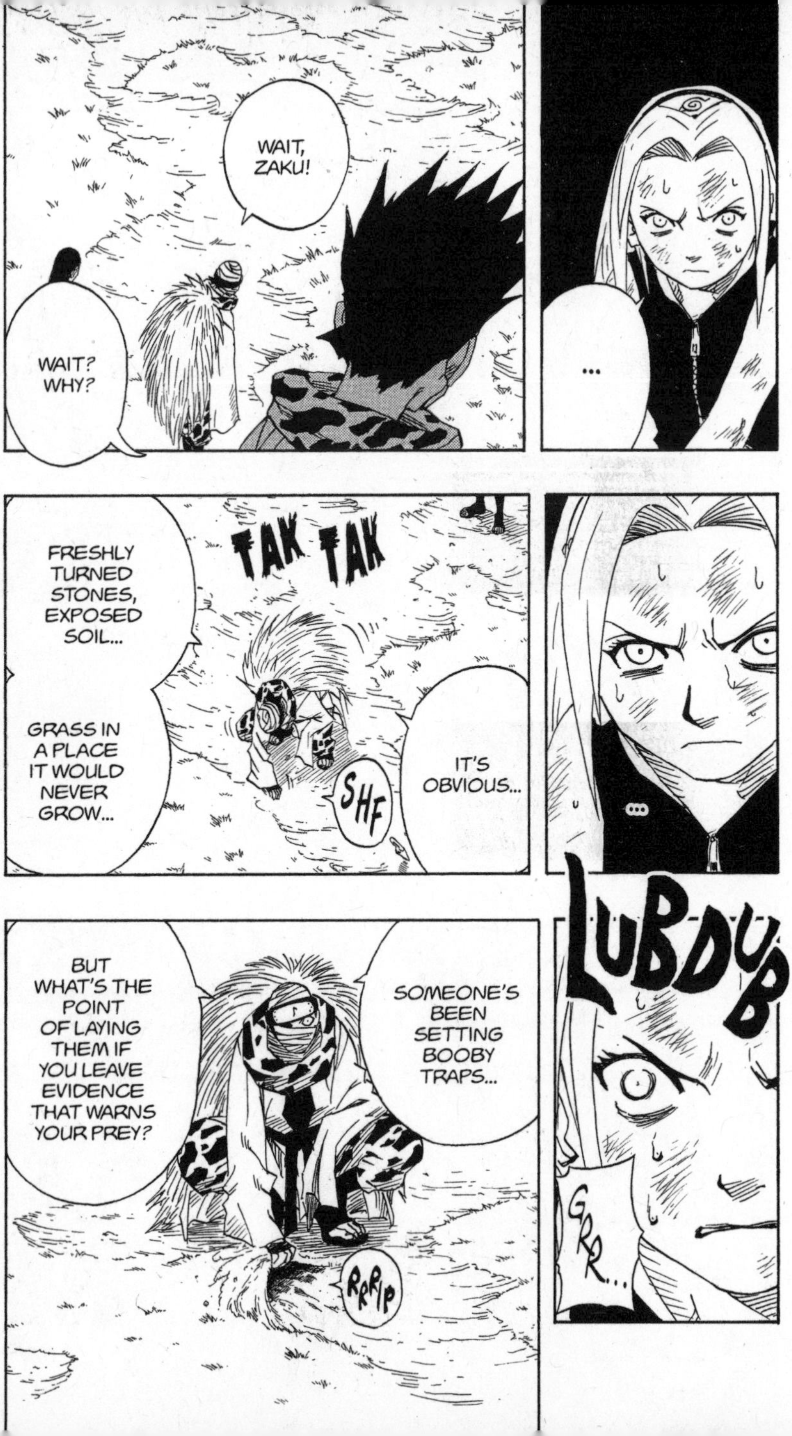
...
WAIT, ZAKU!
WAIT? WHY?
TAK TAK
IT'S OBVIOUS...
SHF
FRESHLY TURNED STONES, EXPOSED SOIL...
GRASS IN A PLACE IT WOULD NEVER GROW...
LUBDUB
GRRR...
SOMEONE'S BEEN SETTING BOOBY TRAPS...
BUT WHAT'S THE POINT OF LAYING THEM IF YOU LEAVE EVIDENCE THAT WARNS YOUR PREY?
RRRIP

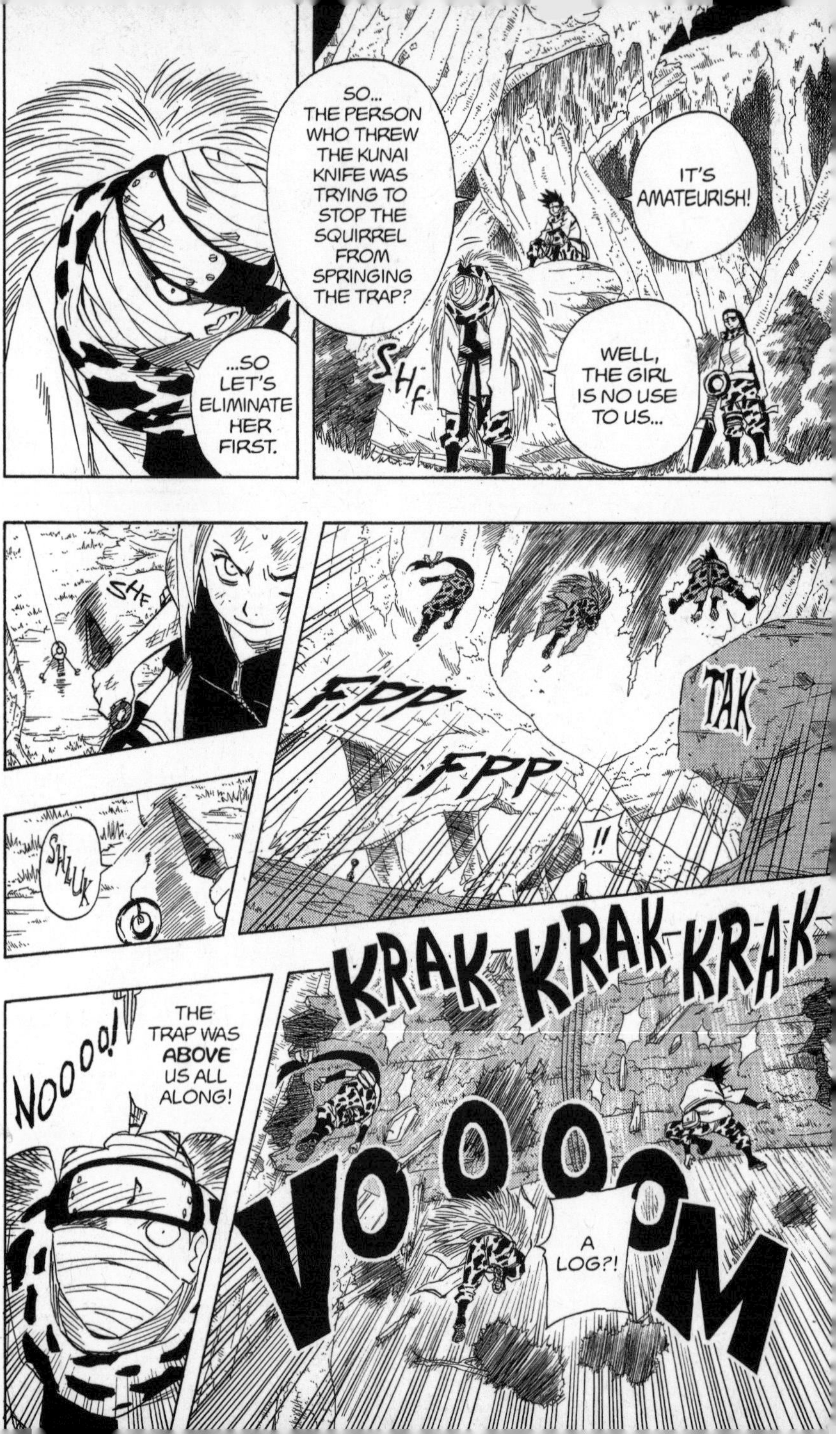
SO... THE PERSON WHO THREW THE KUNAI KNIFE WAS TRYING TO STOP THE SQUIRREL FROM SPRINGING THE TRAP?
IT'S AMATEURISH!
WELL, THE GIRL IS NO USE TO US...
SHF
...SO LET'S ELIMINATE HER FIRST.
TAK
FPP
FPP
!!
SHF
SHLUK
KRAK KRAK KRAK
A LOG?!
VOOOOM
THE TRAP WAS **ABOVE** US ALL ALONG!
NOOOO!

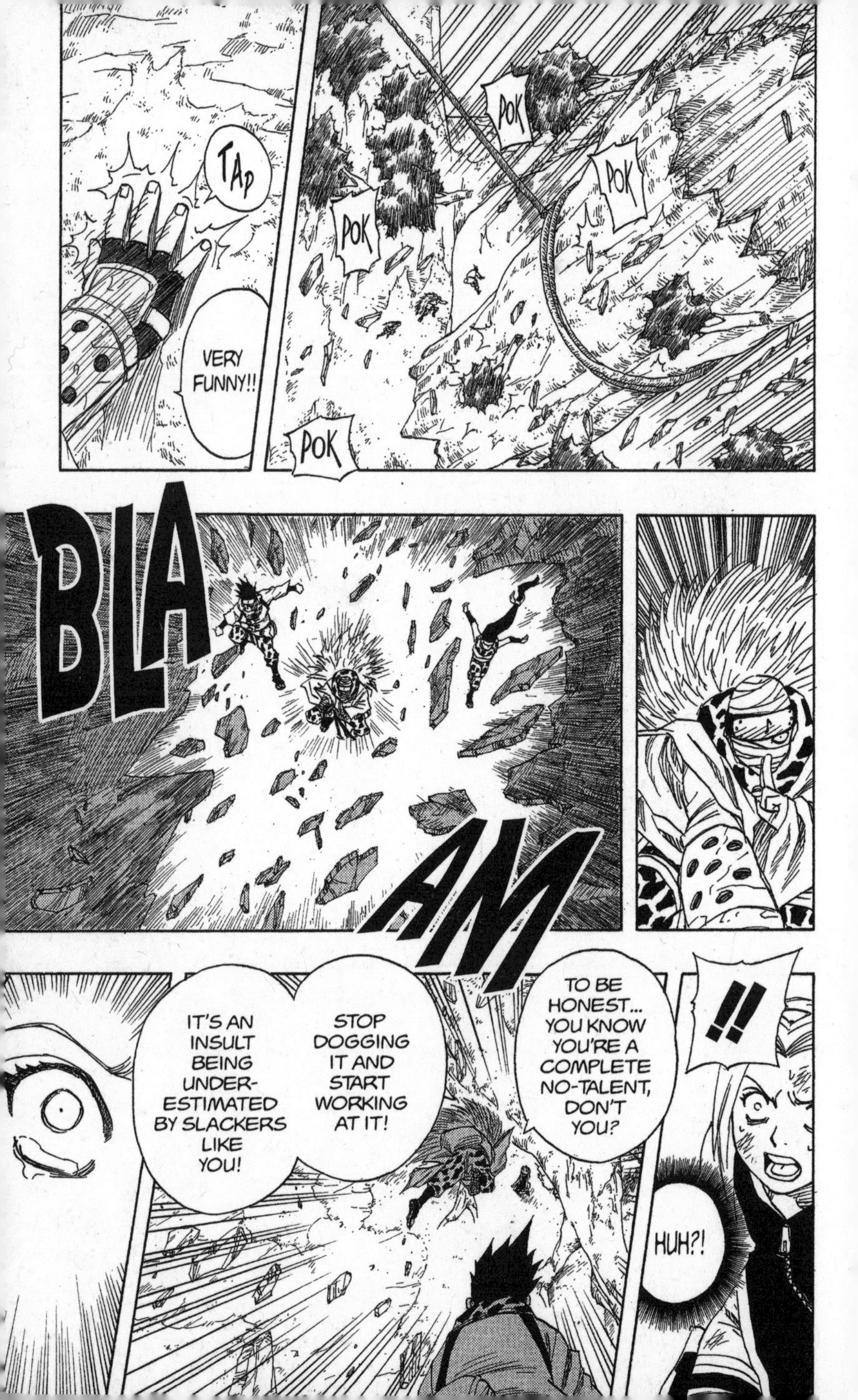
POK
POK
POK
POK
TAp
VERY FUNNY!!
BLA
AM
!!
HUH?!
TO BE HONEST... YOU KNOW YOU'RE A COMPLETE NO-TALENT, DON'T YOU?
STOP DOGGING IT AND START WORKING AT IT!
IT'S AN INSULT BEING UNDER-ESTIMATED BY SLACKERS LIKE YOU!

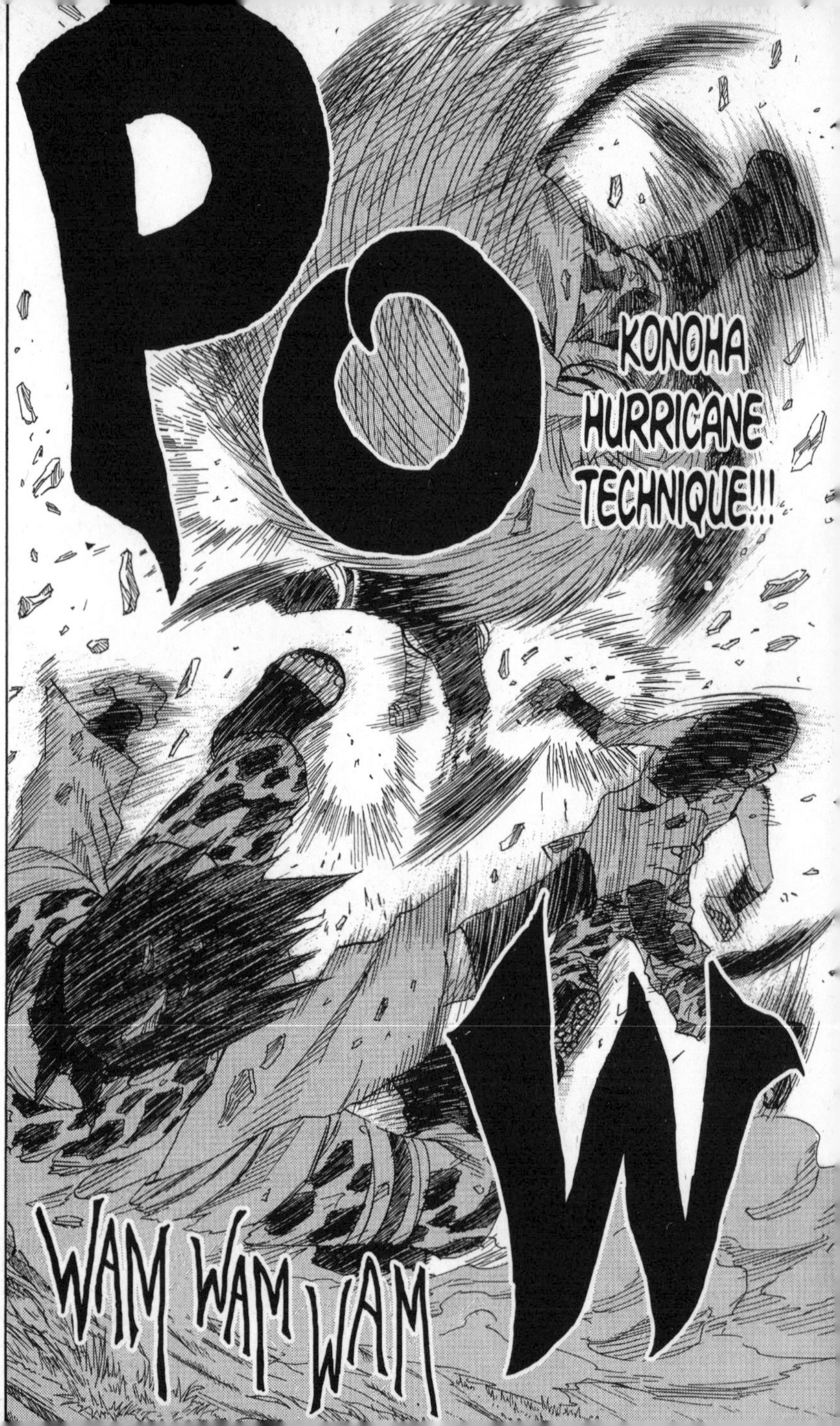
POW
KONOHA HURRICANE TECHNIQUE!!!
WAM WAM WAM

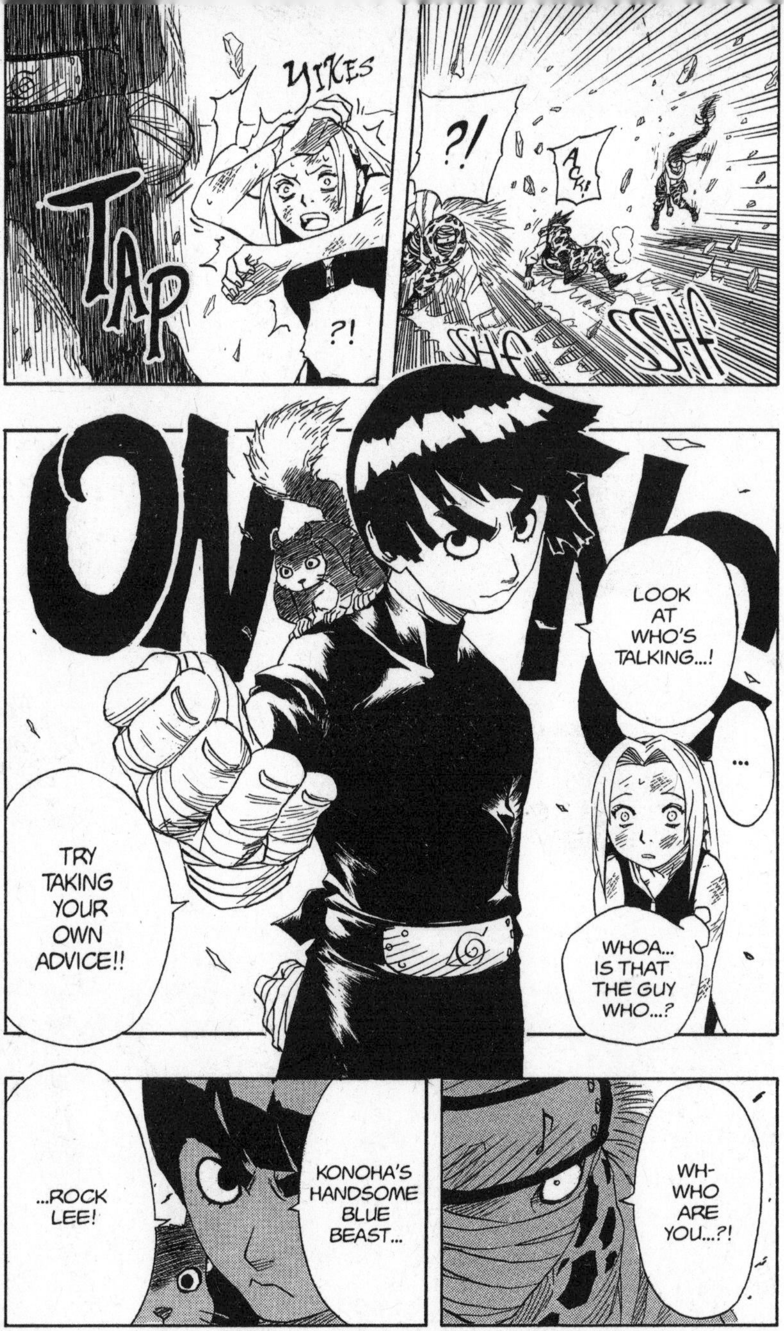

?!
ACK!
SHF
SHF
YIKES
TAP
?!
LOOK AT WHO'S TALKING...!
...
WHOA... IS THAT THE GUY WHO...?
TRY TAKING YOUR OWN ADVICE!!
WH-WHO ARE YOU...?!
KONOHA'S HANDSOME BLUE BEAST...
...ROCK LEE!

Number 52:

The Principles of Use!!

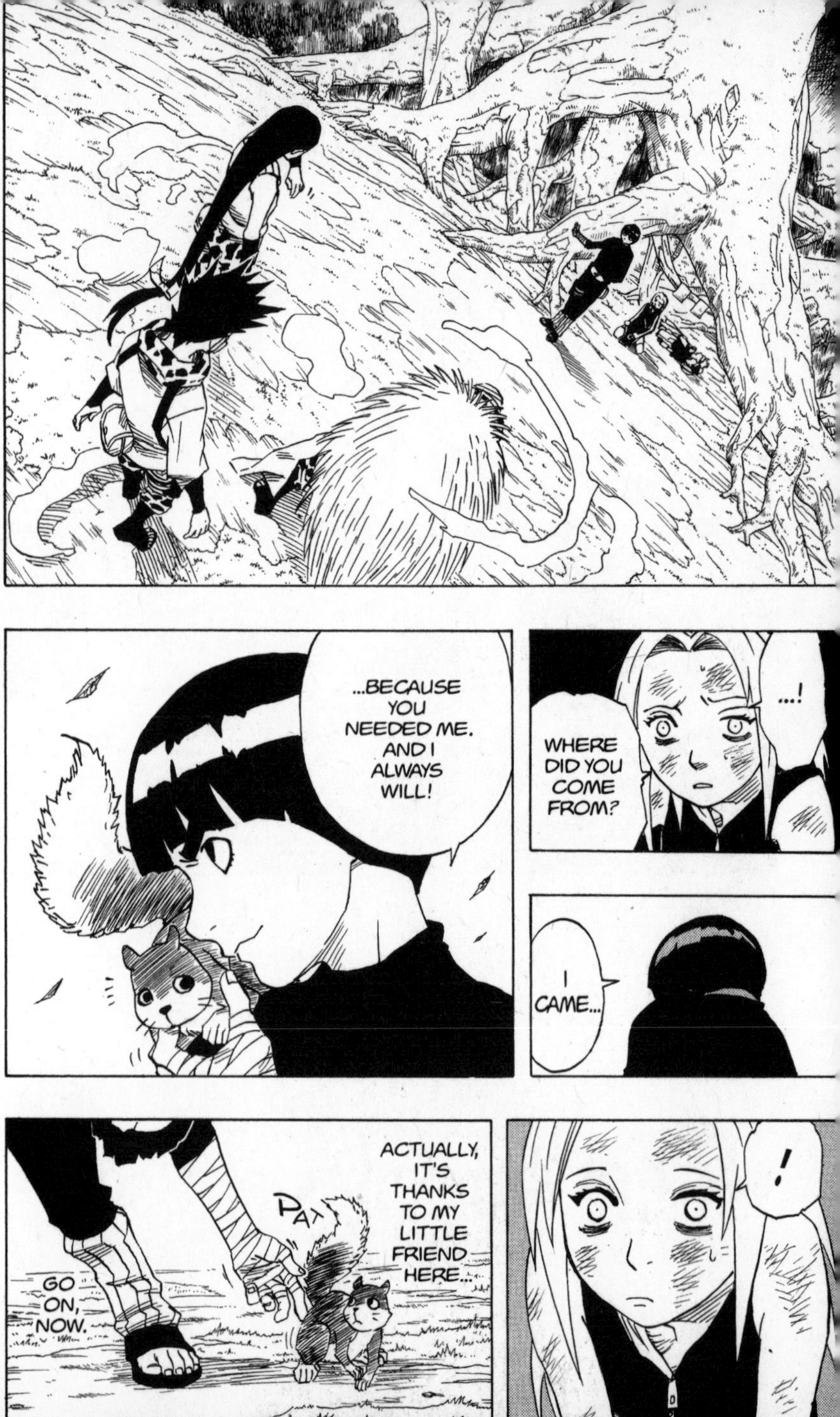
...!
WHERE DID YOU COME FROM?
I CAME...
...BECAUSE YOU NEEDED ME. AND I ALWAYS WILL!
!
ACTUALLY, IT'S THANKS TO MY LITTLE FRIEND HERE...
PAT
GO ON, NOW.

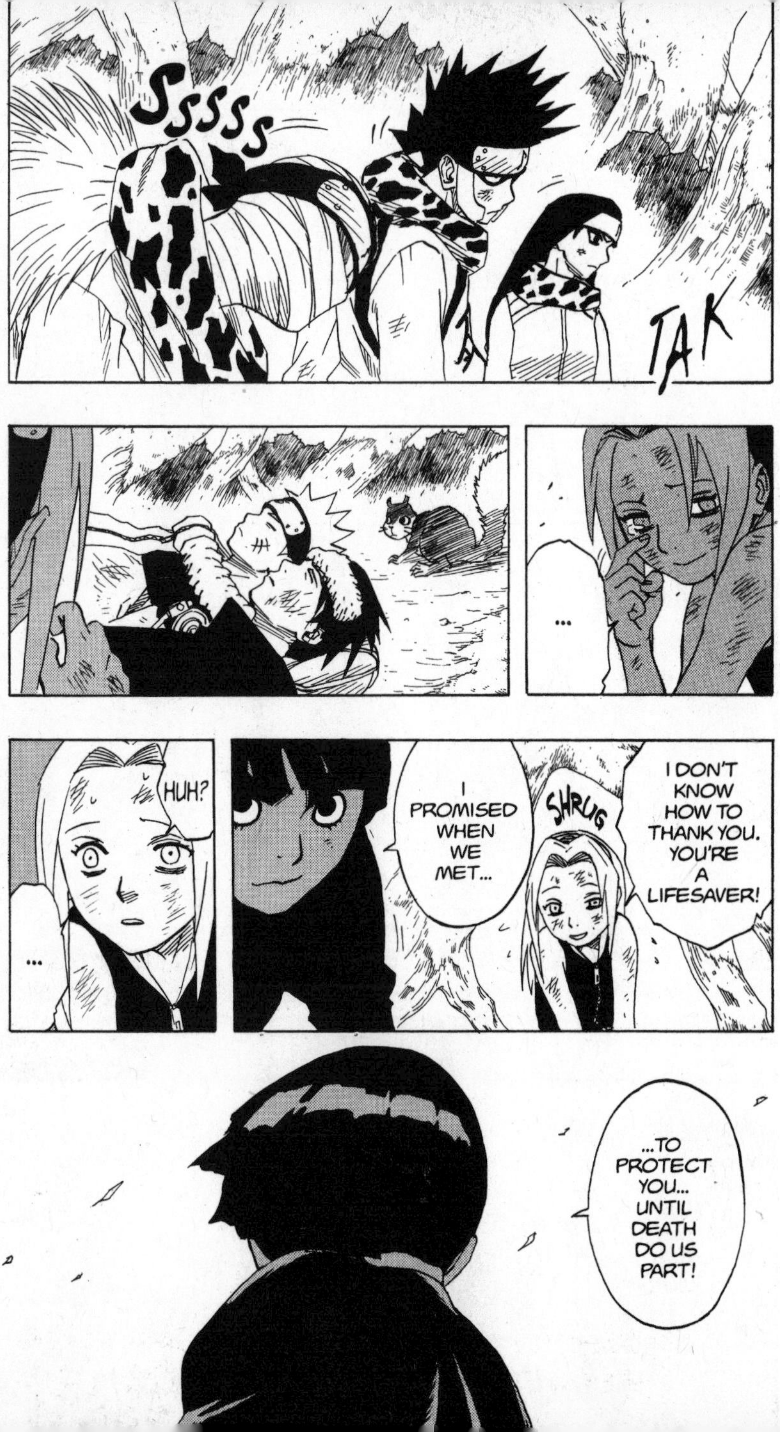
SSSSS
TAK
...
I DON'T KNOW HOW TO THANK YOU. YOU'RE A LIFESAVER!
SHRUG
I PROMISED WHEN WE MET...
HUH?
...
...TO PROTECT YOU... UNTIL DEATH DO US PART!

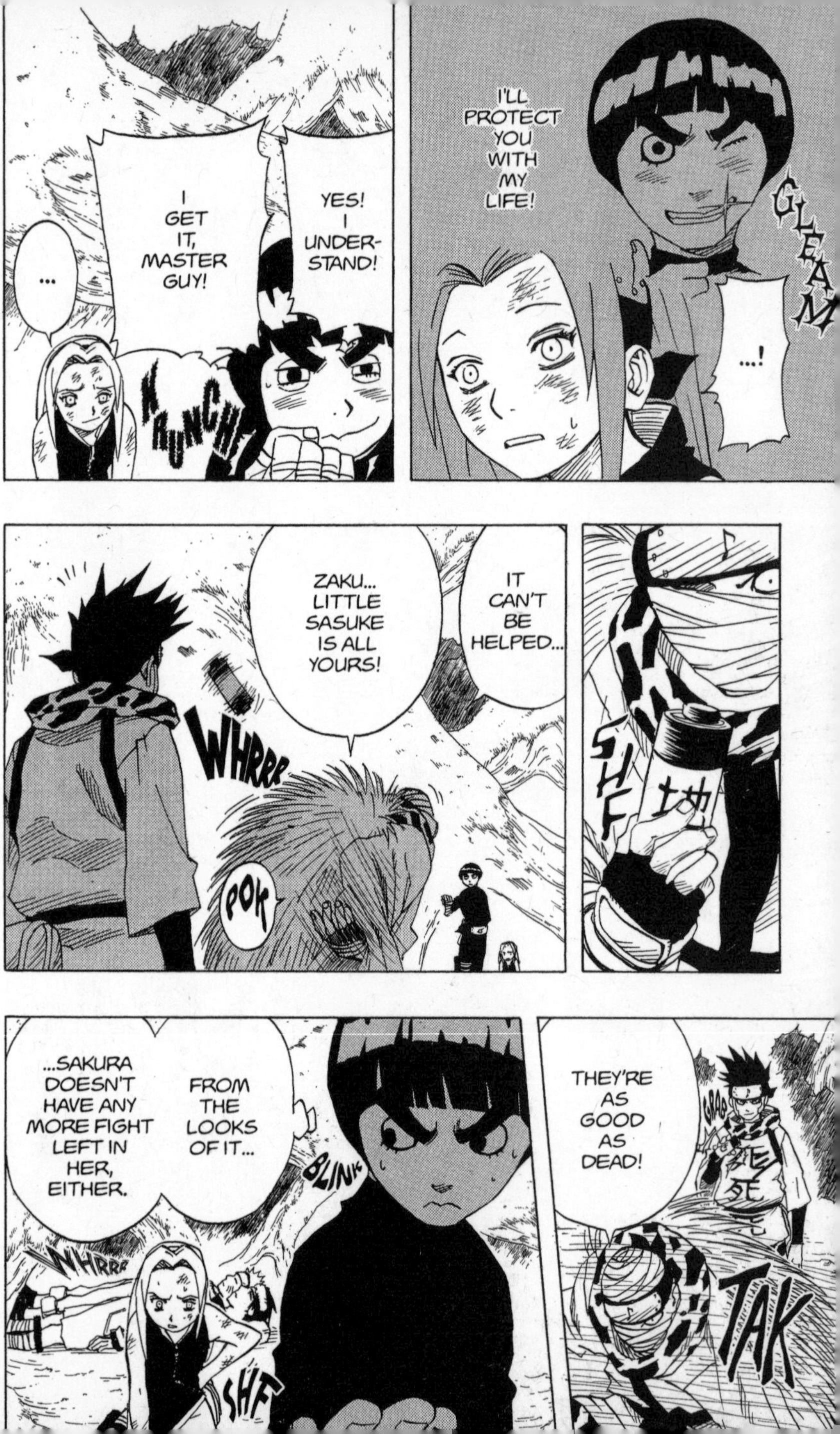
I'LL PROTECT YOU WITH MY LIFE!
GLEAM
...!
YES! I UNDERSTAND!
I GET IT, MASTER GUY!
...
KRUNCH!
SHF
地
IT CAN'T BE HELPED...
ZAKU... LITTLE SASUKE IS ALL YOURS!
WHRRR
POK
THEY'RE AS GOOD AS DEAD!
GRAB
TAK
FROM THE LOOKS OF IT...
...SAKURA DOESN'T HAVE ANY MORE FIGHT LEFT IN HER, EITHER.
BLINK
WHRRR
SHF

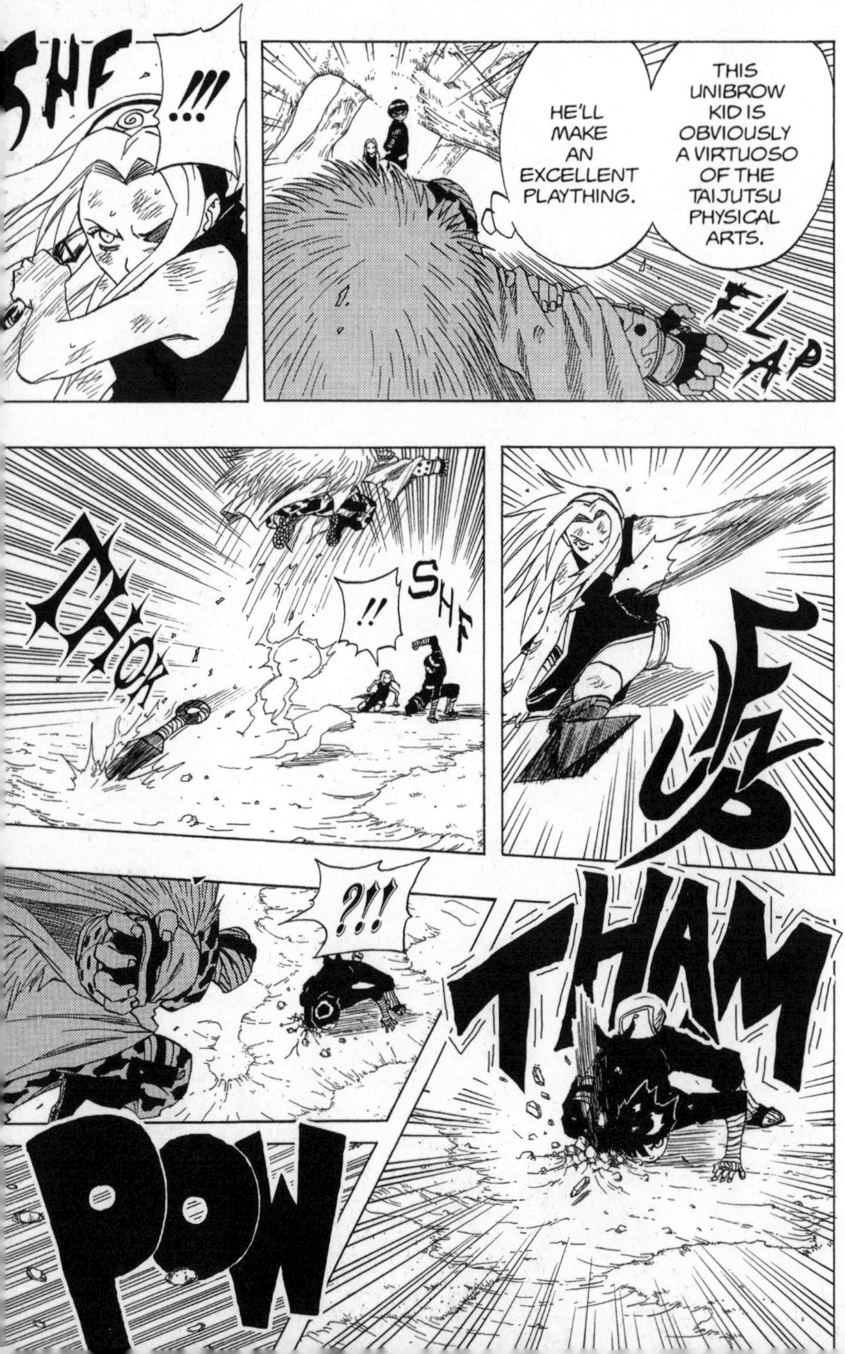
THIS UNIBROW KID IS OBVIOUSLY A VIRTUOSO OF THE TAIJUTSU PHYSICAL ARTS.
HE'LL MAKE AN EXCELLENT PLAYTHING.
FLAP
SHF
!!!
SHF
!!
THOK
THAM
?!!
POW

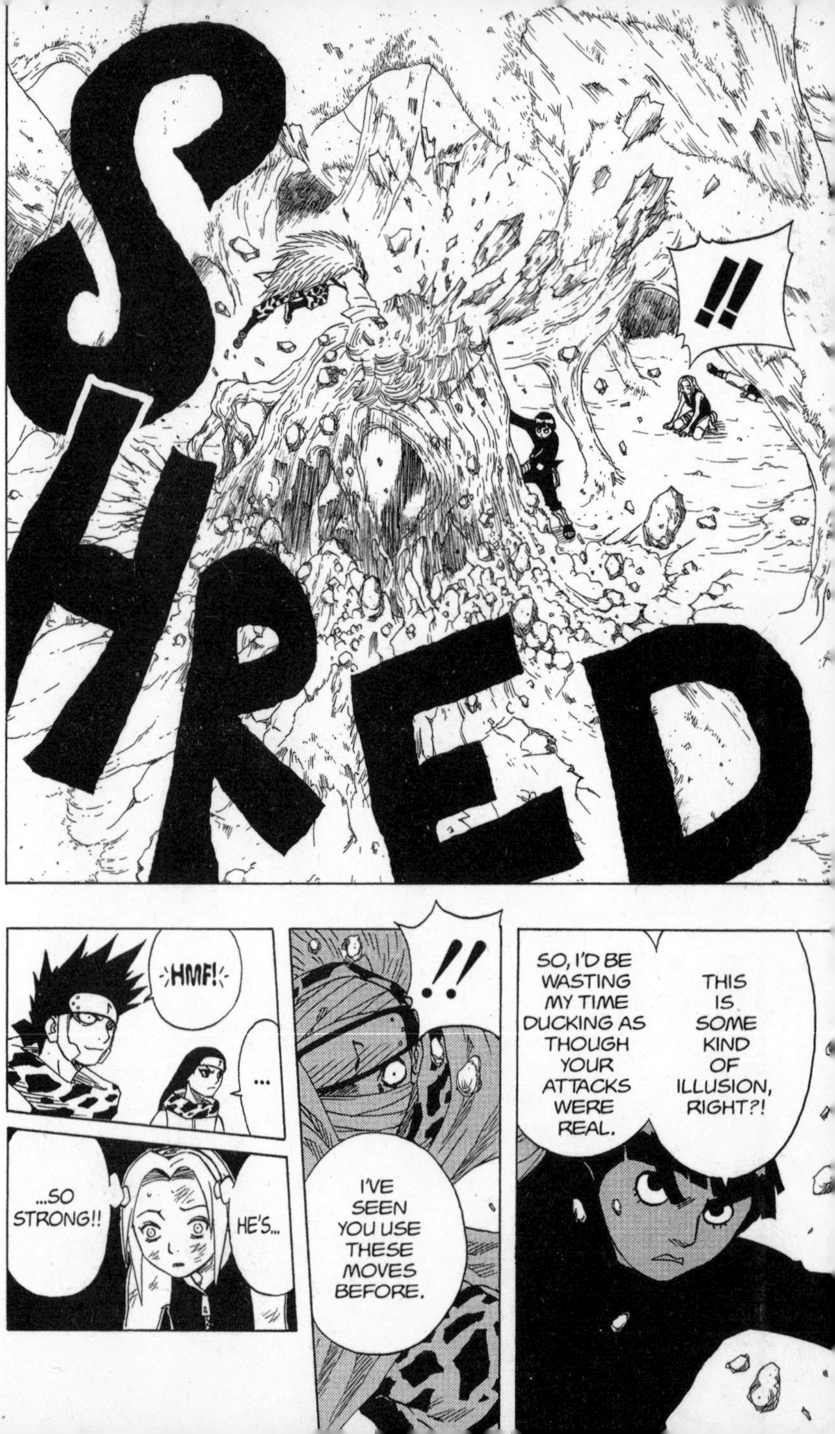
SHRED
!!
THIS IS SOME KIND OF ILLUSION, RIGHT?!
SO, I'D BE WASTING MY TIME DUCKING AS THOUGH YOUR ATTACKS WERE REAL.
!!
I'VE SEEN YOU USE THESE MOVES BEFORE.
HMF!
...
HE'S...
...SO STRONG!!

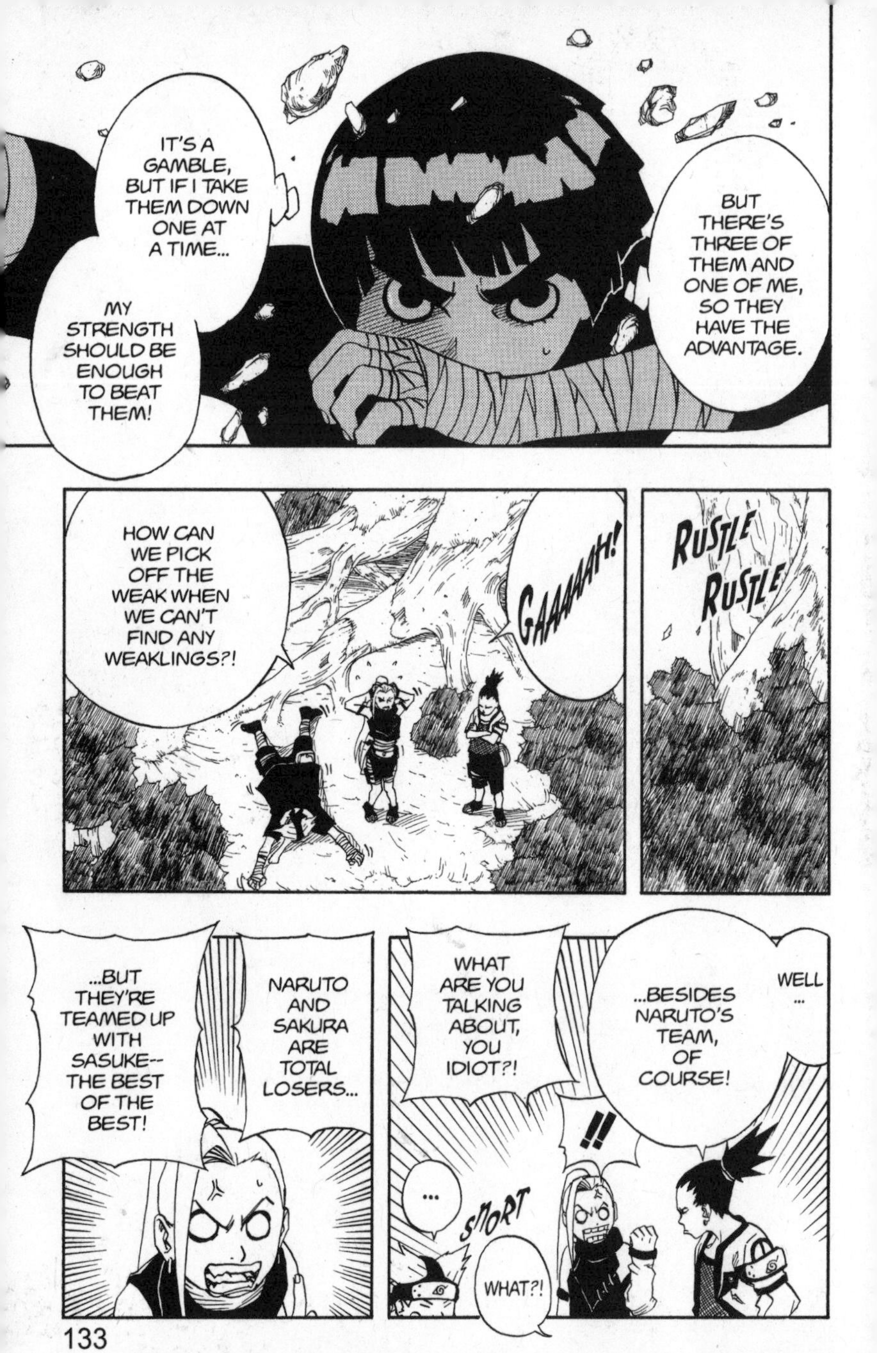
BUT THERE'S THREE OF THEM AND ONE OF ME, SO THEY HAVE THE ADVANTAGE.
IT'S A GAMBLE, BUT IF I TAKE THEM DOWN ONE AT A TIME...
MY STRENGTH SHOULD BE ENOUGH TO BEAT THEM!
RUSTLE RUSTLE
GAAAAAH!
HOW CAN WE PICK OFF THE WEAK WHEN WE CAN'T FIND ANY WEAKLINGS?!
WELL ...
...BESIDES NARUTO'S TEAM, OF COURSE!
WHAT ARE YOU TALKING ABOUT, YOU IDIOT?!
!!
...
SNORT
WHAT?!
NARUTO AND SAKURA ARE TOTAL LOSERS...
...BUT THEY'RE TEAMED UP WITH SASUKE-- THE BEST OF THE BEST!

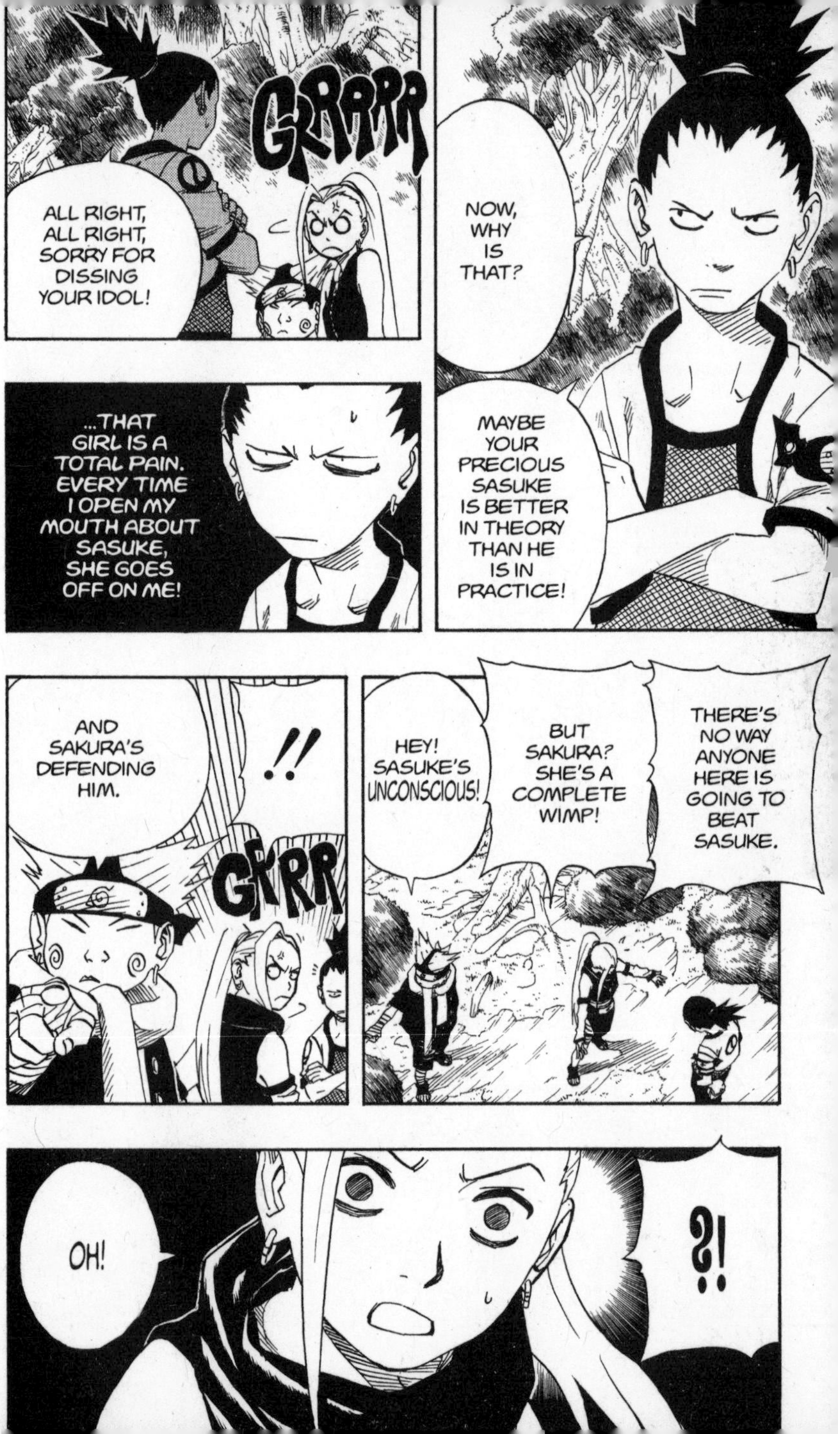
NOW, WHY IS THAT?
MAYBE YOUR PRECIOUS SASUKE IS BETTER IN THEORY THAN HE IS IN PRACTICE!
GRRRR
ALL RIGHT, ALL RIGHT, SORRY FOR DISSING YOUR IDOL!
...THAT GIRL IS A TOTAL PAIN. EVERY TIME I OPEN MY MOUTH ABOUT SASUKE, SHE GOES OFF ON ME!
THERE'S NO WAY ANYONE HERE IS GOING TO BEAT SASUKE.
BUT SAKURA? SHE'S A COMPLETE WIMP!
HEY! SASUKE'S UNCONSCIOUS!
!!
AND SAKURA'S DEFENDING HIM.
GRRR
?!
OH!

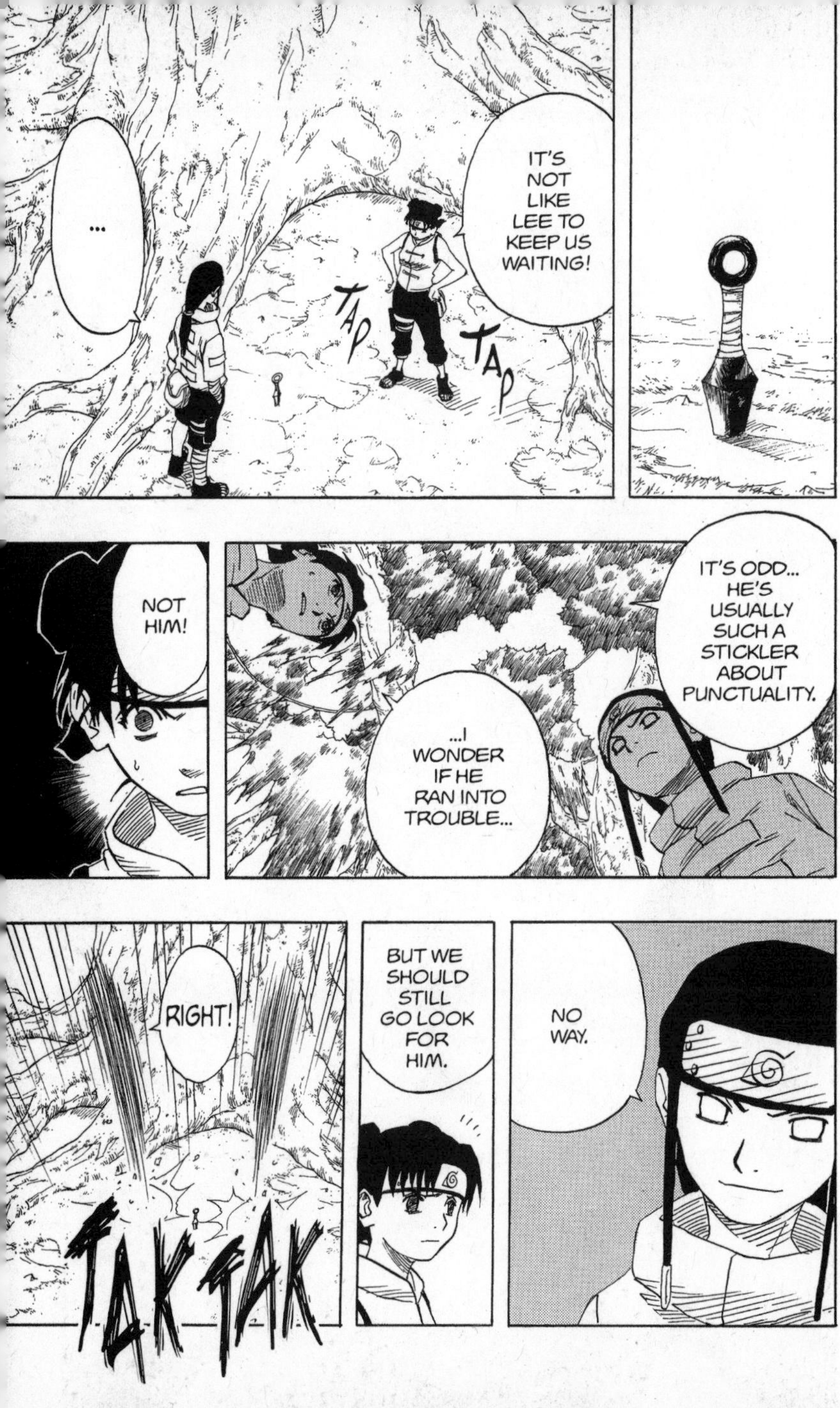
IT'S NOT LIKE LEE TO KEEP US WAITING!
TAP
TAP
...
IT'S ODD... HE'S USUALLY SUCH A STICKLER ABOUT PUNCTUALITY.
...I WONDER IF HE RAN INTO TROUBLE...
NOT HIM!
NO WAY.
BUT WE SHOULD STILL GO LOOK FOR HIM.
RIGHT!
TAK TAK

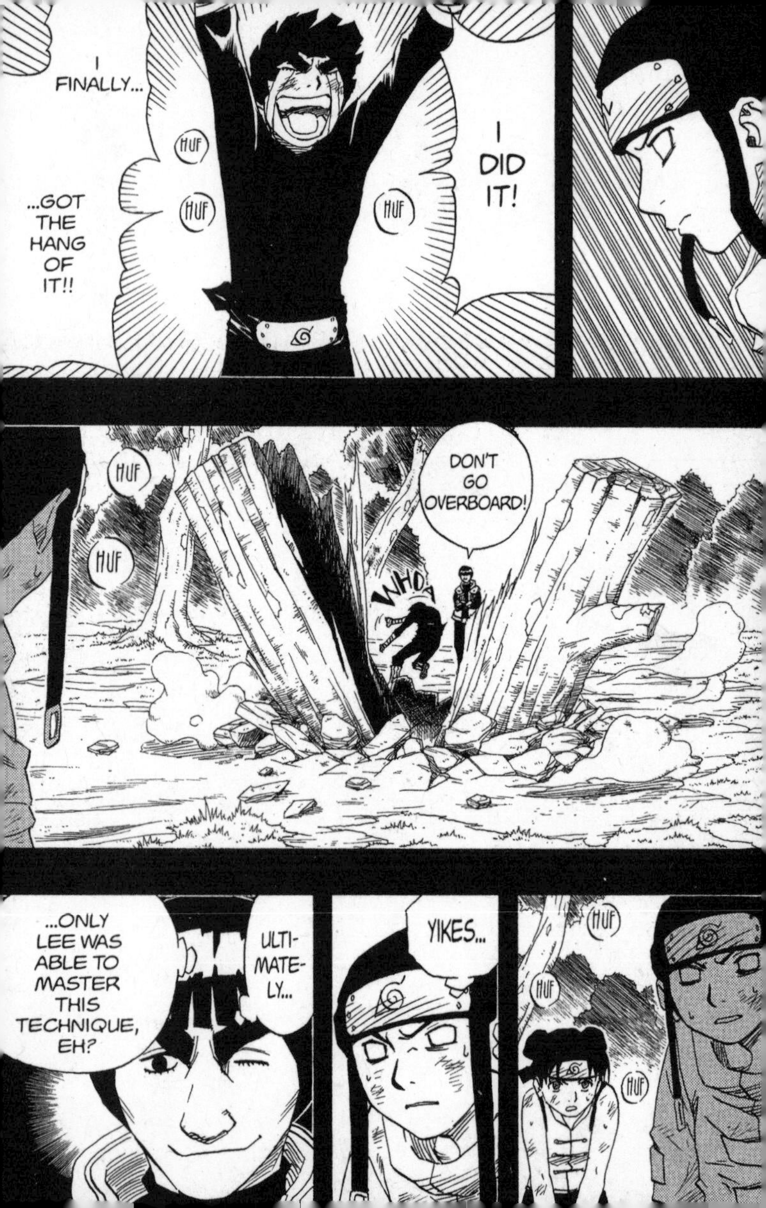
I FINALLY...
HUF
HUF
HUF
...GOT THE HANG OF IT!!
I DID IT!
DON'T GO OVERBOARD!
HUF
HUF
WHOA
HUF
HUF
HUF
YIKES...
ULTIMATELY...
...ONLY LEE WAS ABLE TO MASTER THIS TECHNIQUE, EH?

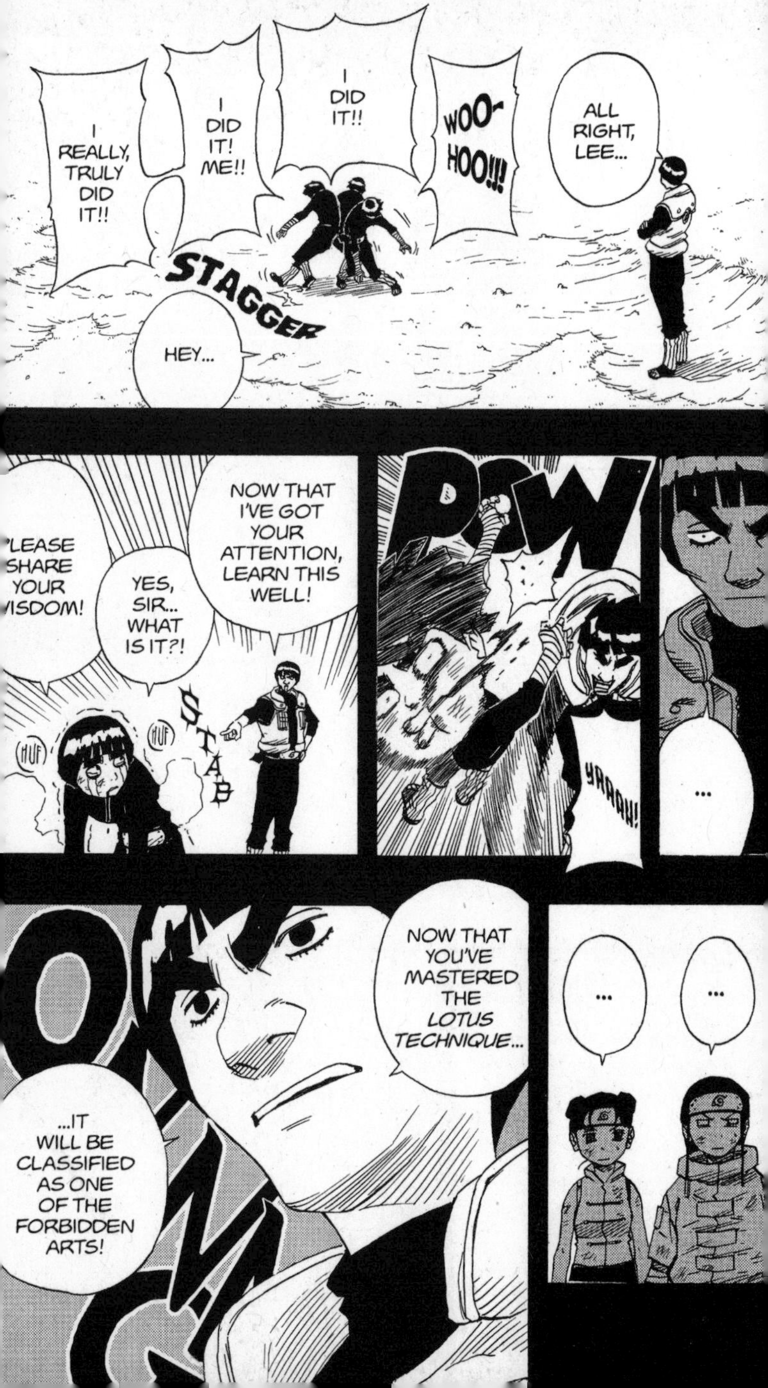

ALL RIGHT, LEE...
WOO-HOO!!!
I DID IT!!
I DID IT! ME!!
I REALLY, TRULY DID IT!!
STAGGER
HEY...
...
POW
YAAAH!
NOW THAT I'VE GOT YOUR ATTENTION, LEARN THIS WELL!
YES, SIR... WHAT IS IT?!
PLEASE SHARE YOUR WISDOM!
STAB
HUF
HUF
...
...
NOW THAT YOU'VE MASTERED THE *LOTUS* TECHNIQUE...
...IT WILL BE CLASSIFIED AS ONE OF THE FORBIDDEN ARTS!

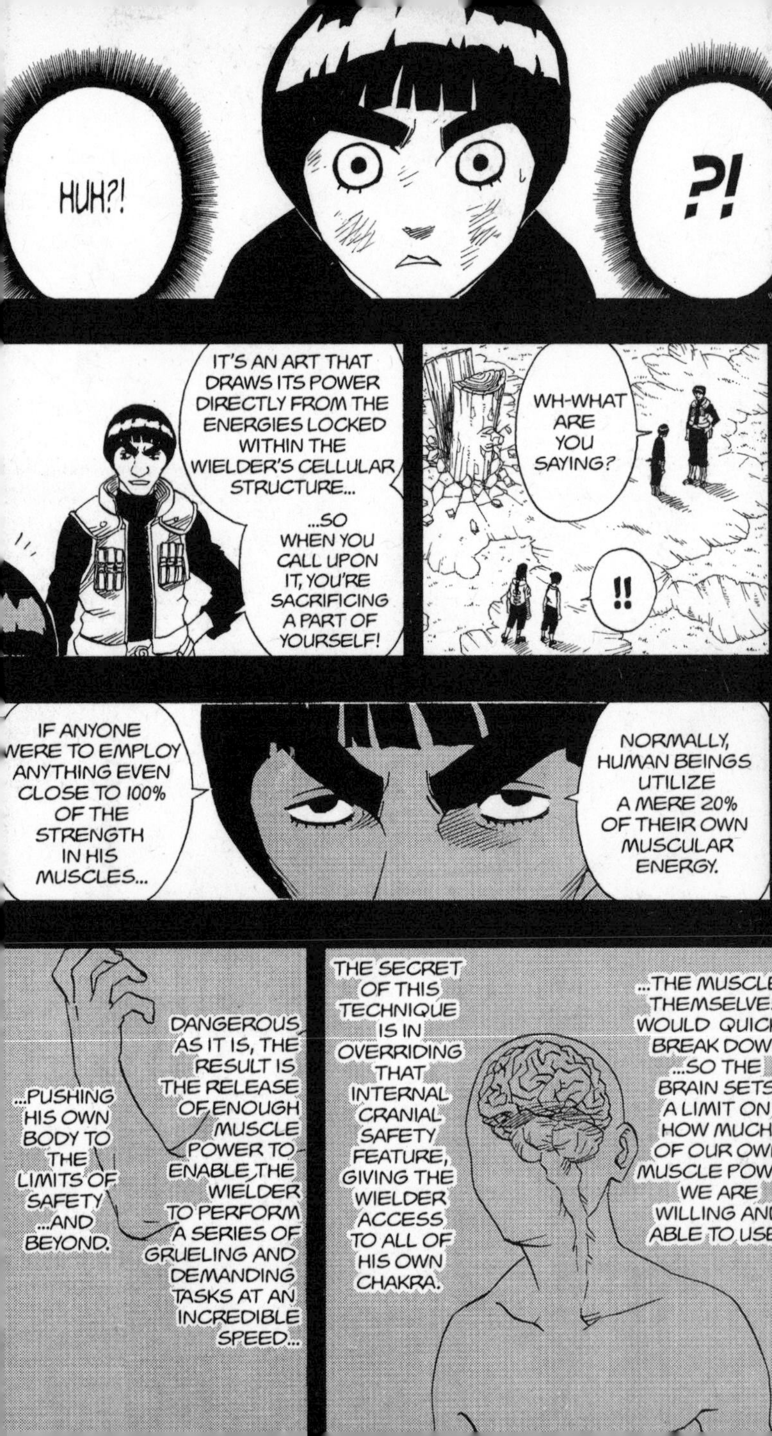
?!
HUH?!
WH-WHAT ARE YOU SAYING?
!!
IT'S AN ART THAT DRAWS ITS POWER DIRECTLY FROM THE ENERGIES LOCKED WITHIN THE WIELDER'S CELLULAR STRUCTURE...
...SO WHEN YOU CALL UPON IT, YOU'RE SACRIFICING A PART OF YOURSELF!
NORMALLY, HUMAN BEINGS UTILIZE A MERE 20% OF THEIR OWN MUSCULAR ENERGY.
IF ANYONE WERE TO EMPLOY ANYTHING EVEN CLOSE TO 100% OF THE STRENGTH IN HIS MUSCLES...
...THE MUSCLES THEMSELVES WOULD QUICKLY BREAK DOWN ...SO THE BRAIN SETS A LIMIT ON HOW MUCH OF OUR OWN MUSCLE POWER WE ARE WILLING AND ABLE TO USE.
THE SECRET OF THIS TECHNIQUE IS IN OVERRIDING THAT INTERNAL CRANIAL SAFETY FEATURE, GIVING THE WIELDER ACCESS TO ALL OF HIS OWN CHAKRA.
DANGEROUS AS IT IS, THE RESULT IS THE RELEASE OF ENOUGH MUSCLE POWER TO ENABLE THE WIELDER TO PERFORM A SERIES OF GRUELING AND DEMANDING TASKS AT AN INCREDIBLE SPEED...
...PUSHING HIS OWN BODY TO THE LIMITS OF SAFETY ...AND BEYOND.

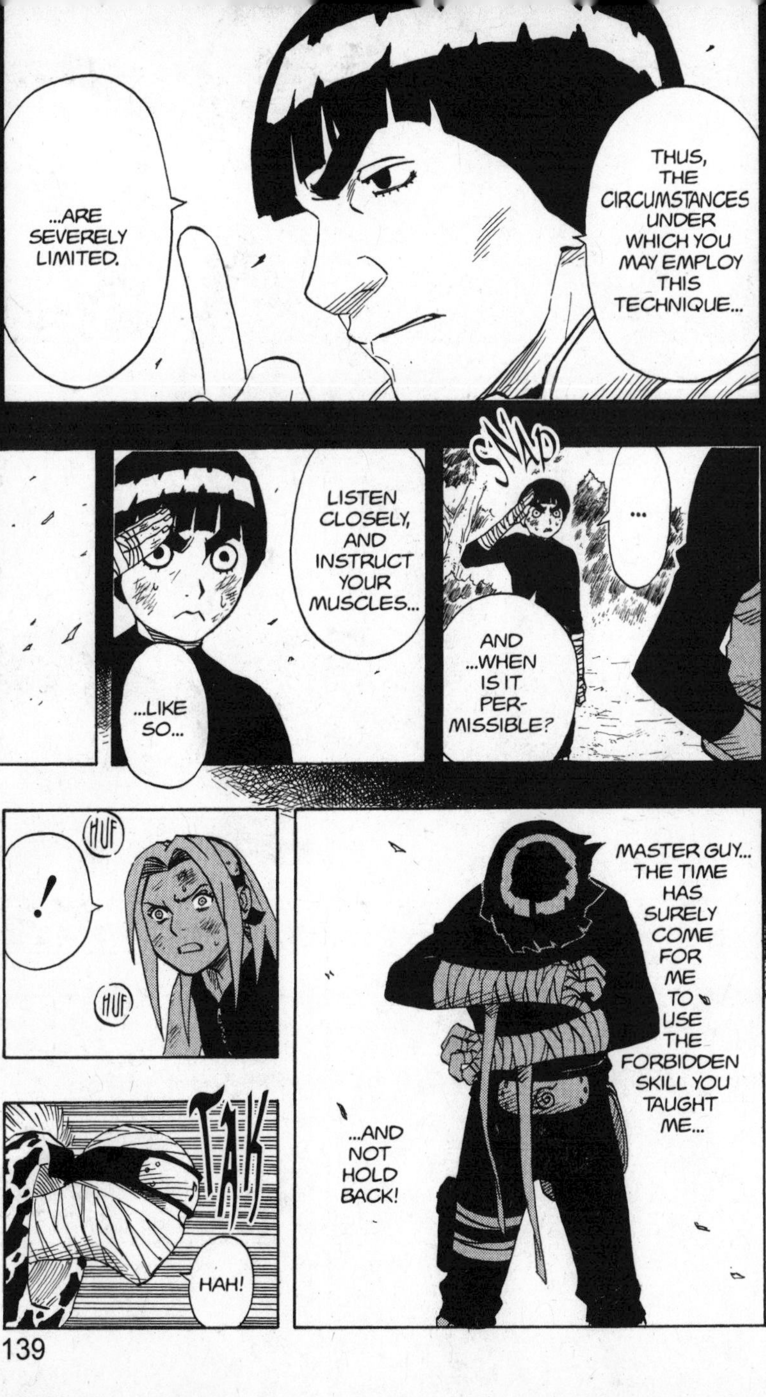
THUS, THE CIRCUMSTANCES UNDER WHICH YOU MAY EMPLOY THIS TECHNIQUE...
...ARE SEVERELY LIMITED.
SNAP
...
AND ...WHEN IS IT PER-MISSIBLE?
LISTEN CLOSELY, AND INSTRUCT YOUR MUSCLES...
...LIKE SO...
MASTER GUY... THE TIME HAS SURELY COME FOR ME TO USE THE FORBIDDEN SKILL YOU TAUGHT ME...
...AND NOT HOLD BACK!
HUF
!
HUF
TAK
HAH!

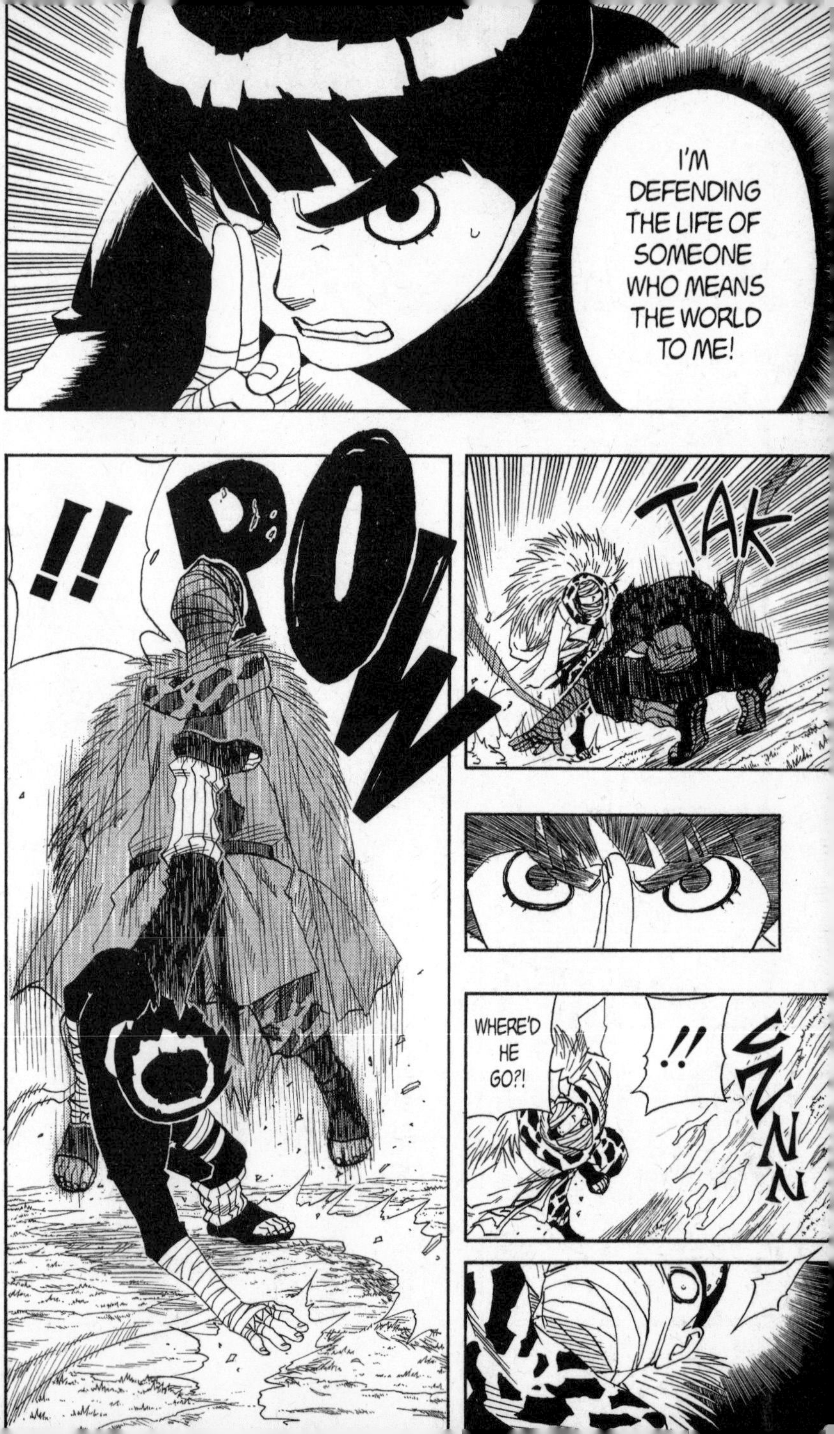
I'M DEFENDING THE LIFE OF SOMEONE WHO MEANS THE WORLD TO ME!
TAK
!!
POW
!!
WHERE'D HE GO?!
VNNN

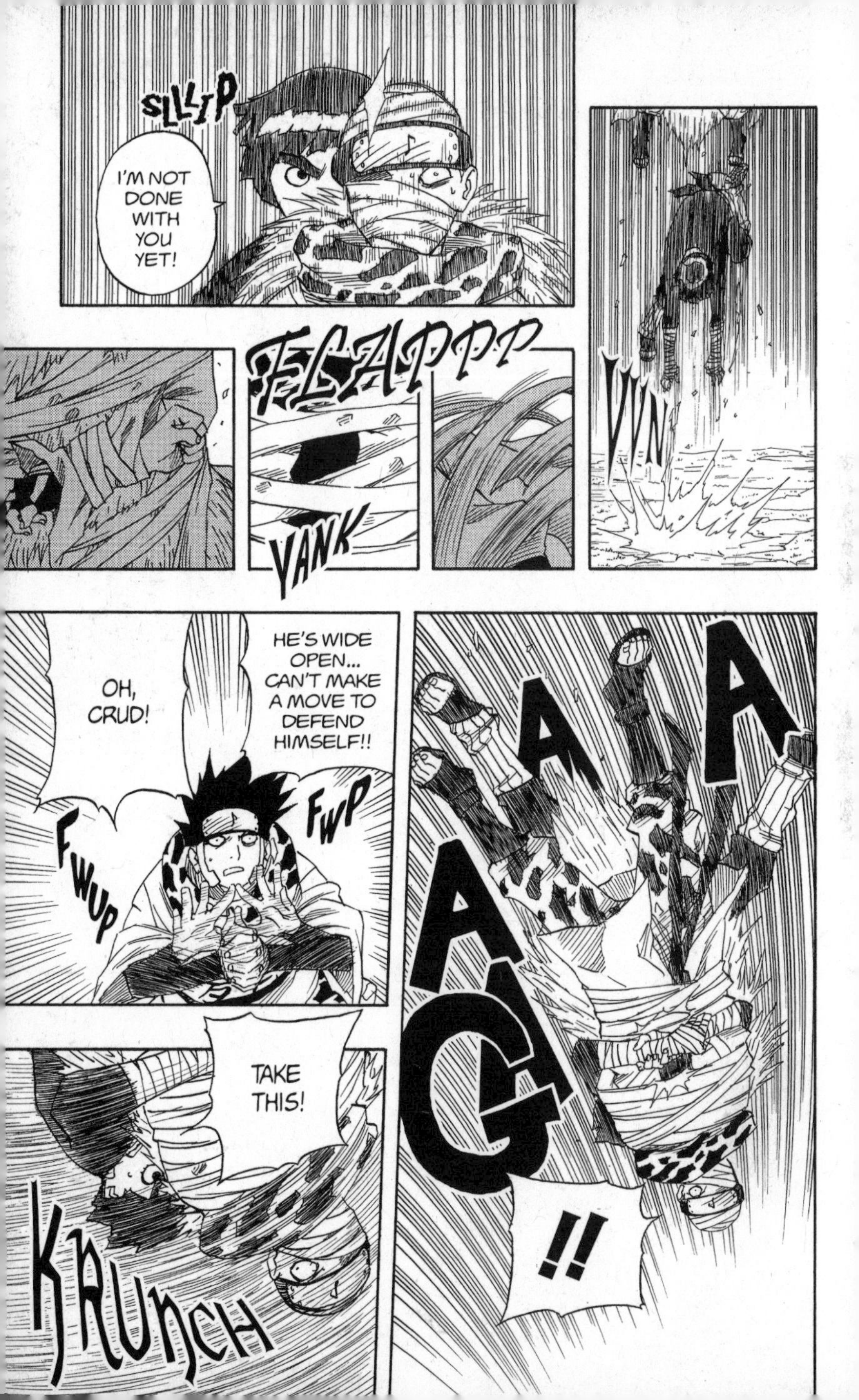
VVN
SLLLIP
I'M NOT DONE WITH YOU YET!
FLAPPP
YANK
HE'S WIDE OPEN... CAN'T MAKE A MOVE TO DEFEND HIMSELF!!
OH, CRUD!
FWP
FWUP
AAAG!!
TAKE THIS!
KRUNCH

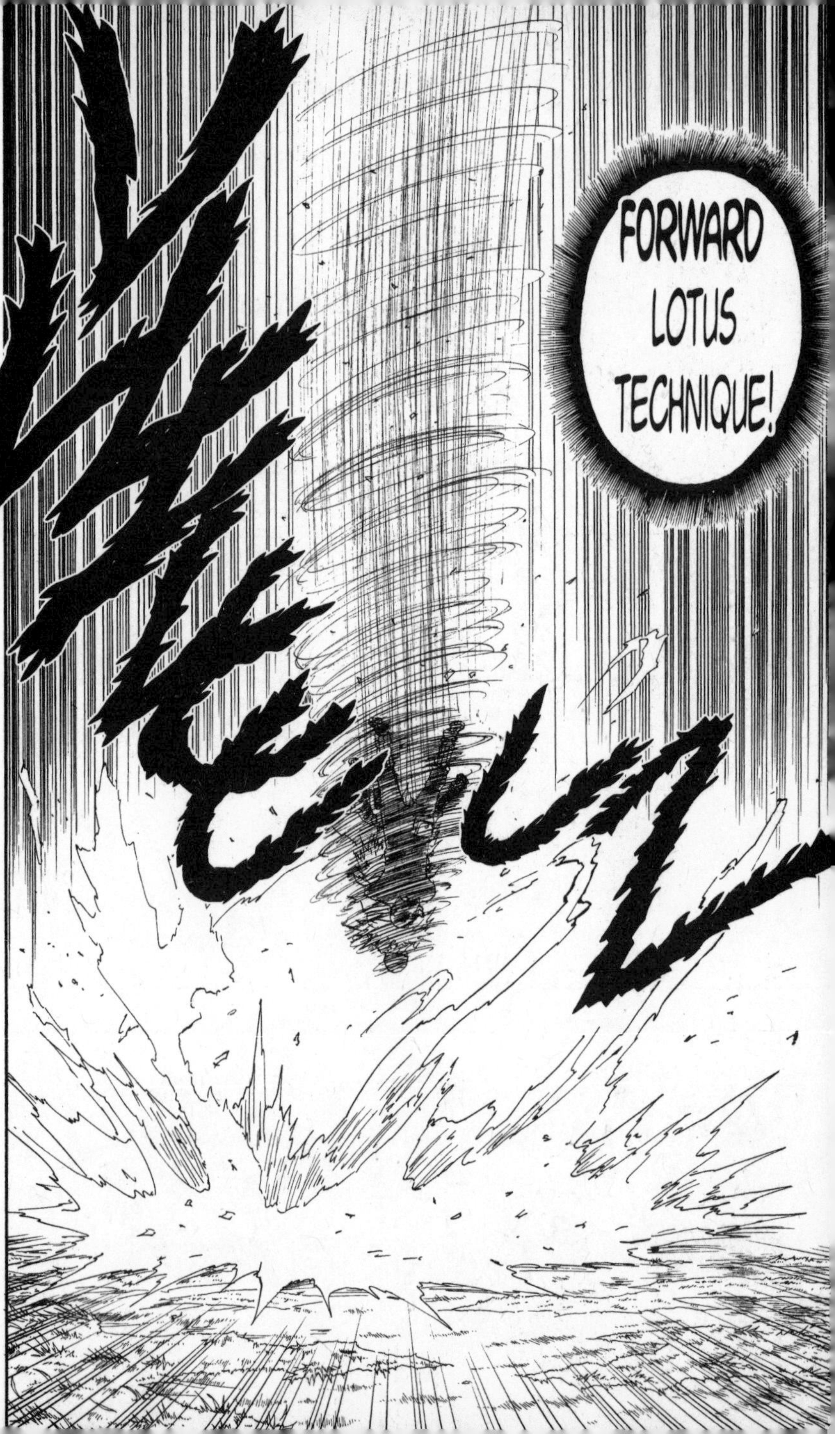
FORWARD LOTUS TECHNIQUE!

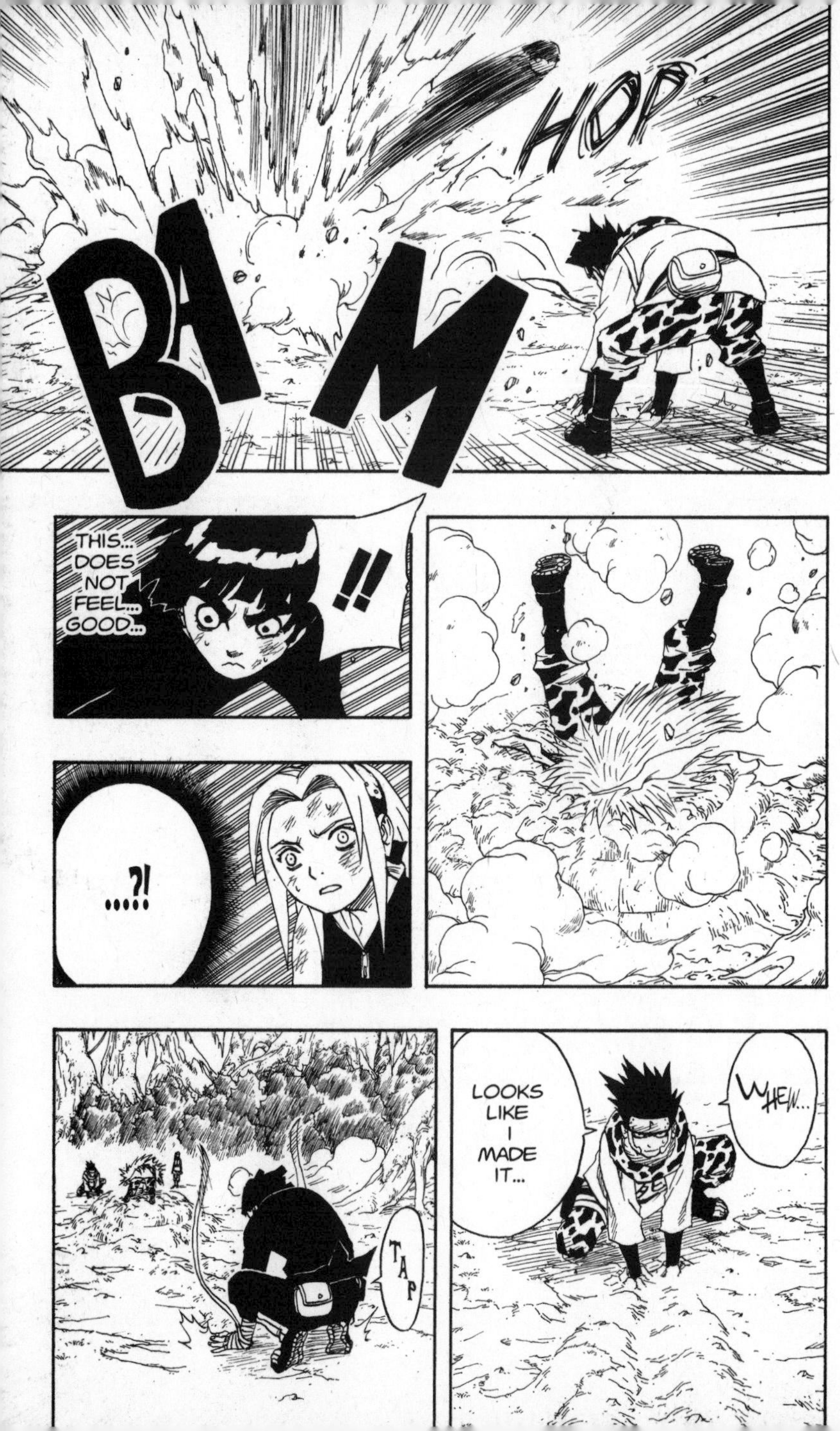
HOP
BAM
!!
THIS... DOES NOT FEEL... GOOD...
...?!
WHEW...
LOOKS LIKE I MADE IT...
TAP

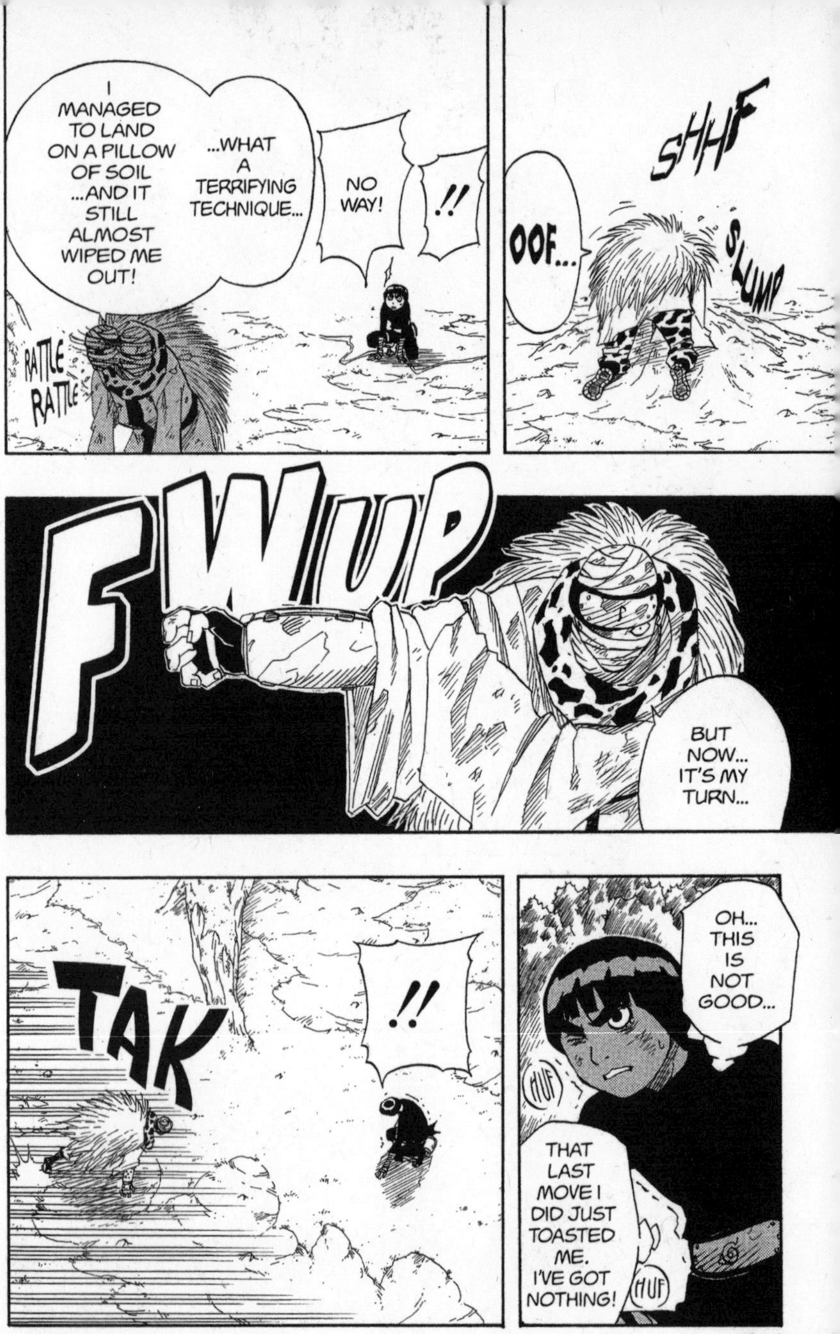
SHHF
OOF...
SLUMP
!!
NO WAY!
...WHAT A TERRIFYING TECHNIQUE...
I MANAGED TO LAND ON A PILLOW OF SOIL ...AND IT STILL ALMOST WIPED ME OUT!
RATTLE RATTLE
BUT NOW... IT'S MY TURN...
FWUP
OH... THIS IS NOT GOOD...
HUF
THAT LAST MOVE I DID JUST TOASTED ME. I'VE GOT NOTHING!
HUF
!!
TAK

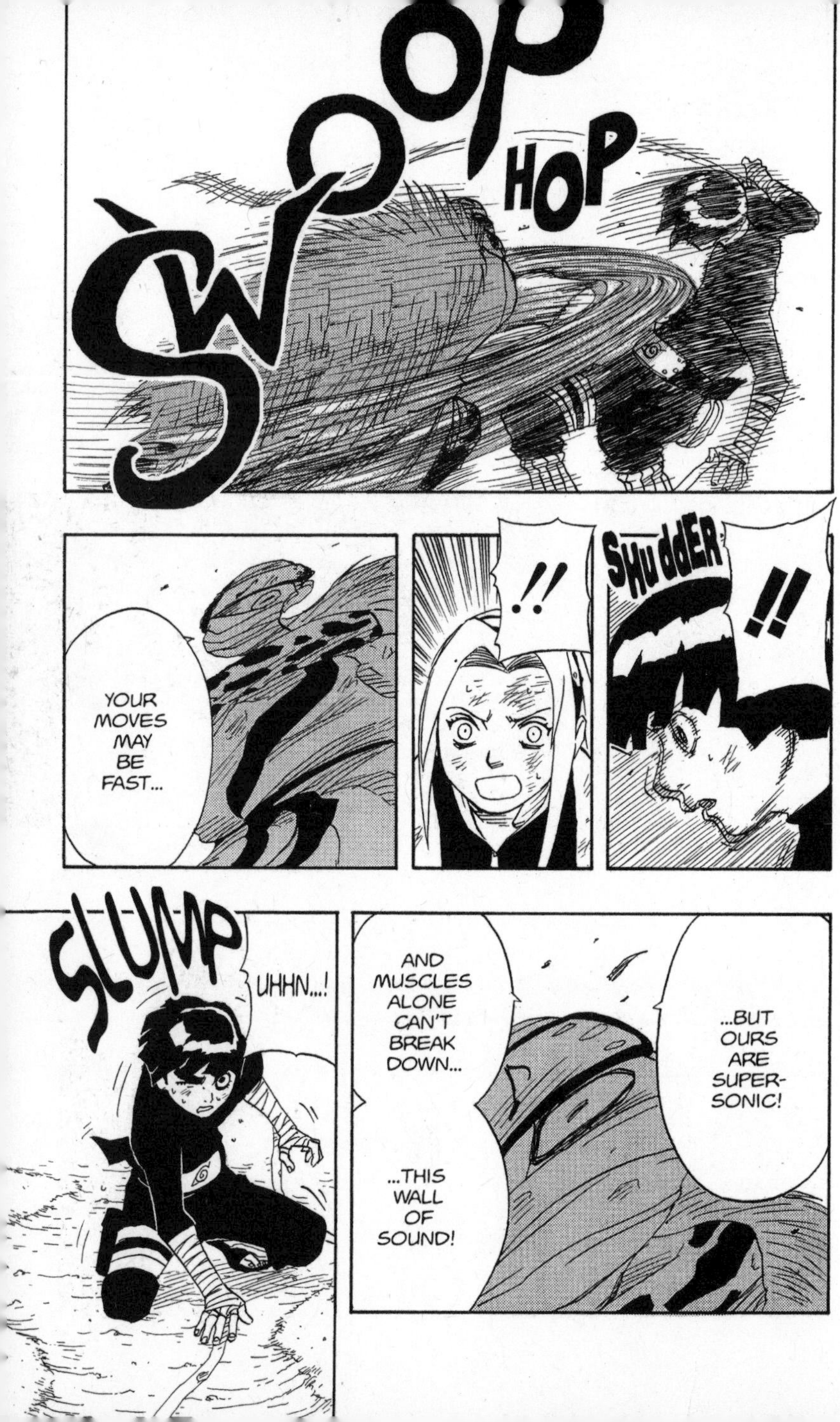
SWOOP
HOP
SHUDDER
!!
!!
YOUR MOVES MAY BE FAST...
...BUT OURS ARE SUPER-SONIC!
AND MUSCLES ALONE CAN'T BREAK DOWN...
...THIS WALL OF SOUND!
SLUMP
UHHN...!

MEET KISHIMOTO MASASHI'S ASSISTANTS
PART FOUR
ASSISTANT NO. 4: KAWAHARA TAKEMI

PROFILE

° A TOTAL PERVERT
° BLABBERMOUTH
° A NATIVE OF KANSAI WITH A GREAT SENSE
  OF HUMOR. (HIS OLDER BROTHER IS ALSO
  QUITE A JOKER. I'VE FALLEN FOR HIS PRANKS
  AT LEAST TWICE.)
° LOVES AMERICAN AND EUROPEAN-TYPE MUSIC.
° A TOYS"R"US KID AND A STAR CHILD.
° A REAL RAY OF SUNSHINE, HE BRIGHTENS
  UP THE MOOD IN THE OFFICE.

IN TERMS OF JOBS, HE'S AN ALL-AROUND
MASTER OF ANYTHING AND EVERYTHING.

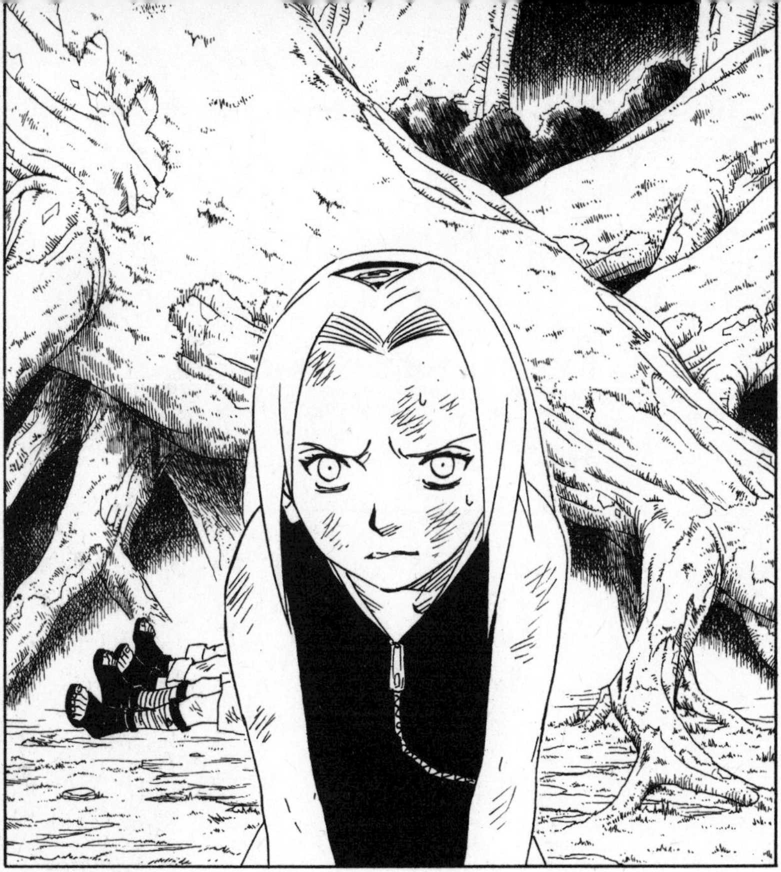

Number 53:

Sakura's Decision!!

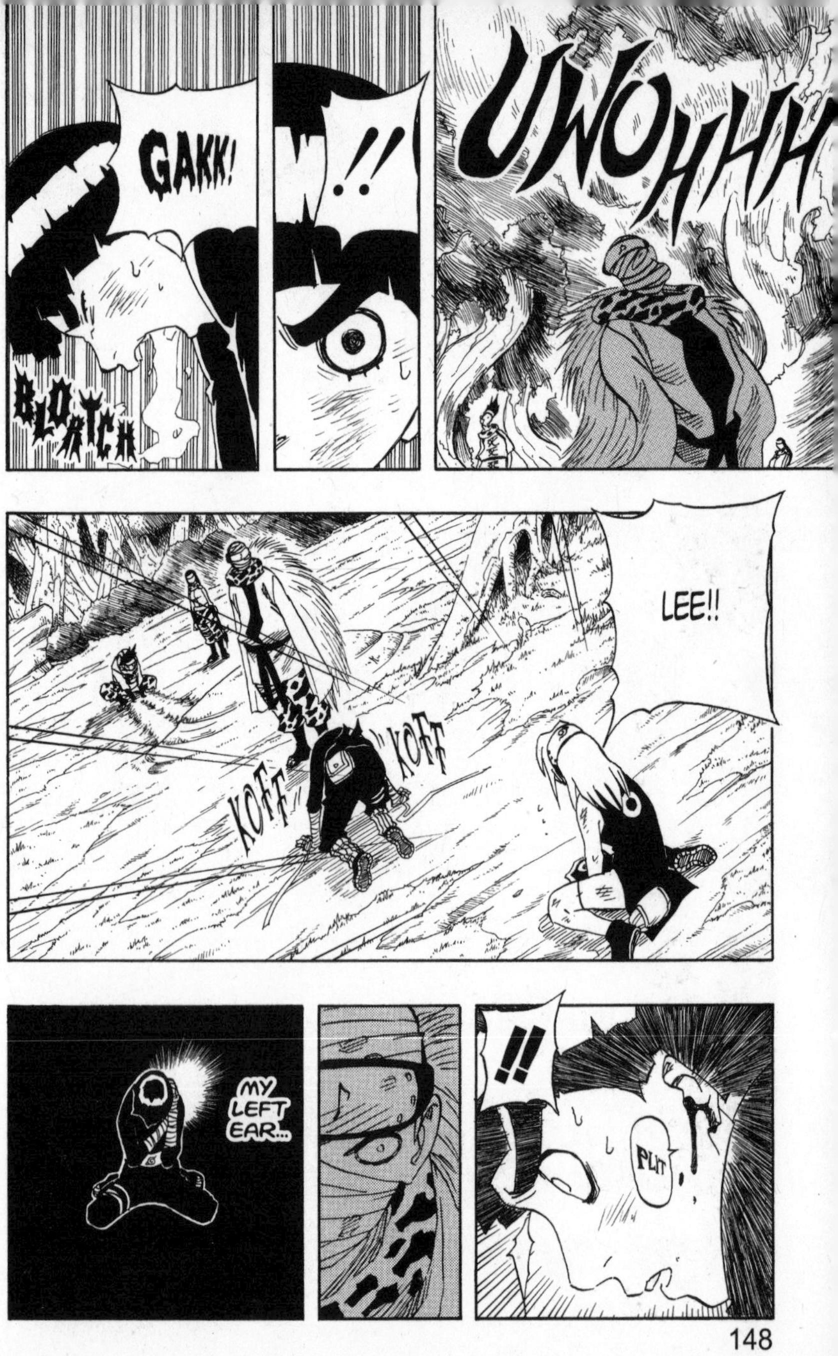
UWOHHH
!!
GAKK!
BLORTCH
LEE!!
KOFF
KOFF
!!
PLIT
MY LEFT EAR...

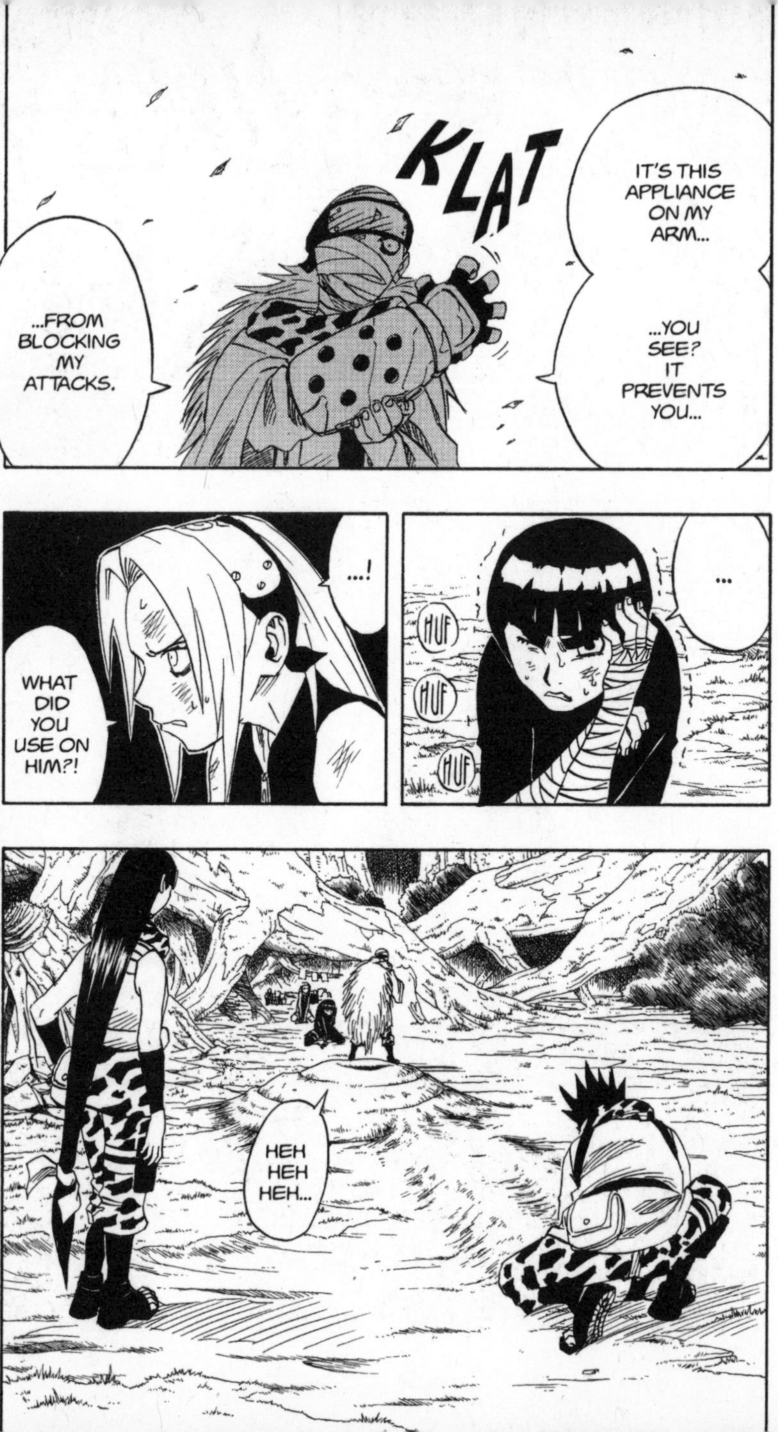
IT'S THIS APPLIANCE ON MY ARM...
KLAT
...YOU SEE? IT PREVENTS YOU...
...FROM BLOCKING MY ATTACKS.
...
HUF
HUF
HUF
...!
WHAT DID YOU USE ON HIM?!
HEH HEH HEH...

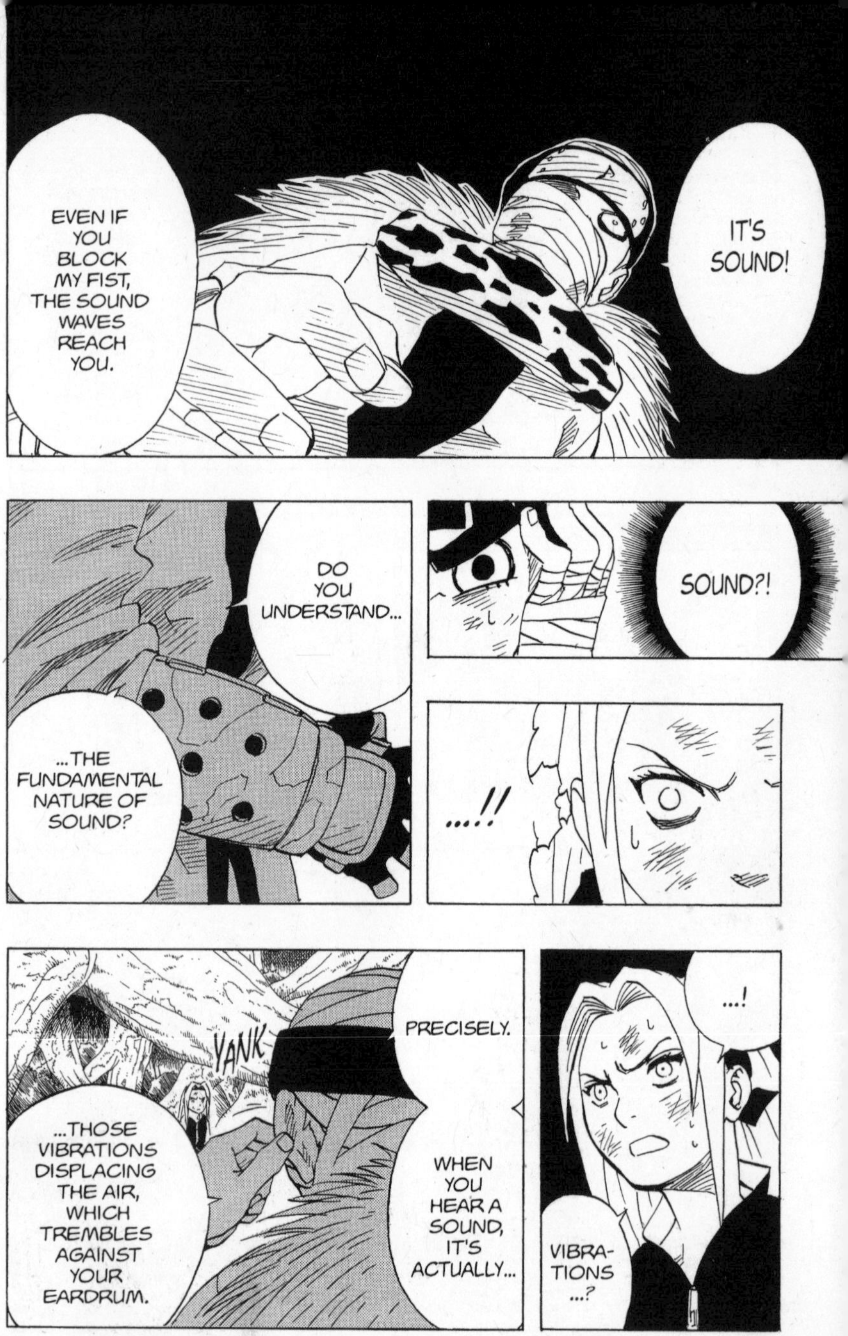
IT'S SOUND!
EVEN IF YOU BLOCK MY FIST, THE SOUND WAVES REACH YOU.
SOUND?!
...!!
DO YOU UNDERSTAND...
...THE FUNDAMENTAL NATURE OF SOUND?
...!
VIBRATIONS...?
PRECISELY.
WHEN YOU HEAR A SOUND, IT'S ACTUALLY...
YANK
...THOSE VIBRATIONS DISPLACING THE AIR, WHICH TREMBLES AGAINST YOUR EARDRUM.

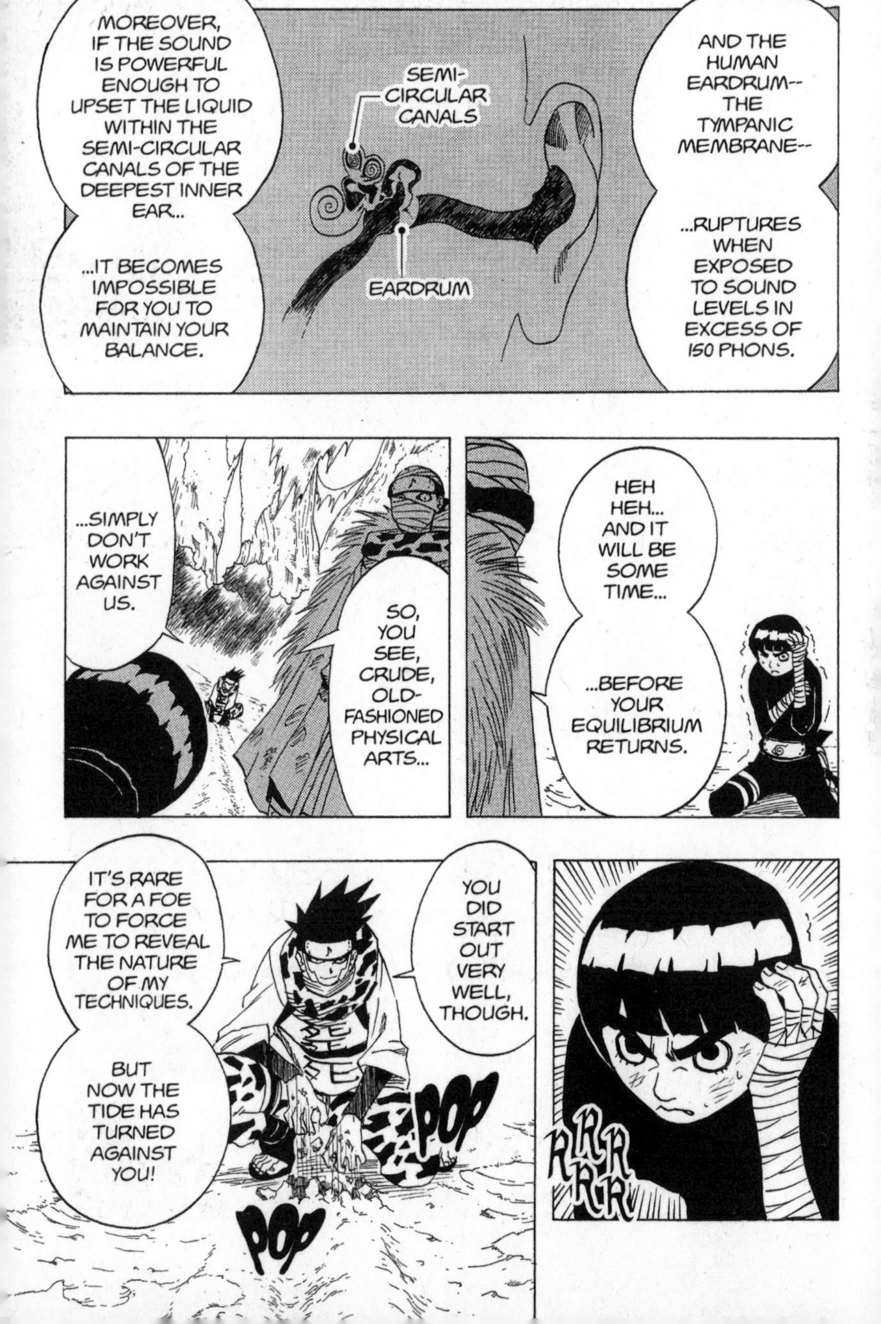
AND THE HUMAN EARDRUM-- THE TYMPANIC MEMBRANE--
...RUPTURES WHEN EXPOSED TO SOUND LEVELS IN EXCESS OF 150 PHONS.
SEMI-CIRCULAR CANALS
EARDRUM
MOREOVER, IF THE SOUND IS POWERFUL ENOUGH TO UPSET THE LIQUID WITHIN THE SEMI-CIRCULAR CANALS OF THE DEEPEST INNER EAR...
...IT BECOMES IMPOSSIBLE FOR YOU TO MAINTAIN YOUR BALANCE.
HEH HEH... AND IT WILL BE SOME TIME...
...BEFORE YOUR EQUILIBRIUM RETURNS.
SO, YOU SEE, CRUDE, OLD-FASHIONED PHYSICAL ARTS...
...SIMPLY DON'T WORK AGAINST US.
RRRRRR
YOU DID START OUT VERY WELL, THOUGH.
IT'S RARE FOR A FOE TO FORCE ME TO REVEAL THE NATURE OF MY TECHNIQUES.
BUT NOW THE TIDE HAS TURNED AGAINST YOU!
POP
POP

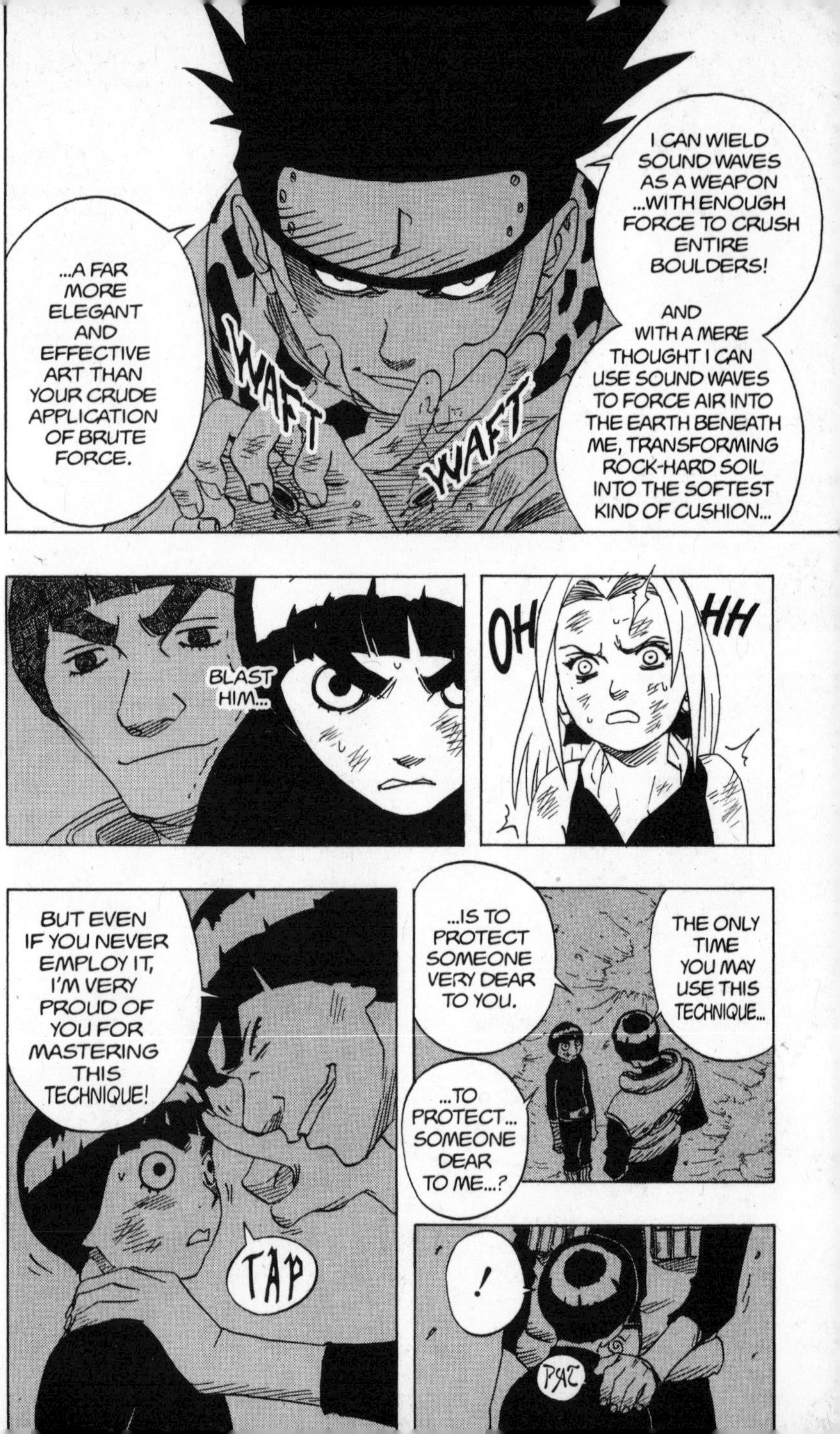
I CAN WIELD SOUND WAVES AS A WEAPON ...WITH ENOUGH FORCE TO CRUSH ENTIRE BOULDERS!
AND WITH A MERE THOUGHT I CAN USE SOUND WAVES TO FORCE AIR INTO THE EARTH BENEATH ME, TRANSFORMING ROCK-HARD SOIL INTO THE SOFTEST KIND OF CUSHION...
WAFT
WAFT
...A FAR MORE ELEGANT AND EFFECTIVE ART THAN YOUR CRUDE APPLICATION OF BRUTE FORCE.
OHHH
BLAST HIM...
THE ONLY TIME YOU MAY USE THIS TECHNIQUE...
...IS TO PROTECT SOMEONE VERY DEAR TO YOU.
...TO PROTECT... SOMEONE DEAR TO ME...?
!
PAT
BUT EVEN IF YOU NEVER EMPLOY IT, I'M VERY PROUD OF YOU FOR MASTERING THIS TECHNIQUE!
TAP

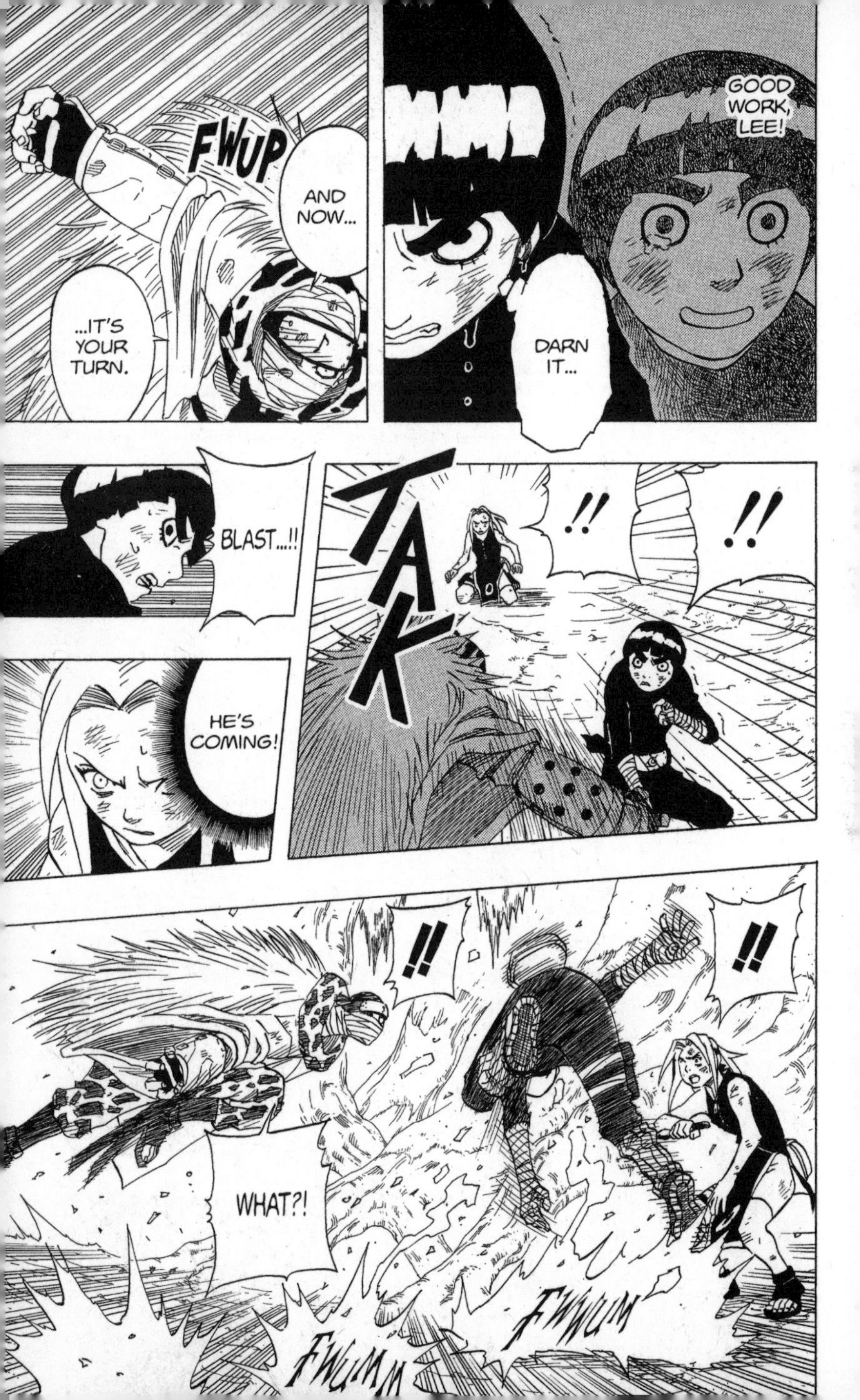
GOOD WORK, LEE!
DARN IT...
AND NOW...
FWUP
...IT'S YOUR TURN.
!!
!!
TAK
BLAST...!!
HE'S COMING!
!!
!!
WHAT?!
FWUMM
FWUMM

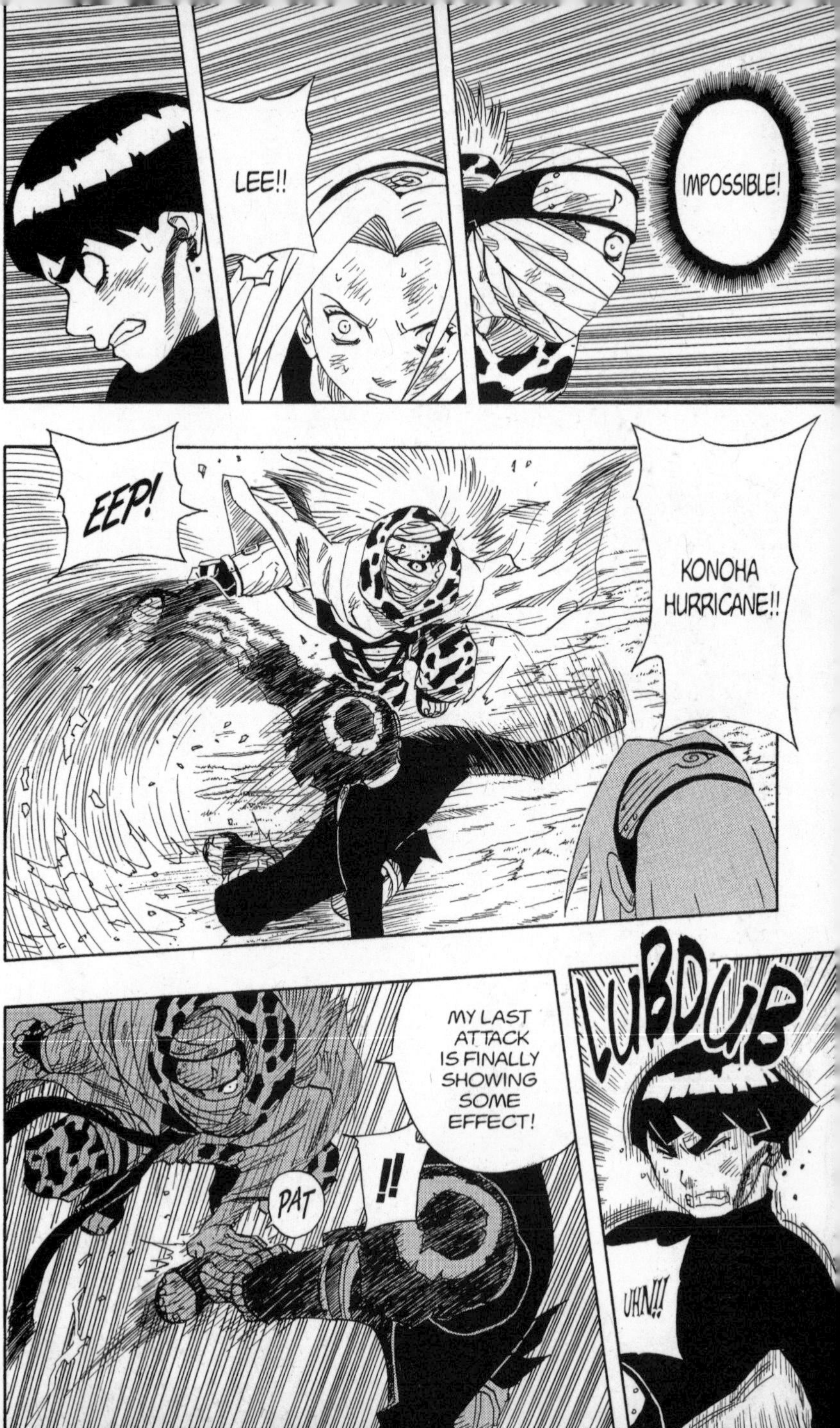
IMPOSSIBLE!
LEE!!
KONOHA HURRICANE!!
EEP!
LUBDUB
UHN!!
MY LAST ATTACK IS FINALLY SHOWING SOME EFFECT!
!!
PAT

READ THIS WAY

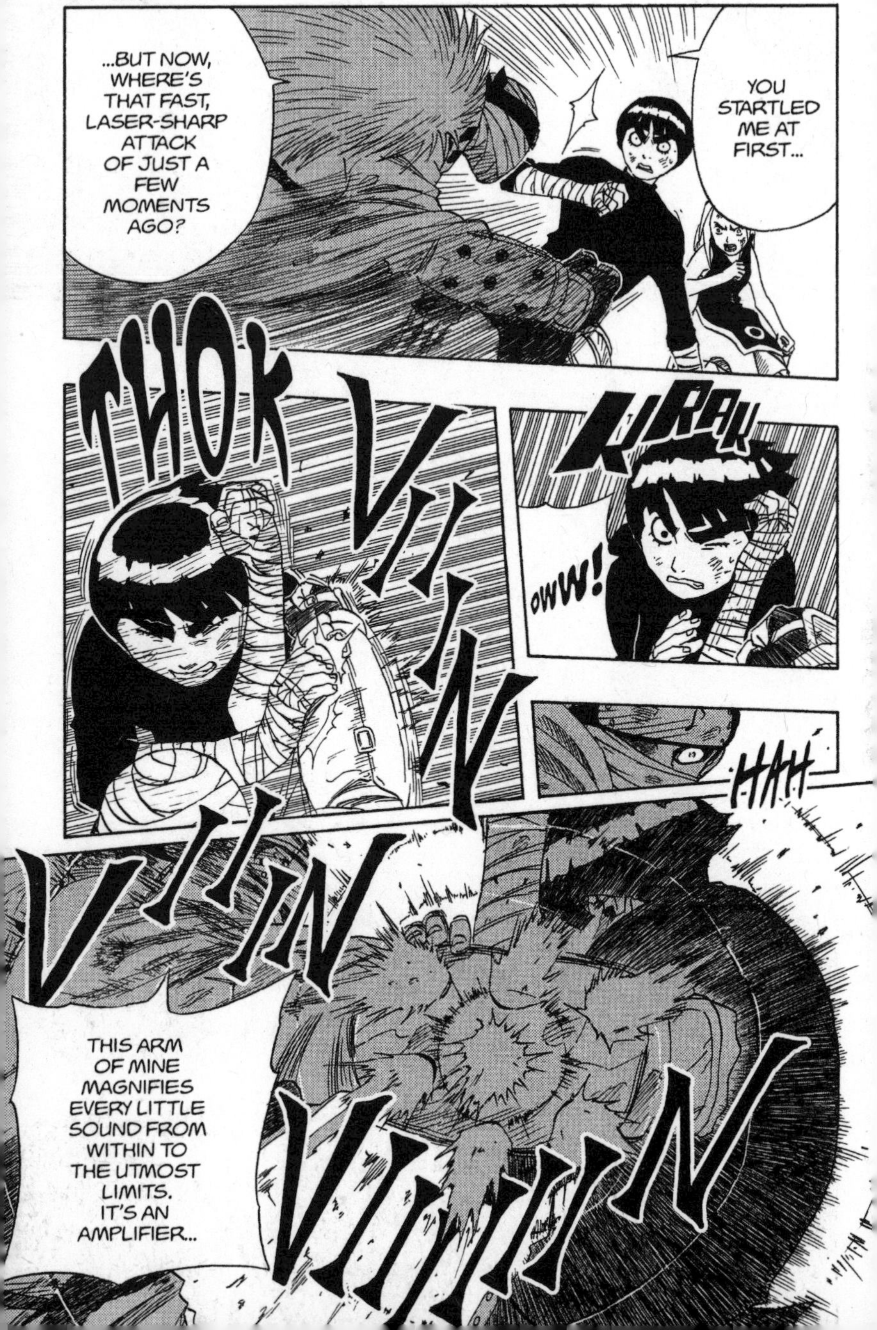
YOU STARTLED ME AT FIRST...
...BUT NOW, WHERE'S THAT FAST, LASER-SHARP ATTACK OF JUST A FEW MOMENTS AGO?
KRAK
OWW!
HAH
THOK
VIIN
VIIIN
THIS ARM OF MINE MAGNIFIES EVERY LITTLE SOUND FROM WITHIN TO THE UTMOST LIMITS. IT'S AN AMPLIFIER...
VIIIIN

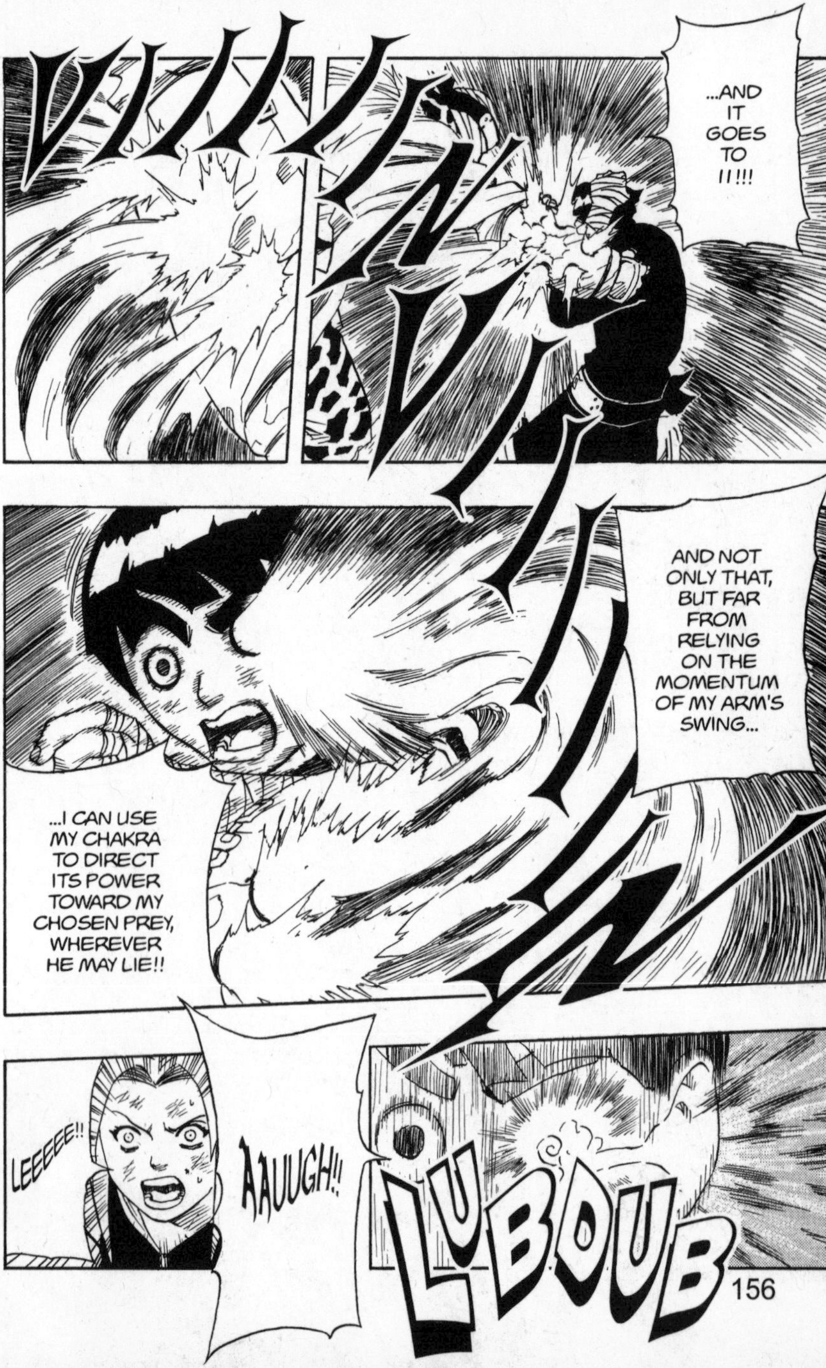
...AND IT GOES TO 11!!!
VIIIINVIIIIIN
AND NOT ONLY THAT, BUT FAR FROM RELYING ON THE MOMENTUM OF MY ARM'S SWING...
...I CAN USE MY CHAKRA TO DIRECT ITS POWER TOWARD MY CHOSEN PREY, WHEREVER HE MAY LIE!!
LUBDOUB
AAUUGH!!
LEEEEE!!

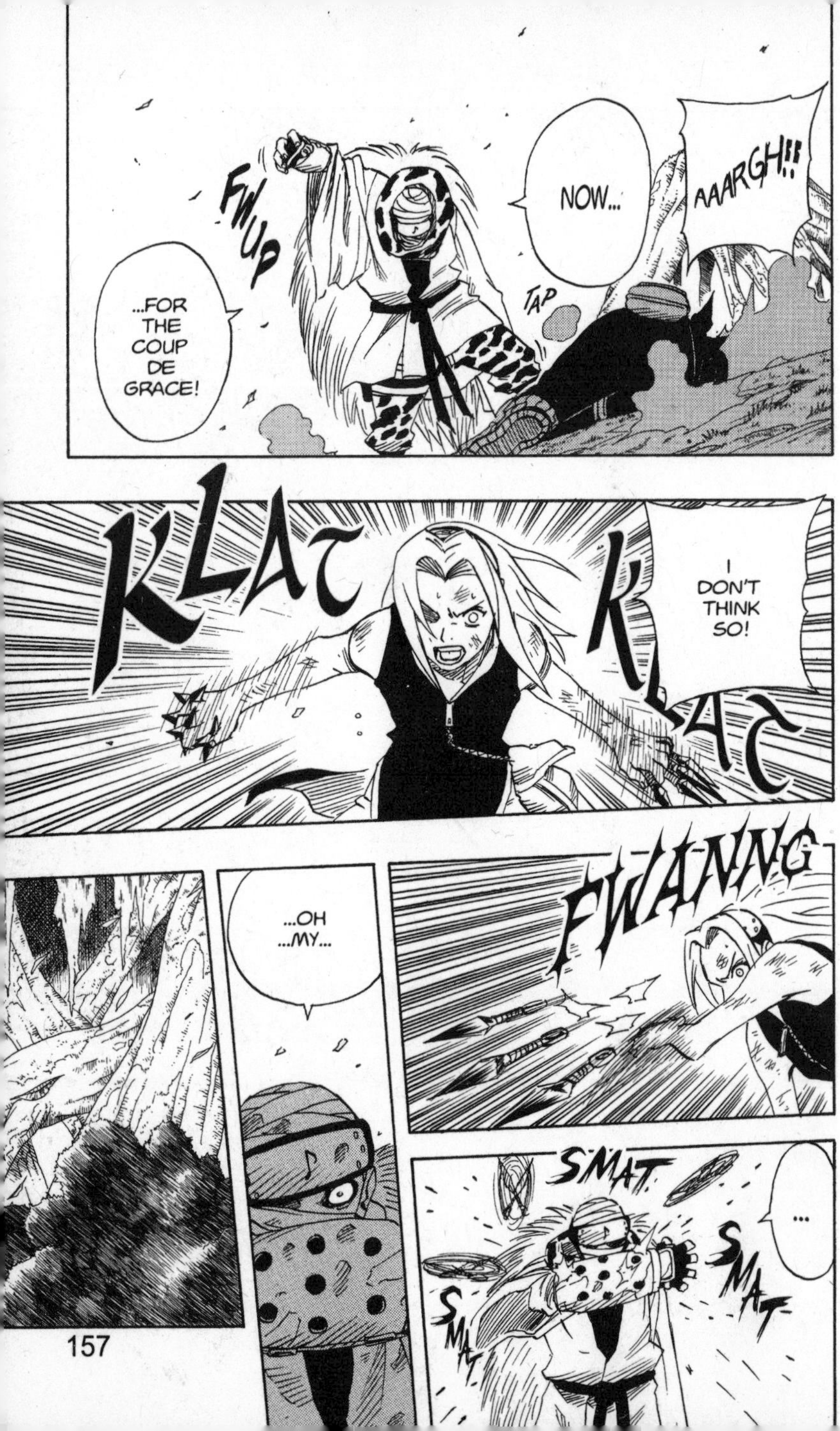
AAARGH!!
NOW...
FWUP
TAP
...FOR THE COUP DE GRACE!
I DON'T THINK SO!
KLAT
KLAT
FWANNG
...
SMAT
SMAT
SMAT
...OH ...MY...

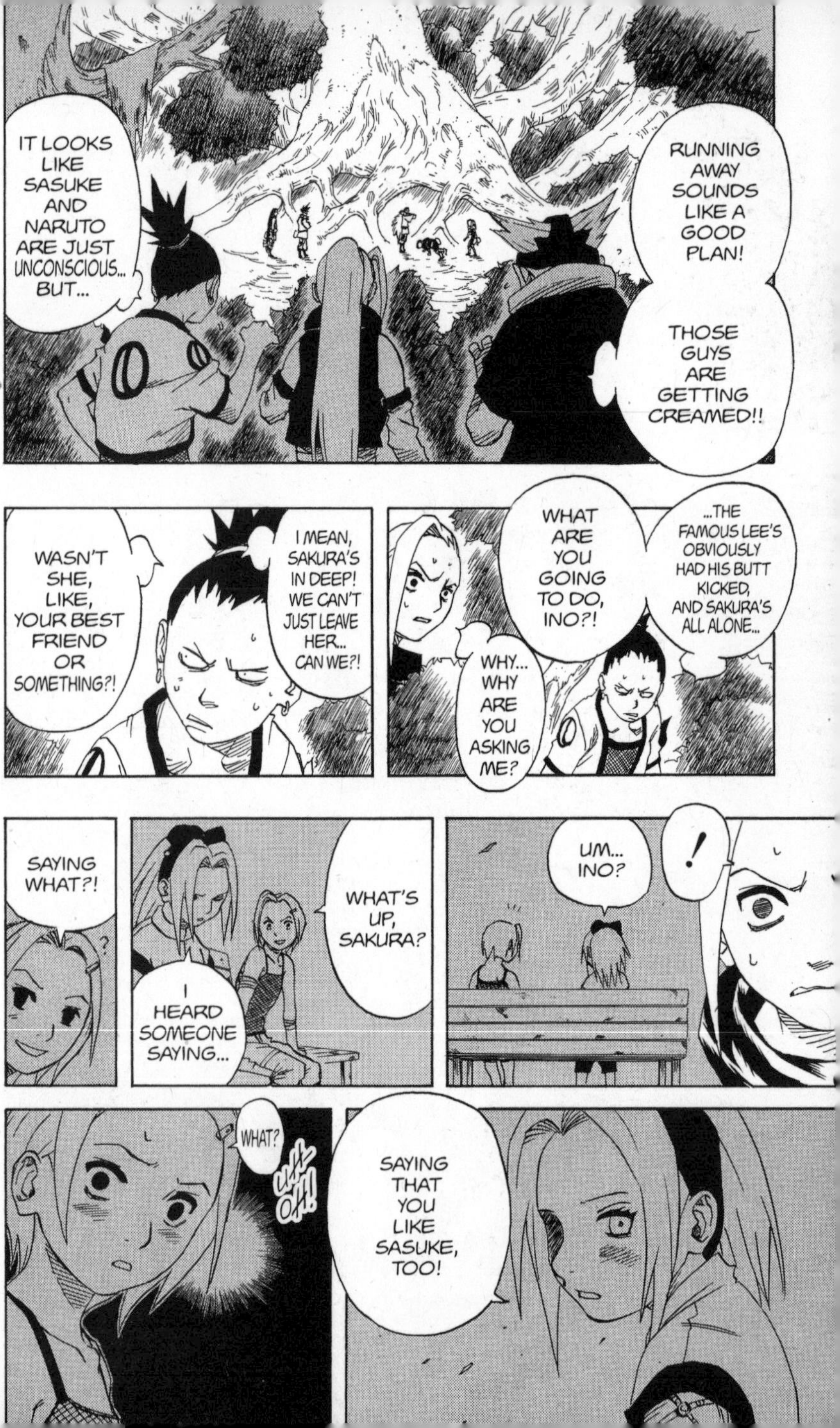
RUNNING AWAY SOUNDS LIKE A GOOD PLAN!
THOSE GUYS ARE GETTING CREAMED!!
IT LOOKS LIKE SASUKE AND NARUTO ARE JUST UNCONSCIOUS... BUT...
...THE FAMOUS LEE'S OBVIOUSLY HAD HIS BUTT KICKED, AND SAKURA'S ALL ALONE...
WHAT ARE YOU GOING TO DO, INO?!
WHY... WHY ARE YOU ASKING ME?
I MEAN, SAKURA'S IN DEEP! WE CAN'T JUST LEAVE HER... CAN WE?!
WASN'T SHE, LIKE, YOUR BEST FRIEND OR SOMETHING?!
!
UM... INO?
WHAT'S UP, SAKURA?
I HEARD SOMEONE SAYING...
SAYING WHAT?!
SAYING THAT YOU LIKE SASUKE, TOO!
WHAT?
UH OH!

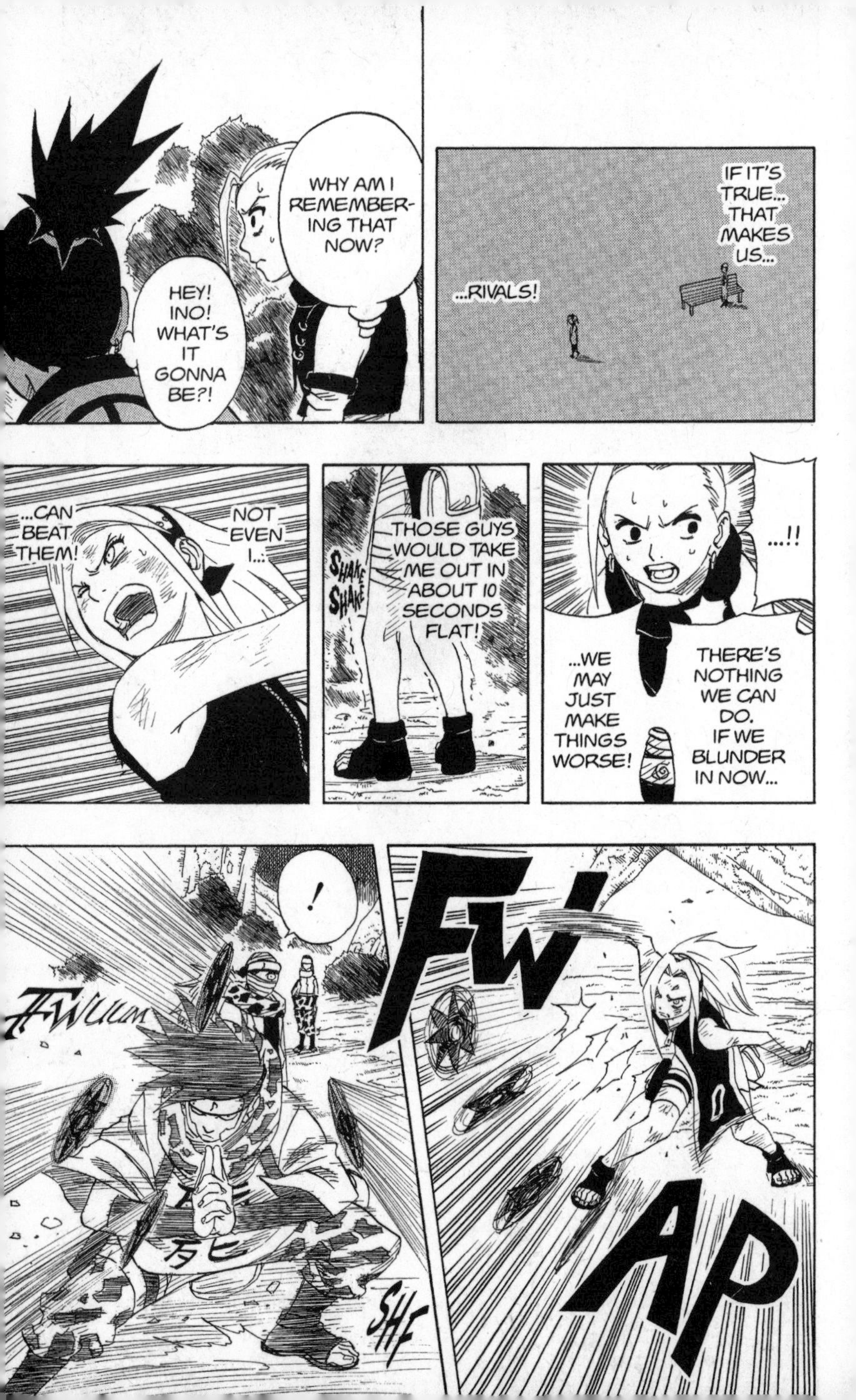
IF IT'S TRUE... THAT MAKES US...
...RIVALS!
WHY AM I REMEMBER-ING THAT NOW?
HEY! INO! WHAT'S IT GONNA BE?!
...!!
THERE'S NOTHING WE CAN DO. IF WE BLUNDER IN NOW...
...WE MAY JUST MAKE THINGS WORSE!
THOSE GUYS WOULD TAKE ME OUT IN ABOUT 10 SECONDS FLAT!
SHAKE SHAKE
NOT EVEN I...
...CAN BEAT THEM!
FWAP
SHF
!
FWUUM

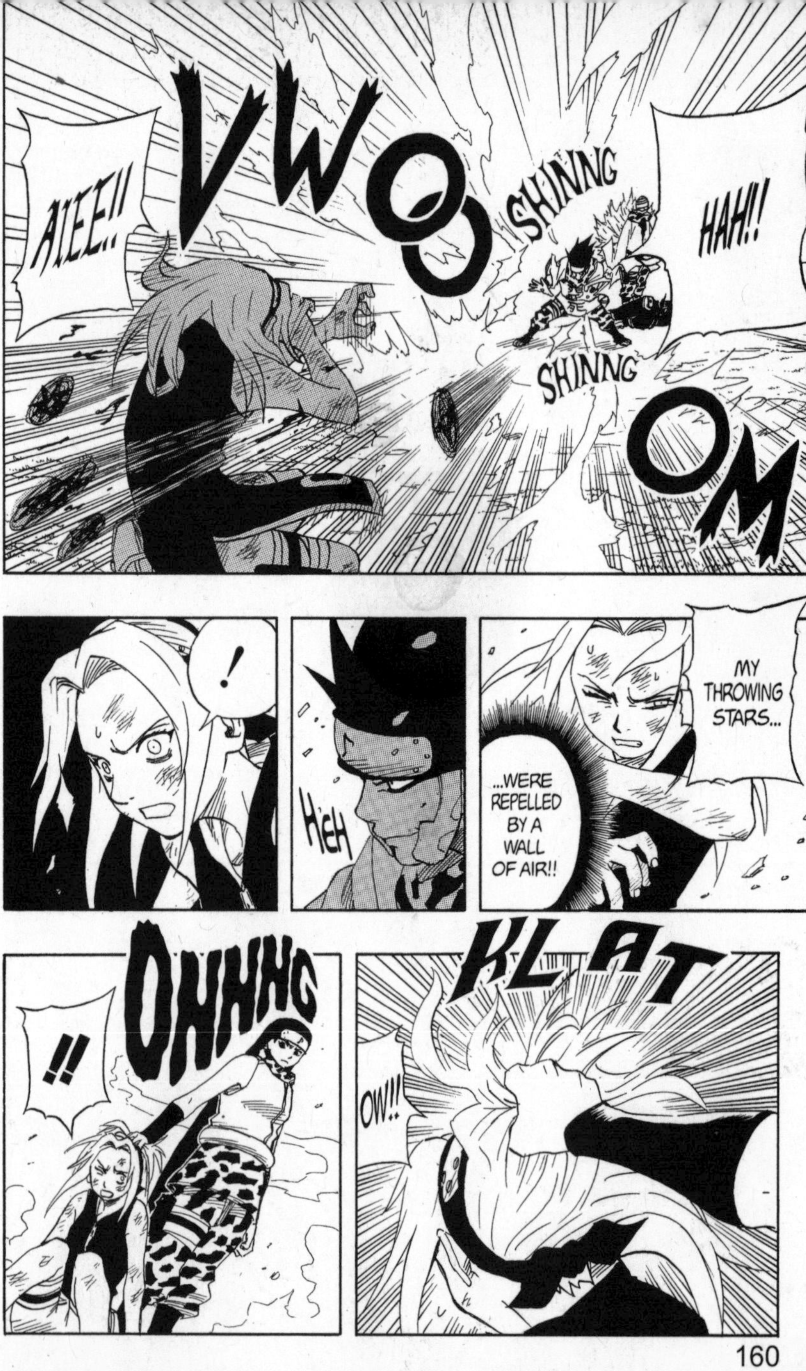
HAH!!
SHINNG
SHINNG
VWOOOM
AIEE!!
MY THROWING STARS...
...WERE REPELLED BY A WALL OF AIR!!
H'EH
!
KLAT
OW!!
OHHHG
!!

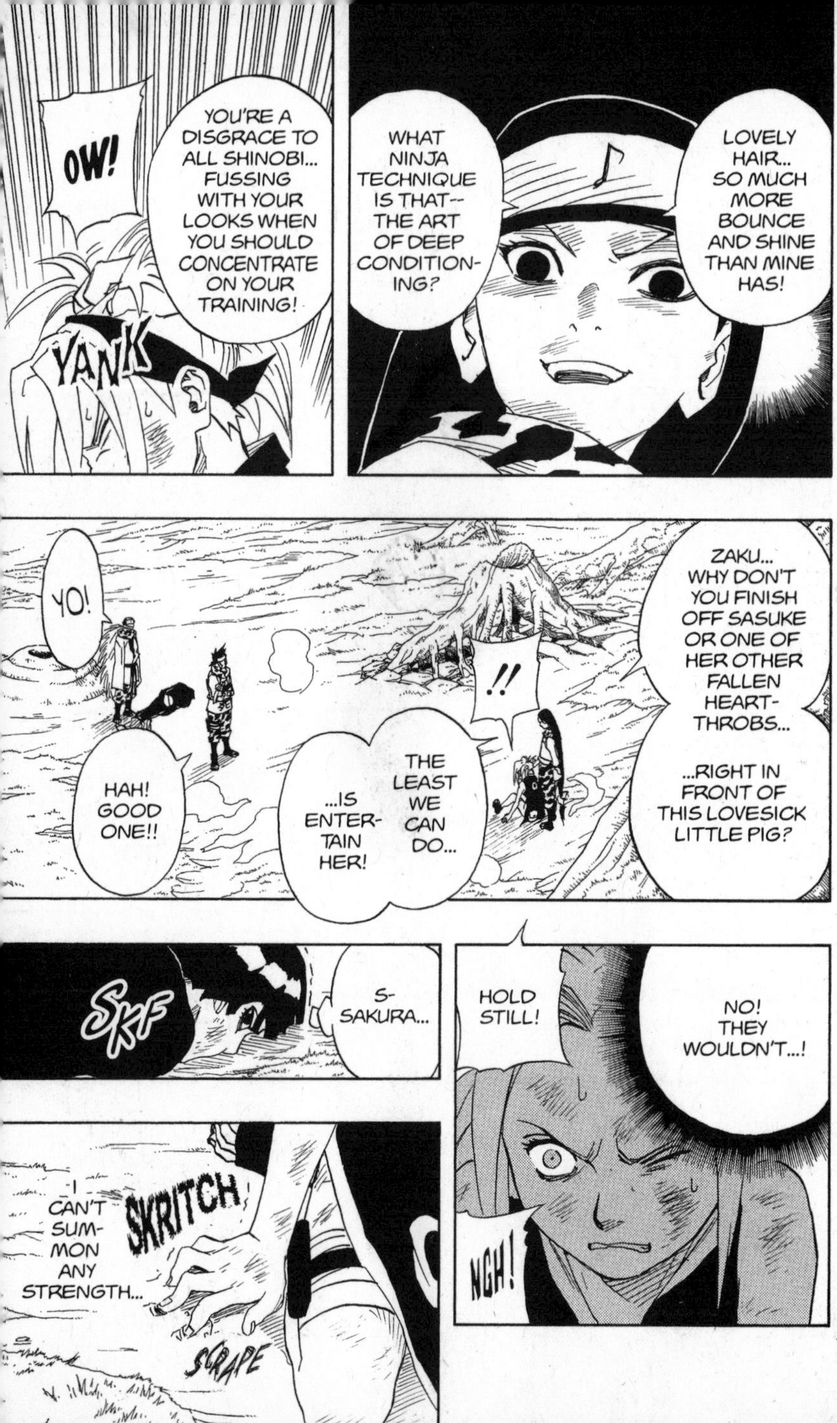
LOVELY HAIR... SO MUCH MORE BOUNCE AND SHINE THAN MINE HAS!
WHAT NINJA TECHNIQUE IS THAT-- THE ART OF DEEP CONDITIONING?
YOU'RE A DISGRACE TO ALL SHINOBI... FUSSING WITH YOUR LOOKS WHEN YOU SHOULD CONCENTRATE ON YOUR TRAINING!
OW!
YANK
ZAKU... WHY DON'T YOU FINISH OFF SASUKE OR ONE OF HER OTHER FALLEN HEART-THROBS...
...RIGHT IN FRONT OF THIS LOVESICK LITTLE PIG?
!!
THE LEAST WE CAN DO...
...IS ENTERTAIN HER!
YO!
HAH! GOOD ONE!!
NO! THEY WOULDN'T...!
HOLD STILL!
NGH!
S-SAKURA...
SKF
SKRITCH
I CAN'T SUMMON ANY STRENGTH...
SCRAPE

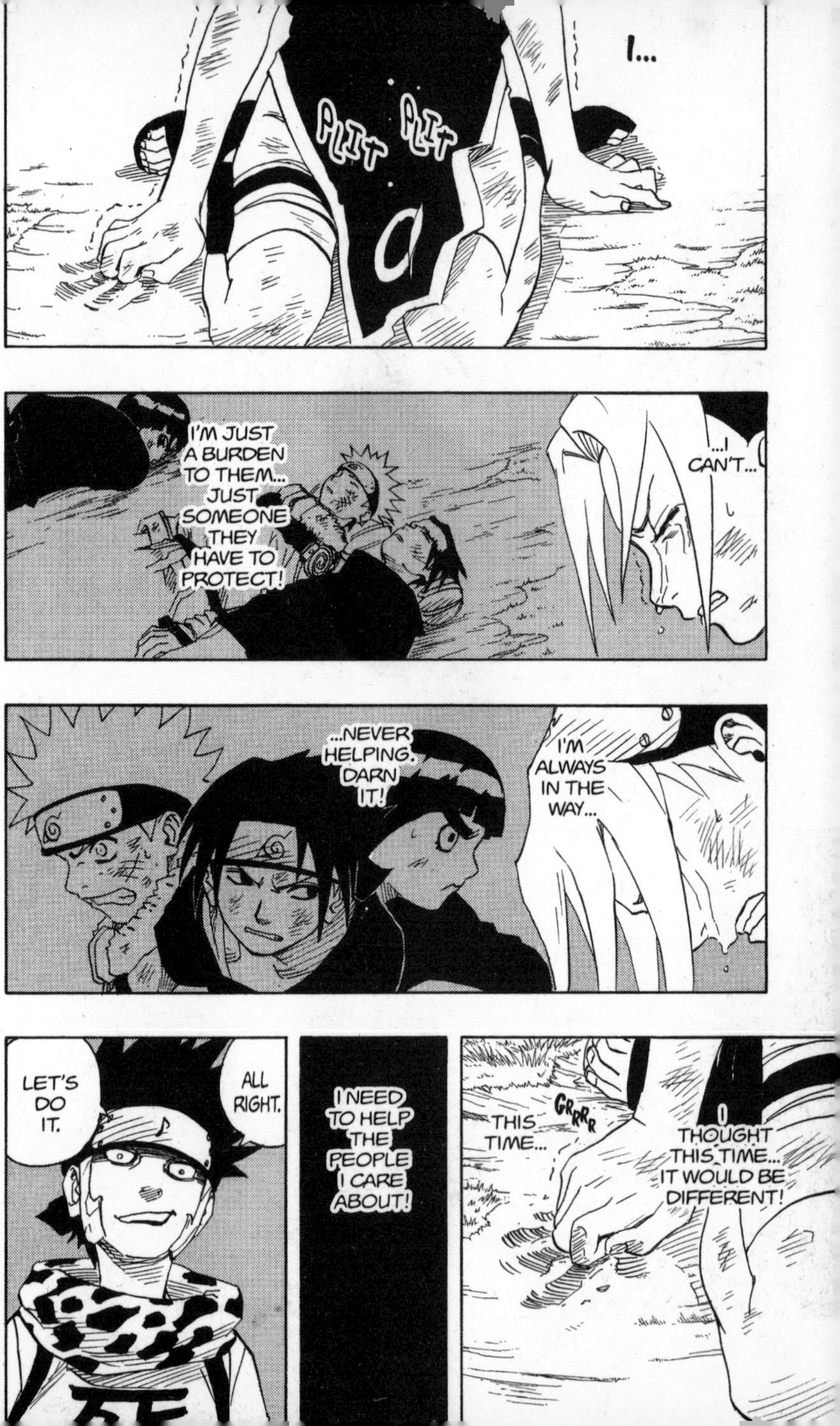
I...
PLIT PLIT
...I CAN'T...
I'M JUST A BURDEN TO THEM... JUST SOMEONE THEY HAVE TO PROTECT!
I'M ALWAYS IN THE WAY...
...NEVER HELPING. DARN IT!
I THOUGHT THIS TIME... IT WOULD BE DIFFERENT!
GRRRR
THIS TIME...
I NEED TO HELP THE PEOPLE I CARE ABOUT!
ALL RIGHT.
LET'S DO IT.

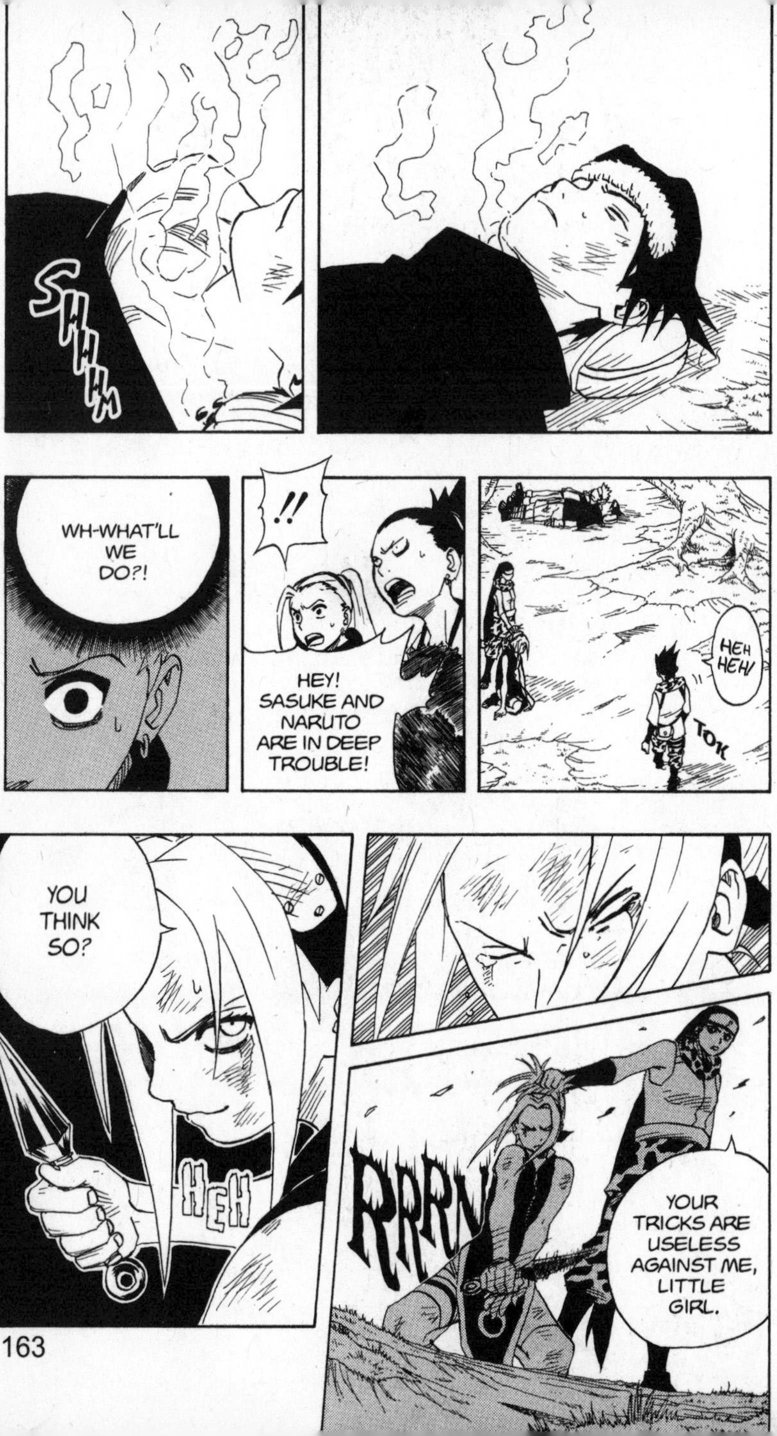
SHHHM
HEH HEH!
TOK
!!
HEY! SASUKE AND NARUTO ARE IN DEEP TROUBLE!
WH-WHAT'LL WE DO?!
RRRN
YOUR TRICKS ARE USELESS AGAINST ME, LITTLE GIRL.
YOU THINK SO?
HEH

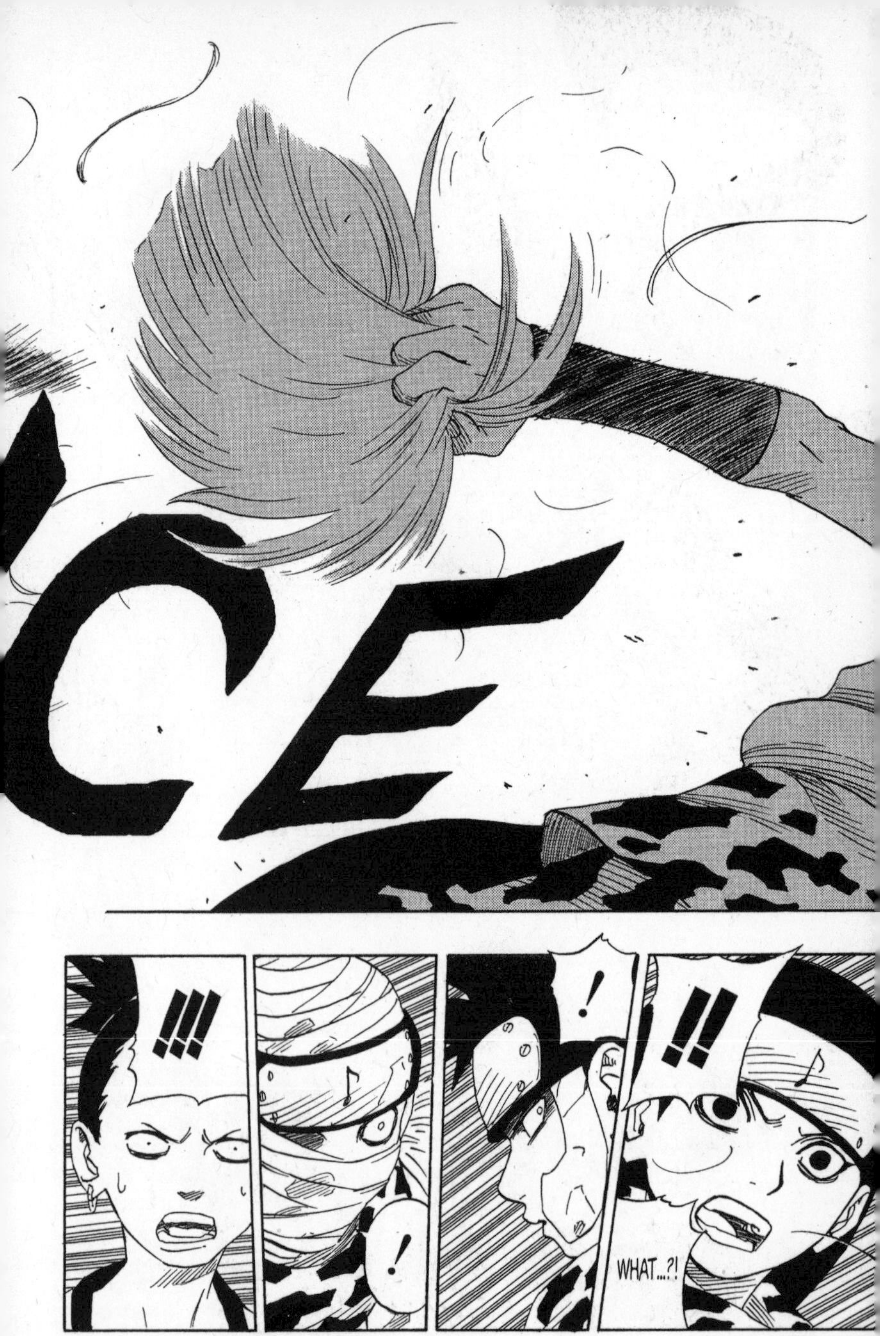
CE
!!
WHAT...?!
!
!
!!!!

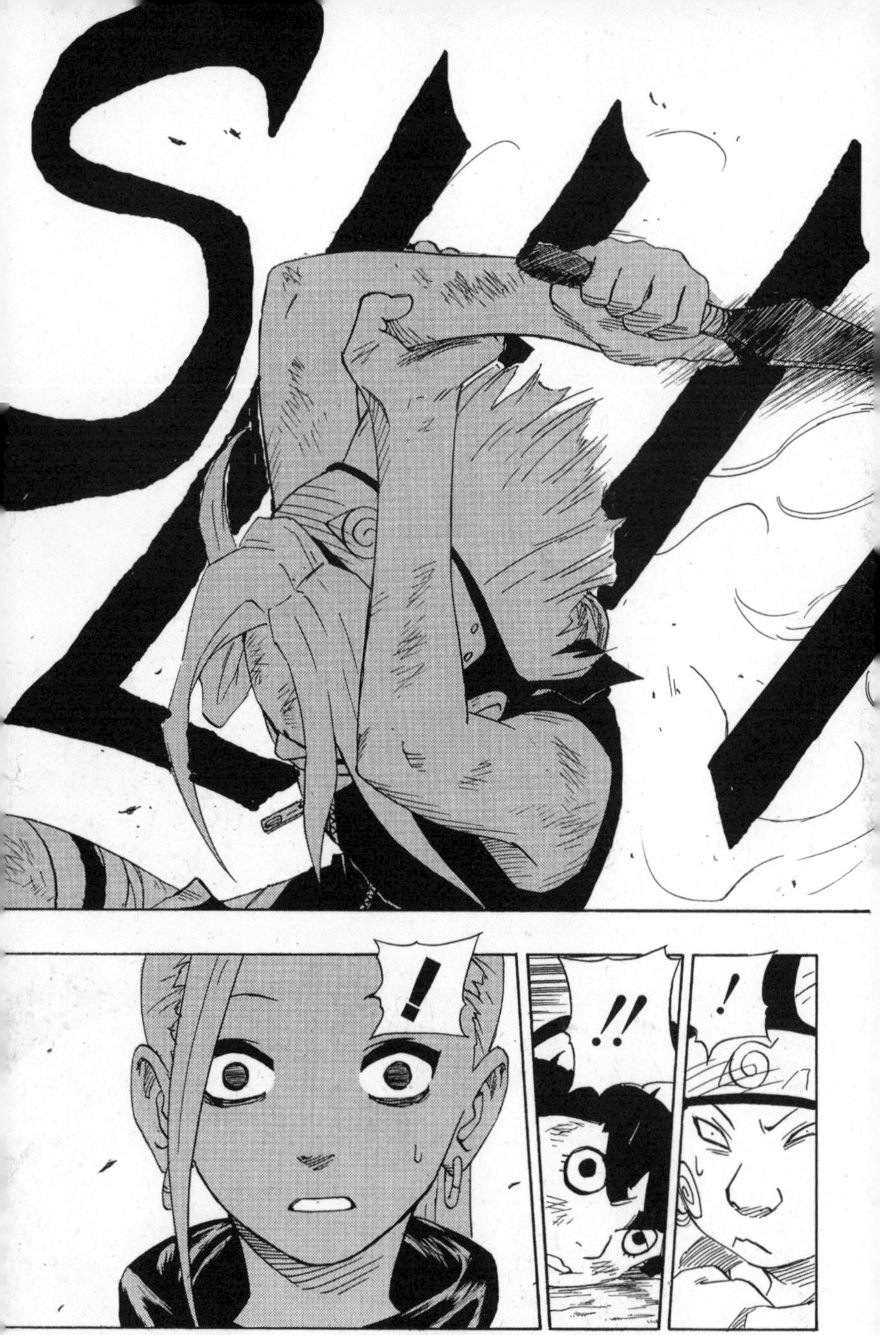
!
!!
!

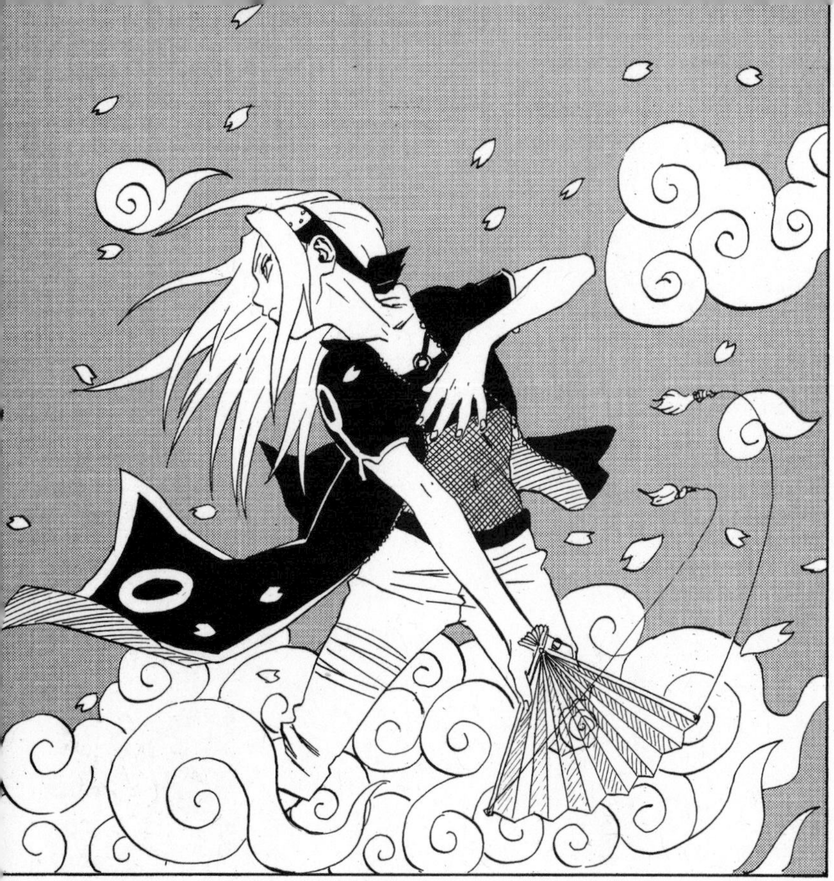

Number 54: Sakura and Ino

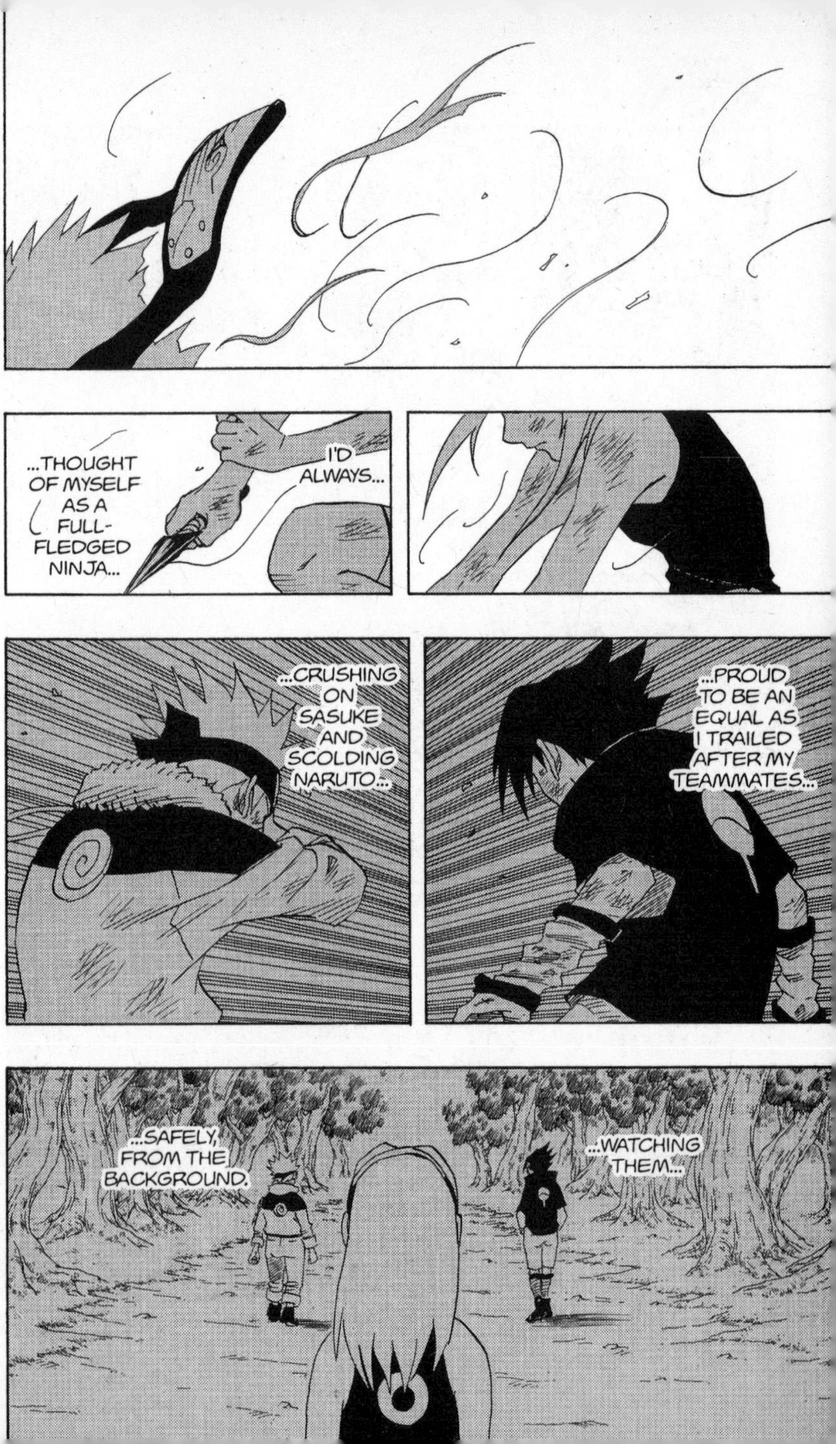
I'D ALWAYS...
...THOUGHT OF MYSELF AS A FULL-FLEDGED NINJA...
...PROUD TO BE AN EQUAL AS I TRAILED AFTER MY TEAMMATES...
...CRUSHING ON SASUKE AND SCOLDING NARUTO...
...WATCHING THEM...
...SAFELY, FROM THE BACKGROUND.

READ THIS WAY

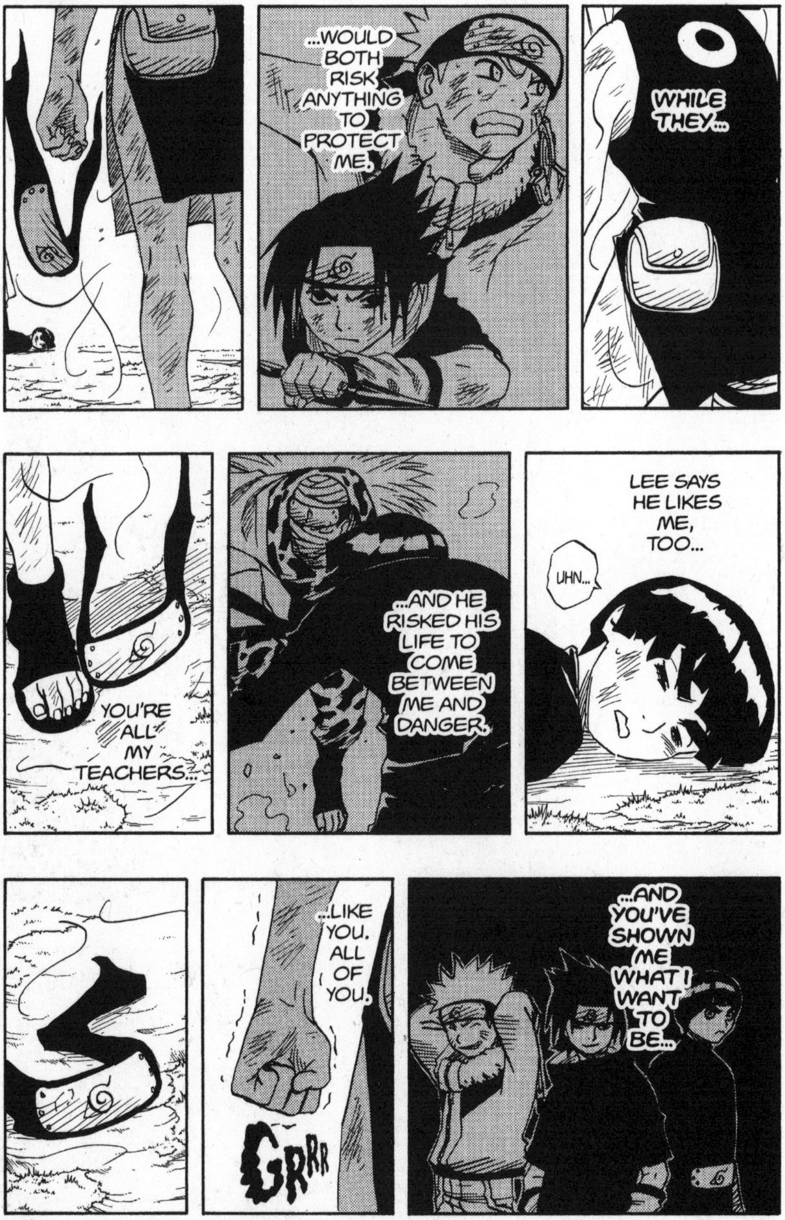
WHILE THEY...
...WOULD BOTH RISK ANYTHING TO PROTECT ME.
LEE SAYS HE LIKES ME, TOO...
UHN...
...AND HE RISKED HIS LIFE TO COME BETWEEN ME AND DANGER.
YOU'RE ALL MY TEACHERS...
...AND YOU'VE SHOWN ME WHAT I WANT TO BE...
...LIKE YOU. ALL OF YOU.
GRRR

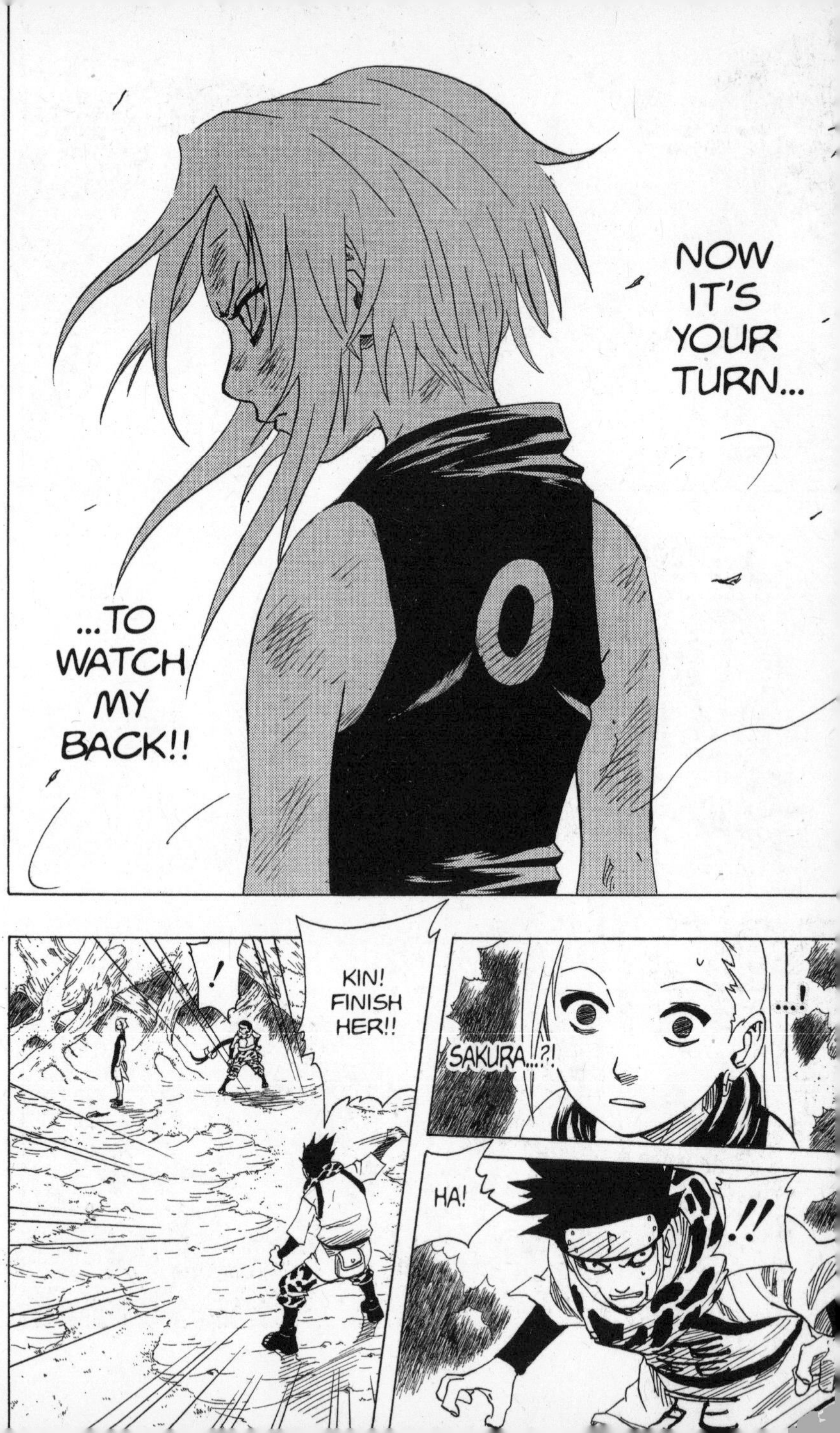
NOW IT'S YOUR TURN...
...TO WATCH MY BACK!!
...!
SAKURA...?!
HA!
!!
KIN! FINISH HER!!
!

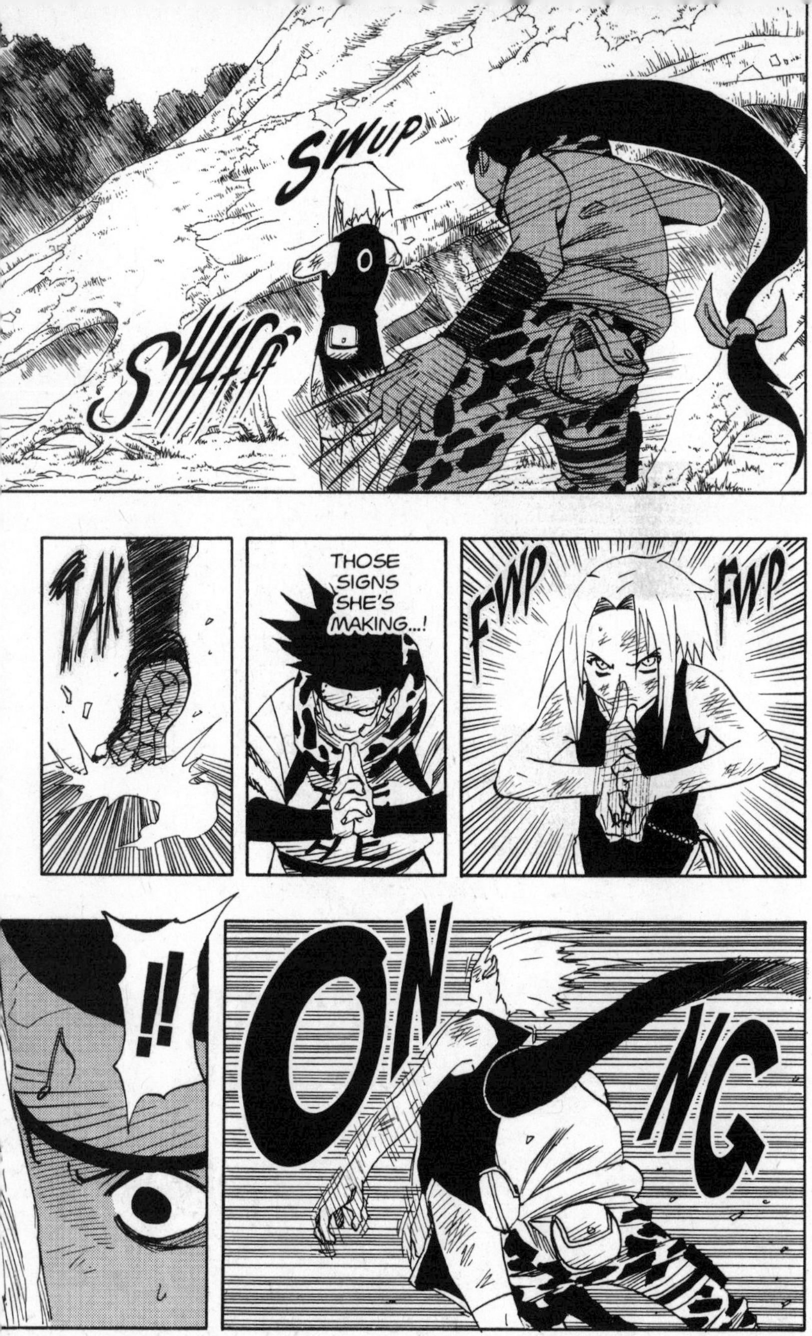
SWUP
SHHFFF
FWP
FWP
THOSE SIGNS SHE'S MAKING...!
TAK
ONNG
!!

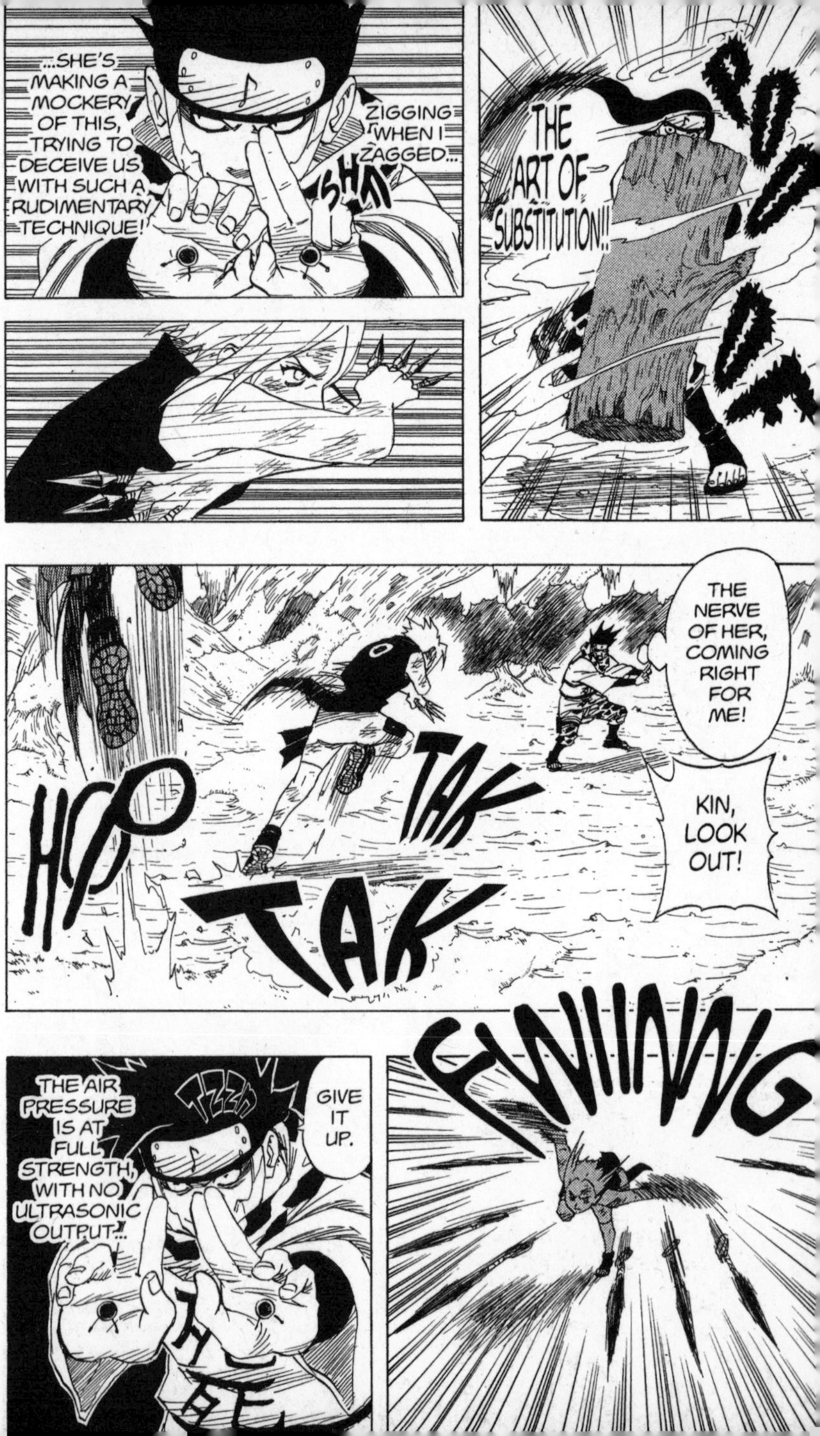
POOF
THE ART OF SUBSTITUTION!!
ZIGGING WHEN I ZAGGED...
...SHE'S MAKING A MOCKERY OF THIS, TRYING TO DECEIVE US WITH SUCH A RUDIMENTARY TECHNIQUE!
THE NERVE OF HER, COMING RIGHT FOR ME!
KIN, LOOK OUT!
TAK
TAK
HUP
FWIINNG
GIVE IT UP.
THE AIR PRESSURE IS AT FULL STRENGTH, WITH NO ULTRASONIC OUTPUT...

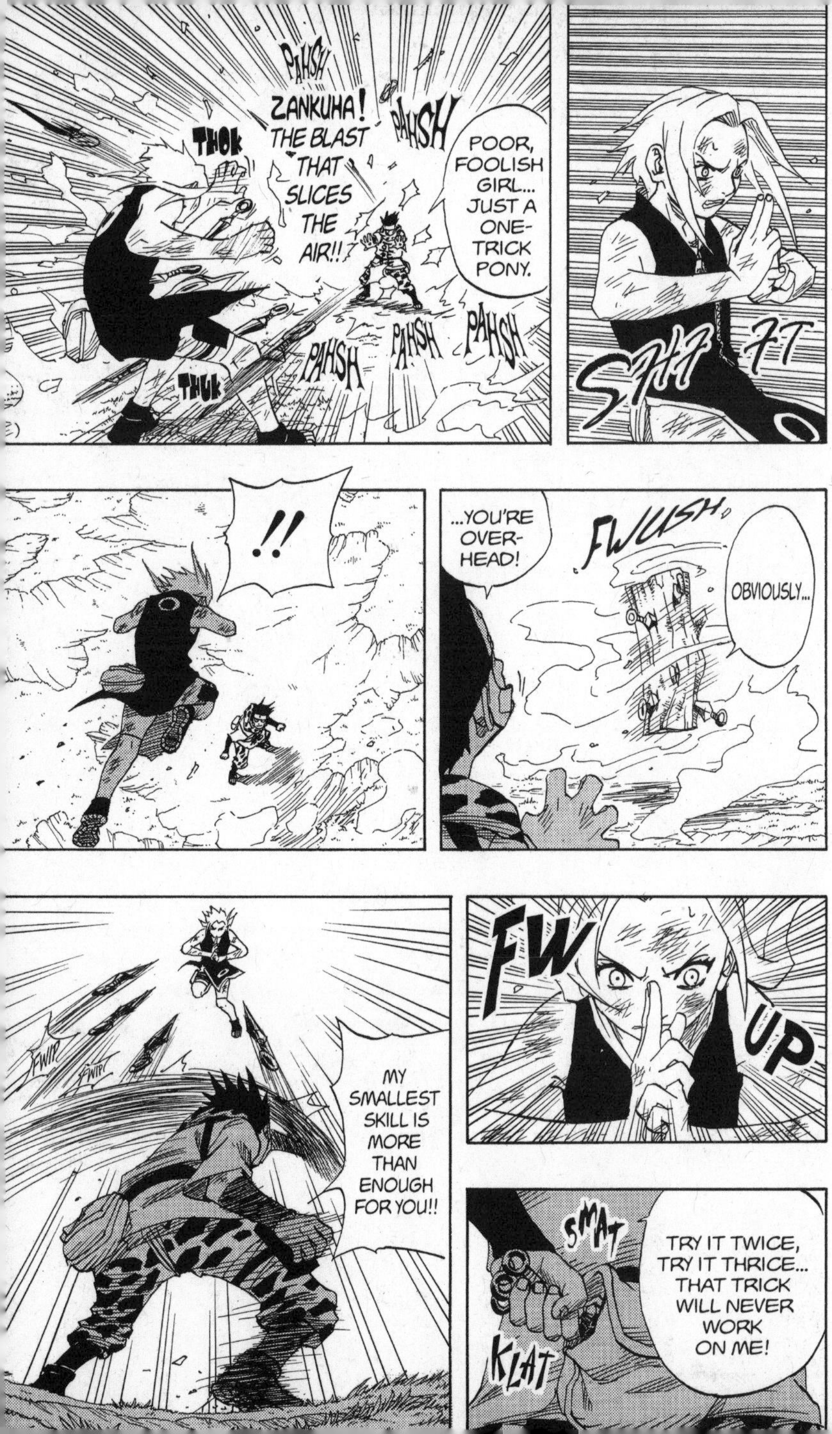
SHHFT
PAHSH
PAHSH
POOR, FOOLISH GIRL... JUST A ONE-TRICK PONY.
ZANKUHA! THE BLAST THAT SLICES THE AIR!!
THOK
PAHSH
PAHSH
PAHSH
THUK
OBVIOUSLY...
FWUSH
...YOU'RE OVER-HEAD!
!!
FW
UP
SMAT
TRY IT TWICE, TRY IT THRICE... THAT TRICK WILL NEVER WORK ON ME!
KLAT
MY SMALLEST SKILL IS MORE THAN ENOUGH FOR YOU!!
FWIP
FWIP

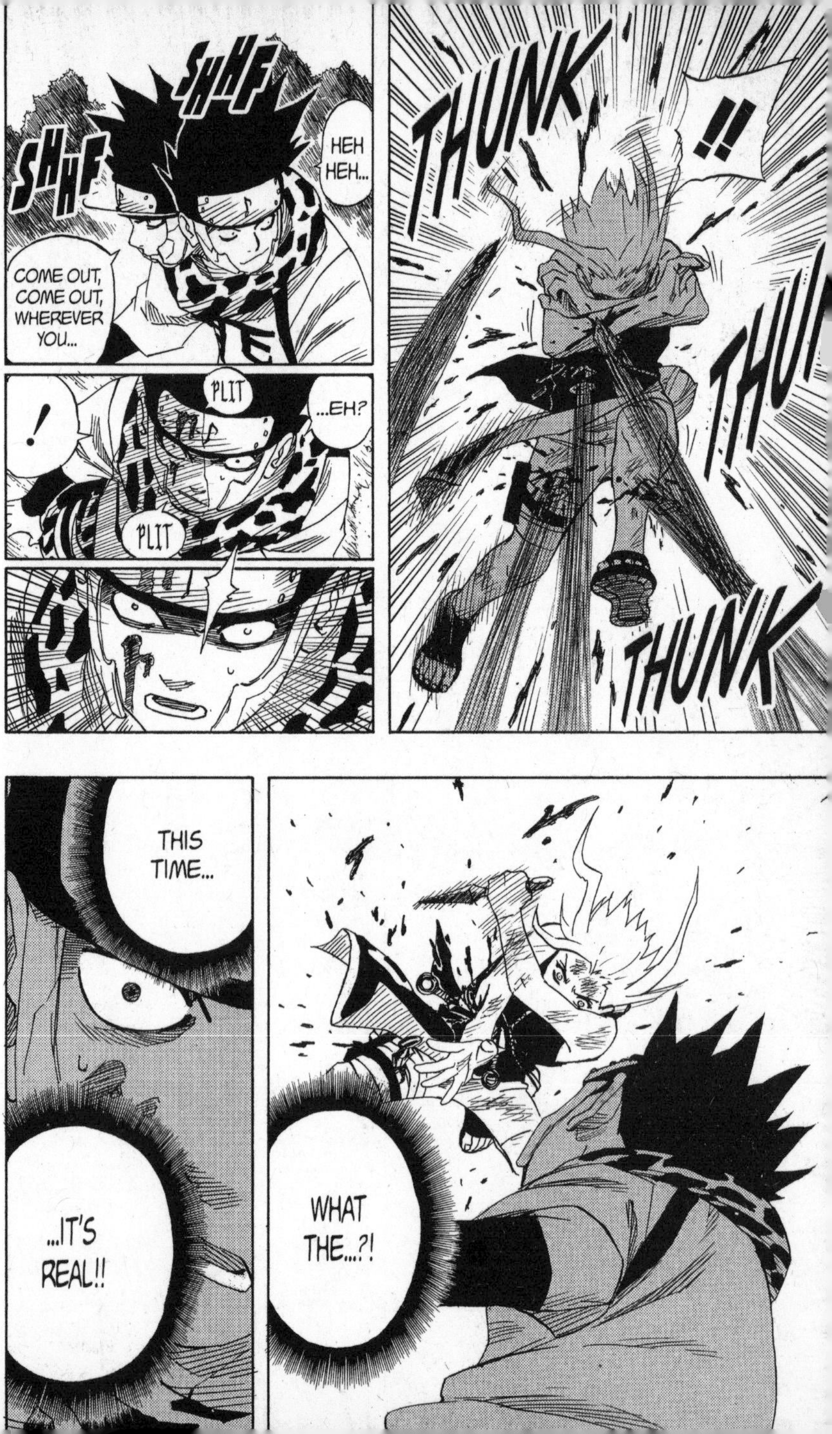
THUNK!!
THU
THUNK
SHHF
HEH HEH...
SHHF
COME OUT, COME OUT, WHEREVER YOU...
PLIT
...EH?
!
PLIT
WHAT THE...?!
THIS TIME...
...IT'S REAL!!

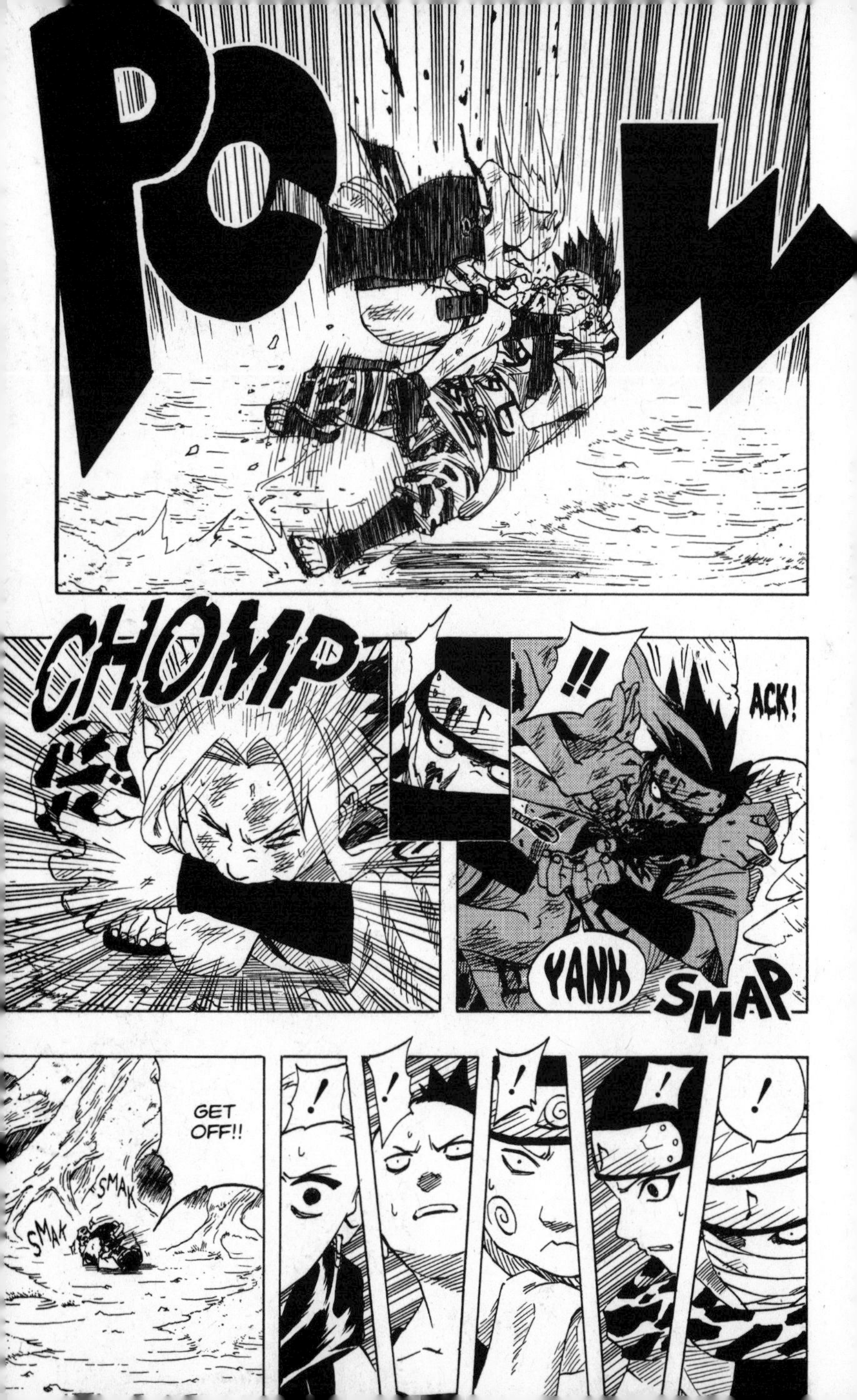
POW
!!
ACK!
YANK
SMAP
CHOMP
!
!
!
!
!
GET OFF!!
SMAK
SMAK

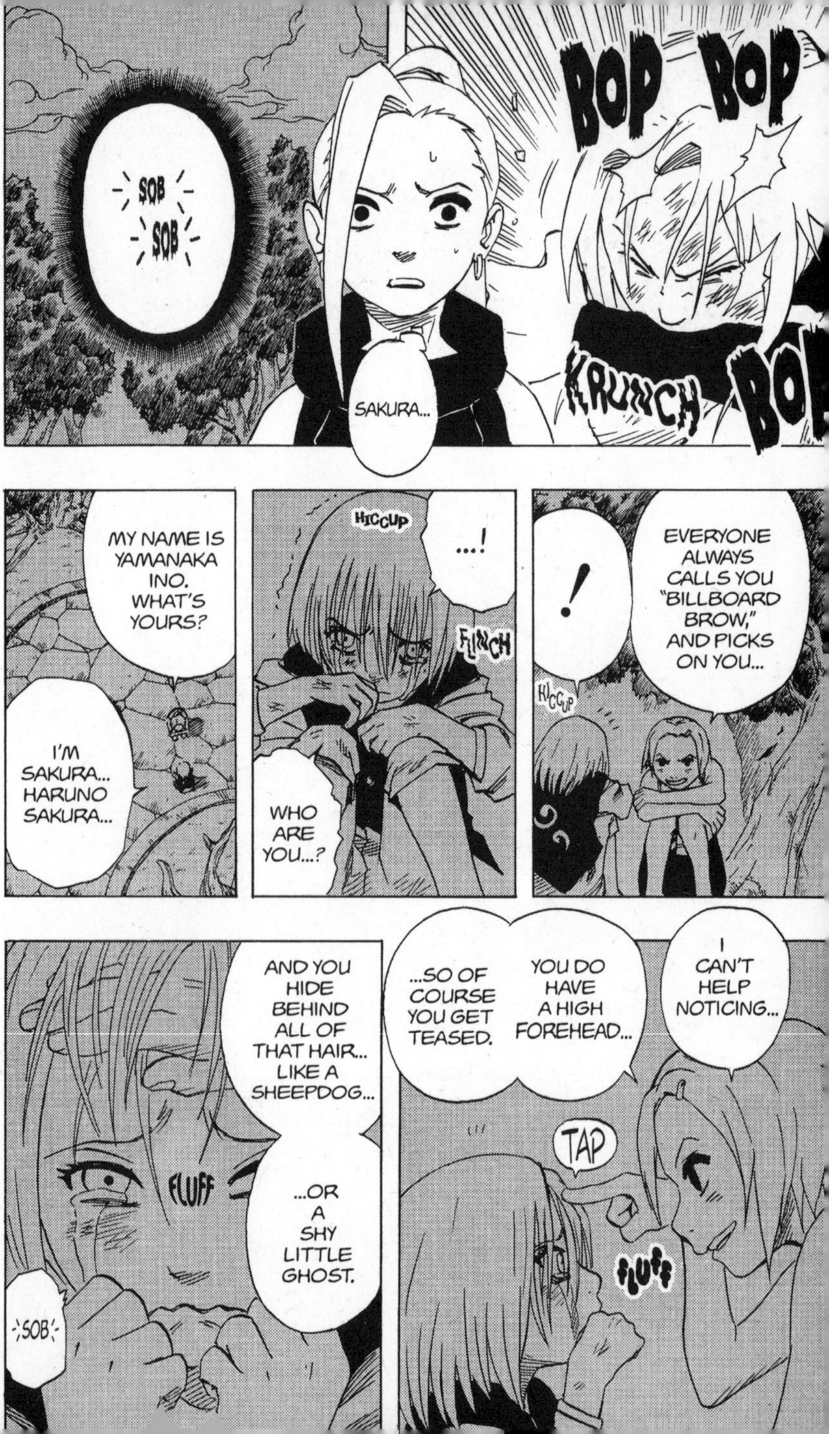
BOP BOP
KRUNCH
BOP
SOB SOB
SAKURA...
EVERYONE ALWAYS CALLS YOU "BILLBOARD BROW," AND PICKS ON YOU...
!
HICCUP
...!
HICCUP
FLINCH
WHO ARE YOU...?
MY NAME IS YAMANAKA INO. WHAT'S YOURS?
I'M SAKURA... HARUNO SAKURA...
I CAN'T HELP NOTICING...
YOU DO HAVE A HIGH FOREHEAD...
...SO OF COURSE YOU GET TEASED.
TAP
FLUFF
AND YOU HIDE BEHIND ALL OF THAT HAIR... LIKE A SHEEPDOG...
...OR A SHY LITTLE GHOST.
FLUFF
SOB

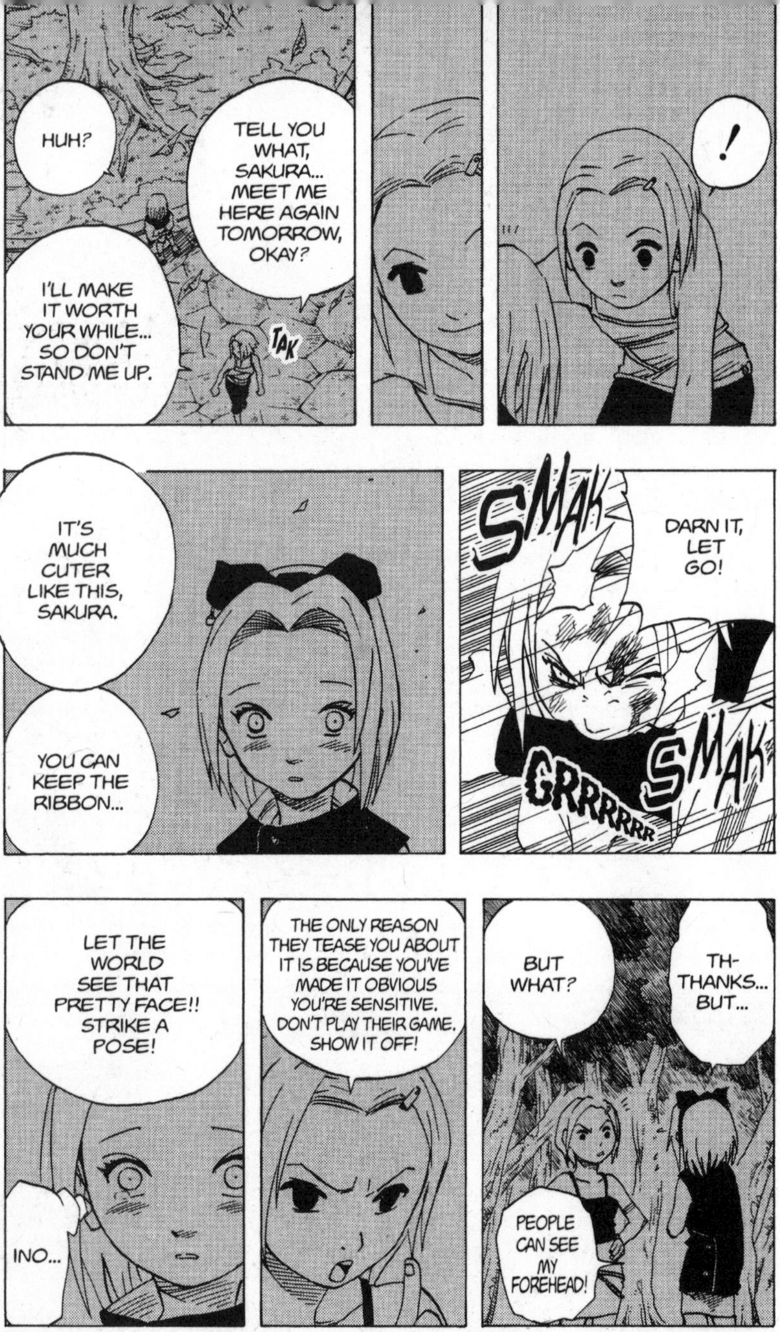
!
TELL YOU WHAT, SAKURA... MEET ME HERE AGAIN TOMORROW, OKAY?
HUH?
TAK
I'LL MAKE IT WORTH YOUR WHILE... SO DON'T STAND ME UP.
SMAK
DARN IT, LET GO!
SMAK
GRRRRRRR
IT'S MUCH CUTER LIKE THIS, SAKURA.
YOU CAN KEEP THE RIBBON...
TH-THANKS... BUT...
BUT WHAT?
PEOPLE CAN SEE MY FOREHEAD!
THE ONLY REASON THEY TEASE YOU ABOUT IT IS BECAUSE YOU'VE MADE IT OBVIOUS YOU'RE SENSITIVE. DON'T PLAY THEIR GAME. SHOW IT OFF!
LET THE WORLD SEE THAT PRETTY FACE!! STRIKE A POSE!
INO...

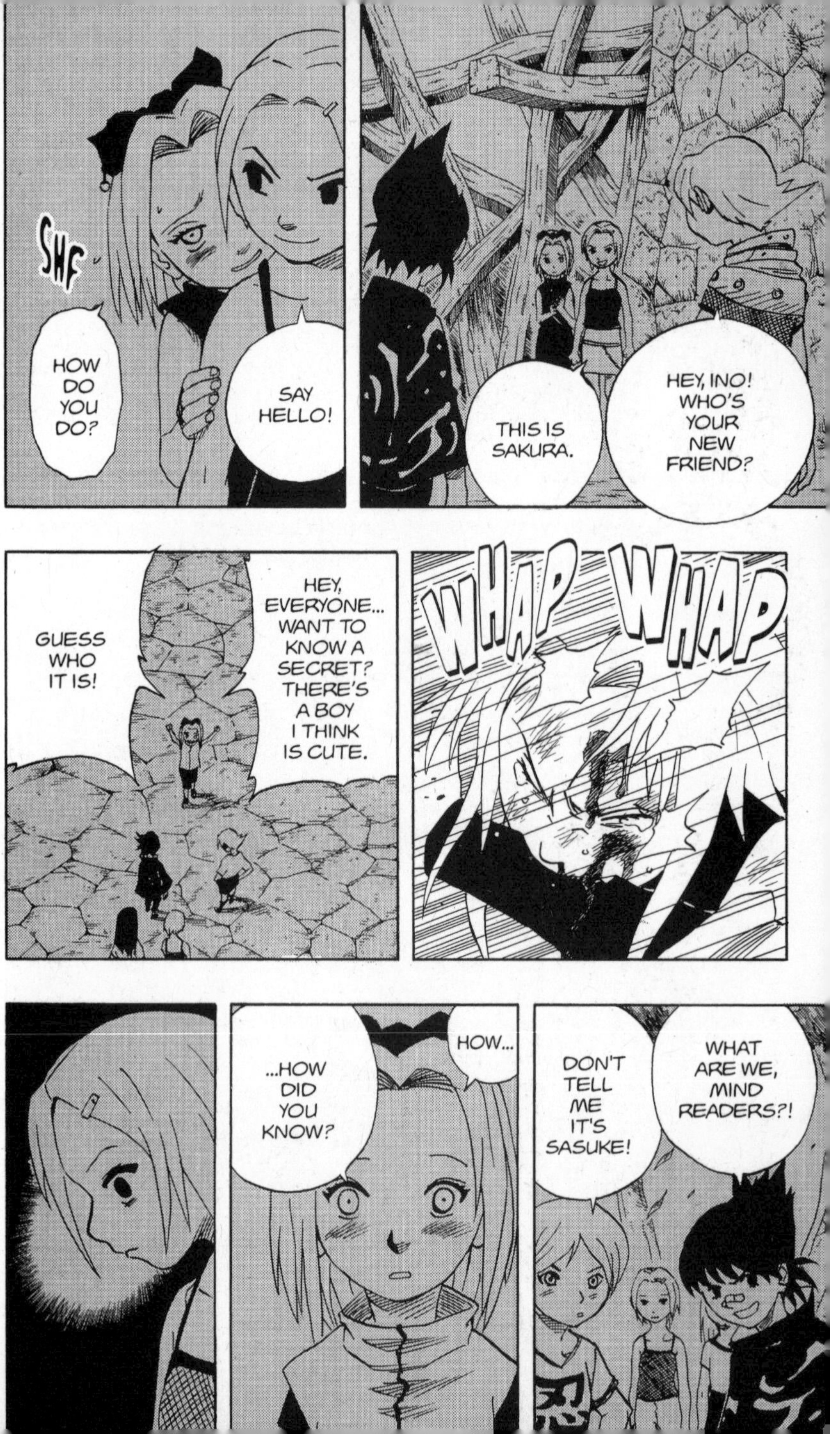
HEY, INO! WHO'S YOUR NEW FRIEND?
THIS IS SAKURA.
SAY HELLO!
SHF
HOW DO YOU DO?
WHAP WHAP
HEY, EVERYONE... WANT TO KNOW A SECRET? THERE'S A BOY I THINK IS CUTE.
GUESS WHO IT IS!
WHAT ARE WE, MIND READERS?!
DON'T TELL ME IT'S SASUKE!
HOW...
...HOW DID YOU KNOW?

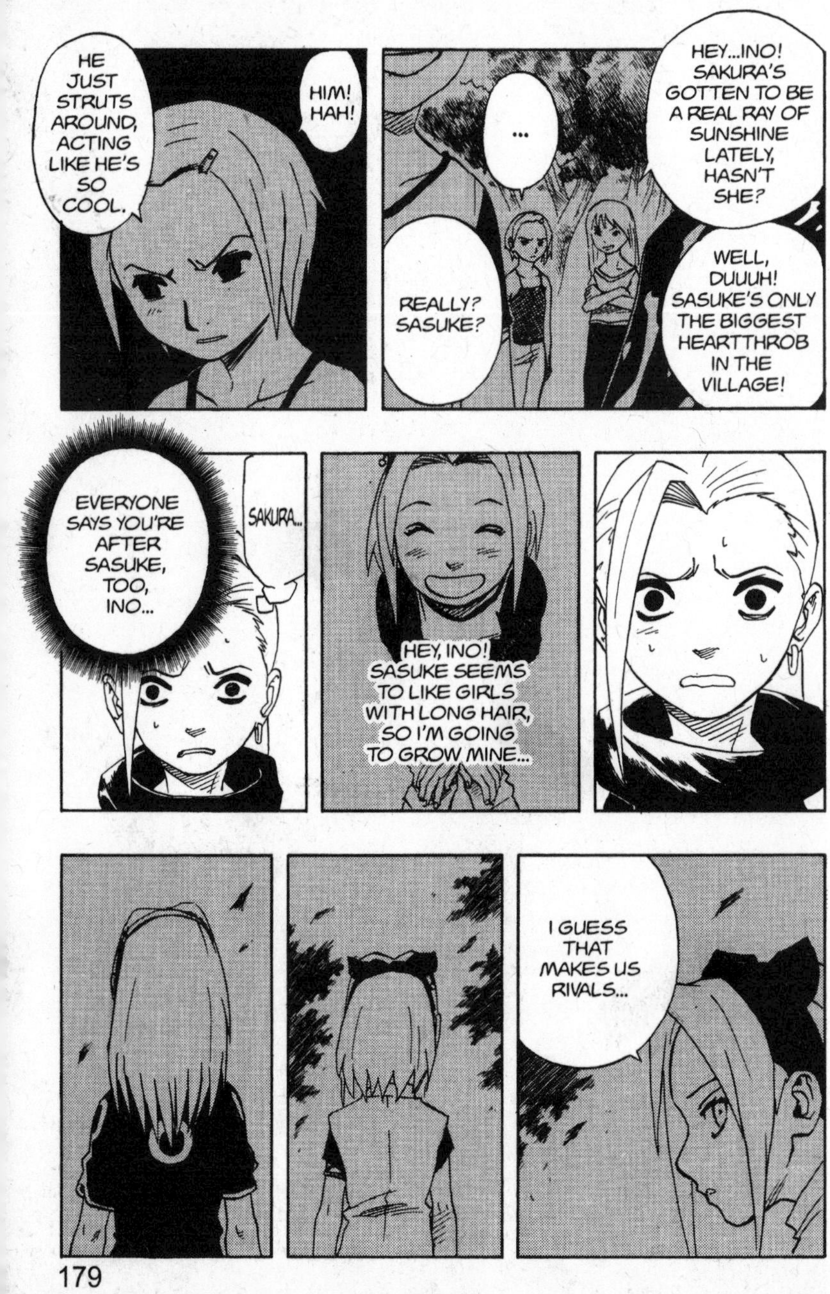
HEY...INO! SAKURA'S GOTTEN TO BE A REAL RAY OF SUNSHINE LATELY, HASN'T SHE?
...
WELL, DUUUH! SASUKE'S ONLY THE BIGGEST HEARTTHROB IN THE VILLAGE!
REALLY? SASUKE?
HIM! HAH!
HE JUST STRUTS AROUND, ACTING LIKE HE'S SO COOL.
HEY, INO! SASUKE SEEMS TO LIKE GIRLS WITH LONG HAIR, SO I'M GOING TO GROW MINE...
SAKURA...
EVERYONE SAYS YOU'RE AFTER SASUKE, TOO, INO...
I GUESS THAT MAKES US RIVALS...

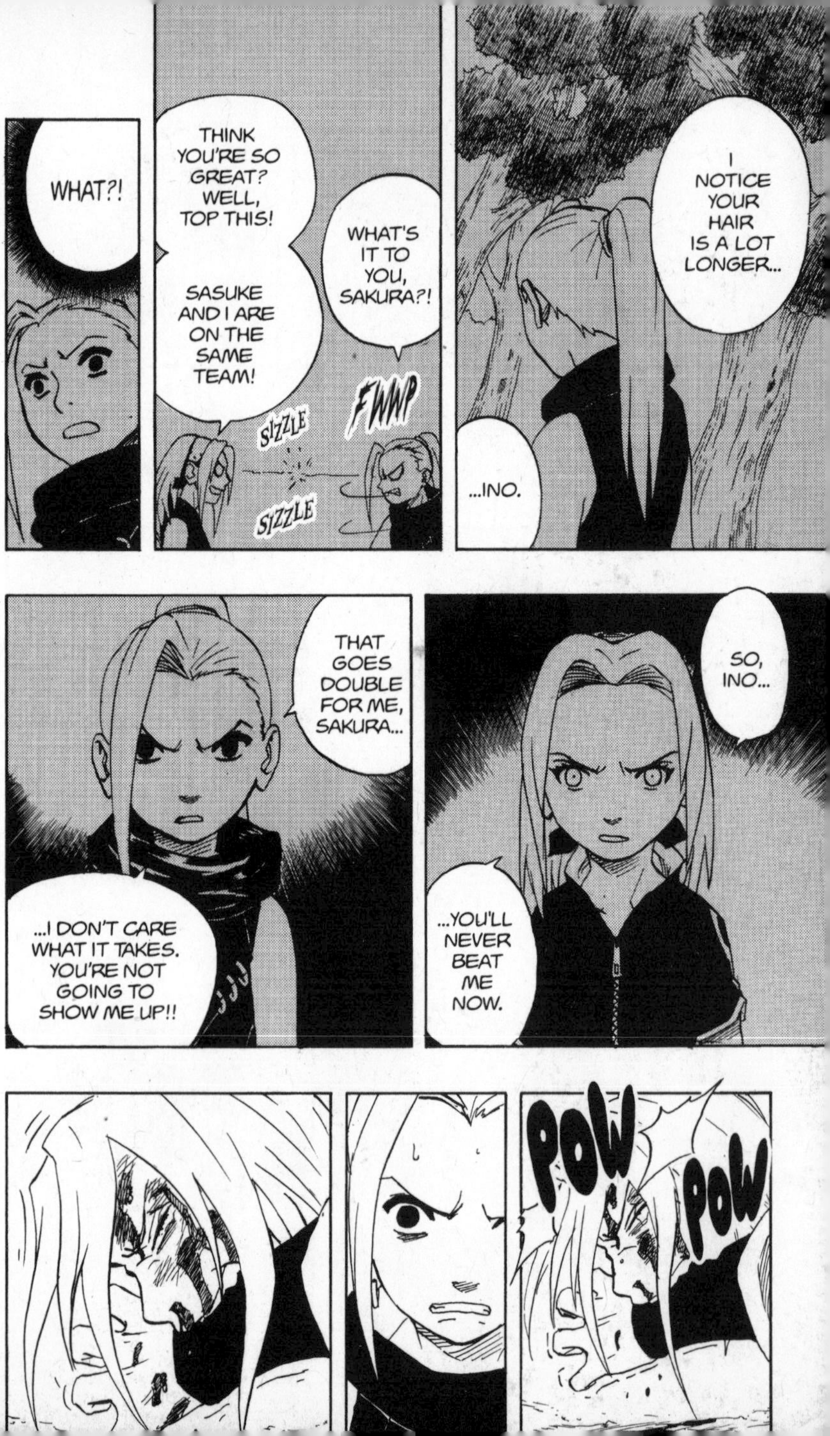
I NOTICE YOUR HAIR IS A LOT LONGER...
...INO.
WHAT'S IT TO YOU, SAKURA?!
FWWP
THINK YOU'RE SO GREAT? WELL, TOP THIS!
SASUKE AND I ARE ON THE SAME TEAM!
SIZZLE
SIZZLE
WHAT?!
SO, INO...
...YOU'LL NEVER BEAT ME NOW.
THAT GOES DOUBLE FOR ME, SAKURA...
...I DON'T CARE WHAT IT TAKES. YOU'RE NOT GOING TO SHOW ME UP!!
POW
POW

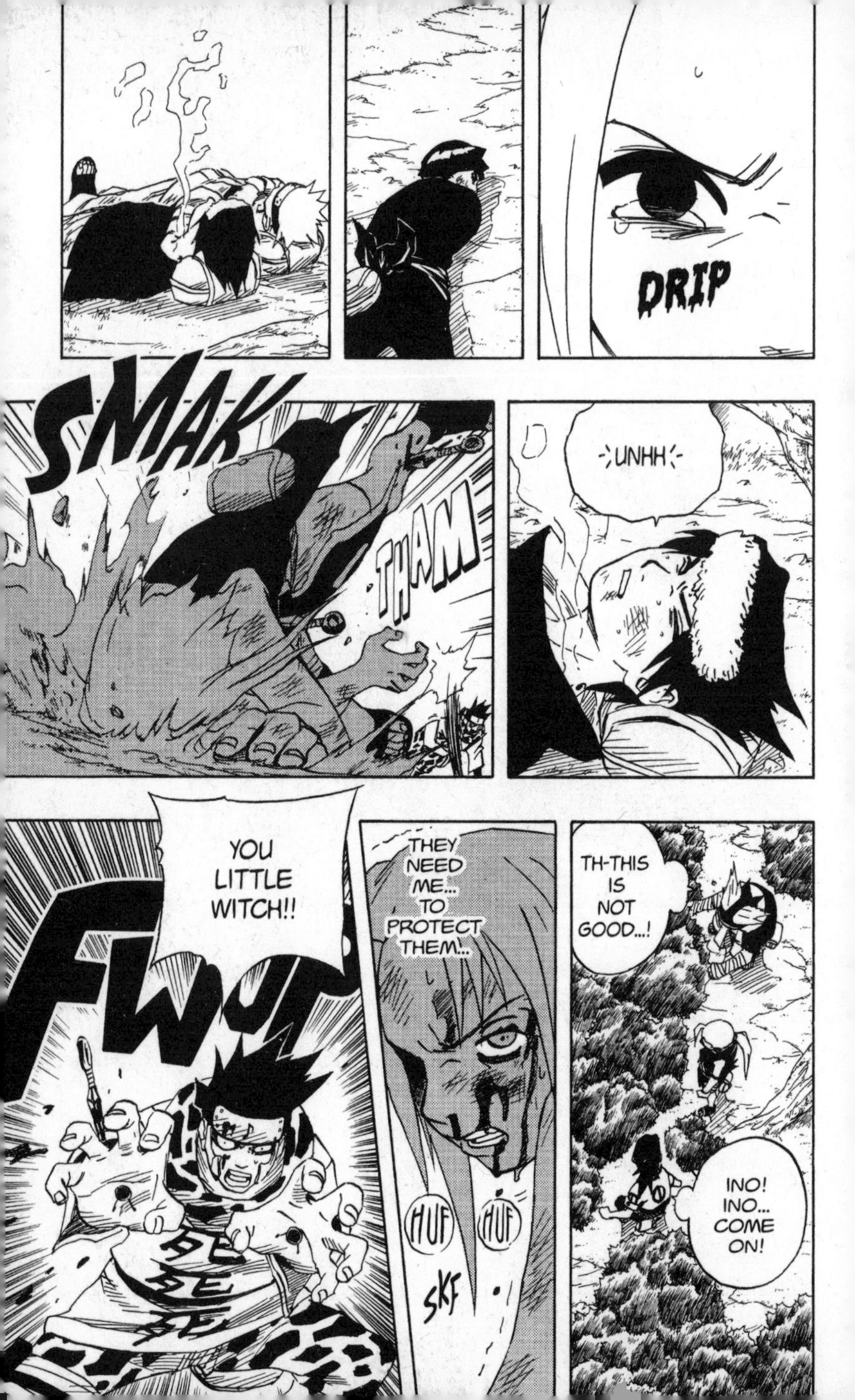
DRIP
UNHH
SMAK
THAM
TH-THIS IS NOT GOOD...!
INO! INO... COME ON!
THEY NEED ME... TO PROTECT THEM...
HUF
HUF
SKF
YOU LITTLE WITCH!!

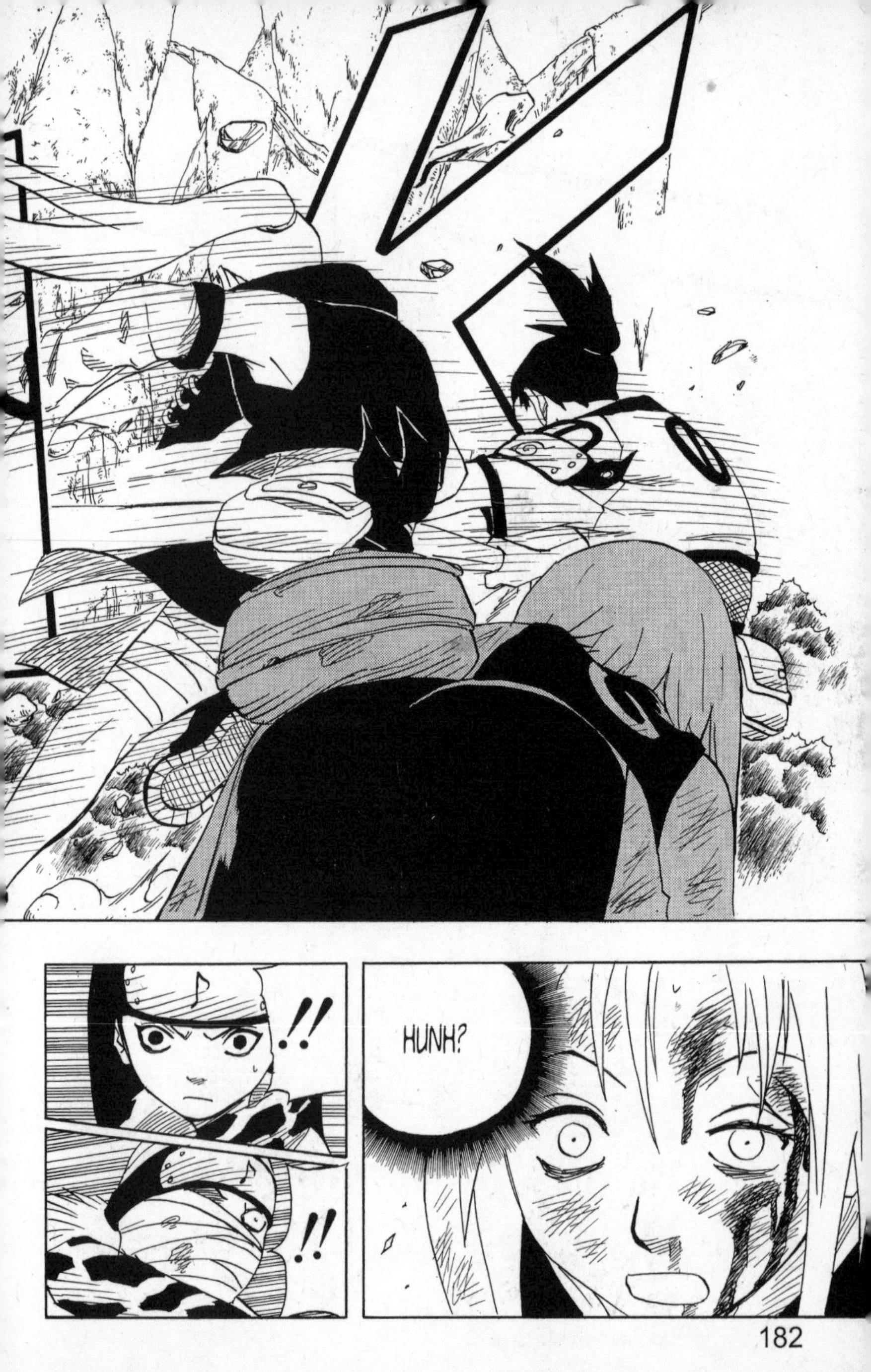
HUNH?
!!
!!

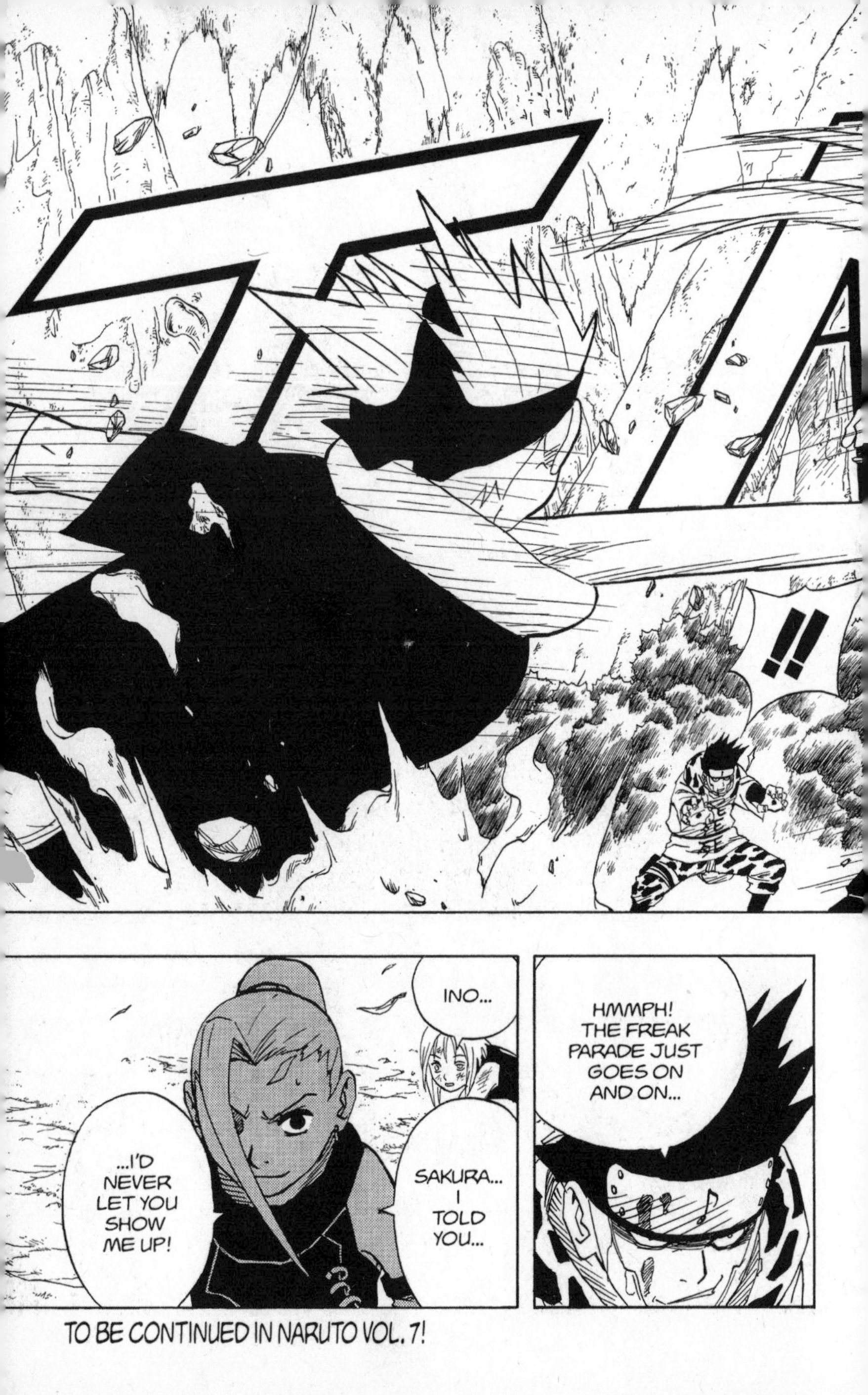
!!
HMMPH! THE FREAK PARADE JUST GOES ON AND ON...
INO...
SAKURA... I TOLD YOU...
...I'D NEVER LET YOU SHOW ME UP!

TO BE CONTINUED IN NARUTO VOL. 7!

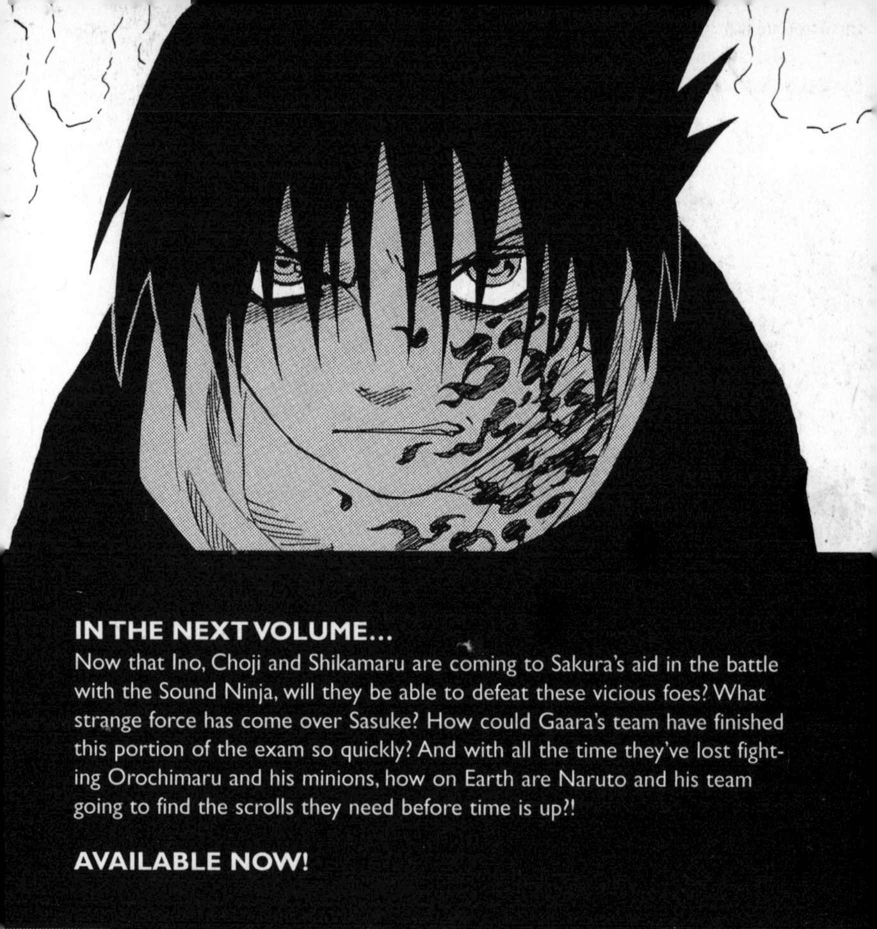

IN THE NEXT VOLUME...

Now that Ino, Choji and Shikamaru are coming to Sakura's aid in the battle with the Sound Ninja, will they be able to defeat these vicious foes? What strange force has come over Sasuke? How could Gaara's team have finished this portion of the exam so quickly? And with all the time they've lost fighting Orochimaru and his minions, how on Earth are Naruto and his team going to find the scrolls they need before time is up?!

AVAILABLE NOW!

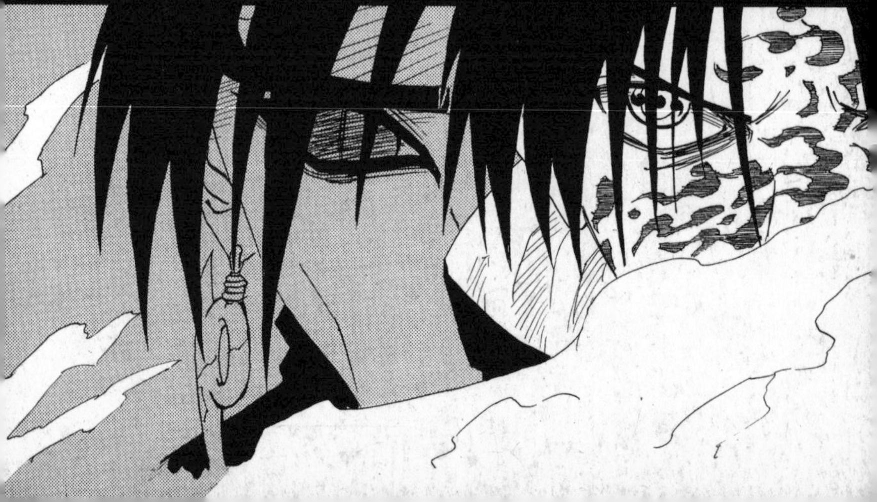

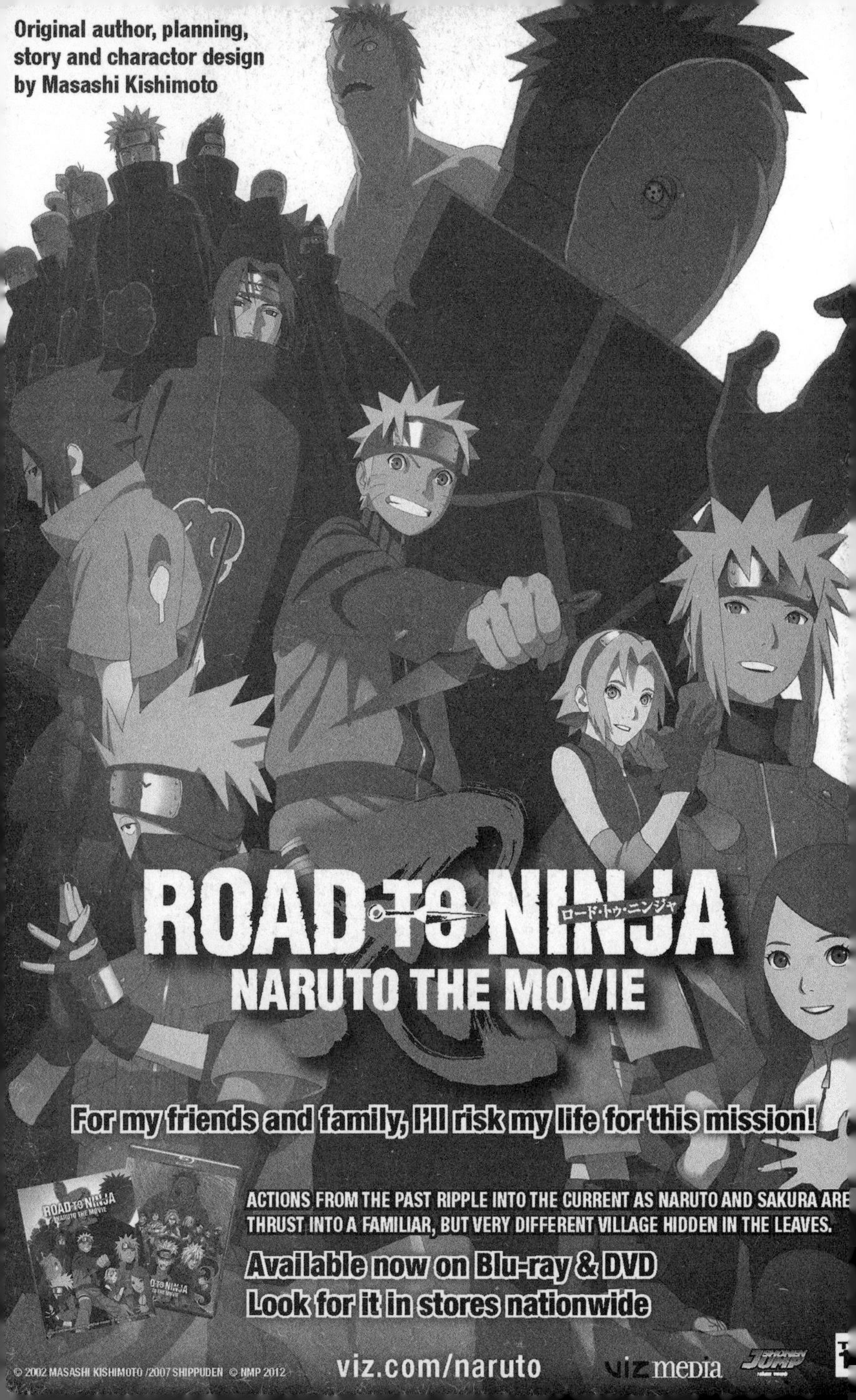
Original author, planning, story and charactor design by Masashi Kishimoto
ROAD TO NINJA
ロード・トゥ・ニンジャ
NARUTO THE MOVIE
For my friends and family, I'll risk my life for this mission!
ACTIONS FROM THE PAST RIPPLE INTO THE CURRENT AS NARUTO AND SAKURA ARE THRUST INTO A FAMILIAR, BUT VERY DIFFERENT VILLAGE HIDDEN IN THE LEAVES.
Available now on Blu-ray & DVD
Look for it in stores nationwide
© 2002 MASASHI KISHIMOTO /2007 SHIPPUDEN © NMP 2012
viz.com/naruto
VIZ media

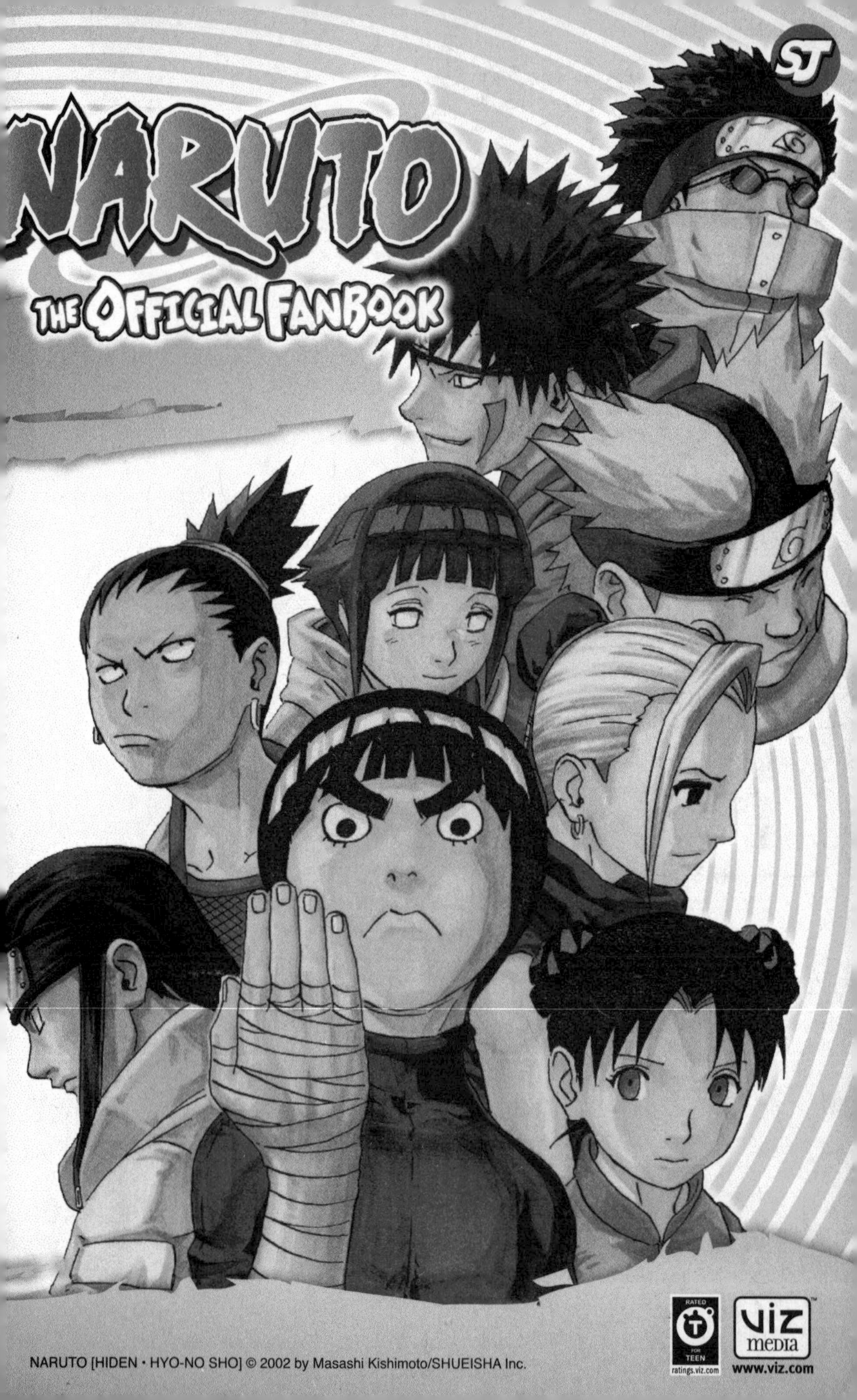

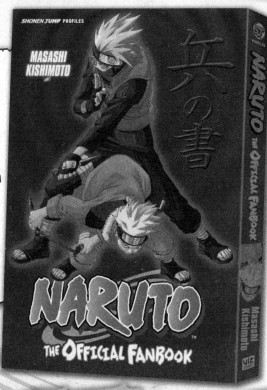

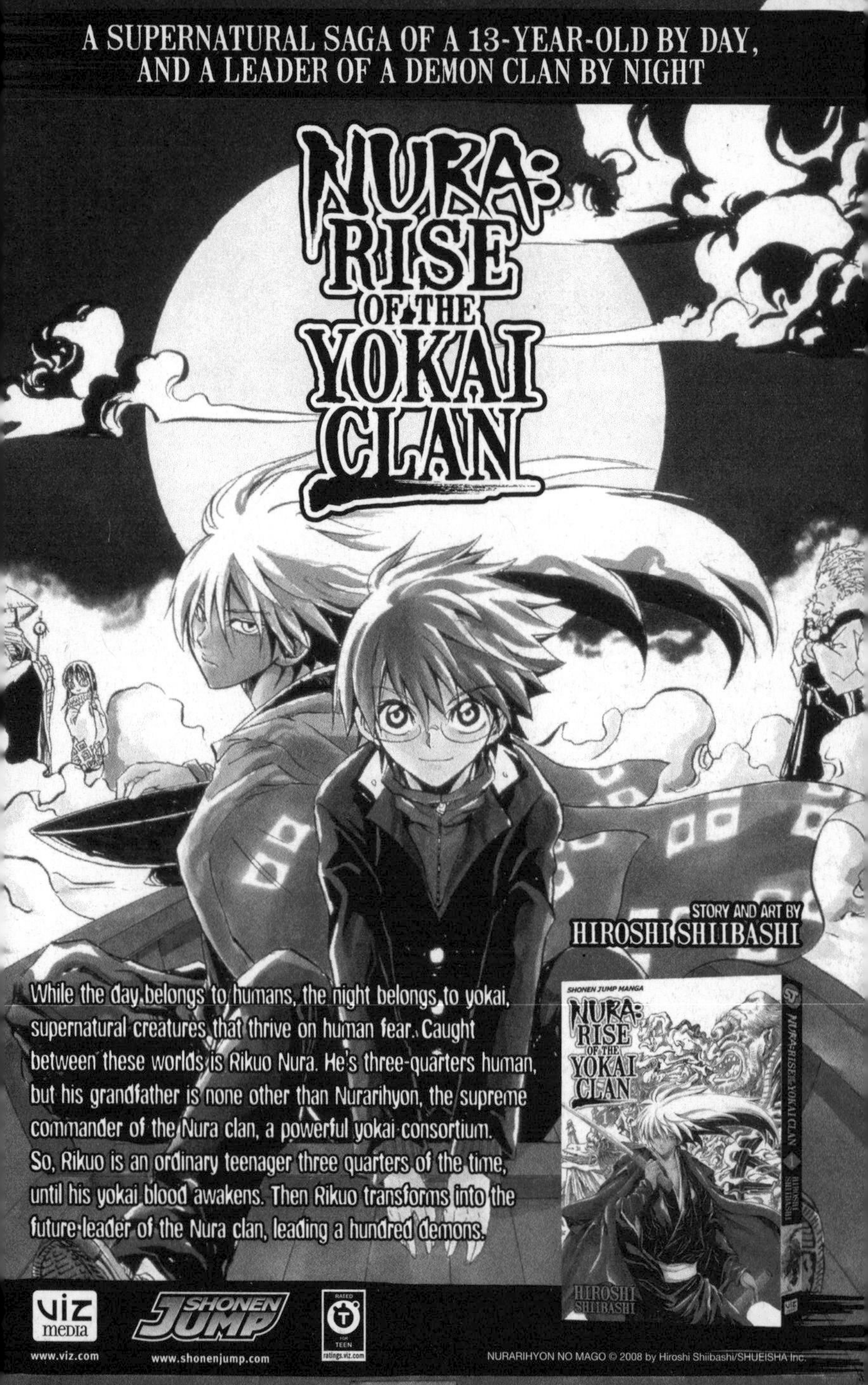

A SUPERNATURAL SAGA OF A 13-YEAR-OLD BY DAY,
AND A LEADER OF A DEMON CLAN BY NIGHT
NURA: RISE OF THE YOKAI CLAN
STORY AND ART BY
HIROSHI SHIIBASHI
While the day belongs to humans, the night belongs to yokai, supernatural creatures that thrive on human fear. Caught between these worlds is Rikuo Nura. He's three-quarters human, but his grandfather is none other than Nurarihyon, the supreme commander of the Nura clan, a powerful yokai consortium. So, Rikuo is an ordinary teenager three quarters of the time, until his yokai blood awakens. Then Rikuo transforms into the future leader of the Nura clan, leading a hundred demons.
SHONEN JUMP MANGA
NURA: RISE OF THE YOKAI CLAN
HIROSHI SHIIBASHI
viz media
www.viz.com
SHONEN JUMP
www.shonenjump.com
RATED T FOR TEEN
ratings.viz.com
NURARIHYON NO MAGO © 2008 by Hiroshi Shiibashi/SHUEISHA Inc.

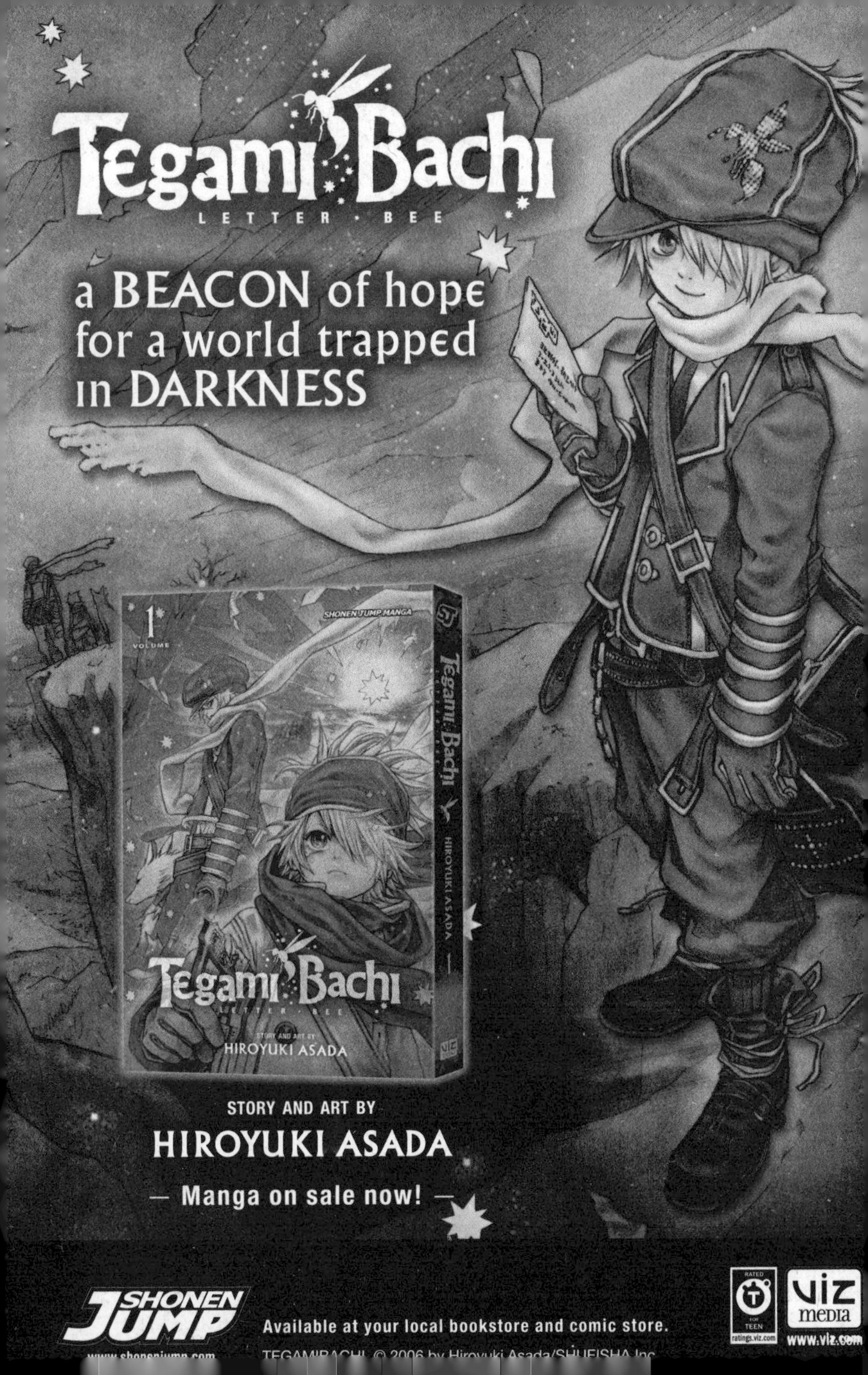
Tegami Bachi
LETTER • BEE
a BEACON of hope
for a world trapped
in DARKNESS
SHONEN JUMP MANGA
1
VOLUME
Tegami Bachi
HIROYUKI ASADA
Tegami Bachi
LETTER BEE
STORY AND ART BY
HIROYUKI ASADA
STORY AND ART BY
HIROYUKI ASADA
— Manga on sale now! —
SHONEN JUMP
Available at your local bookstore and comic store.
RATED
T
FOR
TEEN
ratings.viz.com
viz media
www.viz.com

A PREMIUM BOX SET OF THE FIRST TWO STORY ARCS OF ONE PIECE!

A PIRATE'S TREASURE FOR ANY MANGA FAN!

STORY AND ART BY EIICHIRO ODA

Comes with
EXCLUSIVE
POSTER
and the
ROMANCE
DAWN
mini-comic!

As a child, Monkey D. Luffy dreamed of becoming King of the Pirates. But his life changed when he accidentally gained the power to stretch like rubber...at the cost of never being able to swim again! Years later, Luffy sets off in search of the "One Piece," said to be the greatest treasure in the world...

This box set includes VOLUMES 1-23, which comprise the EAST BLUE and BAROQUE WORKS story arcs.

EXCLUSIVE PREMIUMS and GREAT SAVINGS
over buying the individual volumes!

You're Reading in the Wrong Direction!!

Whoops! Guess what? You're starting at the wrong end of the comic!

...It's true! In keeping with the original Japanese format, **Naruto** is meant to be read from right to left, starting in the upper-right corner.

Unlike English, which is read from left to right, Japanese is read from right to left, meaning that action, sound effects and word-balloon order are completely reversed...something which can make readers unfamiliar with Japanese feel pretty backwards themselves. For this reason, manga or Japanese comics published in the U.S. in English have sometimes been published "flopped"—that is, printed in exact reverse order, as though seen from the other side of a mirror.

By flopping pages, U.S. publishers can avoid confusing readers, but the compromise is not without its downside. For one thing, a character in a flopped manga series who once wore in the original Japanese version a T-shirt emblazoned with "M A Y" (as in "the merry month of") now wears one which reads "Y A M"! Additionally, many manga creators in Japan are themselves unhappy with the process, as some feel the mirror-imaging of their art alters their original intentions.

We are proud to bring you Masashi Kishimoto's **Naruto** in the original unflopped format. For now, though, turn to the other side of the book and let the ninjutsu begin...!

—Editor

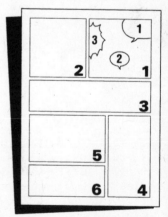